Ryan — It
A pleasur
with you
the book!
Enjoy

CW01034212

CREATING VALUE IN PORTFOLIO COMPANY OPERATIONS

CREATING VALUE
IN PORTFOLIO COMPANY OPERATIONS

A Practical Guide to Growing
Cash Flow in Business

by William Bundy

STYGIAN PRESS

STYGIAN PRESS

Copyright © 2023 William Bundy

979-8-9887599-0-4   eBook
979-8-9887599-1-1   Hardcover
979-8-9887599-2-8   Trade paperback

Library of Congress Control Number: TXu002380006

Book design by Glen Edelstein, Hudson Valley Book Design
Content Edit by Brian Baker

First printing 2023.

This book is dedicated to my Parents.

My Father - The wisest and strongest warrior I will ever know and the giant shoulders I have stood upon.

My Mom - The human who showed me how to tie a tie and to live, love, and laugh. Making all things possible as long as you believe.

CONTENTS

PREFACE

Warren has a saying, «Intensity is the price of excellence.»[1]
—Alice Schroeder

With today's market valuations, purchasers of companies and other assets need to think about how to create additional value in their investments. The days of financial engineering and leverage to create outsized returns are waning. Current valuations and financing rates are at all time highs making a number of potential deals unattractive. In addition, investors and others are seeking more from their private investment partners. Management teams and sellers often want to understand the value that the private investor will bring to the company in the form additional paid in capital, new management teams, or improvements to existing infrastructure. Some limited partners and other key stakeholders have also asked to see environmental, social, and governance (ESG) improvements to the assets acquired by the general partners.

These new investment improvement theses go beyond just ensuring the financials are where they need to be for the desired return or monitoring KPIs in a dashboard and then holding the management team accountable. If you believe that a new era is upon the investing world, then all of the cadre of people around the investment—the deal team, the investor's operating support team, the advisors, and the management—should all be well versed on what actually drives material improvement and how do their actions (or inaction) impact EBITDA and future economic realization of the asset. To provide appropriate oversight and ensure these improvements are made in companies investment practitioners and management need a fundamental and holistic understanding

---

1 <u>Alice Schroeder</u>, *"The Snowball: Warren Buffett and the Business of Life," Microsoft Research, September 6, 2016, YouTube video.* 17:16, https://www.youtube.com/watch?v=NrPBr8iFL9k.

of the key elements of the company that drive value. They need to understand when to call an executive's bluff when they have not delivered a desired outcome and, on the converse, when the management team should push back on the investors when a timeline or anticipated result is not actionable in the operation of their company. This book is meant to help begin to bridge the gap between the investors, advisors, employees, and operators (the management team) of these companies. The goal is to help create a baseline understanding of the operations of a company and the critical elements of operations where cash and value really resides. There is no way to cover every single element of every operation within every type of company and industry—instead I aim to create a framework and rubric to begin the discussion.

This book is not meant to be read cover to cover. It is meant to be used as an initial starting point and guide. While on a flight or as you are preparing for a meeting you can pull out a copy of this book, read the material relevant to you that day, develop a framework for the operations of a company, and be conversant in a given topic. Then, when an operator or advisor begin to talk about the topic you can ask the appropriate questions, and if necessary call their bluff.

There are five major questions I attempt to answer in this book:

1. What is the definition of value?
2. How do you understand how much value is available and how do you assess it?
3. What are the functions of a company and how are they typically optimized?
4. What are the typical levers to create topline value?
5. What are the critical elements of inorganic growth and carve-outs?

One of my high school football coaches always emphasized nailing the basics of anything you are involved in. We would conduct drills on how to correctly leave a three-point stance, how to properly engage with the defender when blocking. When on defense, we would practice tackling and open field tackling. Each repetition would make us stronger on the fundamentals. In school, you take thirteen years to learn the basics from kindergarten through High school. In college, you leverage those fundamentals and basic building blocks to create robots, build autonomous underwater vehicles, design breakthrough art compositions, and draft world class literary manuscripts. From the fundamentals, anything can be derived. Advanced concepts are only used to show you may have some relevant experience.

I fundamentally believe in becoming the absolute best at the basics and then you can derive any concept off of that. That is the basis of a classical education. If you read and learn the root thought process of how the great thinkers like Seneca, Kant, Descartes, Voltaire, Rousseau, Smith, Baudrillard, Camus, Rand, and countless others derived their concepts and ways of being. You will fundamentally understand the basis of our society, laws, and the rationale behind the world. From there, you will be a better and more clear thinker, understanding our world at a fundamental level allowing you to know when rules apply and when they don't. I have sought in some form, limited by my own mental capacity to provide those fundamentals of business operations to you through this medium. Consider this book the beginning of your classical education to understand a company's operations. I am not one of those great thinkers—I am an operator at heart and a strategist because of my intelligence.

I have worked as an operator, advisor, and implementation specialist for some of the largest private equity firms in the world. As chief transformation officer, I developed the framework and led one of the most complex carve-outs in the PE world while executing a financial and operational turnaround for a half-billion-dollar consumer products company on behalf of a major global investor. I'm known for getting stuff done. I am exceptionally effective. I have my fair share of enemies in the world who are more than willing to share their negative sentiments about me. I operate with the highest levels of integrity and one of the hardest work ethics people have seen. Most people can't keep up with my speed and desire to always do the right thing, even if it costs me money or takes additional time.

In the consulting world, my teams know that they will work hard and we will deliver the maximum impact and benefit to the client. They also know that I can be relentless to get to an answer that is actionable by the management team—not just something that is theoretically correct. I always put myself in their shoes if I were to receive our recommendations and advice. I ask myself, could I deliver what is being stated or what would I have to believe for this to be true. I have a reputation that when I say there is an improvement available, that improvement can be manifested with the appropriate motivation and support.

In another, I came across a situation where one of my minority female employees, who was an absolute star, was being paid about 15 to 20 percent less than her majority peer. I worked with HR to immediately correct this issue. I also told them I wanted any other pay discrepancies in my remit to be resolved immediately.

When I was in the Navy, I was selected as part of the team to help the USS *Hampton* (SSN 767), a nuclear-powered fast attack submarine, recover from some unsafe practices that occurred by my predecessors. Here is what Wikipedia had to say about that as of the end of June 2023:

In an isolated incident from her safe operational record, in October 2007, six naval personnel were disciplined for fraudulently documenting the chemistry records of the *Hampton's* nuclear propulsion plant. Shortly thereafter, the ship's commanding officer Commander Michael B. Portland was also relieved of his command because of a loss of confidence in his leadership, but he has not been charged with any offense. In March 2008, the U.S. Navy revealed that a total of 11 officers and enlisted men had been disciplined in connection with the fraudulent documentation and for cheating on qualification tests. In addition to the Captain, the submarine's engineer officer, the engineering department master chief petty officer, and the entire reactor laboratory division were dismissed from Naval nuclear plant duty and submarine service. No damage was discovered in the reactor core and the submarine has returned to operational status.[2]

In late 2007, the Navy inserted me, a top-notch engineering department master chief, and one of their best commanding officers, to help fix this issue. It required the highest levels of character and an extreme work ethic to ensure that everything on the ship was done right and with the highest levels of integrity. When we were out to sea, I would work for 18 hours a day to ensure the team had proper oversight. The officers and chiefs worked tirelessly to ensure that they were trained exceptionally well. I also tried to get all of the top performers from my prior crew to help

---

[2] "USS *Hampton* (SSN-767)," Wikipedia, accessed July 10, 2023, en.wikipedia.org/wiki/USS_Hampton_(SSN-767)#:~:text=On%2017%20September%202007%2C%20the%20Hampton%27s%20homeport%20was,chemistry%20records%20of%20the%20Hampton%27s%20nuclear%20propulsion%20plant.

build out the best engineering team on the waterfront. We meticulously scrutinized every element of the operations, streamlined the workflows for maintenance, and got the crew to the point that they were the crew that all of the best operators and maintainers wanted to transfer to. The ship won the Engineering E under my leadership for several years and then won the Battle "E" for Submarine Squadron ELEVEN in 2010 and 2011.

This is also where I picked up the ability to step in and run large turnarounds and transformations. I prefer to work with companies that are underperforming. I find simple problems boring. I have found the work in the area of transformations and turnarounds to be invigorating. It makes me whistle when I put my shoes on in the morning. You are dealing with situations and management teams that really do need the support. They need your leadership and guidance. I prefer situations where there is a lot of operational complexity with negative EBITDA margins. My specialty is fixing broken companies. I am part of the 10 to 20 percent of Americans that change the world, and I want you to be part of that too.

To best understand value creation, I have found it helpful to change the standard paradigm about a company. I mentally shift my thoughts about a company from being a human organization to that of a machine that should generate the maximum amount of cash possible given its industry. The problem you then are trying to solve is this: How do you fix the machine so that it generates the maximum amount of cash possible? If you are a true capitalist, you should believe that money flows to value and opportunity—this book is here to help you understand the problems you are solving and gives you the starting point on where to hunt to find those opportunities and maximize the cash flow of your business through its operations.

Many may think this focus on cash generation is antiquated. It might be. However, I believe the true strategic value of a company is its ability to generate cash. If a company can generate excess cash from operations, its equity holders can do with it as they please. This cash generation can be used for good: investing in initiatives with double bottom line improvements such as ESG. Or it can be used to generate wealth and the excesses enjoyed by the few and the investors and constituents of the Limited Partners of the private capital funds.

Private equity firms in general take these returns and enable larger-than-market returns for institutional investors—the preponderance of limited partners that fund private equity (PE) firms. The majority of the largest institutional investors are pension funds with assets under management of around $56 trillion.[3] So, supporting PE firms gain excess returns enables these pension funds to maximum their returns. With this money, they then fund the retirement of our municipal workers and teachers—I guess that is a way of justifying the support provided to private investors.

My experience with private equity firms was largely focused on assessing the acquired targets' profitability, topline improvement initiatives, and cost structure. My teams and I would then work with the management team and the investors to implement the new vision and capture significant upside for the investment groups improving their rates of return to their limited partners. The initial phases of these value creation plans would take anywhere from two weeks to about nine months. Sufficient time to rapidly implement large scale structural change in the organization. The nature of the work we conducted is in confidence with the management teams and investors we worked with. Throughout the book, I have altered facts and purposefully obfuscated details about situations and scenarios I may have taken part in. I engineered these scenarios to still capture the axiom I was trying to impart but prohibit knowing anything about the actual scenarios I have taken part in as an advisor.

Working to develop these complex tightly coordinated plans can take months of work with really smart Harvard and Wharton MBAs. Companies and investors will spend millions of dollars to gain operational insight into a potential acquisition. In today's market, valuations require private equity firms and investors to be able to generate value in addition to the management plan. To gain that advantage in the acquisition process, there is a blend of industry experience, analytics, and operational know how that is required to deliver accurate information and more importantly actionably accurate benefit estimates and costing. This is the art operational improvement and value creation. I hope this book provides you the information you need to understand at a high level what is going on and what is needed to drive the value.

The art of value creation is the ability to take those learnings and

---

3 "Global Pensions Soar to New US$56 Trillion Record," Thinking Ahead Institute, accessed July 12, 2023, https://www.thinkingaheadinstitute.org/news/article/global-pensions-soar-us56-trillion-record/.

then, with the investor's leverage and capital, and a properly incented management team to realize the upside in a given investment.

I do hope that you enjoy this book. It was a pleasure to write. It is a good feeling to take the experiences one can accumulate in their professional experience, distill it into key lessons, and then serve it to willing readers around the world.

I hope this book helps you grow as a professional.

With Respect,
Will Bundy

CHAPTER 1

Cash Generation = Strategic Value

*When people talk about cash being king, it's not king if it just
sits there and never does anything.*
—Warren Buffett[4]

A lot of people will read the title of this chapter and immediately make arguments about why cash generation is not the sole measure of a company's strategic importance. They will make arguments such as:

- Companies are an important element of our society and fabric of how we live. They should be measured on their contributions to society and the greater good.
- Companies that are just starting up have a strategic importance because of their disruption and their ability to generate more revenue in the future. Their ability to generate cash now is less relevant.

If you are someone that would make arguments like those above, it's not that your arguments are wrong. Both of the statements above are true. However, we may want to think about the definition of strategic value for a business. For investors and management teams, strategic value in a business is generated when a company generates cash flow from operations. If a company is cash flow positive, the management and investment team now has the option to invest in additional initiatives that generate additional revenue. It could also use the cash to influence

---

4 Warren Buffett, "Warren Buffett: I Haven't Seen As Much Economic Fear In My Adult Lifetime— Charlie Rose Interview," interview with Charlie Rose, October 1, 2008, www.cnbc.com/2008/10/01/ warren-buffett-i-havent-seen-as-much-economic-fear-in-my-adult-lifetime-charlie-rose-interview. html.

politicians and sculpt a favorable regulatory landscape. It could use the cash to improve brand awareness and consumer sentiment, enabling it to charge higher prices. It can also use the cash to pay off debt or provide investors a special dividend. In short, the value of cash is that it provides the company and investors options.

Cash generation from operations is different than dividends or funds that flow to an investor. Strategic value is related to the actual cash that the management *and* investors has to make decisions. For instance, if you reduce $5 million of spend in advertising and promotion, the management team then has a decision to make. Do they accrete that to the bottom line, thereby improving profitability by $5 million, or do you reinvest the $5 million into an initiative that grows revenue or is otherwise return on investment positive, such as additional allocation of the budget into media spend? In high growth companies the cash generation from operations can be masked because the management team has already invested in another higher growth initiative that will grow revenue in the next year. You can typically discern some of this in the management discussion related to A&P spend or growth trends in sales or marketing teams.

Now let's look at the converse, where a company does not generate cash. If a company is not generating cash from operations it is beholden to its external investors. Startup companies go from seed funding to Series A, B, and eventually C rounds of funding, hustling to generate revenue and then eventually be cash flow positive. Each funding round typically deteriorates some economic value from the equity holders to buy more time for the company to generate sustainable operations and then position for sale or initial public offering (IPO) to generate liquidity in the asset.

Think of a startup founder that has just finished an Angel round of funding. The company may be making cash, it may have a breakthrough, novel technology, but the management team and investors have limited strategic options and the management team is financing the operations based on a burn rate, e.g., how long do I have cash to fund operations. The strategic value of this company is effectively zero. The management team does not have an option to fund efforts to fix climate change. As soon as the investors lose faith and the management team runs out of cash, the company no longer exists.

However, that startup could potentially be economically valued at $1 billion. Just like pricing for consumer products or house markets, the economic value of a company does not always equate to the current strategic or intrinsic value of the asset. For early stage companies they can be valued a number of ways including as a multiple of sales or other indicator of future state performance. For mature companies, there is usually always a correlation between their financial performance and valuation.

Uber is a prime example of a company that does not focus on generating cash from operations. It was an IPO that investors had desired for some time. It had an innovative technology that people leveraged and changed the way the globe thinks about taxis and black car services. When the IPO prospectus was released in 2019 it finally disclosed the size of the funding and profitability gap that Uber had. The *Financial Times* summed up its concerns: "The 431-page prospectus was filled with lawyerly phrases and volumes of information on potential risks, but it left many serious professional investors wondering why a company that loses $3 billion annually would be worth [$9.5 to $10 billion]."[5] This lack of strategic value in part caused its IPO to come in lower than the anticipated pricing of $45 per share instead coming in closer to $42 per share. It also called into question its ability to operate independently as a public company without further deterioration of economic value for its equity investors.

Speculative markets, such as startup funding and venture capital (VC), do not always act rationally. Think of a family member— mother, father, brother, or sister—that is approached by an eager member of the family to help found their business. The founder asks for $10,000 or $50,000 to get started. The typical family member will say yes, if they have the means, just seeking to support their child or family members' dreams. Yes, they will typically receive some sort of security in the company—percent of ownership or liability (may be personal)—but the funding occurs. In the event they are successful, the family member will get paid back – sometimes with no interest. If they made it equity, they would likely still accept a smaller than market return or sometimes a smaller than market valuation on their equity. This type of market is inherently speculative and irrational as the initial investment was made from an emotional standpoint to

---

5 Rett Wallace, "Uber's Enormous, Vague IPO Prospectus Is an Outrage," *Financial Times*, April 30, 2019, https://www.ft.com/content/60ab80e2-6a8b-11e9-9ff9-8c855179f1c4.

support the family member. The return is a non- factor, but this is often how small startups are founded.

Even with rational investors, some times it is hard to truly identify the rational economic value of an asset. In some situations the technologies or companies do not have a strong corollary available in the market. Inherently, this requires experience-based decision making on whether a rational investor will invest. It also takes some form of diligence. Often times, these investors will focus on product-market fit, speaking with paying customers of the product to understand whether or not the service or product is of value. Without firm understanding of the market, the future direction of the company (for instance Uber has pivoted from taxi/black car to food and other sundries) the foundation of the diligence analysis of a rational investor may be invalid.

I once worked with a founder to develop a business model for their startup. The initial focus was on a scalable model where they would provide physical security and credentialing of VIPs. They used an advanced technology as its backbone to ensure the appropriate credentialing of the attendees. The business, in that design, could not scale as efficiently as other methods. Subsequent to those discussions, the startup actually shifted its operating model to a white label solution and has been extremely successful. I invested time and support in the company at an early stage based on a relationship with limited thought on economic return. Had I thought it through as a rationale investor, I may not have invested as conceived at that point. However, I am glad I did both economically and as a friend.

These dynamics and subsequent funding rounds can similarly divorce the economic value from the strategic value of the firm. Similar issues are not typical in later stage companies as investors are typically buying an asset with well-defined products, markets, proven historical financial results, cost structures, and operating models.

There are two broad-brush methods to generate strategic value in a given market: 1) cost leadership or 2) pricing power. For those business savants, Michael Porter would also include the competitive scope of the company (e.g., are you narrowly focused on one market or broader advantage across a number of markets and offerings). For this analysis, we will worry about a single market, as trying to layer in advantage across multiple markets will increase the complexity unnecessarily.

To a point, excess returns in the market can be derived by either of these two broad conceptual designs for strategic value of a company's operations. However, cost leadership is the most sustainable method because the levers to remain at advantage are largely able to be controlled by a proactive management team.

Building pricing power typically takes on the form of improved brand equity. Companies establish this through several methods (note that these methods are often comingled). The first is through super or differentiated products. Apple's reputation as a differentiated brand stemmed at first by developing a superior product with the iPod and then the iPhone. This market leadership, which was established as these technologies took root in the early 2000s, has led to a dominant market position. Because of scale, it now also enjoys some elements of cost improvement: driving a larger advantage over other competitors in the mobile technology market. The second is when the products cannot be differentiated there is a chance that you can generate an emotional connection to the product line and company. In the beauty market, successful companies are able to sell $2 to $10 goods for upward of $40 to $100 to consumers. This methodology is tied to driving an image and brand identity that aligns with the consumer. This impact of brand is well understood. However, this method of differentiation (focused solely on brand) can be extemporaneous. For instance, brands that rely on celebrity endorsement are dependent on a sole point of failure. If your brand is backed by a celebrity and that celebrity does something that gets negative press, you could lose the brand equity and thereby the outsized profits you had previously enjoyed. In diligence processes, a key analysis is often to understand how reliant a brand is on a single personality. If overly reliant, it could make more sense to walk away.

COST ADVANTAGE

Cost advantage is not synonymous with lower price. Companies with a cost competitive advantage can chose to pass this onto its customers (e.g., "Everyday low prices") or it can chose to retain those earnings and maintain pricing in line with others in the market. To better define it, cost competitive advantage is established when the company creates a meaningful, structural cost difference between it and its competitors in a given market. The key factors are that it is structural and that it is meaningful.

One of the things you try to do is create that sort of change when a private equity firm takes over a company. It can be seen as a normalization of cost, but ideally it should create a fundamental change in the cost structure. Oftentimes this means undertaking projects such as improved IT systems, new organizational structures, improved use of financial instruments, improved cash efficiency, changes to procurement methodology, or changes to design or product costing. In addition, changes that increase productivity of assets or lower overhead can change the structural costs for a company, enabling the unlocking of higher strategic value and operating leverage as the company scales.

These cost improvements do need to be meaningful. Often a PE sponsor can reduce a company's cost basis between 10 to 15 percent within the first 12 to 24 months. In more extreme cases or where operations are not as well run, reduction can easily exceed 25 percent or more. Prime cases are where cost becomes a driving factor include when assets are divested from larger companies, when the company has been mismanaged, or when a company may have grown through acquisition and the management team never undertook the hard work of integrating the new assets into the larger entity.

When we look at key examples of firms with definitive cost leadership, we look at companies like Walmart or Ikea. Albeit these companies also now have the advantage of scale, but the largest lessons learned are as they grew and how they focused their energy to achieve outsize returns in their respective markets. Companies that end up with a significant advantage typically leverage a focused strategy to establish their position and take deliberate actions to maintain. Let's take a look at each of the examples above and what drives their strategic advantage.

WALMART

Walmart operates close to 11,500 stores globally with only about 4,800 of those stores in the United States. It is estimated that Walmart earns a profit per hour of around $1.8 million based on 2021 financials.[6] Its scale and breadth of operations gives it a distinct competitive advantage when negotiating with customers. However, the company goes a step further and proactively meets with its vendors and helps them lower their own costs lowering their cost and passing those savings onto the consumer. It actively invests in automation and other technologies to enhance productivity and efficiency. To reduce spend on trucking, Walmart has its own fleet of 6,500 trucks, 7,000 drivers, and around 55,000 trailers. On the customer side, negotiating with Walmart is a challenge. Even when you do have legitimate, defensible cost increases, they will not readily absorb all of the cost increase. The ability for their current scale to maintain their cost advantage speaks volumes about the entrenched nature of their cost advantage.

IKEA

Ikea is known for more than just their meatballs. Their main operation is focused on furniture and home goods manufacturing and retailing. Ikea's cost-conscious culture was driven from its founder Ingvar Kamprad. He was raised in a spartan environment. His goal reducing the cost between the cost to manufacture and the price charged to the end customer, once commenting, "I'm a bit tight with money, but so what? I look at the money I'm about to spend on myself and ask myself if IKEA's customers can afford it.... I could regularly travel first class but having money in abundance doesn't seem like a good reason to waste it."[7] This sentiment has persisted in the company with key enhancements throughout its supply chain. The company focuses its product design prioritizing design elements against a matrix of what matters most to the customer: required customer labor, quality, form, function, sustainability, and low price. This approach enabled IKEA to make tradeoffs that include unfinished elements of the final product (do you need the back of the cabinet to have an expensive finish?). They also closely partner with their suppliers to take high-end designs and produce them at a lower

6 "Walmart: 2022 Annual Report," Walmart, accessed July 12, 2023, https://s201.q4cdn. com/262069030/files/doc_financials/2022/ar/WMT-FY2022-Annual-Report.pdf.

7 Riz Pasha, "37 Ingvar Kamprad Quotes—Founder of IKEA," SuccessFeed, June 24, 2019, succeedfeed. com/ingvar-kamprad-quotes/.

cost point—in one instance they worked to create a new particle board alternative with lower overall raw materials by around 85,000 tons. In addition, everything about their store and operations to include placement of stores typically outside higher cost city centers facilitates a low overhead approach to the business, improving efficiency.[8]

Oftentimes, the PE firm's initial actions to streamline operations may seem more tactical—the end goal is to create a streamlined version of the asset that they purchased and put in place world class organizational design and systems to ensure long term cost improvement, thus improving their return.

One commonality between the two is that the companies have strong cultures, which continues to drive these structural cost improvements. I have worked with companies that have attempted to make these changes. The typical undoing is not the desire or incentive structure, but rather senior management's ability to maintain what has been put into place shortly after close. If you have a CEO who routinely does around the world trips flying business class that sets a precedent for the company. Identifying the right culture and then reinforcing it is critical to ensure cost remains a competitive advantage.

There are instances when this is not the case. There are PE firms that just want to "flip" a company or the situation warrants that the company be "flipped." A number of these short-term holds occur when the asset is significantly under priced—for instance coming out of a bankruptcy with an improved balance sheet or when the company's operations are significantly underperforming with limited growth upside potential. In these situations you may see rapid value creation to unlock rapid EBITDA growth and use of increased leverages with dividends to unlock the economic value for return to the investors.

The importance of the PE firm's ability to understand what additional strategic value it can unlock rapidly in an investment is critical in the deal process and deal design. With higher multiples, putting in place sound value creation plans and management teams that can generate that value

8 "IKEA: Cutting Costs, Creating Value," Technology and Operations Management, Harvard Business School, December 5, 2015, d3.harvard.edu/platform-rctom/submission/ikea-cutting-costs-creating-value/; "Meet Ingvar Kamprad," IKEA Museum, accessed July 10, 2023, ikeamuseum.com/en/explore/the-story-of-ikea/meet-ingvar-kamprad/; Joel Brown, "36 Quotes by the Self Made Billionaire Ingvar Kamprad," Addicted2Success, February 8, 2017, addicted2success.com/quotes/36-intriguing-quotes-by-ingvar-kamprad/.

will set apart top decile returns from the rest of the pack. In addition, in situations that require leverage, identification of plans that generate additional cost focused EBITDA improvements enable the investors financing partners to give them credit for those actions and unlock additional dollars at a lower cost of capital, thus potentially improving their internal rates of return and money on money returns.

CHAPTER 2

Assessing an Investment

Diligence is the mother of good luck.
—Benjamin Franklin[9]

Part of any acquisition process is what's loosely called "due diligence." Taking both technical and legal forms, it's the snooping around an acquiring company does to make sure it's actually getting what it thinks it is.
—Antonio Garcia Martinez[10]

In current market environments for buyout funds, acquisition targets are not usually healthy, high growth companies. There are exceptions, but usually the valuations on those companies (near market highs) may not be attractive for most buyout private equity firms. PE firms can acquire them or a meaningful interest in them in some unique situations where a founder wants an exit, where a company is not fully penetrating its market or potential markets (growth-based value creation), where capital injection is required through a debt, hybrid, or a minority equity investment to fund growth, and strategic decisions to take a large company or a portion of it private to avoid punishment by public equity markets, including activist petitions for value creation purposes. At the end of the day, buyout private equity firms are a strong source of capital for public and privately held companies. Those that know how to use its advantages and are not afraid

---

9   Benjamin Franklin, *Franklin's Way to Wealth, or Poor Richard Improved* (London: W. and T. Darton, 1810).
10   Antonio Garcia Martinez, "How I Sold My Company to Twitter, Went to Facebook, and Screwed My Co-Founders," *Wired*, June 27, 2016, www.wired.com/2016/06/how-i-sold-my-company-to-twitter-went-to-facebook-and-screwed-my-co-founders/.

of the value private equity firms can bring benefit greatly, as do their shareholders.

However, one thing that should be highlighted is a public company's strategic use of a take private sale to make required changes outside of the public eye. The most common occur in two basic scenarios:

1. The selling company sells one of its non-core businesses or brands. This occurs because the larger company typically has underinvested in the business line and there are operational efficiencies. These assets are typically called carve-outs or divestitures, as the selling business is "carving" a piece of its business out for sale.

2. When a company shifts its commercial model A common example from point sales to a XaaS business model. Strategic use of a private holding can avoid public equity punishment of perceived decreased earnings during these transitions.

Carve-outs work well for public companies. In general, the public company receives a capital injection into its core businesses from the sale of the non-core assets. The core businesses can do better because the management is solely focused on their growth. Typically, the non-core businesses have also been less profitable or in some way reducing the valuation of the total enterprise. When they are removed, the remainder typically benefits.

A recent example of a carve-out is Shiseido's sale of brand assets for Laura Mercier, bareMinerals, and Buxom to an investor. I was the chief transformation officer that helped structure and oversee the carve-out and standup of the middle and back-office of the future business. This was a transaction where the assets could leverage focused effort from a new management team and a revised go-to-market strategy to potentially improve the forecast for one of the brands and then leverage the profit from the others to fund it. I will discuss more about the mechanics of a carve-out in Chapter 6.

Commercial model shifts are usually punished by public markets. This is very common in the tech sector as a company shifts from a buy and consume to a service model. In this situation, companies will typically see a real dip in earning as the bulk revenue from platform buys shifts to periodic installments. Upon completion of the transformation, the company will create a more sustainable model with revenue more closely aligned with customer value. These are perfect situations for private equity ownership. In these situations, the firms typically also benefit from the focused attention of the PE firm and the investment made in the management team, systems, and infrastructure.

As a PE shop acquires a company, there are multiple phases of the acquisition process. These will depend heavily on the type of process being conducted and how the process unfolds. The most common process is a competitive bid. So I will walk you through this.

For the rest of this chapter, I will discuss the various diligence items that PE shops will perform prior to signing a deal. Given human nature, there is also an implicit need to investigate the asset and claims of the management and ownership selling the asset. It is always better to walk away from a good deal than to transact on a bad one. To ensure that does not occur, investors will conduct various investigations into the validity and understanding of the seller's claims and projections. In addition to the validation, diligence also is used to validate and ensure that the investment thesis that the investment team presents to the investment committee (IC) is backed up. This latter part can also include forward-looking projections and assessments.

There are multiple elements of a properly executed diligence. At a minimum, the PE shop will likely conduct four professional assessments of the company:

1. Financial assessment
2. Commercial assessment
3. Legal assessment
4. Operational diligence

The first three elements are essential to ensure the investors get what they are paying for. I will provide a very brief description of the critical elements of their typical work packages. Please note: these descriptions are developed on a "by and large" basis, meaning 80 percent of the time this will cover their key work outputs. Not all advisors or assessments are done the same. Some advisors, although initially scoped for an FDD, CDD, or ODD, cover other elements of the needed assessment well at little to no additional cost.

Operational improvements in the asset and the associated diligence has grown to be a necessity in the past five to 10 years because of valuations and the increasing complexity of firm operations. Operational diligence is now an essential tool in the diligence kit to ensure that the financial model has incorporated all of the critical cost structures required to realize the investment thesis and to provide the required insight to hold management teams accountable to run streamlined operations without impinging on revenue growth. Because of the growing importance in the private equity world for the need to improve asset operations, it was time to provide the market and the PE community a toolkit to understand what each function does and how effective operators can create a world-class operation. This is why I am writing this book.

At the time of this writing, there are only three firms that do operational diligence and improvement of the operations at a world-class level: McKinsey, Alvarez & Marsal, and AlixPartners. They have the breadth and depth of operational expertise and the professionals that have participated in PE value creation activities at scale and volume to do it well. They are the Harvard, Yale, and Princeton of private equity performance improvement.

In addition to the critical four assessments, there are other diligence elements that can be used including

1. Technical (e.g., new technology, software platforms)
2. IT systems
3. Management/HR
4. Digital
5. ESG

After this I will provide a brief description of each of these. Please note that elements of each of these may be used in commercial or operational diligences. These offerings, along with financial diligence, are relatively commoditized. They are also backward looking, with limited prognostication for the future health or value of the firm.

On the contrary, the commercial and operational diligences require bespoke approaches because they provide future financial projections to the investment team. In addition, these assessments may also use or include elements of the commoditized assessments to validate the forward-looking projections. The bespoke assessments will likely be used at the investment committee, when speaking with limited partners, or with investment banks to ensure that the PE firm achieves its financing and, most importantly, its desired return, usually measured in internal rate of return or money on money (MOM) return.

Each element is usually conducted by expert, objective advisors to ensure that the investment team's enthusiasm is validated by professionals with limited interest in the economics of the deal itself. The diligence and diligence elements can take many forms considering the industry, the company, the condition of the company, and the investment thesis. Private equity firms carefully select which elements are required for each investment. Each element is expensive costing between $100,000 to multi-millions of dollars for more bespoke and critical diligence elements. Critical to understanding this is that the investor is stuck with "dead deal costs" in the event the transaction is not consummated.

FINANCIAL DUE DILIGENCE

The financial assessment, also known as a financial due diligence (FDD) or a quality of earnings (QoE) report validates and independently assesses the financial statements that are prepared by the management team and the sellers. The final report will also include adjustments and offsets that the investment team needs to consider in their final deal economics. In addition, the QoE may also look at the working capital and capital expenditures of the business, dependent on industry or deal specifics. These additional analyses help the deal team establish working capital pegs and value items in the required capital expenditure for the asset. Each of these are critical and will be covered in future segments of the book.

FDD and QoE are required to ensure that the stated financials can be validated and that earnings and profit from the company match the cash generation stated by the company. These are then verified against individual records such as accounts receivable accounts, receipts, bank statements, accounts payable accounts, and other financial statements available from the seller and the company being sold.

In general, the financials prepared for sale of an asset are optimized to increase the value of the company for the sellers. Historical financials typically include adjustments that make the current profitability and health of the company seem better than reality. These adjustments typically include explicit callouts such as stated one-time items (e.g., deferred revenue, legal expense, cancellation fees, or other large one-time operational expenses), potential restructuring expense (e.g., severance, consultants), unique accounting changes, and sometimes operational improvements projected or anticipated by the management team. Ensuring that you understand and validate or adjust these off of economic models for the deal value can be critical to the potential return desired by investors.

Two other critical analyses that the Financial Diligence team provides can be differentiators in certain deals.

Working capital analysis and forward projections are utilized by the deal team to negotiate and establish the working capital peg. From an operational perspective, the working capital peg is a critical value point in a transaction. In the working capital analysis, the accountant's analyze and assess the past trends for working capital accounts of the asset that include inventory, accounts receivable, and accounts payable. The analysis typically takes into account benchmarks from other companies to ensure that the working capital on day one meets the companies operational needs. As the investor takes over the asset, they need to ensure that these accounts, which can contain millions of dollars of value, are maintained. If they are not then the dollars captured by the seller will, in theory, need to be reconstituted at the buyer's expense. In consumer companies, the inventory element of the working capital peg can be a major issue. If not understood or negotiated properly, the buyer could receive a company with depleted saleable goods. In this situation, the seller usually has an economic incentive to burn down the inventory before close, as they could receive wholesale price when they may just need to replenish at cost. Accounts receivable and accounts payable should also be maintained. In general, the seller can seek to collect accounts receivables early or pay payables late. These differences from standard operation can shift cost or eliminate the ability to collect dollars at close to the buyer.

Capital expense analysis is another area that can be of value for the seller and the buyer alike. The analysis examines the capital expenditure trends for the business. They are usually compared against benchmarks and the anticipated past and future needs of the business. In CAPEX intensive businesses like industrials, telecommunications, or oil and gas industries, underinvestment in the core business and operational facilities can indicate poor performance in future years. It is commonplace that businesses that are planned to be sold receive less investment in the preceding years. This underinvestment then may require the buyer to invest in the business upon acquisition. The capital expense analysis may identify these deficiencies. These value items need to be incorporated into final valuation

The FDD and QoE is the most necessary diligence element. It is the one that ensures the investor receives the economic value it believes available in the transaction. It is an assessment that is required in every transaction.

COMMERCIAL DILIGENCE

Future projections provided by the company typically follow a common trend—the graph for revenue and profit typically looks like a hockey stick. Regardless of the company or industry or historical trend, the typical story in a confidential information memorandum (CIM) is that the management team has a great new plan that will cause revenue to increase and profitability to climb!

Although fictious, here is how this talk track typically goes (my sarcastic commentary is in parentheses):

"Despite Company X's declining revenue base, our management team is putting in place a new five point plan (just for you Mr. or Mrs. Investor). This plan will stem the declines in year 1 and grow revenue in year 2 (despite your 10-year negative revenue CAGR? What has changed?). We expect revenue growth at 5 percent per annum after that. (But your market grows at 3 percent—that's impressive....)"

"Our profitability although currently negative. Has a positive cash flow (from operations, but negative with working capital and capital expense needs). Our adjusted EBITDA (although fictitious) indicates a company with exceptionally strong underlying financials and operations. With the last three points of the five-point plan, we intend to increase our cash flow by 25 percent of revenue in less than three years and continuous improvement will ensure we maintain or improve our EBITDA margins in the outyears. (Since you are currently managing this company, then why are you selling this 'prize' and the great opportunity it presents?)"

There is a similar story in each report and the initial basis of offers for the asset. From a negotiating perspective, it is the smart thing for the seller to do. This ensures that the initial offers from potential buyers are based on the most optimistic scenario. Some management teams are more aspirational with limited ability to deliver. Others will keep these potential economics within the realm of realistic outcomes. The commercial diligence helps the investment team assess the ability for the company to achieve or exceed those topline projections. The operational diligence does the same for the operating profit. I will cover the operational diligence last as that will be the focus of the remainder of the book.

The commercial diligence is yet another critical element of the overall assessment of the asset. It is used to validate the commercial assumptions of the business. This is key to ensure that the economic model put together by the investment team is correct.

Commercial diligence focuses on validating the strategic and commercial viability of the asset. It also will often push further to include opportunities for potential improvement to understand what realistic growth and revenue assumptions are. The commercial diligence element is typically conducted by top-tier strategic advisors such as McKinsey and Bain. They have "factories" of strategic analysts that will assess the company's revenue generation through a series of primary and secondary sources. The effort will focus on key hypotheses that the investment team needs to ensure are correct. Here are some typical hypotheses that the commercial diligence team will be charged with:

- What is the projected growth rate for the industry? Will the potential asset grow at, above, or below the market?
- What is the consumer sentiment for these brands? What are key breaks in the purchasing funnel?
- With three scenarios, how can we improve the revenue generation of the company during the hold period?

The hypotheses can be rather large in scope. Top-tier talent is required to rapidly assess these questions and provide meaningful information to the investment team.

The diligence team will use company provided information and other primary and secondary sources to validate and answer the questions requested by the investment teams. The teams will leverage interviews from industry executives and other experts to answer these questions. Administration of surveys will help to underpin customer or industry sentiment about the company. In addition, they will leverage research reports and other secondary sources to confirm commercial viability of the asset.

The insight they provide is exceptionally valuable to the investment team. In transformation scenarios (e.g., the asset will use a new operating model or the investors will invest to improve a brand and need new revenue projections), the commercial diligence is indispensable and can serve in certain ways as the topline model for the investors.

LEGAL ASSESSMENT

The entire transaction is predicated on a legal transition of ownership of a company to another ownership structure. Legal teams will take part in the diligence of an asset across a number of different vectors. In general, they focus on a few key areas:

1. What is the perimeter of the transaction and does the seller of the asset have the right to sell and transfer the asset?
2. How can the transaction be financed and the contracts required to support the intricacies of the deal?
3. What legal entity structure is required to support the legality of cash flows to the various stakeholders? (This is done in concert with the tax assessment.)
4. In an asset sale (anything less than a full company), what other key contracts or intellectual property will need to convey to ensure that the company is not impaired?
5. Contractual, liabilities, and litigation assessment. Are there any contracts or liabilities that the company and seller has not made the buyer aware of? For contracts provided, are there

> any concerns or limitations on the operation of the company
> or ability to work in markets that the company needs to be
> aware of (e.g., exclusive distribution contracts)?

The legal team for each transaction will also work to pull together the actual legal agreement in parallel with the rest of the diligence. These documents require a significant amount of detail and it ensures that you have sufficient time to review all of the particular elements prior to signing the transaction.

OPERATIONAL DILIGENCE

Operational diligence is a tool in the diligence and value creation toolkit that can and should be used for every control type investment made. Through this vehicle, investment teams can leverage world-class professionals to understand the potential issues and areas of improvement available in the company's operations. The output of the diligence will also help the investors better understand what is needed for the investment thesis and underwriting case to hold the management teams accountable to deliver on the full potential value of the asset. This maximizes returns for the investors and their LPs. Firms that do not conduct this type of analysis leave money on the table and at worst could be blind to major issues that could put into jeopardy the return.

In a lot of cases in the current environment, buyout private equity buyers are often purchasing assets that are past their high growth phase, that have been inadequately invested in, or are potentially in decline. When a buyer is potentially going to face these situations, they need to ensure that they understand what they are buying and what improvements may be needed.

So, I am walking down the street in New York. On the street, I see an iPhone being sold for $500. The current market price for that model of iPhone is closer to $799. However, it has a cracked screen and the owner tells me that otherwise it works perfectly well. Repair costs for the screen are estimated at $100. This could be a good deal. However, when you start to look at the device closer, you see that it does not have the right lens configuration and the Apple logo on the back looks more like a pear and not an apple. I decide this may not be the best purchase. By doing that additional bit of investigation and assessment, I walk away from something that would have lost me money relative to the true value of the asset.

In operational diligence, teams rapidly assess all elements of the operations of the firm from commercial, logistics, manufacturing, services, SG&A, marketing, sales, executive team, facilities, HR, finance, accounting, R&D, and engineering. In the analysis, they provide a viewpoint on the quality of operations and the ability for new management teams to step in and streamline the operations under the new investment thesis and strategic agenda. With top-notch diligence teams, in addition to providing red flag analysis for the deal, they will also provide you the key initiatives that will drive the value (e.g., organizational redesign, replatforming an antiquated monolith software platform), the timeline that the management team (with proactive support) needs to realize the value, the order of magnitude cash improvement of the initiative, the cost to achieve, and the key risks and tradeoffs by undertaking that critical initiative.

With this assessment and the appropriate levels of conservatism, the underwriting case and ability to improve returns are vastly enhanced. In addition, it also alerts investors to potential problem areas that they need to be concerned with or allows them to identify and trade value for them in the economics of the deal.

OTHER ASSESSMENTS

For any given industry or unique situation there are a bevy of other backward looking assessments that can be conducted. Here are a quick selection and description of the most relevant. For any other need that arises, there is also likely a professional that can render an opinion.

Technical Assessment

For highly technical industries such as the payments space, software, high tech manufacturing, and less mature technologies or startups, a technical assessment of products and services can be requested and conducted. These assessments focus on gaining an understanding of the current state of the product or service, identify any potential concerns with the technical elements or the limitations of the product or service.

Please note that although requested, this access is not always provided. The theft of intellectual property and know-how can be debilitating to the potential seller. This is an assessment that should be asked for when appropriate.

This is helpful for startups or less mature products. It provides the investment team an objective opinion on the quality of the technical coding or structure of the program. It can also point out potential points of weakness in the technical operations of the product or service being provided by the company.

IT System Assessment

An IT system assessment is specific to the internal information technology deployed by the company. This assessment reviews the current state of the IT landscape and identifies potential areas of concern. These assessments can be required in situations where an in depth understanding of the systems is required. This occurs often in the payment space, the telecommunication space, and when there are bespoke systems that are critical to business operations.

With legacy companies, you will often see homegrown solutions playing critical roles in the value chain of the business. In one instance, there was a payment provider with a homegrown solution for processing payments. They had planned to update their system to a new, cloud-based alternative that they planned to build. In this instance, it was imperative for the investor to diligence the current and future state systems.

A typical operational diligence will also look at the critical IT systems and their connections. This will provide the investor a view on how to modernize and improve the systems. It will also show the level of maturity and automation of their processes. This is helpful to understand how efficient the business has been run.

Management Assessment

A management assessment objectively assesses the existing management team for a company. There are many different approaches to this assessment. At a minimum, investment and operational teams will conduct a review of the résumés and reputations of the management team. For some executives, they may also conduct a more detailed review, which could include a battery of questions and interviews to determine what type of person the individual is, what are the individual's motives, and how they lead. These can be important for critical roles or when there is a question as whether to hire or retain a given executive.

HR Assessment

The HR assessment reviews key policies and procedures for the company. They will also review key systems and the operations of the HR department. The value to investors is also for the teams to review benefit plans and potential liabilities with defined benefit plans or union plans. With assessments on the benefits plans and the retirement liabilities, the investor can potentially create value through enhanced benefit plan offerings. It can also understand and not be surprised by the potential liabilities in the benefit plan. When appropriate, they can also ask for economic tradeoffs to offset potential issues or losses the investor could incur if assumed as is.

E-Commerce Assessment

A digital or e-commerce assessment will review the digital business for a given company. These assessments are largely conducted in the consumer and retail space when improvements in the digital business can improve profitability for the business. These assessments will review site traffic, buy funnel, discount programs for the e-commerce business, and conduct a qualitative assessment of the e-commerce and social media business operations. In today's marketplace, integration of the e-commerce business with social media and, if applicable, brick and mortar presence may also be conducted.

Environmental, Social, and Governance (ESG) Assessment

The ESG assessment is relatively new and growing in relevance because of some investors limited partners' desire to improve ESG globally. Some have argued that the main point of PE should focus on economic return. Others argue that ESG is something that the limited partners desire and, in addition, consumers and others value for the brand to be successful in today's market. From an objective standpoint, there is value in assessing companies for ESG compliance. There are areas that investors should not be exposed to. For instance, an ESG assessment could potentially uncover DEI issues or others that could cause a brand to be degraded after close.

The key output from an ESG assessment will vary, but it will focus on identifying red flags that the investor should be aware of. It will also review the company's stance on DEI, climate, governance, and other areas. The professionals will largely examine the company's policies, their approach to potential reporting requirements, contractual commitments, ownership of ESG initiatives, training on ESG, communication, and metrics. For DEI, it will also review recruiting, employee engagement, and metrics. For climate, they will also review strategy for emissions containment.

With this assessment in place, the investor can understand key risks to the asset and to their overall portfolio position. Oft times, investors need to report to their LPs on these critical topics.

Contractual/Litigation Assessment

Contractual and litigation liability can destroy value in an asset or introduce large, unexpected costs into a company's P&L post close. To minimize this risk your legal advisor can review the contracts and other elements of the company's records for potential risk. It can also review any outstanding litigation on the asset. If there are key litigation items outstanding, the investor can avoid liability through structures in the contract on when they assume liability and when the seller would be responsible for potential liabilities.

CHAPTER 3

Analyzing a Company's Operations

Excellence is an art won by training and habituation: we do not act right-
ly because we have virtue or excellence, but we rather have these because
we have acted rightly; "these virtues are formed in man by his doing the
actions"; we are what we repeatedly do. Excellence, then, is not an act but
a habit: "the good of man is a working of the soul in the way of excellence
in a complete life... for as it is not one swallow or one fine day that makes a
spring, so it is not one day or a short time that
makes a man blessed and happy."
—Will Durant[11]

When assessing operations of a company, what you are
looking for is a company that is maximizing the efficiency of its operations. It will also have systems in place to continually streamline the
organization and operations removing waste and excess from the company. This should be true regardless of industry and regardless of growth
trajectory. Often executives in growth stage companies do not focus on
removing waste from the system. It is equally important to what they
believe they can do with the topline. **Always remember that topline is
aspirational; bottom line is actionable.**

The method I am presenting to analyze the operations of a company
is an invaluable skillset. It is applicable across all industries and all size
of companies. The process is what makes the diligence effective and
complete. For professional teams, the time to analyze a company is
limited to the deal timing. Typically, this entire assessment needs to be

---

11   Will Durant, *The Story of Philosophy: The Lives and Opinions of the Great Philosophers* (New
York: Simon & Schuster: 1926), 87.

completed within one and four weeks to impact the investment team's decision. For this effort, the professional consultants that perform this work typically deploy teams of experts to develop the critical insights needed at speed.

For individual investors or others interested in the key topics, this timeline may not exist or the level of investment to bring on dedicated teams of professionals may not be practical. Because of this, I am providing the basic building blocks of what you look for in a company and the typical levers used to streamline the operations. This is followed by individual sections in the book that speak to each function, what is in that function and typical levers for optimization. I have made the sections for easy reference and to allow you to hone in on the specific function you are concerned with or need to prepare for that day. These sections can be used on an ad hoc basis or in totality to understand how a company works and how it can be streamlined holistically.

To be most effective, users of these materials should continually focus on a Pareto approach to value. Pareto can often be called "80/20" meaning 80 percent of the value comes from 20 percent of the effort. Whether in this or in other large-scale programs, this method of prioritization has been proven to be highly effective.

Let me walk through this using an example:

An analyst on one of my projects encountered a marketing organization that was spending 5 percent of the company's revenue base. Industry peers were closer to 1 percent at the median and .75 percent at the top quartile performance. We knew there was a significant opportunity to reduce marketing spend and streamline the organization. In the end, we would have to examine both—but which should be done first?

When we looked at the individual benchmarks we identified that the non-personnel spend was four times that of the top quartile companies and three times the median. The organization was also large, but initial views on spans and layers indicated an average of five. The typical normal for an organization is at six, unless additional restructuring could be conducted.

Although marketing spend and headcount spend were each about $30 million He decided to examine the marketing spend first and the marketing organization second.

He immediately identified key areas of opportunity in the marketing spend including reduction in advisory spend, reduction in negative ROI paid media, and event spend, saving the company about $10 million. When we examined the organization, the team only identified about $2 million in headcount reduction, largely focused on excess managers.

The analyst maximized his effort by focusing on the area of the highest probable gain. He knew the company was mismanaging the non-personnel spend. The benchmarks told him that. He used that key figure and unlocked the majority of the value $10 million out of $12 million. If he had focused on the organization first, he may not have found the full value.

When you analyze the company operations, operators tend to get bogged down into the minutiae of how a company operates. They are not wrong. The operations of a company are very complex. To be effective assessing operations, investors, advisors, and analysts should work to find where the inefficiencies in the organization and spend profile are and then ask key questions of the professionals managing that area. Typically, these excesses are rationalized by the management team because it requires investment, requires a level of effort or risk they are not incented for, or because intractable personalities limit their ability to enact the change. When assessing the company and with the incentive structure and investment of private equity investors, these barriers can be effectively managed. In short, the goal is to identify the range of improvement that is achievable and then put a cost to achieve and timing against it.

It is also because of these unique issues that a full top-down approach to improvement operations and accompanying strategic rationale of why the company is not performing in the top quartile does not always hold. I have made large sweeping generalizations about the operations of firms. On a by and large basis we could always tell it was a number of factors combined that led to the various inefficiencies. The management teams are typically trying to do the right thing. However, the Institutional Imperative comes into play. When it does, it creates pockets of opportunity that require discrete initiatives to go and fix. This is why excellent operational assessments are always bespoke and not cookie cutter. They require the teams to analyze the operations and identify those nuggets that open value for the firm. Approaching operational improvement solely top down is on par with trying to identify every person on earth from the moon, a lot will be missed.

Here is how Warren Buffet described the Institutional Imperative in a chairman's letter to Berkshire Hathaway in 1989, "…(1) As if governed by Newton's First Law of Motion, an institution will resist any change in its current direction, (2) Just as work expands to fill available time, corporate projects or acquisitions will materialize to soak up available funds, (3) Any business craving of the leader, however foolish, will be quickly supported by detailed rate-of-return and strategic studies prepared by his (or her) troops; and (4) The behavior of peer companies, whether they are expanding, acquiring, setting executive compensation or whatever, will be mindlessly imitated. Institutional dynamics, not venality or stupidity, set businesses on these courses, which are too often misguided."

Don't discount any opportunity immediately. If you are uncertain about it, size the full opportunity as the maximum available opportunity and then use a zero as the minimum value for the opportunity, indicating that there is a potential initiative, but you are uncertain whether it can be executed or if it may be too expensive to execute.

Here is the reason why: for a PE investor, when they look at cash flow generation improvement, they do not focus on the in-year number. This is the typical method by which management teams are incented. The management team is typically held to focus on profitability, usually in the near term with this quarter or this year being a priority. Private investors look at the company as an asset. They want the asset price to increase. To do this, they need to increase the strategic importance of the asset (cash generation). When a management team improves cash generation by $1 million a PE investor stands to enrich its investors by somewhere between seven to 20-plus times that number, depending on industry and growth characteristics of the asset. **Even if they need to invest $1 million to increase EBITDA by $1 million, it is a positive return on investment overall.** It's amazing that more companies and the stock markets do not begin to hold public equity management teams to the same incentive mechanisms.

When analysts state the potential improvements that can be made it is critical to use ranges of improvement. There is a saying, "If you tell me a number, I will tell you that you are wrong with about 99.9 percent certainty. If you tell me a range of potential outcomes, I can tell you that you are right with 99.9 percent certainty." At this stage of assessment, there are several factors why this is true. However, the two most germane reasons are:

- The information you will likely receive cannot always be fully trusted. The seller has incentives to give you the information they want to give you. This may or may not indicate the current state of the operations.
- In execution there are trade-offs that need to be made to get certain initiatives across. In companies, there can be everything from personalites that cannot be touched, executive initiatives (e.g. sacred cows, special initiatives, executive pet projects) Personal relationships (e.g. the founder's friend, the CEO's family friend) or other unknown unknowns, like system limitations that can potentially impact the execution of a given initiative.

In this element, be wary of the numbers that you publish. I would always tell my teams to always give me a low-end estimate that you would be willing to bet your next paycheck on. For the high end, be aggressive. Typically when these numbers are given to the investment team they will apply a downside reduction to them. Bank underwriters will always reduce any of these forecasts by about 25 percent. I have also heard one operating professional use a formulaic approach. He would average the low and high end and then apply a 40 percent reduction to it for the majority of assessments. In my professional experience, I have a track record of getting to 100 percent of the aligned value for my scope of work in actual execution.

In general, investors and management team's track record for achieving revenue upside post acquisition is spotty. Revenue synergies are not completely under the control of the management team. As such, they tend to think about this as a value creation lever that is less reliable than cost focused levers such as headcount reduction or cost improvement. For potential revenue increases, the downside scenario offsets tend to be more severe. Underwriters and other stakeholders can sometimes give you no credit for the synergy, but typically between 50 to 75 percent reduction on potential topline opportunities.

ALIGNING TIMELINES

Given the tight timeline for these assessments, it is important upfront to align on expectations and deliverables. In general the difference in outcome of assessments is certainty and actionability of the answer given additional time, appropriate resourcing, and information. Timelines for operational assessments can be expanded or contracted as needed given these tradeoffs. In general, an ideal amount of time is between two and six weeks, depending on the size and complexity of the company. The simple acquisition of a small, simple company (<$300 million in cost baseline) can likely be done well in about two to three weeks with an adequately staffed team of experts. A large or complex company or one with a merger or carve-out would be on the longer end of that spectrum.

DATA REQUESTS AND INTERVIEWS

To inform the process, data provided by the seller and discussion with the management team is a critical component to formulate the required assessments of the target company. There are a few critical sources of information that you should always request. Depending on the industry, there are other elements of data that should be requested, as well.

The data request will usually always be made once the investor enters a non-binding bid and that bid is down selected amongst other potential investors. There are times when just the CIM is released prior to that point. There are also times when the seller will give a bit more information prior to the non-binding bids. This down select usually starts a clock in the process of usually between two to four weeks until a binding bid needs to be made. This period, for complex industries or transactions, can extend out to six to eight weeks. This is commonplace for companies going through a divestiture. The extended timelines can also occur in sole-source (one-bidder) deals.

The critical elements of the data request for operational diligence are:

1. Employee census with pay and fringe benefit detail.
2. Accounts payable transaction level detail.

3. Detailed income statement and balance sheet data by
    business segment preferably business line level trial balances.

These three items are the most important because from this, you would understand the cash spend of the company from operations. The limitation is then on context of the spend and how everything comes together, which is provided in the additional data requests. However, with these data sets you have what is needed to set the cash baseline for the company. For some activities, looking at trial balance level detail is critical to ensure you have knowledge of the subaccount build up to the income statement and balance sheet. For accounting and accounts payable information, you would want at least one year worth of data. For census data you, would like the most current snapshot.

In addition to these items, a larger ask should also be made that would include additional items such as. Please note that this list is not exhaustive by any means, but provides an initial starting point for what you would likely ask for:

1. Detailed business plans / strategic plans
2. Market and competitor overview
3. Summary of recent, ongoing, and planned strategic initiatives
4. Current organizational charts
5. Facility summary with ownership or leasing information
6. Critical IT systems, critical interfaces, and schematics
7. IT capital budgets, IT temp labor, and IT service contracts
8. Networking configuration and expenses
9. Major IT contracts
10. Major third party spend contracts (typically top 10 or 20)
11. Manufacturing overview, production information, and facility layout and information
12. Monthly inventories by product and location
13. Supply chain flow information
14. Warehouse inbound receipt information
15. Warehouse shipment detail
16. Transportation transactional detail
17. Product and technology roadmaps
18. Multi-year plan for product development

19. Core product technologies and languages used
20. Infrastructure detail
21. Cyber security architecture
22. Call center technology, process, and metrics
23. Retail store sales, inventories, and detail
24. Key process diagrams (if available)
25. Key customer contracts
26. Marketing strategies for core products or brands
27. Marketing spend detail
28. Sales goals
29. Sales performance and sales performance by quota bearing professionals
30. Customer segmentation, feedback and surveys
31. HR policies (e.g. severance, employee handbook) and key agreements (e.g., union)
32. Employee turnover data
33. Recruiting and hiring data
34. External compensation and benchmarking studies and policies
35. Legal cost summary including outside legal spend
36. Travel expenditure ledger and policies

In addition to these data elements, you should also ask to speak with critical executives. Typically, you do not need to speak with the CEO. If you do, it is normally in discussion on the strategic ambition of the company or vision for the future. Interaction with the CEO and others on the selling board are best left for the members of the deal team that would be working with them. They are more relationship building and deterministic of the go-forward relationship. From an operator or advisor perspective, these interactions, although ego-boosting, tend to not be value added for the target of this exercise which is to find value and inform the investment thesis for the new ownership of the company. This may or may not align with the management's current vision.

However, everyone from the CFO down may be viable interactions as they tend to be knowledge holders within the organization on key initiatives and operations.

When setting these agendas, it is important to develop an agenda and even provide some of the questions you plan to start the conversation with. Conversations meander, but it is helpful to the executive that you allow them to prepare as much as possible so that they can provide quantitative responses to the questions you have for them. In addition, it helps you to build rapport with them and gain an element of trust with the executive during these important interactions.

A typical diligence call agenda may look like this:

Executive	Time Requested	Key Topics	Key Questions
CFO	2 hours	1. Current financial picture 2. Finance processes and systems 3. Finance org structure 4. Working capital and cash management	1. Can you explain the degrading cash generation from operations in the past three quarters? 2. We noticed that your accounting organization has a significant number of revenue analysts could you help us understand what is driving this need? 3. How many ERP systems do you manage? 4. There appear to be 50 FP&A professionals in your organization—could you help us understand how they are utilized? 5. Your AP outstanding appears to be high (~70 days vs 60 days per contract) are there any policies you have in place around this?

Depending on the situation, the additional information gleaned from executives can provide on operations can be critical to the assessment developed by the professional team. In the examples above you will notice that the questions indicate that the professional team has reviewed the data and begun to identify red flags or areas of potential optimization where they could leverage additional information to make an informed recommendation. For instance, running five enterprise resource planning systems (ERP) would not make economic sense for most companies. This introduces a potential area of opportunity if there is limited business reason for the distinct systems. Consolidating them into a new enterprise solution may be a viable solution to improve overall outcomes at the company.

These interactions with key executives at the target are critical to the analysis put forward by the professional team. They provide color to the analysis conducted. In addition, they begin to form relationships between the advisors, investors, and the management team. These relationships can be helpful if the investors are successful and acquire the company.

OTHER SOURCES OF INFORMATION

In addition to company provided information, teams should also leverage second and third party sources of information. The goal for your recommendations and analysis that you have a well thought through and triangulated view on the issue or opportunity. Triangulation is a process in which you leverage multiple independent data points or sources of information and arrive at or close to the same conclusion.

In one interaction my expanded team had done a full bottom-up build of the projected revenue for a company and the growth of the revenue in the marketplace. The model was so intricate that it took customer by customer analysis of wins and losses and risks to the revenue profile. It also incorporated key changes to the operating model where we planned to ramp down a number of retail outlets. In the end, it projected a close to 5 percent decline in the market. At the same time, I was working with a business line leader. His methodology to assess revenue impact was a top down, percent of market share approach. He assessed that there would be a 0.2 percent degradation in market share based on some key drivers he had seen. The two approaches landed our revenue projections into a neat $5 to $10 million window. But the triangulation between a bottom up build and a top down triangulation limited the uncertainty that we had for the enterprise. We chose the low end of the band and then based the remainder of our projected budget off that combined analysis.

The use of triangulation and other sources of information and insight is key to success and narrowing your range of uncertainty. Several sources of information can routinely be used. Here are a few that have proved helpful:

1. **Expert interviews**
   - Sources can range from paid expert consultations through firms like Alphasights, Dialectica, and others.
   - Discussions with former executives are critical. They typically have no skin in the game and can provide unvarnished opinions of the company. There are limitations on when you can speak to them. At a minimum, you would want somewhere between six months and one year of separation to eliminate the potential disclosure of material, non-public information (MNPI). If a public company, it is always important that a financial report by the company has been released (e.g., quarterly (10-Q) or annual report (10-K)). If there was something material, the company would have needed to disclose that during the reporting process.
   - Leverage your existing network to discuss critical topics—this is a key reason to maintain your contacts.

2. **Research reports**
   - Third party, independent research reports on public companies are beneficial to understand the company and key issues they may be facing.

3. **Social media and other websites**
   - Social media and sites like Glassdoor provide insight into a company's culture and operations. Reading through the social media feed on a company can help you understand potential issues. A lot is disclosed by disgruntled employees.
   - Layoff.com also provides insight into past layoffs. It will also often disclose other information about companies.

4. **News and press releases**
   - Companies will often times disclose issues in press releases or speaking engagements of key executives.
   - News releases can also potentially disclose key elements of operations, especially with local newspapers discussing size and scope of operational facilities in their areas.

BENCHMARKS SHOW YOU WHERE TO HUNT

The term benchmark stems from a military use to measure the effectiveness of a given firearm. When comparing firearms, marksmen would fire the various competitive set from the same spot on a bench, usually denoted by a mark. From there, they would compare the results. With those results, they would then select which firearm to use. The term has also been used by cobblers who make marks on a bench to measure shoe size, and also with builders, setting a mark for vertical structures to show distance above ground. For business, benchmarking, in some context, has been used since the 1800s when people like Henry Ford and Francis Lowell studied the processes of their competitors to improve their own operations.

Use of the term benchmark for business applications has been credited to Xerox in the 1980s. Xerox was losing market share to its Japanese competitors in the late 1970s. Its management launched a study to understand why. It found that a comparable product was being manufactured in Japan for 40 to 50 percent less than their cost. This allowed their competitors to undercut their price. In response, Xerox launched an initiative called "Leadership through Quality." It undertook to benchmark and assess over 230 areas of their operations. This did not just improve the quality of its product, but also its manufacturing efficiencies, internal processes, and overall value chain. This case study launched a phenomenon in the U.S. in the 1980s and 1990s to leverage benchmarks to improve overall outcomes. With that said, there are various types of benchmarks that business strategists use to derive insight:

1. Competitor: Studying competitor methods and know how and applying them to your business.
2. Process: Reviewing processes, even across industries, to derive insight or best practices that can be used in your line of business.
3. Internal: Using internal best practices and optimized operations to identify optimal performance.
4. External: Leveraging objectively produced benchmarks to compare business outcomes against others in your industry or comparison set.

During operational diligences, all of these will be leveraged. However, what differentiates an average diligence from a world-class diligence is how they are used. Oftentimes, analysts will leverage the easily available external benchmarks—typical sources include American Productivity and Quality Center (APQC) and the Corporate Executive Board (CEB)—as the potential range of outcomes. This is the easiest and most defensible answer that you can provide to an investor.

Here is an example of potential output based on benchmarks:

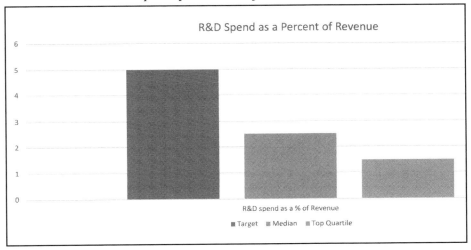

From this analysis you can derive that the company is grossly inefficient in R&D spend. If the target company's revenue was $100 million, then the potential opportunity would be between $2.5 and $3.5 million, shifting the cost from where they currently are at 5 percent of revenue down to 2.5 or 1.5 percent. Ideally, companies should be able to get to the top quartile.

Although helpful, this may or may not be achievable. World-class analysts for private equity performance improvement would use this to identify that this is a place where there is likely opportunity. However, the size and scale of that opportunity is not fully understood. To understand, it then requires the professional to delve into the operations of the company leveraging a mix of analysis and experience. This then allows them to develop a core set of hypotheses about potential methods for value creation in this area.

This is a critical step in the analysis and prevents teams from boiling the ocean, meaning analyzing every element of the business. Instead, it focuses the analysis using an 80/20 approach to pull together discrete initiatives that outline where value may be in a given company.

However, there are some instances where the analyst is not provided a sufficient amount of data or insufficient information can be gained through all sources about the operations of the company. In those instances, use of a benchmark to justify an opportunity can be a plausible solution. However, use of them in this manner should be limited.

HYPOTHESIS DRIVEN ANALYSIS CAPTURES THE MAJORITY OF VALUE

There are many elements of a company that need to be reviewed. Prioritizing and dividing the work up amongst a team or the individuals available is a critical step to success in shorter timeframes. For individuals required to analyze a company's operations, you may not have the luxury to do that. When that occurs, prioritization of effort is key—the goal being to identify the 80/20 of the key issues and opportunities for improvement in each company.

For large teams analyzing a company's operations, a best practice is to segment the work along a given expert's area of expertise or near adjacencies. For instance, if you have a teammate that was a software engineer at Google, it may make sense to have them work on the product, development, and potentially infrastructure areas. He could also potentially cover areas like IT and cybersecurity, as there are some similarities. The understanding he has of one area is highly transferrable to other adjacent areas.

When we look at dividing the work, a typical structure of the analysis and dividing of the workload can be along functional lines. In the list below, I have a comprehensive, but not exhaustive list of typical workstreams. The art for the manager or the individual is to focus the effort on critical areas and collapse others. For instance, in the example above, the team would likely collapse the IT and R&D workstreams under one individual. I have also seen G&A and operating model and operations and manufacturing commonly combined. The design is based on the industry and priorities that those assessing the company identify.

Here is the list:

1. Operating model
   - Organizational design
   - Executive roles and compensation
2. G&A
   - Finance and accounting
   - HR
   - Legal
   - General admin
   - Facilities
   - Other (corporate jets, yoga instructors, etc.)
3. IT
   - Applications
   - Infrastructure (cloud, co-lo, on-prem)
   - Cyber
   - Telecommunications
4. Sales and marketing
   - Brand management
   - Corporate marketing
   - Internal/external sales
   - Marketing spend
   - Trade spend
5. Research and development (tech company)
   - Product management
   - Engineering
   - Client-facing infrastructure
   - Project management
6. Research and engineering (traditional company)
   - Research and development
   - Engineering
   - Prototyping
7. Operations
   - Customer service
   - Warehouse
   - Order management
   - Returns
   - Inventory management

- Working capital management
8. Manufacturing
   - QA
   - Contracting for outsourced manufacturing
   - Four walls
   - Inbound supply chain and direct procurement
   - Design to value
   - Make vs. buy
9. Procurement
   - Contract and spend analysis for third-party spend

In each company, there is always an area that has the "most" opportunity and most issues. For times you have a large team available to you, it is a best practice to identify and place someone with a solid pedigree and work experience against that area of the case. In one situation, we knew that there was a lot of opportunity in the IT portfolio for a company. The end product would require a large-scale redesign of the IT ecosystem (typically the ERP + adjoining systems). To support this work, we assigned a former CIO in a relevant industry. He would be the most credible person to discuss this in detail with the investors and the management team when the time came.

Another best practice is to identify the highest probability areas of opportunity and then systematically analyze the hypotheses from the highest impact, highest probability to the lowest impact, lowest probability opportunities and issues. However, to be effective this structured approach to the analysis needs to start up front. These initial thoughts and lists are a work in progress. Often when you are doing the work, you uncover other areas that may be of higher value. When that occurs, the individual responsible just prioritizes that hypothesis and area. Once complete, they then go back to the remainder of the priority list.

As a best practice, teams should begin to formulate these hypotheses as they review the materials on the company. In addition, within the first one to two days of the work, a best practice is also to begin having the teams put in place a rough order of magnitude of opportunity for each of the initiatives they believe may be available to the company. This helps the manager to identify the estimated ranges of opportunities and if the allocation of resources is correct on the team. Another added benefit is that it allows an initial discussion with the investment team to calibrate expectations of where opportunity may lie and whether their initial assessments were correct or if you may need to rethink the way the company is being run (e.g., op model design) in order to optimize the operations of the company. Being able to have this discussion and add strategic value to the discussion also can help them inform their view of the management team and what they need for the management of the organization to achieve their investment thesis.

When the teams put these lists together, there are three things that should be incorporated.

1. Identify the area of the company potentially impacted.
2. Identify whether this is an area of opportunity or potential red-flag on the transaction.
3. Define and provide rationale for why this area may be an opportunity or area of concern.
4. Provide a rough order of magnitude or qualitative assessment of risks for a potential red-flag.

Here is an example of what a potential list of hypotheses may look like for a given function:

Work-stream	Specific Area	Opportunity / Red-Flag	Description	ROM/Risk
G&A	Finance and accounting	Red-flag	Needs for working capital have continued to increase as the company undergoes international expansion. Future cash flow does not incorporate WC build requirements.	ROM: -$4 to -$5m/yr Risk: Yellow

G&A	IT	Opportunity	The company currently has five different ERP systems for similar operations. The company appears to have grown through acquisition, but not integrated operations.	ROM: $5 to $10m
G&A	Legal	Opportunity	A mid-market company has been utilizing top-tier legal advisors with higher than normal day rates causing legal spend to exceed benchmark by 2x.	ROM: $0.5 to $1m
G&A	T&E	Opportunity	The company allows all personnel to fly business class without approval. Putting in place a standard T&E policy could reduce spend.	ROM: $2 to $3m

These hypotheses are well formed and consider initial work done by the team to evaluate the company and understand the current state of operations. This also creates a robust conversation with the investment team within the first week of the engagement. It exhibits value and creates insight into how the company is being operated.

When these are reviewed the manager should also begin to synthesize these findings into an overall view on the company and critical elements of the operations that may be a problem or create significant opportunity. This can then be woven into a cohesive narrative about the company and high-level discussion on the operations.

SETTING A COST BASELINE

For opportunities, it is important to understand what you are improving against. It is also important for the investment team to understand against what year or baseline your improvements should be measured against. In one situation, I was working with an analyst and I looked at the integrated model and the improvements in profitability seemed exceptionally high in the first and second year. When we looked at how my findings were integrated into the model, the analyst had integrated 100 percent of the profitability improvement into the first year. If allowed to persist, this would have caused a significant issue with the management team's ability to deliver against the profitability profile. We addressed it and I provided in year and estimated ramp in values for the opportunities against the appropriate baseline and fiscal year profit estimates.

When setting a cost baseline there are few options on how to establish this estimate. The three methods I consider valid in preferred order are:

1. Direct
2. Hybrid
3. P&L adjusted

The biggest differentiator in the use case for each is what information is provided by the company. I will provide an overview for each and then discuss how to calculate and establish the number in subsequent pages.

Direct Cost Baseline

The most preferred method is the direct cost baseline. This provides a measure of the full cash outlay of the company. Please recall, for all of our discussion, I will only focus on cash outlay improvements. Accounting and book improvements in profitability are not beneficial to investors or the company over the long term as there is no true impact to the strategic value of the company.

In a direct cost baseline, the analyst takes the total personnel cost of the company, including benefits, bonuses and then adds the non-personnel expense on top for the past twelve months. Using this method, you know where all of the dollars for the company have been spent and what they have been spent on. If you are successful getting the critical information from a company, you would receive the employee census—this would have the fully burdened pay rate for an employee. Fully burdened pay rate includes an employee's base salary, their bonus, their benefits, and any other payments (tax, union, etc.). From the accounts payable pull you have all of the third party payments.

This method will not tie to a GAAP accounting P&L for the company. The main driver of the difference will be the capital treatment of various expense items and it will also not take into account the timing difference—AP days outstanding. This is the preferred method for analysis because you now have the most granular explanation of the expenses the company has incurred. From this you can analyze the issues and also places for optimization with precise dollar values that are most likely conservative as they are one year in arrears.

The analyst will also need to true this assessment up against the P&L. This should be achievable with the appropriate VIM runs from the ERP that will show outstanding days payable. On the headcount side, it will focus on the vacancy rate of positions. The capital treatment of the expenses should be well understood.

However, when you work with a PE firm using this method of a baseline, all dollars that you identify as an opportunity can be eliminated from the appropriate P&L category or for CAPEX adjusted based on the implied capitalization rate. These adjustments are routine post fact.

Hybrid Cost Baseline

This is one of the most common baselines that are employed. A typical hybrid baseline utilizes a mix of direct transaction and census data and adjustments from the P&L to form the basis of analysis for the analyst.

In most diligences, the team will receive the employee census. This is a critical element of the analysis and deals are not likely to proceed without this information. So, the team will have that element of the direct cost baseline. However, you typically receive a partial AP run or you do not receive an AP run at all. When this occurs, the analyst will then need to leverage the trial balance and P&L data to understand the accounts and sub-accounts in their scope of responsibility and relative size of spend. This is oftentimes supplemented by other sources of data—for instance, a marketing spend detail provided by the marketing management team.

The risks with this are non-cash items that a given analyst may not be aware of. The most common are depreciation and amortization that are usually accounted for. However, working through and reversing capitalized expenses can be difficult to understand and appropriately apply to get the full cash expense in a given functional area.

You also need to leverage this in unique situations like carve-outs. In this situation, there are a number of P&L adjustments that also need to be made in addition to understanding the allocations that need to be attributed to the new carved out entity. Because of this, the certainty on a carve-out baseline is usually lower than an acquisition or merger. In addition, sellers can hide expenses and accounting irregularities because of the allocation process between business units.

This is a second best alternative to the direct expense and leverages whatever portion of the direct cost baseline that you can. By limiting the amount of analysis that goes into the hybrid cost baseline, you also limit the risk of the analysts starting with the wrong baseline for an analysis that focuses on spend reduction for a given account or sub-account.

P&L Adjusted

The P&L adjusted baseline is just that. This is typically done when you have limited access to the company or do not receive company data. There are a number of times and scenarios where you may conduct an "outside-in" due diligence where you have no access to a company or their management team. These are increasingly common when working with activists, with direct credit lenders, and buyouts in a hostile situation.

When you put together a P&L adjusted estimated cost baseline, you start with the company's provided or publicly available income statement information. Then leveraging their own financial statements you adjust out the non-cash items from the P&L. This then gives you a cash focused cost baseline proxy to begin your analysis.

With these, I typically walk through the adjustments with the investment team to ensure they are aligned with how we did them. In addition, there are adjustments that often times need to be made because of accounting treatment differences, these items are typically detailed in the notes of the financial statements. When putting these baselines together, it is helpful to leverage professional accountants or financial analysts that have experience analyzing financial statements.

Final Cost Baseline

When the final cost baseline is aligned with the investment team the team will have a fully defined split between personnel and non-personnel for each function. An example of potential output is below. Please note this uses a tool called Mekko Graphics to improve the appearance of the charts and layout of the tables.

I have provided a potential output for an estimated direct cost baseline. This numbers are fictitious, but provide a view of how to align this output and the detail needed.

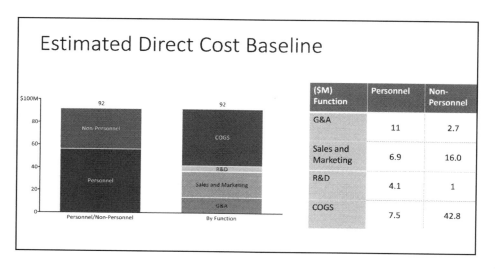

Estimated Direct Cost Baseline

($M) Function	Personnel	Non-Personnel
G&A	11	2.7
Sales and Marketing	6.9	16.0
R&D	4.1	1
COGS	7.5	42.8

Functional Cost Baselines

Once the total enterprise baseline is aligned, and usually in parallel as it is being finalized, each functional workstream owner also establishes their own more detailed baseline. These outputs will not just identify personnel and non-personnel, they will also seek to provide another layer of detail to the personnel and non-personnel spend. Below is a cascade chart of a fictitious scenario. You will notice that additional analysis will be required to get to the level of detail required for the functional baseline. However, based on this, it allows the analyst to benchmark and better characterize spend within their given functional area.

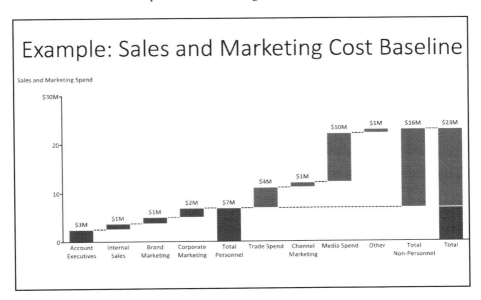

INSIGHT COMES FROM EXECUTION AND EXPERIENCE

In the next section we will shift over to looking at each of the functions and major drivers of value. I will seek to show what each function does, critical deliverables, key analyses and where the value comes from within the organization or company. This content is meant to serve as a method to kickstart your learning, supplement what you already know, or serve as a method to gain exposure to cross-functional areas that you may not yet have familiarity.

To be truly effective in assessing operations you have to understand the material through experience. That experience can be gained as an operator, consultant, or advisor—it absolutely does not require being on a factory floor or having served as a CIO. Those experiences help and build credibility, but you do not need them to be an expert in a given subject matter. In-depth and prolonged exposure with top-tier talent allows you to build the relevant competency.

I previously mentioned that McKinsey, Alvarez & Marsal, and AlixPartners are the Harvard, Yale, and Princeton of this space. In those advisory shops, the average consultant gains direct exposure to companies and in-depth operations of the company focused on creating value or turning around or transforming them. In addition, the consultants gain indispensable experience actually conducting negotiations on behalf of their clients, directly engaging with the C-level executives in a peer or near-peer type relationship, and, for the more senior resources, as interim executives in transformational or turnaround scenarios.

Other consultancies stop short of providing their consultants these types of experiences. There is nothing that stops non-audit focused advisory practices. The main driver is a concern over risk in the engagement and support. By assuming more risk, some firms have been able to deliver superior value and impact over others in the space of private equity performance improvement.

CHAPTER 4

Assessing Key Drivers of Cash Generation

Easy does it. After 25 years of buying and supervising a great variety of businesses, Charlie and I have not learned how to solve difficult business problems. What we have learned is to avoid them. To the extent we have been successful, it is because we concentrated on identifying one-foot hurdles that we could step over rather than because we acquired any ability to clear seven-footers.
—*Warren Buffett*[12]

The really smart thinkers are clear thinkers. They understand the basics at a very, very fundamental level. I would rather understand the basics really well than memorize all kinds of complicated concepts I can't stitch together and can't rederive from the basics. If you can't rederive concepts from the basics as you need them, you're lost. You're memorizing.
Advanced Concepts in a field are less proven. We use them to signal insider knowledge, but we'd be better off nailing the basics.
—*Naval Ravikant*[13]

In this chapter of the book I will walk you through some of the key points of opportunity in each functional area and how to assess the relative value to an investor. In each section there is a mix of discussion on how the opportunity manifests value for the organization and how to quantify potential benefits. Given that this book is meant to be easy to digest for practitioners, I will not be exhaustive on how to analyze each potential scenario. I will focus on the basics of the function and core

---

12 Warren Buffett, "1989 Chairman's Letter, Berkshire Hathaway," accessed July 12, 2023, www.berkshirehathaway.com/letters/1989.html.
13 Naval Ravikant, *The Almanack of Naval Ravikant* (Belgrade: Magrathea Publishing, 2020).

elements to understand. Sometimes, I will discuss typical analyses and how it is done well and what insights you can garner. I will also seek to identify typical methods to generate value in each of the functional areas.

In general, whenever you look at a company, there is always some opportunity to optimize its operations and improve cash generation. They are usually not thematic, but rather piecemeal initiatives that when strung together can sometimes creates a larger picture, but often times are just discrete areas of improvement that management has not addressed. Most people initially argue that if that was the case, why don't all management teams just do it? I would tell you that that is a great question. The majority of it comes down to the Institutional Imperative. However, in a lot of scenarios, managers are not incented to change, even if it would improve the company or improve outcomes for customers. The majority of executives have gotten to their position by avoiding risk and a healthy amount of fear. Unless incented, a number of them would rather avoid the risk.

As an exercise, I challenge you to think about any corporate environment you have been in. If 5 percent of the people in the company did not come in the next day, would the company still function? The majority of you are nodding your heads yes. Let's push that further—how would the company fare if 10 percent of the people sitting in the cubicle farms did not show up? Then what? Would the company still function? Most would answer yes. What about at 20 percent? Most people would start to argue that we would start to drop material elements of the operation. I would say that I agree with you. Because of this, the range of 5 to 18 percent is typically a good initial starting assumption for the size of opportunity for performance improvement in a properly incented and managed organization. There are certain times when more opportunity presents itself. Some of these unique high opportunity situations are during carve-outs, for a merger, following a high growth phase, (and are usually compounded if the growth occurred through acquisition), mismanaged businesses, and when founders are exiting a business. Conversely, there are some scenarios where less opportunity will be available—some of those situations are when you are buying or assessing a company post-bankruptcy and following ownership by a PE firm. In high opportunity situations, the high end of that band can increase to 25 percent. In lower opportunity scenarios, I would reduce the top end of that range to 10 percent.

As we begin to discuss these potential areas of opportunity, the first thing that analysts should incorporate into their analysis should be the strategic context of the company that they are examining. Is this a growth company? Or is this a company firmly in decline? What is the competitive context of the asset? These questions and others like it help to inform some elements of what is achievable for a given company. For instance, if a company is in a high growth phase of the business, opportunities to improve business operations may not result in improved free cash flow. Instead, management may undertake the optimization, but then reinvest the cash to maintain the high growth trajectory. In other situations, it may limit what initiatives a company would undertake. This should not prevent you from putting the opportunity on the table. One of the most salient opportunities and one that we will discuss first is the ability to reduce the number of executives in an organization. Streamlining upper management is a highly efficient mechanism to streamline operations. It removes unneeded overhead, has a significant impact on cost reduction with limited personnel impact, and removes additional layers of bureaucracy. However, management teams typically do not like to see their positions in the elimination crosshairs. We will discuss this in additional detail, but it should not prevent you from recommending the action as an alternative, as that is profit maximizing and can be better for the overall business.

With my relevant work experiences and, if needed, secondhand events, I will also provide examples of how these opportunities manifest in actual investments and how the analysis comes to life. This will help you better understand the next section which will focus on how to take the assessment and convert that into buy-in, action by the management team, and development into a large-scale transformation program.

OPERATING MODEL

The operating model for the company is one of the most critical elements of the future state design. It dictates the overall cost structure for the future state. Changes in this element of the company can lead to significant cost shifts in a company.

Operating model design consists of six key areas. These areas need to be thought through in each function, but also horizontally across the enterprise:

Key Area	Description
1. Organization	1. What people are required to manage the company or functional element of the company? 2. How do you align the resources to manage the strategic objectives of this element of the organization?
2. Talent management	1. How do you ensure you have the appropriate people to support these objectives? 2. How are those people properly incentivized to meet the strategic objectives for the future state company? 3. What are typical norms of behavior?
3. Technology	1. What technological enablement and information retention is required? 2. What key processes or elements of the value chain should be automated?
4. Process	1. What critical processes and functions will be undertaken by which elements of the company? 2. How do we manage interactions across the enterprise?
5. Governance and tracking	1. How are decisions made? 2. Who has the decision rights? 3. How do you track performance and maintain accountability?
6. External partners	1. How are external partners used to supplement or replace functional capability in the company? 2. How are external partners managed and incentivized?

The operating model also needs to be thought through in a strategic context. The choices you make here will predicate how much control management has on its business or functions of its business. Whenever looking at this, you first need to identify what is the true core of a business. Understanding what is the core of the business allows you to make stronger recommendations on which elements of the business can be managed at an arm's length, offshored, or given to an external partner.

For a clothes apparel provider, what is the core of the business? Is it the manufacturing of the product? Or is it the design and marketing? Plausible arguments can be made for both. Some designers believe that they need to maintain custody of their supply value chain. Others believe they can outsource that element or selectively outsource, maintaining key proprietary elements in house. A strategic discussion is important and understanding of the asset and company you are reviewing is helpful. For most apparel manufacturers, you can make an argument that the cut and sew operations are not core to their business. The key differentiator is the design, marketing, and channel distribution of the product set.

When you look at the economics of shifting cut and sew to outsourced providers, it changes your cost structure, usually for the better. Now, for that business you can outsource through partnerships the manufacture of your product. This allows the business to focus on the design and marketing. For those functions, you will then ensure that you have a robust organization to support and gain a competitive advantage. In addition, the channel distribution and sales function will remain critical to ensure that your product can continue to be distributed. All other functions, with some regulatory holdouts (e.g., audit, risk, financial and fiduciary ownership), can largely be outsourced or shifted to a cost advantaged focus for the future strategic direction of the company.

Looking at this at a functional level, you can look at a legal function in a company. The core of support for the business and that which requires specialized legal knowledge is the management of IP, litigation associated with the product, and internal personal matters. The remainder of the legal functions can be examined for service by others. Here is a potential breakdown of how a legal function cost be optimized to get to the lowest possible cost structure:

Core Legal Function	Internal	External
Personnel matters	X	
Contract review	X	X (for peak periods)
Partnership contracts	X	
IP decisioning	X	
IP search and review		X
Board governance	X	
Litigation		X
Legal entity management	X	
M&A		X

By leveraging outsourced providers for unique or non-core functions, the need for higher numbers of resources are reduced. It does introduce potential non-budgeted excesses for unique situations like litigation or M&A. For those issues, it is common for special budgets to be leveraged as they are extraordinary items. However, if extraordinary becomes ordinary (e.g., litigation or serial M&A), then the management team can always make the decision to insource that capability.

Quality analysis for this will typically show other representative cases of companies that have organized differently. Experience in various situations and operating models also helps bring credibility to the discussion. These conversations, if required, are sometimes best managed at the board level at first, as management and the CEO may not be interested in potential changes.

Quantification of the impact of these changes will compare the current cost structure—usually headcount and then the runrate cost for the outsourced services (do not include extraordinary items).

REQUIRED EXECUTIVE COST STRUCTURE

Executives are the most expensive resources in a company. Each executive position should be well thought through and ensure that the position is absolutely required. What typically occurs in public companies and mismanaged companies, CEOs will build very large executive teams reporting into them. This command and control approach to leadership is costly. Let me walk you through an example.

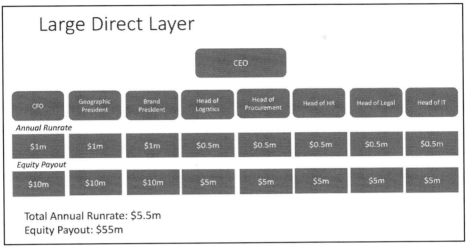

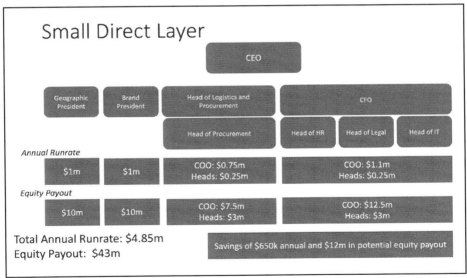

In the example scenarios above, you will see the first example of a large direct span of control—the number of people reporting into a given manager. In this example the CEO has eight. For a CEO, that size of span is not always necessary because the executives below them are highly capable and should be relatively autonomous. With strategic direction and the appropriate incentives, they should deliver the business as required for the investment thesis. The runrate cost is about $5.5 million with an equity payout of around $55 million. The equity payout is just for example. These numbers, depending on the industry and value creation plan, can be significantly higher.

By upgrading one executive and shifting organizational design under the CFO, you can create an organization that removes around 11.8 percent of that cost baseline. This is $650,000 in annualized savings and, for enterprise valuation purposes, this is an increase of $4.5 million to $7.15 million (7-11x EV/EBITDA multiple). In addition, for the PE firm, they have also reduced the amount of equity they need to payout to executives by $12 million. In general, lower levels of the organization get a disproportionately lower equity return on their contribution then the direct CEO reports. This small change has improved the PE firms outcomes by around $16.5 to 19.15 million with minor, largely non-impacting changes to the executive organizational structure.

For assessment purposes, you can approach this through qualitative realignment of the executives, similar to what is above. I will also typically use a functional alignment chart to ensure I have captured all of the functions and how they report into any potential new proposed organizational structure. Here is an example:

Functional Alignment Chart

Geographic President	Brand President	Head of Logistics and Procurement	CFO
Geo Sales	Marketing	Supply Chain	Finance and Accounting
	Product Dev.	Contract Manufacturing	Legal
	Pricing	Procurement	Facilities
		Order Management	HR
			Strategy

With charts like this, you can review key differences in organizational designs and executive scopes of responsibilities rapidly. For highly complex organizations, it also ensures that you have incorporated all of the key functions for the business.

One key assumption is that the executives that you leverage are actual leaders and not just managers. In some cultures, such as in Europe, they have a preference for experts managing each area. In the U.S. and other areas, this is not always a requirement. It is important that the executives have a baseline understanding of the content, but they do not need to be deep experts. The more cross-functional the role, the less likely you are to be able to find someone that has expertise across all of the key functional areas in that domain.

Another consideration for always starting at the executive level is that you can create significant value in the organization with limited impact to the operations. A lot of advisory practices like to use spans and layers as the rationale for reducing headcount. I have leveraged this as a starting point, but there is a base assumption that the current operating model and leadership structure is correct. To truly unlock the full potential in a company, you should start at the top of the house and then restructure to support the strategic objectives of the company, but also take into account the cost optimized approach, combining key executives as and when appropriate.

SPANS AND LAYERS

A spans and layers assessment of an organization is a very quantitative, high-level approach to understand how many resources can be reduced in a given organization. I view this in the same light as a benchmark. It shows you where to hunt, but it does not show you what to address or identify actual opportunities. I view this as a method to triangulate an opportunity. However, I always push my analysts to go further and show me where in the organization they see the specific opportunity. I will show you both of these approaches and key things to look for in an organizational chart that identifies when there may be opportunity.

For spans and layers, the general assumption is that managers should be able to manage between six to eight direct reports. This is a cascading effect so one VP should manage six directors, who should manage 36 managers, who should manage 216 individual contributors.

However, here are a few other considerations: For more technical roles (e.g., legal, finance) the spans can be between three to five. Also, for roles in finance and strategy it is common for individual contributors to have the title of manager or even director. Although an exception, this is usually a talent acquisition and retention tool. The title does not have as much bearing as does the reporting relationship. This is critical for true managers of people. Also, although there are cases when it can be acceptable, typically, use of the VP title for individual contributors should be limited.

For service-based organizations like field service or line manufacturing these spans can be between 10 to 25. With field service, it is common for a span of about 20 employees.

From there, the analyst will quantitatively assess the average spans and layers in each individual organization. This will typically be done at a functional level. This is what a typical example will look like:

G&A Spans and Layers

	Current State				Achievable State			
Layer	Manager HC	IC HC	Avg Span		Manager HC	IC HC	Target Span	Opportunity
L1	1	0	1.0		1	0	1.0	$0
L2	1	0	7.0		1	0	3.0	$0
L3	7	0	4.0		3	0	5.7	$2.0m
L4	18	10	2.8		7	10	6.0	$2.1m
L5	14	36	2.9		6	36	6.8	$1.3m
L6	7	34	6.3		7	34	6.3	N/A
L7	7	37	N/A		7	37	N/A	N/A
Total	55	117	3.2		32	117	4.8	$5.4m

The savings comes from the reductions in the managerial headcount in this example. This assumes that the top-tier of the organization is correct. However, this is a high-end estimate. The layer of analysis that the analysis would then conduct is to examine the actual organizational charts to better understand what is and is not achievable.

The best tool in this situation is a headcount radial. A headcount radial is a tool that creates a visual with a central node as the CEO and then spirals out with interconnecting dots that represent an individual person in the company. This is a tool that can greatly reduce time to actionable insight. In addition to the graphics, it also automates a lot of the analysis to compute total compensation. It also allows you to conduct scenario analysis. This allows you to simulate the changes to an organization and rerun key analyses like spans and layers and total compensation changes.

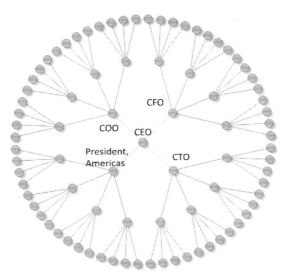

Example of a Radial Diagram

However, depending on the size of the company, this can also be done through a basic organizational diagram. Below, you will see some examples of how spans and layers are conducted in practice

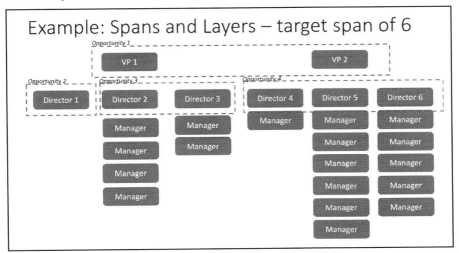

For Opportunity 1: The company may not need two different VPs in this scenario. With only six directors, there is potential to collapse the organization down to one VP.

Under VP 1 The individual contributor director could potentially have their functions assumed by the other two directors in the organization, or add an additional manager to assume the responsibility. This would save the difference between the cost of a director and a manager. This is usually about 20 percent of the burden for a given employee.

Under VP1, there is also the opportunity to consolidate the functions of Director 2 and 3. They have four and two managers, respectively. As such, they can eliminate one of those director roles completely.

Under VP 2, you can consolidate the three director roles into two, eliminating a full director cost structure in the organization.

In the end, this is the level of analysis that would be appropriate for analysts to conduct and for investors to be fully comfortable with the analysis and range of opportunities.

Spans and layers is not a panacea. It helps identify where there may be opportunity. However, there are legitimate reasons why managers may not be at benchmark spans within an organization. Sometimes, when you see an organization like under Director 4 in the figure above, the company is trying to give a new manager the opportunity to lead. They are willing to make the investment in order to develop a high performing resource. In others, like for Director 1. They may hold unique information on the organization or systems. They are not someone that the company trusts managing resources but is a highly valuable resource for the company. In this scenario, the spans and layers analysis would overestimate the opportunity in the organization by two directors. Or it could require management to force the issue on the functional leader.

IT AND TECHNOLOGY

When companies believe they will sell or when companies believe they will divest an asset, Information Technology (IT) is a place that typically does not receive attention or investment. Because of these dynamics, IT is usually a functional area that can be improved when a company is acquired.

There a few situations that I will highlight that drive this to be a major opportunity item:

1. Carve-out: In a carve-out, you are either receiving the old company's systems "as-is" or you will need to stand them up completely independent of the old company. In a situation that permits time to build a greenfield IT ecosystem, the initiative should be undertaken. Typically, legacy systems will have a large number of applications that provide marginal value. In one instance, a spin-out company potentially needed to retain the implementation of a leading eCommerce Solution. When you do a greenfield build out, you can potentially build the infrastructure from the ground up and fundamentally alter the cost structure. In this instance, the legacy spend was closer to $2 million per year on that platform. The company shifted to Shopify and reduced the spend by over $1 million. A typical greenfield ecosystem, with the right level of investment can be completed in less than one year.

2. **Growth through acquisition:** When companies grow through acquisition, the IT systems are often times not integrated. This causes a large number of operational issues. Sometimes, it will balloon out the size of accounting, customer service, or order management teams because they are handling a number of manual operations when they could be automated with a limited amount of investment. In these situations, modest investment can unlock significant runrate savings. In addition, it sometimes will require consolidation of ERPs. This initiative, although complicated, can be completed.

3. **Distressed company:** When a company has limited cash available from operations, one of the first years they pull back on in investment is IT. Depending on the duration of the distress dictates the potential opportunity. A careful examination of high ROI projects that have not been undertaken can very quickly yield significant runrate benefit for limited upfront investment.

IT Applications and Application Organizations

When a team is assessing the IT ecosystem they should start with the main financial ecosystem. This is the system that interacts with the enterprise resource planning (ERP) system. This is the main ecosystem and usually also controls the company's operations and provides a clear financial picture to management and investors.

Here are the core systems typically involved in the core ecosystem:

1. ERP: The ERP is the main source of financials for a company. An ERP is a series of databases with a structured frontend that allows the company to interact with the system, input information, and extract data. An ERP is comprised of a core set of functionalities that typically including accounts receivable, accounts payable, and record to report. This allows the company to receive money, pay money, and record transactions in a general ledger. There are also routing and approval systems for accounts payable and accounts receivable. Depending on the sophistication, there are typically automated feeds or file transfers between this system and the company's financial institution.

    a. ERPs also can be expanded to include other functionality through modules. For instance, if your supply chain is critical to manage and monitor through the ERP, you can procure and then integrate that functionality directly into the ERP during the implementation. For consumer companies, it is typical to have this type of functionality such that you can review and better track the orders being processed. Some of the key modules for ERPs include: financial management (core ERP), procurement, inventory management, supply chain management, warehouse management, manufacturing, order management, marketing automation, HR management, e-commerce, work force management, project service workforce management, and customer relationship management.

b. ERPs take up to two years to implement. A short ERP implementation one to three months could be as simple as a back end GL to support limited operations or consolidation of other ERPs for overall financials for a combined company. To get to bare minimum functionality, an ERP implementation will likely take between six to nine months. A robust ERP will usually take between nine and 12 months to implement from ideation to go-live. With additional geographies or with additional systems, creating a longer timeline out to 18 to 24 months is not unreasonable. When thinking about project planning it is always better to be conservative.

c. ERPs are often used to interface with other core systems. Some of those other systems replace the modules; others add new capability. When interacting between systems, data mastery and data congruence are critical. I will discuss some of the other systems in the following pages.

2. Other systems

a. Human resources information systems (HRIS): The HRIS system is used to maintain information about employees, performance, pay, benefits, certifications, and other personnel related information. The HRIS system will usually provide these capabilities through expanded module offerings. With the expansion of training content online, some companies have also integrated training into the HRIS portfolio.

i. The HRIS system interacts with the ERP for payroll purposes. One of the critical flow paths is for payroll. Typically, the payroll file will be processed in the HRIS and then transmitted to the ERP for payment. A number of companies will usually work with providers like ADP for the actual disbursement of the payments to their resources.

ii. The system also interacts with work management systems (WMS) to ensure workers have the appropriate qualifications for a given job. It can also work with training modules or external systems that will track the lessons that a given employee takes. This can work both for continuous training as well as statutory training (e.g., sexual harassment).

iii. The HR system can also be used to track performance ratings. The module is highly customizable and allows for companies to tailor their rating system into the system and retain the information in the HRIS's database.

iv. The HRIS can also be used as the system to input and retain benefit election information.

v. This is a critical system for employee experience. It is also invaluable for tracking headcount and census information.

vi. There is also typically a feed from the HRIS system into your single sign on service (e.g., Okta, Microsoft Active Directory). This ensures that your HR decisions populate through to access to critical IT systems.

b. Procurement systems

i. The typical procure to pay solution in the ERP is sufficient for most companies. However, there are new AI or machine learning enabled competitors that help companies achieve reduced expenses for third party spend.

ii. These systems handle the full procure to pay cycle for the company. They will manage requisitions, purchase orders, invoices, approvals, and the payment and disbursement of funds to the supplier/vendor.

iii. The newer systems provide enhanced overall spend visibility and tracking. The newer systems focus on reducing the burden on the AP and procurement teams. They focus on other tools that automate invoice handling and matching to meet compliance requirements.

c. Work management systems (WMS)

i. The work management system is usually not offered as part of the ERP module suite. This is typically a standalone system that integrates into the ERP for permissions and certifications.

    ii.   The WMS is a system that tracks work packages through origination, formulation, and approval. This system then integrates with the ERP for approval of part and service procurement. It can also then interact with the HRIS for validation of resource certification or qualification.

d.   Warehouse management system (WHMS)

    i.   The warehouse management system is a tool that supports receipt, handling and shipping of products in a company's warehouse or that of a company's partner (3PL).

    ii.   The warehouse management system and ERP interface on three major areas: 1) Order management: the ERP provides and the WHMS ensures fulfillment of the orders; 2) Receipt management: the WHMS will be a source of received products to meet the requirements in the payables module to pay invoices from suppliers; 3) The WHMS also manages the inventory and provides that feed to the ERP on a periodic basis.

e.   Manufacturing resource planning (MRP)

    i.   The MRP is a central manufacturing scheduling, planning, management, and quality assurance platform for the company. The company can use the MRP to track production through the manufacturing process or control the process for batch or line processes.

    ii.   The MRP can help companies maximize the efficiency of their existing plants by improving scheduling and use of equipment. With the correct input, it can also be used by the factory line personnel with the actual procedures for each product or step in the process to reduce the potential for error introduction.

    iii.   Finally, it also manages the quality assurance process and approval process for the company. For large industrial or manufacturing focused enterprises, this is a critical enabler. MRP implementations are expensive and time consuming. However, they typically have short payback periods with enhanced utilization of the factory and equipment.

iv. There are also applications that calculate the required materials. These are called material requirements planning. They also often utilize the same acronym: MRP.

f. Customer relationship management (CRM)

i. The CRM is an application suite that manages customer information and supports sales, marketing, and customer service teams to manage client experience and contact.

ii. For sales management, it is a critical enabler for the management team to understand the status of the sales funnel and the performance of their sales team.

iii. For marketing and customer service, the data provides critical insights to the clients. For customer service, the data is typically fed into the company's Interactive Voice Response (IVR) system and other customer service systems that provide guide and improved response information for the customer service teams.

iv. The information in the CRM is also typically fed into the order management system to ensure shipping and other information for order management is up to date.

g. Data storage

i. Companies are growing in their sophistication on how to store data.

ii. The majority of companies use a combination of a data lake and data warehouses to manage their information.

iii. Data lakes allow large amounts of unrelated data to be stored with limited relational relationships (how does this data set interact with another). The data can then be stitched together by data analysts through a master data schema to deliver insights or reporting.

iv. Data warehouses are relational databases that make data extraction easier for people less versed in information retrieval in an unstructured database. The data warehouse takes extracts from the data lake or other systems and retains key information for quick digestion and analysis.

v. A new and growing trend is the use of a customer data platform (CDP) to manage and drive value from customer information. The CDP integrates data from a number of internal and external sources that include personal and demographic information, onsite behavioral data, customer engagement information, transactional data, and device data. It then provides real time information and predictive intelligence to digital marketing teams. It can then conduct targeted outreach via various channels.

h. Travel and expense management (T&E)

i. The T&E system allows employees and others associated with the company to book travel and then expense the costs against the company.

ii. Typically, this system is interfaced with the ERP for disbursement of money back to the employee or associated person. Other key data feeds include information from the various travel providers to inform purchasing decisions.

iii. These systems now have strict controls on purchasing. These controls can be leveraged to minimize T&E expense with approval overrides.

i. Product lifecycle management (PLM)

i. PLM solutions manage the innovation process for consumer product companies.

ii. In addition to innovation, they can also be used to maintain a repository of the key ingredients and acceptable substitutes for various products. The use of a system like this is then fed into the ERP to inform the bill of materials for various components. It can also be used for costing information.

j.   Middleware and enterprise service bus (ESB)

    i.   There are middleware solutions that allow for seamless connections and data transformation between systems. A middleware solution also sometimes called an enterprise service bus connects applications in a service-oriented architecture IT ecosystem. A service-oriented architecture is a framework where each application provides a service to another. For instance, the HRIS system develops the payroll feed. Then the ERP takes the payroll feed and sends it to ADP and logs it into the appropriate GL accounts.

    ii.   To support this, the data from the HRIS has to be converted into a file format that the ERP can accept and then sent to that application. The middleware or enterprise service bus can and does do both. With the ESB in place, you can more easily integrate the systems together and more seamlessly move data between the systems.

k.   There are many other systems and applications. I have provided you a quick overview of some of the highest likelihood systems you would interact with. Below is a high-level schematic of how these key systems interact with each other.

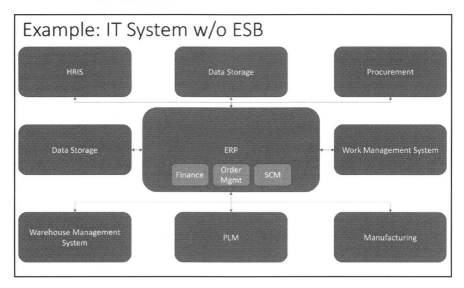

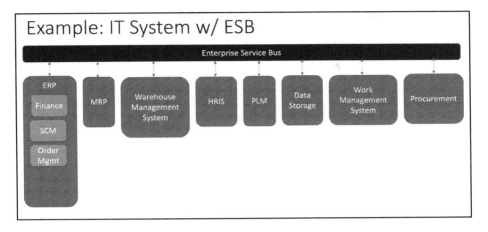

Value from the IT stack comes from four main areas:

1. Consolidation of applications: It is not uncommon for applications to proliferate within a company. There are many instances where a team may be using Slack at the same time as using Teams. The enterprise should strive to just use one solution for each requirement. When a company does that, most companies can pare their applications down tremendously. I have seen a list of over 90 applications come down to less than 20. When doing this, you have to map out the applications and see where there may be redundancy and then eliminate it. There are times when you do this that you will notice key features of similar products that the company would find hard to manage without the additional functionality. In those instances, you may need to choose which application provides the best solution.

2. Reduction of licenses and modules: There are many applications where personnel have licenses and do not use the product. In these situations, you can reduce cost through reducing the licensure. In addition, there are times when you have excess modules. It is common for companies to have procured too much functionality in a given application. When this occurs, you can try to pare that back for additional opportunity. This is a key lever, but unlikely for you to

recognize this in a diligence process. Another is with Microsoft Office 365, you should assess what license you have and whether you need all of that functionality. Sometimes your team may buy E5 for the entire office at $38 per month when only a few resources need it. E5 provides advanced security, some advanced analytics, and some voice capabilities. However, not everyone needs all of this capability. If you shift some of the employees to a lower tier such as enterprise Apps at $12 per month or E3 at $23 per month the company can save between fifteen to twenty-six dollars per month per user. Over a year with 1,000 employees this could save $180,000 to $312,000 (Microsoft pricing as of March 13, 2023).

3. Improved efficiency of operations and reducing headcount through use of a system. Also, there are some systems and processes that can be improved through investment. These insights are typically generated through expert interviews or through discussion with management. When you gain insight into these, you will need to conduct additional investigation. There are potentially significant opportunities, but you will need to validate that the functionality gain and estimated efficiencies are valid.

4. Negotiated rate reductions: There are some IT vendors where you can improve your expense by direct negotiation with your account executive. There are technologies that help you understand your IT spend to ensure you receive the best-negotiated rate.

There are many ways to create value in IT. The key element is to calculate the decrease in application spend through license and module reduction, and reduction of older technologies and systems being consolidated. In an ideal world, you could create your ecosystem from scratch. However, it will likely be a brownfield development. This will yield some loss in efficiency gain but the opportunities should still be presented. There will likely be flowback—increases in spend elsewhere to realize the savings. Oftentimes this flowback comes in the form of increased licenses for the remaining application suite or procurement and installation of a like module or capability in another application.

Additionally, when you conduct an IT ecosystem or singular application implementation, it is sometimes advisable to seek out a small scale or regional provider to implement the systems. This is largely a commoditized offering. System integrators (e.g., Big Four) tend to cost about 20 to 30 percent more for the same type of work. This additional cost can be warranted when the change is highly complex and requires improved project management.

IT Application Selection and Management

The IT organization is a service provider in the company. They are responsible for providing infrastructure and applications that enable the remainder of the business to do their job as efficiently and securely as possible. Some companies empower the business too much in this pursuit and they end up selecting systems and applications. The majority of which do not meet the needs of the business.

A balance needs to be struck between empowering the business and IT providing an integrated, cost effective infrastructure. To support this, the IT function should be empowered with the final decision on applications. In addition, IT should own the IT application and systems budget, then have it allocated appropriately to the various business lines. This creates a positive tension with the business on new applications, but also holds IT responsible for the cost. The business has a final check against IT to provide the best level of service at the lowest cost point, as it ends up being allocated against their P&L. Allocation is required because this allows systems and applications to be used across the enterprise versus creating a parochial view on applications because of arbitrary budgetary lines or ownership.

Here is one of the ways this can work for system selection. This can be thought of as a best practice that can minimize IT expense creep once you have normalized the spend. It also shows how IT can be empowered within the organization to minimize its application landscape and cost.

1. The business is responsible to define the requirements. The business (end user) should define the system requirements needed with the support of their IT business partner. The IT business partner should convert those processes and requirements into the requirement definition, but also push

back on unrealistic or questionable requirements. The business partner should sign off on the requirements and then it goes to the IT department to determine best-fit solutions.

2. The IT team and the IT architecture team review the requirements and determine what can be done with the existing systems and capabilities. Some times, the capability exists, but the team has not leveraged it or been trained on how to use it. If a new system or application is required, then the IT team selects optimal solutions taking into account its architectural requirements and existing systems. Cost can also be a consideration at this phase to eliminate gold plated solutions.

3. In conjunction with the business team, the IT team presents the options and conducts discussions with the customer account teams from the providers. From there, the business owners and IT team conduct a down-select through an aligned criteria set, usually set in advance by the head of IT.

4. The final selection is presented to the head of IT and head of the business function for final decision. For smaller companies, that decision may be brought to a higher level.

The key differentiator and where some businesses go wrong is that they allow the business to determine what application they want. This should be the role of the IT team. As a cost focused business center, they can find optimal solutions and should be better equipped and better informed on the solutions that would fit the need of the business.

When this process is not disciplined, the business presents gold plated solutions and drives up cost. A typical example of this is when HR wants Workday. Yes, it is the market leader, but it is also very expensive. Does your organization truly need that level of capability? Or would a less expensive HRIS be better suited for your needs? There are other products at a lower cost point with similar functionality.

IT Application Organization

To support these applications, companies will develop a structure that needs to meet these core functions:

1. **System architecture**: Designs and manages the organization's IT infrastructure and application suite in a way that meets the needs of the business, is secure, reliable, and scalable, and is aligned with the organization's overall strategic goals

2. **IT business partner:** Serves as a liaison between the IT department and the business units of an organization. The IT business partner works closely with business stakeholders to understand their needs and requirements and to ensure that IT solutions are aligned with the organization's overall strategic goals.

3. **Application maintenance and upkeep:** Ensure that software applications are running smoothly and effectively. This includes monitoring performance, upgrading and patching applications, troubleshooting issues, providing user support, and maintaining documentation.

4. **IT procurement and vendor management:** This involves the selection, purchase, and management of hardware, software, and services required to support the organization's IT infrastructure. IT procurement professionals work closely with vendors to ensure that the organization's IT needs are met.

5. **IT project management:** This involves the planning, execution, and management of IT projects, such as network upgrades, server migrations, and software implementations. IT project managers are responsible for ensuring that projects are completed on time, within budget, and according to specifications.

6. **Cyber security:** This involves the development, implementation, and management of security policies, procedures, and technologies to protect the organization's IT infrastructure from threats and vulnerabilities. Cybersecurity professionals are responsible for identifying and mitigating risks to the organization's IT systems and data.

From an operating model perspective, a number of companies typically will keep all of this in house. However, almost all of IT can be outsourced. The critical areas where I have not seen the function effectively outsourced is for system architecture and business requirement definition. Those core elements of functionality should be retained internal to the company. The remainder of IT can be outsourced or offshored. If a company is of sufficient scale, creating a captive offshore center is ideal and once established the most cost effective method to maintain operations

For opportunity, operating model shifts in IT are the major source of opportunity. If the company has internal IT resources, then shifting them to an outsourced or offshored model typically yields significant opportunity with limited to even positive impact on operations. Depending on where you plan to offshore resources and where you currently have the resources, you can see opportunity between 10 to 50 percent reduction in the cost per resource.

Additionally, you can also look at organizational optimization. A typical look at organizational hygiene will likely eliminate some managerial positions and layers in the organization. While doing so, you also should examine the business requirement team portfolio. There may be opportunity to review this coverage for increased opportunity.

IT Operations, Services, and Infrastructure

IT operations consists of organizations, enabled by workflows to fix and repair IT and networking issues, address incidents, and maintain the company's networks and cyber security. In technology companies there can be a blend of the operations between IT and the product teams, when some of the internal systems are required to address customer needs or the infrastructure is co-mingled. For this discussion, I will just focus on traditional IT operations.

These teams are typically segmented between the IT helpdesk, the network operations center (NOC), the security operations center (SOC), and the infrastructure teams.

Modern companies will typically also seek to shift all of this workload and its infrastructure operations to a managed service provider (MSP). An MSP will take on all of the IT operations for a company and all of the infrastructure operations. There tends to be significant efficiency gains for small to medium businesses to do this. Depending on the size, even large companies can leverage these types of services at discount to their current operations. However, there are certain industries where this is a core capability where MSPs do not make sense. For instance, given the critical nature of a financial institution's IT system and technology backbone, it may not make sense to outsource this capability. However, for the average company use of an MSP should be explored to simplify organizational needs.

IT Helpdesk

The IT helpdesk team are resources that assist the end user employees with their IT issues. The teams typically look at issues on a tiered scale with Level 1 being basic resolution (e.g., password reset, new user login) to Level 4 where outside services are required for resolution. Some organizations will also include a Level 0 which includes issues that can be addressed through self-service with limited to no direct IT team involvement.

Here is a basic outline of the tiering. Please note each organization has minor differences with this generalized framework.

Tier	Description
Level 0	• Self-help • Can include email or web forms which may require teams to respond • Can also include password resets done by the user • Limited technical support required
Level 1	• Basic support (e.g., password resets, new user credentials) • Requires IT technical support to resolve • Usually results are scripted and require low levels of technical capability
Level 2	• In-depth technical support • Escalation from Tier 1 • Requires in depth knowledge of the product or service, but may not require actual engineers or programmers to resolve

Level 3	• Expert product and service support • Highest levels of technical resolution; this may also involve a new feature creation • At this stage, the technicians duplicate the issue, track it to root cause, resolve the issue and correct or document how to resolve for future use • May include use of Engineers, programmers, and architects to resolve
Level 4	• Outside support required • External support service for items handled by external providers (e.g., printers, vendor software, higher level depot repairable parts). • Requires established relationships with external providers

For helpdesk, you can typically outsource or offshore the majority of the functions. The widespread use and availability of connectivity allows the helpdesk to log in to computer assets through programs like LogMeIn for the technician to remotely troubleshoot the issues. There are also elements of Tier 3 that can be outsourced or offshored. Some of the knowledge retention and management of the key architecture may be beneficial to retain. When these functions are outsourced, you should still have a primary point of contact and responsibility holder for the function. There are usually one or two hands-on resources that manage the technical issues that executives experience. This executive care coordinator is typically colocated with the CEO. This person can also serve as an onsite troubleshooter for high impact issues. Depending on the size and complexity of the organization, you may also need one of these on-site resources for sites with over 100 to 150 people. This is typically sufficient scale to keep the person fully occupied. When companies maintain their own networks, there may be need for additional resources, which we will discuss in the infrastructure operations section.

These organizations should be managed with a larger span—typically eight to 10 resources per manager. In addition, the manager can also manage issue resolution.

IT Operations

Larger organizations will maintain a network operations center and security operations center. For some smaller organizations, these functions are critical to business success and also maintain them. For instance, an e-commerce company would likely maintain a NOC or some semblance of a NOC. The NOC monitors the network and serves to ensure that the e-commerce site stays up and running, maximizing the revenue generation of the firm. For a company like that, it may also make the decision to combine the NOC and the SOC or have this as an ancillary duty of another employee.

The SOC leverages tools like Splunk, Darktrace, and data distribution visualization to understand where your data is going and who is trying to break your systems. They also have the ability to interrupt service or suspend sessions that could be determined to be detrimental to the company.

These services should operate 24/7 or can be done on a less full time basis, if the company is willing to accept that risk. Because of the type of operation, these functions can very quickly be offshored. They do not need to be in the higher cost jurisdiction. However, you do want to have your IT team look at the various segments of the internet to ensure that the signal cannot be suspended. For instance, China has software and capability that allows the government to inspect and subsequently interrupt service to and from its borders. Needless to say, China is not one of the best options for placement of a SOC or NOC. Typically, these can be offshored to lower cost jurisdictions.

In addition, these organizations should be reviewed to ensure that the staffing is commensurate with the concerns. CISOs can sometimes overstaff these locations. There is not a good general guideline for the required staffing, but review should be made. In addition, reviewing manager to individual contributor levels is often effective to reduce redundant overhead in the organization.

IT Infrastructure

To understand IT infrastructure, I will walk you through each of the major components and the organizations involved. As you will quickly come to understand, managing all of this and paying for it all in capital expenditure can be less efficient then leveraging a largely cloud based presence. The most efficient companies have now shifted the predominant amount of their IT infrastructure to the cloud.

Please note that there are instances and some elements of the IT infrastructure organization that should be considered to be maintained by internal resources. However, use of a Managed Service Provider can potentially even eliminate that requirement.

Infrastructure Network Elements

The average advisor or investor does not need to know the full inner workings or required connections to manage the IT infrastructure for a company. Below, I am providing some of the main components and their core functionality.

Servers: Servers are powerful computers that provide centralized services to network clients. Common types of servers in a corporate network include file servers, email servers, web servers, database servers, and application servers.

Network devices: These include routers, switches, firewalls, and access points that are used to connect network devices and manage network traffic. Routers are responsible for forwarding data between networks, while switches are used to connect devices within the same network segment. Firewalls are used to filter network traffic and block unauthorized access, and access points provide wireless connectivity.

Network clients: These are the devices that connect to the network to access network resources and services. They can include desktop computers, laptops, tablets, smartphones, and other mobile devices.

Network cables and infrastructure: The physical infrastructure of the network includes the cabling, connectors, and other hardware that connect devices together. This can include copper cabling, fiber optic cabling, and network switches.

Network services: These include services such as domain name system (DNS), dynamic host configuration protocol (DHCP), and network address translation (NAT), which are used to manage network traffic and resources.

Network security: This includes hardware and software solutions such as firewalls, intrusion detection and prevention systems (IDS/IPS), and antivirus software that are used to protect the network from unauthorized access, attacks, and other security threats.

Network management and monitoring: This includes tools and systems used to manage and monitor the network, such as network management software, network analyzers, and performance monitoring tools.

End user computing: This includes all of the devices and security apparatus required by the employee.

Opportunities in infrastructure can be complicated and require a dedicated program to reduce the overall cost structure. Because you are dealing with hardware and networking appliances, partnerships and investment will likely be required.

Shift to the cloud: To reduce the overhead associated with internal IT computing requirements you need to reduce the companies need to maintain that infrastructure. The majority of companies that have successfully done this have shifted all or the majority of their IT operations to the cloud. By reducing your internal workload, you reduce the requirements for servers. In addition, the use of cloud allows the company to rapidly expand and scale its operations without limitations introduced by the internal IT infrastructure.

Eliminate legacy networks: Some companies have continued to maintain dedicated multi-protocol label switching (MPLS) networks and point-to-point networks. These flexible networks allow network administrators to control the prioritization of the data traffic flow. However, they require highly specialized knowledge to maintain and as the complexity of the internal network increases, MPLS becomes more difficult to maintain. Use of a software-defined wide array network (SD-WAN) technology simplifies the same level of prioritization and can also take into account real-time network information and multiple routing pathways to reduce latency. When you shift between the two, you can realize significant savings, depending on the company and level of complexity of the company's existing network.

MSP, group buying, and negotiated cost reduction: The other methods to reduce cost in this area is to leverage group buying arrangements or use of an MSP. The MSP typically has precontracted arrangements for computer purchases or other programs to reduce IT vendor expense. Some of the Big Four firms also have partnerships with cloud providers and co-lo providers to reduce the cost of maintaining infrastructure and storage or compute capacity.

Data center optimization: There is opportunity to optimize data centers as well. This work is highly technical and will focus on the HVAC system (reducing input energy costs), cooling systems redesign, required technical support and staffing, and other levers.

Network redesign and architecture optimization: For larger companies with dedicated bandwidth and large scale point to point operations, network redesign, routing simplification, and elimination of some point to point dedicated networks may also yield some opportunity. Use of SD-WAN and improved layer two tunneling protocols (L2TP) can eliminate some of the latency and security issues. In addition, technical analysis of the network can sometimes eliminate cabinets and energy costs for the network appliances and internal server cabinets. This is highly technical analysis and will likely require partnership with external providers. For some of this work, limitations of your internal cabinet capacity could cause an issue with implementation.

Virtualization: Use of virtualization technologies can increase utilization of the existing server capacity, reducing your need for additional server capacity. In addition, use of virtualization layers can reduce energy consumption, maintenance requirements, and required space.

IT Infrastructure Organization

The IT infrastructure functions work to ensure that the IT infrastructure remains up and running with limited to no down time. The core functions in the organization are:

Network administration: This involves the design, implementation, and management of the organization's computer networks. Network administrators are responsible for ensuring that network performance is optimized, that network security is maintained, and that the network is reliable and available.

Server administration: This involves the design, implementation, and management of the organization's servers. Server administrators are responsible for ensuring that servers are performing at an optimal level that server security is maintained, and that data backups and recovery procedures are in place.

Technical support: Provide technical support to end-users, including troubleshooting technical problems, resolving issues with hardware and software, and assisting users with access to the network and applications.

Database administration: This involves the design, implementation, and management of the organization's databases. Database administrators are responsible for ensuring that data is secure, that the database is available, and that data is backed up and recoverable.

Opportunity can be created in this function in several ways. As always, these lists are not exhaustive and need to be considered against the company's current status.

1. **Standard organizational hygiene:** There are also opportunities to reduce overhead and cost through typical organizational hygiene levers. There may be technical limitations that you run into when executing these opportunities.

2. **MSP:** Evaluate the opportunity to shift these operations in a larger package to a managed service provider. When you shift this to an MSP, the function will be completed by an external agency with the internal team managing the relationship and outcomes. This is a very efficient method to maintain this functionality.

3. **Shift the company's IT footprint to the cloud:** By shifting the IT footprint to the cloud, you can eliminate a significant amount of the overhead associated with server management and maintenance. It also simplifies your internal network requirements. There will still be need for DBAs and some network admin roles.

4. **Shift to colocation facilities:** If the company is not able to shift to the cloud because of internal requirements, examination should be made to shift their compute resources to a colocation facility (e.g., Equinix). These facilities are managed and optimized data centers where companies can buy cabinet space for their own technical requirements. Some of these companies also cover disaster recovery services, as

well. This will eliminate some of the required technical support and requirements to manage physical data centers.

There are significant opportunities throughout the IT stack. Some of the opportunities require technical capability. Firms like McKinsey, Alvarez & Marsal, and AlixPartners typically have prior executives with experience in these areas. In addition, there are niche firm and single-shingle providers that have experience working on these areas that can be beneficial to the desired outcome.

ACCOUNTING, TAX, TREASURY, FINANCE, CORPORATE DEVELOPMENT, AND STRATEGY

The finance and accounting functions are a critical area of the business and can include a number of areas besides pure bean counting and financial analysis. For smaller companies, the CFO (typical leader of this function) can be a very versatile executive that can work across a number of areas depending on their capability. As I have broken this book up across functions, I will focus this discussion on the finance and accounting function and a few adjacencies like corporate development and strategy. These organizations are relatively straightforward when you review them and how to optimize them.

Accounting

Accounting is the language of business and one of the most critical functions in a company. Through accurate bookkeeping and leverage through enterprise resource planning systems, they manage the company's finances and report the profit and loss of a company. These are very technical roles, but also heavily commoditized skillsets. Expert knowledge of US GAAP, IFRS, and Sarbanes-Oxley (for those potentially going public) are required in the organization to ensure your accounting rules are compliant with required guidance and that changes to those rules and organizational policies are appropriately updated in the ERP or other systems of record. The system of record is a critical term. It indicates what is the source of truth for a given piece of data or record.

Typically the ERP is the source of truth for financial information. HRIS is typically the system of record for human resources information.

In addition to the internal teams, the accounting organization will require an external audit partnership and team. Depending on the size of the organization and future plans, these external providers can be conducted by a Big Four (Deloitte, KPMG, EY, and PWC) or another provider (e.g., BDO, CohnReznick, Grant Thornton, Baker Tilly, and Plante Moran). There is a significant pricing difference between the Big Four and other providers. Audit opinions are relatively commoditized. There are some private equity firms that prefer to have a Big Four opinion and are willing to pay more for that additional assurance.

The final differentiator in accounting operations is with the ERP and the processes in the ERP. For companies less than around $2 billion in revenue simpler systems such as NetSuite and Microsoft Dynamics are excellent choices. In addition, with the introduction of AI technologies for Dynamics, there are additional potential advantages to be gained. For industrial businesses and large-scale enterprises, the use of more robust solutions such as SAP and Oracle can also be beneficial. Their ancillary modules and integrated functionality can lead to improved outcomes. In addition, companies of this size can bare the increased overhead cost structure for those systems. For instance, I have seen a $1 billion business leveraging Microsoft Dynamics and paying less than $500,000 per year for the required licenses and implementation. Implementations of SAP and Oracle typically have a much higher price tag.

Use of AI technologies, electronic payment systems, and robotic process automation are also a significant opportunity for accounting teams. A few of the critical technologies that should be leveraged are:

1. AI technologies: Use of technologies such as optical character recognition (OCR) and software technologies that automate data entry and classification information for transactional information are helpful. These technologies are typically focused on invoice processing, reducing the need for additional accounts payable clerks. Generative AI models are already showing benefit in the routing of accounting documents.

2. Robotic process automation: The use of RPA has been increasing throughout the accounting function. RPA is the use

of software robots to automate repetitive tasks. Typically, these bots are effective in several areas of the accounting function. They include:

a. Data entry – automating the entry of data into the accounting system of record.

b. Account reconciliation – the bot will review information from multiple sources and help the user identify discrepancies that require manual reconciliation.

c. Invoice processing—beyond OCR—the RPA bot can extract relevant information and then help to route the invoice or payable as needed versus a human routing items for approval.

d. Financial reporting – gathers data from various sources and compiles reports

e. Audit preparation support – gathers routine information and compiles prior to audit team arrival to streamline preparation.

3. Electronic payment solutions: Effective use of systems like Ariba can yield significant efficiency for the accounting function. Equally, these systems also improve outcomes for procurement teams. Sometimes these savings can be close to 10 percent of the procurement spend. For the accounting function, systems like Ariba automate purchase order creation, management of invoices, and payment reconciliation. In addition, it also streamlines vendor management—another function typically managed or overseen by the accounting and finance function. Ariba can manage supplier performance and compliance. Use of Ariba and systems like it for your accounts receivable function also streamlines your accounting process. By using Ariba and other payment portals, they can be integrated into the ERP and payment reconciliation can also be automated.

The Close Cycle (Month, Quarter, and Annual)

The month end close cycle is the process that collects all of the financial transaction information from the prior month. In the process, they review, reconcile, and report the results of each month. This is critical as it ensures that the accounting of the business is reliable and accurate, helps to inform business decisions, and simplifies any audits and filing requirements. It also sets up the company's financials for the next month. At the end of a quarter or year these close processes will include the typical monthly close, but then a more prolonged process to validate the full results for the quarter or year. For public companies, these also result in statements and press releases to markets. It is important to ensure these are correct as they are the basis of investment decisions and can cause significant issues for the company if they are not correct.

The close cycle is one of the core tasks for accounting. It occurs every month and will limit the availability of accounting resources during the first week to two weeks of the month. The average close cycle takes about 10 to 15 days. For less mature organizations, highly complicated, and larger organizations, these timelines are longer.

The close cycle starts with the accounting teams closing their subledgers and collecting other needed information (e.g., inventory, accrued expenses, general ledger). The general accountants then need to consolidate the various elements of the business. In the process of the month-end consolidations, they will also validate that the AP ledger meshes with the general ledger. Sometimes there are timing differences (accruals) that need to be made. For instance, you incurred an expense during the month but you have not been invoiced. There should be an accrual for that expense. Some element of decision-making occurs during this process. If there are issues, they will issue corrective entries to ensure the general ledgers are up to date.

In some organizations, the finance team will also play a critical role in the close. There are some elements of the accrual process that may need their input or some elements of revenue recognition that requires their support or direct calculations.

The accountants will also reconcile all of their cash accounts. It will also reconcile all of its balance sheet and revenue and expense accounts. They will also review inventory and fixed asset balances.

Once satisfied with the accuracy, they will develop financial statements. These can be compiled in spreadsheets or through automated tools. These reports will typically focus on the summary of the general ledger, profit and loss, and balance sheets.

There are multiple reviews throughout the close cycle with relevant managers to ensure the team is on track for the month end close. In addition, there is a final review with someone separate from the close process to validate the results. From there the reports are sent to upper management for review.

Procure to Pay Process

The accounts payable process is a critical business process that involves managing and recording all of a company's financial obligations to its suppliers or vendors. The key steps of the accounts payable process include:

Requisition: The requisition process typically occurs before the purchase order process and involves a request for goods or services from a department or employee within the organization. The requisition includes details such as the item or service requested, the quantity needed, and any other relevant information. Once the requisition is approved, it is forwarded to the purchasing department to generate a purchase order.

Purchase order: The purchase order is a formal agreement between the buyer and the supplier that specifies the terms and conditions of the purchase. The purchase order includes details such as the item or service ordered, the quantity, the price, the payment terms, and the delivery date. The purchase order is created by the purchasing department based on the requisition and is sent to the supplier for approval.

Invoice receipt: The accounts payable process starts with receiving an invoice from a supplier or vendor. The invoice includes details such as the amount owed, payment terms, and the goods or services received.

Invoice verification: The next step is to verify that the invoice is accurate and matches the purchase order and/or receipt of goods or services. The accounts payable team may check for errors or discrepancies in the invoice, such as incorrect pricing or quantities.

Purchase order matching: If the invoice matches a purchase order, the accounts payable team will ensure that the goods or services have been received and that the invoice is in accordance with the purchase order.

Approval: Once the invoice has been verified and matched, the accounts payable team will send the invoice to the appropriate department or manager for approval. This ensures that the goods or services have been received and are in compliance with company policies and procedures.

Payment: Once the invoice has been approved, the accounts payable team will schedule payment to the supplier or vendor based on the payment terms. Payment can be made through a variety of methods, including checks, wire transfers, or electronic payment systems.

Recordkeeping: Finally, the accounts payable team will record the payment in the company's financial records and update the vendor's account information. This information is important for tracking expenses, managing cash flow, and preparing financial statements.

Through a thorough P2P process, companies can ensure that they pay their suppliers and vendors accurately and on time, maintain good relationships with their business partners, and effectively manage their financial obligations. The accounts payable process can be automated using software systems, which can help improve efficiency, reduce errors, and provide better visibility into financial data.

Order to Cash (OTC)—this is sometimes referred to as Contract to Cash (CTC)

The order to cash process (OTC) is a critical accounting process that involves managing the entire sales cycle from the receipt of an order to the receipt of payment. Here's a sequential process for the OTC process and how orders are converted into shipments and invoices, and how invoices are managed to ensure collections and payment:

Order receipt: The OTC process starts with the receipt of an order from a customer. The order includes details such as the items or services ordered, the quantity, the price, and the delivery date.

Order verification: Once the order is received, it is verified to ensure that it meets the company's requirements and that there are no discrepancies or errors.

Order fulfillment: After the order has been verified, it is fulfilled by picking, packing, and shipping the order to the customer. This involves converting the order into a shipment and updating inventory records.

Shipment creation: A shipment is created to record the shipment of goods or services to the customer. The shipment includes details such as the items shipped, the quantity, the shipping method, and the shipping cost.

Invoice creation: Once the shipment has been made, an invoice is created for the customer based on the details of the shipment. The invoice includes details such as the items shipped, the quantity, the price, and the payment terms.

Payment collection: After the invoice has been created, it is sent to the customer for payment. The accounts receivable team manages the collection of payments from customers and ensures that the payments are received on time and in accordance with the payment terms specified in the invoice.

Payment validation: Once the payment is received, it is validated to ensure that it matches the invoice amount and that it is in accordance with the payment terms. This involves reconciling the payment with the order and verifying that the payment has been applied to the correct customer account.

Payment posting: Finally, the payment is posted to the customer's account and updated in the company's financial records. This involves updating the accounts receivable records and reconciling the payment with the invoice.

The company's AR team is critical to the success of this process. Here is how the AR team typically manages and oversees this process. Please note that some of this process, specifically billing, and bad debt management can often times fall between accounting and the sales teams, with the sales team sometimes being a primary driver on some of the issues.

Order entry and validation: A team in the company will be responsible for entering orders into the accounting system and ensuring that the orders are accurate and complete. This can be done through an order management team, the sales team, or a dedicated accounts receivable team. This team is also responsible for verifying that the orders are valid and that the customer has the creditworthiness to purchase the goods or services. These teams can often work with the customers to change the orders to ensure they can be fulfilled with the available stock. Oftentimes, companies will leverage this team for allocation of goods.

Invoice creation: The team is then responsible for creating and issuing invoices to customers based on the orders received and the product shipped. Each company will vary on when the invoice is issued. For some CPG companies, that timing could be at time of shipping. For consulting companies, it may be every 30 days or at the end of an engagement. For others, it is when an item is ordered. The invoices provided to the customers will include details such as the items shipped, description of goods or services received, the quantity, the price, and the payment terms.

Payment collection: The AR team is responsible for collecting payments from customers and ensuring that payments are received on time and in accordance with the payment terms specified in the invoice. In this function, they will review AR aging output typically from the ERP. They will work with the leadership and sales teams to follow-up with customers that have not paid within their stated terms, known as an outstanding balance.

Payment application: When the customer pays, the AR team is responsible for applying the payments received to the customer's account and ensuring that the payments are accurately recorded in the accounting system and the asset from the accounts receivable is offset with the new cash asset. There are times when the payment is not in full or does not match with the invoice. These are known as exceptions. The exception handling process will vary. The majority of the issues can be resolved when you discuss it with the customer. Sometimes, there are disagreements on the billing. When that is the case, the sales team will typically work with AR to make a call as to whether they need to push the issues or not. When not paid in full, the AR team may treat this as an outstanding balance, depending on the interaction and input from the sales team.

Bad debt management: The AR team is responsible for managing bad debts and identifying customers with delinquent accounts. This requires active dialogues with the credit management team or the leadership, depending on the size of the company. When customers have outstanding balances they are typically prohibited from ordering more products until the issues is resolved. When the issue cannot be resolved, companies can handle this on their own to try to collect the money. A number of companies have also opted to partner with dedicated collection agencies.

Reporting: The AR team is responsible for generating reports on accounts receivable, aging of invoices, and collections activity, and providing this information to management for decision-making.

Opportunity In the Accounting Function

1. Enhanced use of technology: The enhanced use of technology can reduce accounting cost and improve overall outcomes for the company. The catch-22 on this is that the companies the benefit the most are larger companies. Those companies have on a by and large basis already implemented these improvements. However, some have not.

    a. RPA: The increased use of RPA can have a positive impact for smaller companies. Once the bots are trained, you can usually identify a positive ROI and focus on the processes with the highest impact. When looking at these opportunities, realize that the companies that engineer the solution oftentimes will incorporate an annuity that partially offsets the realized savings. This is typically done through a license fee. Implementation that eliminates this continuous fee may be beneficial. Typically you can realize significant savings for a greenfield deployment. When I look at this I typically range the opportunity as 0 percent on the low end and up to about 10 percent on the high end across the AP and AR remaining spend for the company.

    b. OCR: OCR requires a significant amount of documents to be processed to be a positive ROI undertaking. Typically this is a potential option for companies in the healthcare, financial services, and legal sector. OCR can also be used for general admin and other functions within the company. For accounting purposes, you need to process a significant number of invoices. Typically you want the company to process at least 1,000 invoices per month for the OCR technology to make sense. OCR is not 100 percent correct all of the time so manual intervention to the AP process is usually still required. In addition, it is the first step of a larger AP automation project. Use of platforms like Ariba can also be beneficial and help to eliminate some of the need for manual processing of invoices.

2.   Offshoring: The largest benefit to an accounting organization is for the organization to largely be offshored. Although a critical function, accounting is not typically core to the business. In addition, the processes in accounting are relatively mature and largely controlled by the accounting software and ERP. This makes offshoring this function highly desirable.

Companies will have varying willingness to offshore the accounting function. Very mature companies will be willing to offshore almost the entirety except for the leadership and some elements of the record to report function. Others may be reticent to offshore any portion of the function. The less contentious elements of the organization to offshore tend to be transactional in nature, typically AP, AR, fixed assets, financial system analysts (people who pull data from the finance system). The next tranche is typically the management and leadership of these functions and some of the record to report function (general accountants). The hardest to shift tends to be anything associated with cash management and final accounting consolidation of accounting and reporting management. The last tranche tends to require involvement and discussion with business leadership. Because of this interlock, sometimes you cannot offshore or outsource this capability.

An additional consideration given the nature of accounting, it is sometimes better to nearshore the function. This can occur in a lower cost jurisdiction in a near time zone or it can occur in a lower cost area of the country. If your headquarter office is in New York there is no reason that your accounting (or for that matter any of your back office) needs to be in New York. Places like Austin, Columbus, Raleigh, the suburbs of Chicago, Milwaukee, Baltimore, Providence, Salt Lake City, Phoenix, and countless others provide access to high-quality talent at a lower cost point. From an employee perspective, their quality of life is typically higher and productivity is just as high.

Typical arbitrage on labor rates can be anywhere from approximately 20 percent up to close to 95 percent. If nearshoring or low cost onshoring the arbitrage can be lower with rates only 10 percent lower – this is highly dependent on the company's final choice of location and operating model. In one situation, I have seen accounting resources in the high cost country making around $100,000 per year be replaced by internal, offshore resources for as low as $7,200 per year. These outcomes are highly dependent on the initial high cost country and the intended destination for the service. Use of internal resources in a captive offshore center tends to be less expensive than outsourced providers. However, there is greater risk and overhead to maintain the offshore center and continue to populate it with qualified resources. In addition, operating models that allow locals to maintain their local language increases the candidate pool and likely improves the arbitrage. If this is a path, the key element is to ensure that the middle management is fluent in the company's language and acts as the conduit and intermediary for the company with the workers speaking their local language.

3.   Organizational hygiene: Typical organizational hygiene can be conducted on the accounting organization.

4.   Unique situations: A number of the levers above have already been leveraged for most accounting functions. A lot of opportunity in accounting will come from unique situations. Below I will list a few, but there are countless others.

   a.   ERP consolidation: For multiple ERPs, you will need multiple teams of AR/AP and general accountants. Because of that when ERPs are consolidated and the accounting teams consolidated, you will find additional opportunity.

   b.   Industry specific accounting automation: Some industries have unique requirements that have not been automated. The companies tend to use either a homegrown solution or excel to conduct unique accounting practices. For instance, in the gift card industry, revenue recognition is complicated. Some firms will use teams of analysts to conduct the work. They have not had the time or money to invest in automating the processes. Once automated, the teams can be reduced or reallocated to support other functions.

Tax

The tax function, if deployed well within a company, should create significant value for the company. Typically, this function will have a more senior tax strategist as the leader. They are typically a former accounting firm executive that understands how to optimize a company's legal entities, Intellectual Property, operations, and transfer pricing to reduce the company's tax liability. The tax function is also responsible for compliance—tax filing—for the company.

The mechanisms to create value in taxes can reduce tax liability for a company anywhere from 10 to 20 percent. For some industries with certain tax advantages, this can be even higher. An entire book—well, hundreds—can be written on this topic. For companies with operations across a number of different countries, it is recommended that they get a tax lead. Given their background, they are not cheap, but if selected well and empowered they pay for themselves.

The other responsibility is also the legal entity structure. The legal entity structure for a company can be a strategic enabler and if properly chosen, can create an advantage. For instance, it is better to establish a continental European presence through a German entity than it is through a French entity. This is because the company then falls under French authority. For a variety of reasons, Germany is more business friendly than France. There are also advantages for some companies with intellectual property if the IP is housed in an Irish or Swiss company. The Tax advisor would understand these and other opportunities and work with your legal team to implement the tax optimizing legal entity structure.

Compliance, on the other hand, is commoditized. Some companies try to maintain this function in house. However, efficient companies typically outsource and offshore this capability. It has a significant savings opportunity, depending on the company.

The other area to assess is the legal entity structure for the company. Whenever possible, attempt to streamline the legal entity structure. For each entity, it is likely that you will pay on average around $5,000 to $20,000 in compliance costs per year. This is just for filing. Simplification can generate a return, depending on the number of companies and their geographies. There are some times when these efforts will not make sense because of repatriation expenses (typically tax on account transfers) and cost to achieve.

Treasury

The treasury function of a company controls the cash movement and disbursement for the company. In addition, they also oversee cash management if the need arises when cash is potentially constrained. The function of treasury and tax are often times combined in one leader. For a number of companies, this is okay because the tax issues have largely been solved and cash management is relatively straightforward.

To best understand the treasury function, think about your personal finances. You have multiple accounts and you also have a credit card. In business just replace a credit card with a "revolver." This is a line of credit—a revolving loan—that companies have to cover working capital fluctuations and other unforeseen needs. As the treasurer you make sure that there are adequate funds in your disbursement account to cover your cash needs. This is relatively straightforward if your operations are in a single jurisdiction. However, when you have operations in other countries, shifting money between accounts can potentially introduce tax risk. Having an experienced treasurer is beneficial. Tight coordination with the tax team is also important in the event money has to be moved between accounts and across jurisdictional lines.

These teams are typically small. However, they can be optimized. One of the first levers is potentially combining the tax and treasury lead. You should also look at how busy these professionals seem. Because this can be as simple as balancing a checkbook and issuing reports on it, there may be excess capacity in the function. If so, reduction of capacity may be an opportunity.

Another item to look at is the number of accounts being managed and the level of automation in place for typical cash movements. There are times that the bank you use does not have account technology or infrastructure to accommodate the size of your company. When this occurs, you may want to look at transitioning banks. The other watch out for on bank selection is geographic coverage. I have run into a situation where our bank did not have coverage for a given geography. When this occurred, the company had trapped cash in their stores until we established a relationship with another bank.

Finance

The remainder of the finance organization is focused on financial planning and analysis and financial reporting. These functions are business critical and typically are considered a service to the management team to understand how the business is performing and conduct ad hoc analysis on the business operations of the company.

Finance teams are generally oriented by either geography or business line. For larger organizations, this can also result in specific finance support for a business line colocated with business leadership in that region. Typically, there is also a corporate finance team that supports central budgeting, headquarters, and back office. There is a tendency for larger and more complex organizations to add additional pockets of financial resources. The more centralized the finance team, the more relative information the CFO and headquarters has regarding the business. Shifting the finance resources lower in the organization (e.g., to a business line) improves the data and information at that level, leaving corporate to rely on the business units for reporting. This is a relatively large tradeoff and requires significant trust and confidence in the business units. Some of this can be mitigated with dotted reporting lines, but it is not fully corrected through those mechanisms.

Division of reporting can sometimes be mixed between accounting and finance. Typically, accounting is responsible for reporting the "as-is" numbers post consolidation. The finance team is then responsible for conducting variance analysis and tying together the "so-what" for the business.

Besides business reporting and analysis, the finance team also plans a central role in the budgetary process. The budget process is something that takes about six months depending on the complexity of the business. It will typically start off with a budget kickoff planning session focused on the sales team high level forecast in about the March or April timeline. Over the summer, the finance team will work with the business unit leads to develop a granular bottom up build of the budget and supporting models. These models can be developed at a customer or operating unit level with full cost and profit drivers and anticipated performance and costs each month through the next year. Around August to September, the budgets will be presented by the business unit leads to the internal executive committee that can provide oversight on the anticipated financial results. Typically the budgets are overestimated and require refinement. Between September and December (goal being November), the budgets are typically negotiated between finance and the business leads. The CEO or other executives will act as a decision maker for some elements. In addition to the hard line numbers, the teams will also provide risks and opportunities to the budget. Risks being the main economic issues that could result in a budgetary miss. The opportunities being the corollary to that. Ideally, the budget has equal risks and opportunities when it is finally approved.

Typical optimization of this function occurs around several levers:

1. **Report automation:** Most companies have some semblance of automated reporting on business outcomes.
2. **Organizational realignment**: Oftentimes FP&A organizations are overstaffed because there are duplicate finance functions across the globe and business units with each business leader having dedicated resources. Realignment of resources and sharing of resources between business leaders creates a tension that allows resources to be reduced and the analysis undertaken to be more highly valued and focused on the most accretive initiatives. It also elevates the role of the CFO and financial team.
3. **Offshoring:** Financial analytics and financial data gathering are elements of the organization that can be offshored or even outsourced.
4. **Reducing staffing and adding volume during peaks:** Use of interim and temporary resources through firms like Catalant Technologies or Randstad are achievable for peak period

volumes (e.g., budget season and others). This allows you reduce the overall quantity of resources by around 10 to 20 percent and then, if and as required, you bring on one to two resources for two to three months. The markup on resources through these channels is about 20 to 40 percent. In addition, you can also bring them on full time, if there is a fit and the additional long-term capacity is required.

5. **Generative AI will likely have a profound impact on this section of the company in the coming years.** The singularity is when the company's proprietary data sets is able to be understood by generative AI. This is something that can be done over the next two to four years with long implementation periods for large companies. But once complete, it could be a situation where large tranches of the finance department can be replaced with bots and managers to ensure the analysis is correct. Companies like BCG and McKinsey are already developing solutions to automate large amounts of the typical analysis being conducted by these teams.

Risk Management

Depending on the size and complexity of the company, the risk management function may not have any dedicated resources. For small companies (less than $250 million to $750 million in revenue) and companies that do not have significant risk exposure like a bank may not have a dedicated risk management function. It may just be an ad-hoc group or a function that resides directly with the CFO or head of legal. When it is just a collateral duty, it will typically review major enterprise risks and also be responsible for the company's insurance policies to ensure that the risk can be fully mitigated through external liability absorption. I will discuss insurance coverage at a later stage.

When the company has systemic risks or is large, you will begin to see dedicated risk management functions within the company. There should always be someone that has a collateral responsibility to identify, assess and manage risk. At a minimum, the leader of each function is accountable for it. External and dedicated risk managers can also be a good resource for key areas of the company. They are common to review risk in cyber and for financial institutions investments and liabilities.

From there you can design this organization from the ground up and with the appropriate level of attention to the correct functions.

They should also have a small third party spend budget to conduct cyber intrusion and security studies and bring in decision maker on third party audit firms. For areas of special interest, they may also need some additional dollars for legal or other advisory support.

This function should have a direct reporting relationship to the board of directors and the CEO. Organizationally, I have seen this function report into numerous other functions and also be stand alone, as well. It depends on how important the function is to the business and how the business wants to manage its internal risk management function.

Corporate Development / Investor Relations

Corporate development is not always required in a business. This function is typically required for companies that have a goal of growing through inorganic methods or conducting a few partnerships. For a PE-backed company, the role of corporate development will often be conducted by the PE firm itself. This allows teams looking to optimize the business to immediately reduce all or almost all of the corporate development function. For investment thesis that will also focus on inorganic growth and the CFO does not have a strong strategic or M&A background, they may supplement the management team with a corporate development resource. If so, it is usually one or two people that conduct deal reviews and partnership analysis for the company.

Likewise, a privately held company does not need dedicated investor relations resources. These positions are typically eliminated when a company is taken private.

If the resources in the positions discussed above are versatile, then you can place them into other roles within the company. However, these roles tend to be highly skilled and less versatile across the operations team.

Strategy

The role of strategy in a PE-backed company is critical for companies undergoing strategic repositioning. Typically, this will be a single dedicated person or a small team of resources (one to three people). Their function is to assess the company's current competitive position and work with the management team to effectively reposition the company into an optimal position for sustainable competitive advantage. These roles will typically have a direct reporting relationship with the PE fund.

There is also the opportunity to reduce or eliminate this function or incorporate it at a lower level, if the function is not required moving forward or the investment thesis is well understood. If the resources in the strategy positions are versatile, then you can place them into other roles within the company. Often these strategic resources are valuable in a number of other roles in the company. They can easily be leaders of business units, heads of operations, or other roles that require horizontal and strategic level analysis and insight.

HUMAN RESOURCES

The human resources department at a company plays many vital roles for the enterprise. The majority are solely focused on the selection, payment, retention, and welfare of the employees of the company. There are a significant number of movements to make HR a strategic enabler to companies. My general tendency is to minimize the role of HR as a service. The culture of the company is something that should be set on the day-to-day interactions and fostered by the business management team.

The HR organization has some opportunities, largely in labor arbitrage or use of PEO providers, like ADP. The other area of HR that we will focus on is the HR policies. These have significant costs associated with them and should be closely examined. Even minor changes have a multiplier effect across the entirety of the organization.

HR Organization

Here are the key functions within the HR organization:

Talent acquisition: Attracts and hires the best candidates for job openings in the organization. This involves posting job ads, screening resumes, conducting interviews, and making job offers.

Training and development: Oversee or deliver training and development to employees to help them improve their skills and knowledge.

Compensation, payroll, and benefits: HR manages employee compensation and benefits programs, including salaries, bonuses, health insurance, retirement plans, and other perks. Payroll is the processing of employee compensation disbursement. In some companies, this falls under the accounting team. It can be in either. However, with the majority of the process occurring in the HRIS, a number of companies have determined it should sit under the HR team with accounting oversight and audit.

HR business partners: HR handles employee relations issues, such as conflicts, grievances, and disciplinary actions. They also provide guidance on workplace policies and procedures. HR business partners also ensure that the organization complies with all relevant employment laws and regulations, such as equal employment opportunity laws, minimum wage laws, and labor laws. HR business partners also support and ensure that the performance management process is executed on a regular basis and that the employees receive the support and feedback needed to improve job performance and enhance their careers.

Diversity and inclusion: HR works to create a diverse and inclusive workplace culture that values and respects differences in race, gender, ethnicity, religion, and other characteristics.

So where are the opportunities?

Use a PEO: For smaller companies, there is no reason to hire on an HR function. You can outsource almost the entirety, with the exception of the head of HR role to a PEO, a professional employer organization. Through a PEO you can leverage a co-employment arrangement—there is little difference that an employee will experience. You still control the hiring and termination of the employees. The PEO, on the other hand, takes care of everything else. This includes technically being the employer of record for the person. As they are the employer of record, they may also help you think through some of your policies where they may face liability. The other benefit is that you can benefit from lower benefit premiums and fuller benefit offerings than most small companies put together. In general, through a PEO small- to mid-size companies can benefit tremendously from cost, as well as quality of life perspective. They also typically come with a technology solution. Because they have the technology solution, you do not need to spend money to install one. On average, administration costs are around $450 cheaper per employee through use of a PEO.[14]

In addition, these providers can also spin up entities globally to ensure you can start a business and hire resources in any given geography. Please note that the costs can be high for hiring resources across the world. In one company, we stood up operations across more than 10 different geographies through the use of PEOs in less than three months.

Reduction of non-core HR requirements: There are elements of HR that, although important, can be an area to take risk for a truly efficient organization. For instance, training and development for a small company is less of a concern than a larger company. Why? A large company needs to seek strong methods to retain their resources. The name of that organization on a resume typically has some carry in an industry. For instance, the GE meatball on a resume was a gold stamp for many years in the industrial space. McKinsey, Bain, and BCG are gold standards for the consulting space. Strong retention and incentive programs like training and development are critical to employees feeling they are valued in a firm. For smaller firms, there is less systemic risk of loss of the employee base. For those firms, you may be able to take additional risk. Shrinking training and development budgets and reducing the teams in size and scope may be a potential opportunity.

Another area like this is the ESG element of HR. In today's world in the United States, it is recommended that you do have some diversity representation and inclusivity framework and oversight. If not, you will continue to have issues and for it to be swept under the rug. I was in one organization where an executive referred to an African American as an animal. HR was in the room when it happened, the person complained to HR, and nothing was done. This is the definition of a toxic work environment. Having a second line of defense on these types of insidious behaviors reduces overall workplace liability. However, you do not need analytics, you do not need a significant infrastructure to support this—you just need a strong person that is backed at the board level to ensure diversity is a priority in the organization.

---

14   Cinnamon Janzer, "What Does PEO Mean?" Zenifefits, May 8, 2020, www.zenefits.com/workest/what-does-peo-mean/.

Reduction of HR business partners: There are various models of leadership within corporations. Some companies prefer to promote leaders that do not actively manage their people. When this occurs, they rely on HR to do this. This creates a conflict in many ways. The main issue is that it also denies an actual avenue for effective oversight of management practices in the company. A better model is to run extremely lean HR business partner teams. They are there to ensure that managers manage the issues within the organization in compliance with the law and to minimize liability. Otherwise, management of the internal resources and knowledge of the organization should fall to the business leaders. This can significantly reduce your overall requirements for HR business partners to the top quartile.

Opportunities in talent acquisition: Talent acquisition can also be reduced. On average, an internal resource can attract fill about five roles per month. There is a balance that needs to be struck between internal and external sourcing. In addition, there are networks for specialized roles that tend to be limited. Because of this, it can be preferred to leverage a hybrid approach—where you have the talent acquisition team able to manage about 80 percent of the role fills based on standard turnover (around 5 to 10 percent of the employee population for a healthy company). So for a company of 1,000 people you would anticipate around 50 to 100 people would leave per year. This then requires only one to two people in talent acquisition. You may also need another resource to manage the process for recruiting (e.g., scheduling, background checks, etc.). There are some functions in the company that have significantly higher turnover—for instance customer service, manufacturing, and logistics. For these types of companies additional talent acquisition resources will be required to manage the process and recruit the required amount of talent to maintain the company.

Today, there are also service providers that focus exclusively on talent acquisition. For either peak periods or during transitions, you can hire on a temporary resource that works largely on contingency of finding the resource. When fully contingent, you will likely pay between 20 to 30 percent of the person's salary. There is also a hybrid where you pay the person a stipend each month, let's say $5,000 to $10,000, they then reduce the contingency fee per person hired down to 10 to 20 percent.

Another option for larger enterprises is to leverage offshore talent to provide lists of qualified resources. These services are relatively affordable and reduce the need for onshore analytical support for the talent acquisition function. You can also offshore the process management element of the TA function. Caution is required for outsourcing this as it is a core element of the employee experience. It is better for larger organizations that have established offshore centers as a tuck in service.

Compensation, payroll, and benefits organization: For compensation, payroll, and benefits, these roles tend to be highly analytical. The majority of this function can be offshored or outsourced. There likely needs to be a director or manager level resource to inform the policy making, but the majority of day-to-day output can be offshored. I will talk more about policies in the next section. These can and should be optimized.

HR third party spend: Third party spend by human resources should be closely scrutinized. There is not a good benchmark for the spend, but there should be line item level detail for what the HR team wants to use this on. A lot of these dollars can quickly become a slush fund, as there are a number of good deals that do not directly contribute to the bottom line that can be financed through HR. For instance, executive education is often financed through these funds. These schools are tens of thousands of dollars for one or two individuals. These should be reserved for true standouts and not just someone who has gained favoritism from hire echelons in the company. In addition, the spend on hiring conferences should also be examined. A number of times, the team will want the highest level of coverage. Each of these investments should be reviewed by the CFO and the CHRO to ensure proper and optimized use of funds.

HR Policies

There are a number of HR policies that can cost the company significant amounts of money. In this section, I am not recommending that you undertake any or all of these options. HR policies are something that a company has to think through on its own and make informed decisions with the understanding of their own employee population. In addition, I am showing options that I have seen that work to improve efficiency in the organizations I have served. These have never been one-size fits all.

With that disclaimer, here is a list of HR policies and how minor tweaks can improve efficiency in the organization:

Pay: Companies have a choice when determining the level at which people are paid. In a given region, there are pay standards for a given industry and job function. These can be found via the bureau of labor statistics. You can also commission a study. Within these pay bands, companies can decide whether they want to pay at the top of the pay band or lower in the pay bands. This has a direct correlation to the talent levels you can attract and also likelihood for retention of the personnel. Some companies will determine that they can take risk in this area and reduce from the top quartile to the mid quartile. Some shift from mid to lower quartile. These decisions need to be taken by experienced professionals. However, depending on the industry and the asset, there may be opportunity to reduce total costs for the company.

In addition, examination and installation of paybands for given levels in the company are helpful to support the healthy functioning of the company and ensure equity. If a decision is made to put in place paybands, this can yield some opportunity for a company over time. As more tenured resources are typically higher than the pay band, when they attrite from the company and are replaced, this tends to lower your overall cost for employees.

Travel and expense: Travel and expense is an easy lever to focus on. It has direct cost implications to the company. Use of travel and expense management systems like Concur help to systemize these policies and prevent people from misusing company funds. In addition, the direct linkage between the travel and expense system allow auditors full access to the decisions and approvals made when travel was booked.

First, all travel should be booked through your travel management system. This allows you to put in place and systematize rules for what can and cannot be booked. For instance, business class travel overseas is a major use of T&E expense. With the correct TMS and rules, you can minimize that to senior executives or others where those additional dollars are warranted. There are also rules that will allow you to limit the increased cost that a user can use. For instance, you can put a rate difference cap of $100 off the lowest cost option. When you do, this prevents someone from selecting a flight with a difference of more than $100 from the lowest cost option the company could pay for. Use of the TMS allows you to partner with demand aggregation platforms for better hotel and airfare rates, providing altogether reduced costs for your T&E expense.

Use of a company provided corporate card provides money back, typically between 0.5 and 2 percent of total travel expense. In addition, integration with TMS and expense management platforms provides full transparency for the cost you incur and minimizes the chance for frivolous or fraudulent expenses. To enforce, you also need to prohibit the use of personal cards. To enact, you just need to start rejecting those claims without full, itemized receipts and manager approval for each line item expense.

When you put this into place and with the automation and use of machine learning that these providers are putting into the systems, you can also look to lower your overhead for expense processing. This allows the auditors to just focus in on exception handling.

Severance policy: Severance policies can range from generous (three months for ICs, six months for directors and VPs, and 12 months for first level executives) to not as generous. Shifting your severance policy toward the less generous end of the spectrum may be something to consider. This also allows you to increase the policy for layoffs, but minimize cost for desired turnover. This analysis is U.S.-centric— other parts of the world have statutory requirements that I will briefly cover.

On the low end of the spectrum, a typical equation is number of weeks for years of service. One example is below:

Service Period	Severance
First three months	No severance
After three months	Minimum of two weeks of salary
After one year	Two weeks of salary + 1 week for each year of service

Another example on the generous side is:

Service Period	Severance
First three months	No severance
After three months	Two weeks + 1 week for each year of service of salary
Individual Contributor / Manager	3 months of salary
Director/VP	6 months of salary
SVP or above	12 months of salary

When calculating severance for layoffs, I typically use the fully burdened cost basis for the people (base + bonus + benefits) and then divide by four. This is a good rough approximation for the budget needed for the layoff when assessing at a high level. For actual execution, you will look at each person and the actual costing.

For other countries, you will need to consult with a legal team. However, the two most restrictive countries to conduct layoffs are in Germany and France. This is one of the reasons why you avoid establishing operations in either of those countries and, if established, then try to eliminate them.

For Germany, there is no statutory requirement for severance. However, use of works councils and social plans that they maintain are a standard normal for severance payments. IF no works council exists, then you want to provide the employees what they would be entitled as if it did exist. In short, employees can elect to form a works council. For those involved it can prolong the process for some time. This is in no one's interest. If a works council exists, then you will need to justify the terminations to the works council and then payout employees per the agreed upon social plan. These payments are based on age. Here is a typical table that I have seen in the past:

Age	Payout Entitlement
Up to age 50 and less than 15 years of service	12 months payout
Age 50 to 55 and between 15 and 20 years of service	15 months payout
Over 55 or greater than 20 years of service	18 months payout

You will notice the stark contrast of this versus the United States. The UK is actually quite similar to the generous table for the U.S., but does require formal consultation with the employees to ensure all needs are met.

France is one of the most restrictive. In addition, the works councils are much more powerful and some layoffs require appeals all the way up to the French supreme court. This process can take up to two years. In the end, the value paid out will likely be in line with the social plan if you are successful and win your case. Just realize that you will have a carrying cost for the individual for about two years.

For large-scale layoffs or plant closures in the U.S., there is also the Worker Adjustment and Retraining Notification (WARN) Act that needs to be considered. Whenever you are considering large-scale layoffs, it is advisable to seek the counsel of an employment attorney. There are also a lot of resources available online through the Department of Labor. In general, the WARN Act requires that employees receive written notice at least 60 calendar days prior to separation. The intent is for the employees to seek alternative employment or enter into skills training programs. This only applies when the business has more than 100 workers and is laying off at least 50 people at a single site of employment within a 90 days retroactive looking time frame. This last element prevents a company from laying off the equivalent sequentially over a three month span. Each state has various precedents that can be more restrictive than the federal statute. California is typically considered the most restrictive. For your unique situation, please contact employment counsel. There are financial penalties due to the employee notification is not done properly.

Performance management: To meet ambitious EBITDA targets, some companies in a PE paradigm will more actively enforce their performance management system. Some companies will incentivize managers to manage out their bottom percentage of performers. This is a good tool to meet targets, but the downside is the culture that you create in the company. This can create a toxic and cut throat culture if kept in place too long. Doing this for a year or so may make sense to eliminate poor performers.

Benefits

Benefits are always a touchy topic. This topic impacts not only the employees, but also the executives that are making the decisions. Here are some areas you may consider:

Executive benefit packages: These packages often times will have the executives have their 401(k) and retirement paid for or they will receive car or medical pay stipends in addition to their outsized pay packages. There is no reason to create two separate benefit packages. There should just be one at the company level with no additional benefits for the executives. Depending on the size of the company, this is an easy fix and reduces payouts by hundreds of thousands of dollars, if not millions. The rouse is to tell the executives that this will not be offered and the equity compensation offsets this.

In addition, if the company has corporate jets, this program should be closely examined. Typical ROI on a company jet is low. Instead, look at enhanced options for executives to fly elevated classes on flights. If itineraries absolutely demand it, look at use of services like NetJets. When these programs are dissolved, there is usually a cash injection into the company of between $5 and $50 million on the sale of the assets. This can be used to fund other accretive initiatives.

Healthcare: There are a number of variables that go into healthcare expenses. The rates for healthcare insurance are based on the company's size, location, average age of the employees, and demographics of your company's population. For instance, if you are a company, a 70-year-old man will have a different risk profile than a 25-year-old woman. Interestingly, women of childbearing years tend to cost more than a man of the same age. However, on average, older populations cost more to maintain health insurance, given typical body deterioration. As of 2021, the typical total premium for healthcare was $7,470 for single employees and $21,342 for families.[15]

This is a major attraction and retention tool for employees. Given that, you cannot eliminate or significantly reduce the benefit. A typical approach is to improve the options available for employees that have different risk tolerances. For some, they would prefer a higher premium payment and lower deductible, others the converse. On average, employees typically pay about 17 percent of the premium for single members and about 27 percent for families. Companies have the option to shift this over time. Typically the minimum that companies will subsidize employee health benefits is 50 percent of the premium. Some generous companies will fully cover. The option of where your company sits is in the full discretion of the management team.

The other variable that management typically has is the selection of the plans offered. They can range from healthcare management organizations (HMOs) to preferred provider organizations (PPOs) to high-deductible healthcare plans (HDHPs). PPOs are the most common plan offered and adopted by employers. Forty-seven percent of employees enroll in PPOs; HMOs are the second most common with 26 percent of employees, and 24 percent are in HDHPs.

Shifting employees to HDHPs save companies significant cost. Here are the 2021 average premiums for the various plans:

Type of Plan	Single	Family
PPO	$7,556	$22,067
HMO	$7,176	$20,321
HDHP	$6,277	$18,308
Percent difference	16.9%	17.0%

To incent this behavior, companies will typically put some money toward their employees' healthcare savings account (HSA). Even contributing $500 may provide a large incentive to single members to

15 "2021 Employer Health Benefits Survey," Kaiser Family Foundation, November 10, 2021, www.kff.org/report-section/ehbs-2021-section-1-cost-of-health-insurance/.

take on the HDHP versus either of the managed healthcare options.

Retirement: For any company that still has a defined benefit plan, those should be retired. This was a trend in the 1990s and 2000s. If there are hang overs, the best advice is to eliminate the program. There is a proven playbook to do this where you phase it out and then make the people still eligible whole on the company's promise to them, but going forward the cost basis is reduced.

For defined contribution plans, like a 401(k), there are ways to reduce the expense. First, examine your contribution to employees. You can eliminate matching benefits, but this will not be popular with your employees. In fact, you will risk higher attrition. Another method is to change when the payouts to employees occur. A typical program pays this out monthly. You can change this into a lump sum at the end of the year. By doing so, you may not be required to pay for employees that leave in the middle of the year. This can typically save about 5 to 10 percent (based on average attrition) of your projected 401(k) matching budget.

Another lever is to assess your current 401(k) administrator and the fees they charge. If your objective is to reduce your cost, there are some providers that focus on reducing corporate overhead associated with the 401(k) administration. This may result in lower total returns on your employee's 401(k)s. Given that this is a relatively low expense for the company, it is not usually advised to do this.

Corporate cars: Corporate car programs should largely be eliminated. For some regions, like Europe, they are part of the pay package. You need to ensure your pay is at market. However, for all others, you should seek to eliminate them. In substitute, you provide a stipend that offsets the cost of a car, typically $300 to $500 per month for field service resources and local field sales people. All others would have their expenses reimbursed by the company for travel.

Bring your own device: We all need mobile devices. However, companies should seek to eliminate the full pay model. Instead, you should seek to shift to a monthly stipend of around $80 for employees that are required to manage their device. This is typically managers and above and field resources. For international calling, they should be reimbursed at cost. This typically saves between $20 to $100 per employee and eliminates the capital cost of buying and replacing phones every few years.

Other programs: There are other programs that companies will have in their benefits programs. They are typically low cost, but should still be examined. The typical benefit program will have these minimum components, healthcare, life insurance, ADD, and a retirement plan. Everything about this is at the management team's discretion and what is required to support attraction of the talent needed for the company.

Legal

The firm's legal team is responsible for managing the company's interests and operates within the boundaries of the applicable jurisdictions laws. There are several critical functions that they serve:

Advising on corporate governance: Advise the company's management and board of directors on matters related to corporate governance, such as compliance with laws and regulations, board structure and composition, and executive compensation.

Drafting and reviewing contracts: Draft, review, and negotiate contracts with vendors, suppliers, customers, and other parties.

Managing litigation: Represent the company in legal disputes, including managing litigation and settlement negotiations with third parties.

Intellectual property protection: Monitor and protect the company's intellectual property, such as patents, trademarks, and copyrights.

Compliance and regulatory matters: Ensure that the company complies with applicable laws and regulations, such as employment law, data privacy regulations, and environmental regulations.

Risk management can also be placed under legal, depending on the company's structure. This area has already been covered in the finance section of the book.

For legal, there is a balance of how much this function is done in house versus external and when done external which provider you leverage. The optimal solution likely leverages lower cost solutions for external counsel. Some of the top firms in the United States such as Ropes & Gray, Weil, Gotshal & Magnes, and others tend to cost more than second tier firms. There may be reasons to use top tier firms for transaction advisory or high profile litigation. However, the majority of corporate issues can be handled by a tier down or regional specialty firms.

By doing this, you can reduce your external legal spend by up to 30 to 40 percent. For instance, a partner at a top tier firm can easily charge about $1,000 per hour. Regional firms partners will typically charge around $500 to 600. There tends to be less arbitrage at the lower levels in the legal firm.

Using an in-house counsel that is well connected in the industry and in the legal field is highly advisable. These resources can typically find these alternative solutions, if properly incented. The head of legal will be a larger expense line item. They will range between $300,000 to $500,000 for a mid-size firm. For larger firms they can be seven figures. They should be able to optimize their budgets and also provide sound legal advice to the executives of the firm.

The largest variable for internal work tends to be the review of contracts. It is recommended that you set the internal workload to about 80 to 95 percent of peak capacity requirements. Additional capacity can be outsourced. There are agencies that allow you to outsource contract review to a ready pool of legal talent. The rates are affordable and enable a lower internal permanent staffing.

Litigation and special issues tend to be the domain for external support. Again, you do not always need the top law firms. Second-tier law firms can provide excellent counsel.

Whenever I look at the legal team, I look at the legal staffing benchmarks and ensure we shrink the in-house counsel down as low as practical. The workload needs to be picked up so you will need to offset that with external spend.

The other option is to look at lower cost locations to setup your legal teams. For instance, do you need your legal team in San Francisco or New York? Or could they be in Austin or Salt Lake City? Labor arbitrage can typically reduce cost structure by between 10 to 30 percent.

You should also seek to find lower cost providers for the needs of the business. For instance, for IP monitoring, you can do this in house. However, there are legal firms that specialize in this for a very low cost. In this area, you can optimize your cost structure and maintain your long-term run rate as low as possible.

Typically, this area does not have a significant amount of opportunity except if the current providers are charging higher rates.

TALENT STRATEGY AND LOWER COST OPERATIONS

Efficient organizations also spend time thinking through their strategy on talent. The selective and smart placement of talent can be a competitive advantage to companies that master it. I worked with one engineering company that maintained two hubs for their core business—one in the Bay area and the other in Montreal. There was a significant price advantage to the resources in Montreal—they were almost half the cost of the resources in the bay area. In addition, Canada offers scientific research and experimental development (SR&ED, also known as "shred" credits). These lucrative tax credits also provide a tax break of 35 percent of the eligible expenditure. It made sense to shift as much of the engineering and development to Montreal as achievable.

However, the ecosystem and market in the bay area attracts some of the top engineering talent. To maintain resources there, the company would have to believe and then show that the talent in the bay area were more than twice as efficient and effective as those in Montreal. From a number of lines of code perspective, that was near impossible. But there is also a creativity and solution solving element that comes with an industrial ecosystem. In addition, the replacement cost for a resource is lower when the market is saturated with top talent.

In the end, the company decided to maintain the two hubs—one in the Bay Area to focus on the innovation and maintain a second engineering hub in Montreal for less innovative development. The workload balance did shift to Montreal, and over time Montreal became more and more effective, even at the high end of the innovation requirements for the company. However, it never surpassed the Bay Area.

For core areas of the company, it can and does make sense to keep key elements of the core in areas that create an advantage. For instance, for marketing and artistic talent, New York and London have some of the world's best talent for advertising and media. It makes sense for a marketing company to keep their creative agency there. However, for top online marketing talent, the best talent is in San Francisco and the Bay Area. However, there is also excellent marketing talent in locations like Cincinnati and Columbus because of the consumer product industry heritage of those geographies. When a company leverages these types of advantages for the core of their business they can create a distinctive competitive advantage in their industry.

However, it is less relevant where the non-core elements of your business are located. For instance, for a retail company, finance, although important to the business, does not need to be colocated with the headquarters in New York or London. Instead, this function can easily be onshore in Phoenix and offshore in Bangalore. To manage this, companies that begin to grow in size past about 200 people should start to look at a diversified location strategy.

Here is one example:

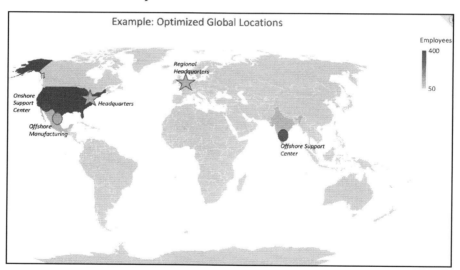

In this example, the company has chosen to maintain their headquarters in New York with cost optimized onshore support in Phoenix, offshore manufacturing in Mexico, a regional HQ in London, and an offshore support center in India. For a 1,000-person company this can begin to drive significant economic improvement while minimizing issues and deterioration of performance. In addition, it provides the framing for a scalable global company. Now, when the company wants to grow non-core functions or transactional volumes increase, they add those resources in India or Phoenix versus New York. In addition, they have the strategic talent framework to grow their company in Europe (or globally) with a regional toehold in London.

A key piece of this strategy is to focus on areas of consolidation for the business. Establishing these points of aggregation helps with recruiting, establishing and stabilizing the company's culture, and also to ensure site overhead is reduced (e.g., office managers, facility leases). Ideally, companies up to about $2 to 3 billion in revenue can work off of two onshore hubs (HQ + support), regional HQs, one or two offshore support centers, and operational locations (e.g., manufacturing and logistics). To accomplish this, field sales resources should work from home. If an office is needed, use of coworking space is ideal. Providing an All-Access pass for a WeWork to your field sales reps costs less than $5,000 per year and provides an office in all major locations in the U.S. sales overhead and support can be aggregated in the onshore hubs and provide the required support to the various field professionals.

Some may ask, what are the functions you put into each of these centers? There is no one size fits all, but here is the general way to think about each of the centers.

Location	Rationale for Talent in that location
Headquarters	• Executive leadership team • Functions that would need to have private conversations with senior management (e.g., legal and corporate finance team)
High Cost Location	• Talent that creates a strategic advantage (e.g., NYC for marketing, SF for tech)

Onshore Support center	• Functions that require near daily interaction with business units and cannot afford significant time zone lag • Support functions that require daily leadership engagement • Support function leadership (can include CFO, CHRO, and others) • Functions that require in-country cultural understanding • Typical functions include operations, logistics, HR, finance, accounting, IT, non-core engineering, merchandising, retail operations, sales operations
Offshore Support Center	• Preponderance of non-core resources and all transactional resources • Typical functions include logistics, HR, finance, accounting, non-core engineering, IT, and copywriting
Regional Headquarters	• Regional sales team • Regional leadership • Regional managerial and reporting finance team (can be offshore as well) • Regional logistics and operations management (can be offshore as well)
Offshore Manufacturing	• Manufacturing operations and overhead

When you follow this general guideline, it will not only reduce your overhead burden, but it would also help to reduce your facility cost structure. The biggest driver is typically headquarters cost. By structuring it in this manner, you change your need for real estate in places like NYC or other high cost cities to a much smaller footprint. We will discuss real estate optimization in a few chapters.

Process Maturity

There is a strong school of thought and a number of practitioners that insist that processes be mature—some even want them optimized—before shifting to a lower cost location. There is a gradient and also an assessment that management needs to make on the level of risk it is willing to take. There are some reasons you would not shift the process or function to the lower cost jurisdiction. However, there are some functions and processes that you can shift and assume some risk while doing it.

In one instance, I was working with a team that felt it had a very stable process for one of its accounting functions. There had been an incumbent in the role for over a decade and the numbers always seemed to work out. When this function was offshored, the offshore resource identified a number of irregularities in the reporting and methodology. Indeed, the issues were identified and then fixed by the offshore center.

An analysis of the processes is warranted, but realize that when it is offshored, you are working with professionals that also can address some of the issues that may arise. Selection of the process and function is more critical than the maturity. For instance, if it is a process that requires business judgment that someone closer to the business line would have keener insight, then it may not make sense to offshore. In this sense, it becomes more about where can the best judgment on the decision be made.

If a process is still felt to be immature or not ready for offshore, at a minimum place it in the onshore support center. From there you can stabilize the function or process and make any desired improvements. Once management is aligned, then shift to the lowest cost structure that makes sense. A best practice is to overhire the onshore manger for key functions. This provides another set of experienced eyes to fix processes and over manage a given location.

Moving Operations Offshore

In this section, I provide a high-level overview of the steps and actions to take to setup an offshore captive center. This is the most complicated move to make, but also the lowest cost and creates a sustainable lower cost structure (depending on market selection). Please note, for teams that do not have experience in offshore operations, there are partners that can assist in this transition. There are also providers that build, operate, and, when the management team is ready, transfer (BOT) the operation over to the internal team. This will result in a higher initial cost structure and day rates being applied to the company, but lower long term cost structure. Also, when you transition the services there tends to be a loss of resources back to the larger offshore enterprise. This can be mitigated, but realize there is risk and an increase in attrition.

Another option for management teams that are hesitant to move operations to low cost jurisdictions is that you can look to conduct this in multiple steps. In this option you conduct this in at least two phases. First, you shift the resources to an onshore hub. The purpose of this move is to remove it from the headquarters location. The other opportunity in this preliminary step is that with focused middle management attention in a support center, you can further optimize, streamline, and document the processes. Second, once the processes are mature and you have a critical volume to offshore, you can shift these to a lower cost jurisdiction. This process typically takes about two years. However, it allows you to seamlessly transition the business to the lower cost location. In addition, it will likely allow you to set up a captive center.

To shift operations offshore, we will assume a starting point in a high cost location. On average, this process will take about six to 12 months to implement. This analysis will assume that the company rents a building or floors of a building. Shifting an operation in less than six months can be done but will typically require infrastructure to already be existent in the final jurisdiction. For instance, I assisted a company to offshore a function in just six weeks, but that required them to already have a site selected and a site leader in place. If that is the aspiration and you do not have infrastructure established, you can also just seek to outsource directly with a partner. When doing so, you do need to ensure processes are more stabile or ensure the contract is sufficiently flexible that you can work with them and adjust processes as needed without change orders or increases in cost.

Here is the typical timeline to move operations offshore.

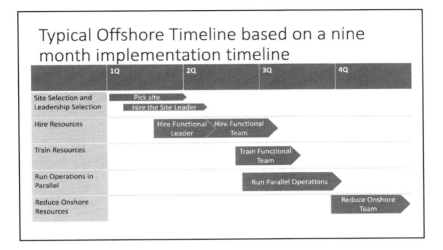

There are two critical decisions that need to be made. First is the site—which country and within that geography—which city and location. I have stated this as a month, but this decision and alignment may take longer. This is a critical step to ensure you get right. One thing that helps is to put together an information pack about the countries and the specific cities that will have the talent that you are looking for. These can easily and quickly be done with an offshore research provider. If your company has large operations in EMEA, then Eastern Europe, India, and the Philippines are potentially good options. If you are predominantly in the U.S., operations in Latin America, Eastern Europe, and India tend to be good options. Another key consideration is the language availability in each of the geographies. For instance, there are likely fewer Chinese speakers in Panama than in the Philippines or Vietnam. Typically, companies will base this decision off of the economic rationale (what is the arbitrage?) and also the time difference. One of the biggest impediments for the U.S. to offshore to India is the time difference. In addition, in recent years the economic arbitrage has degraded and made options in Central and South America attractive to U.S. based companies with less scheduling issues.

Second and most important is who will be the site manager for the center. This is the most critical hire and a key driver of success for an offshore center. Typically, you want someone that is local to the area, well-regarded, and will be a draw for talent to want to work with. Because this site is remote and will largely be run independently you need to have someone you can trust. Use of headhunters in the area is helpful. If you also have a network in the area, that is even better. Use of both is optimal. If the company has prior employees in a country they can trust, that can also drive a decision. From there, you can select the best candidate. On this decision, take your time and ensure you select the best resource. In addition, judgment on their fit into the culture is also helpful. In some instances, companies have leveraged a culture carrier at their firm that was considering a move back to their home country. This is a great person to use to start an offshore center and a way to de-risk this critical hire.

Hiring for the individual functional leaders is also important. These resources will typically act as a pivot point and a main customer relations person between the onshore and offshore centers and the business. They will also have oversight over the various capabilities in the offshore center. For countries where there may be a language gap, you can also leverage them as a translational service. In one model, we chose to hire native speakers and train them to speak English. In the interim, we used a local fluent in English and the native language to be a bridge. In addition, most ERPs and other systems have a language conversion service. Use of it is typically free, but allows these sorts of models.

Training of the resources can be done on site, with members of the team flying to meet them and train them on the various processes. The other option is for the team members to fly to your onshore locations. Both of these models work. If you are bringing people onshore, work with your legal team to ensure you have the appropriate visas. In some situations, these may be hard or elongate the implementation. Often, it is easier for resources from the high cost country to go to the low cost country to train them. You will also likely have them on site during the transition of operations and is not a bad idea for them to familiarize themselves with the local country.

During the transition of operations, you will typically run the onshore and offshore function at the same time in parallel with additional capacity building over time. Also more and more of the functions will shift offshore versus remain with onshore. Once the operation is stabilized, you will reduce or redeploy the redundant resources in the high cost location.

Management of Redundant Resources

When you establish an offshore center, people will likely know there jobs will be reduced. During the period of time to implement these changes, you will likely need to put in place extra incentives and guarantees for those employees. It is not a best practice for employees to train their replacements. Sometimes it is better for upper management to deliver this training or if the employees are used to do this, then put in place incentives for them to do so. Typically, employees impacted will receive a bonus for this period of time in addition to potential severance payments. From a modeling perspective, a good general guideline is to divide the impacted employees fully burdened salary by three to understand the overall impact. For low arbitrage rates (<20 percent improvement)—you will likely need to increase that to divide by 2. The other way to think about it for conservatism is that transitional costs between the new employee ramping in and the exit of the current employee is about four to six months of the higher cost employee.

MARKETING AND MARKETING SPEND

Marketing models vary by the industry. There are stark differences in how companies make money and marketing is one of the key drivers of value for some. In others, marketing is just demand generation for the sales team. For instance, an application or software engineering firm may leverage marketing to ensure the right businesses understand their product. In others, the use of marketing allows reach and sales in the small to medium business segment. For consumer or retail, the marketing team may need to build a brand image. This brand image creates a larger willingness to pay, the competitive advantage of the brand or company. In the last scenario, marketing is a core element of the business. For the others, it is not core.

I will start this discussion with an overview of the key types of marketing and then discuss optimization levers. This will be highly industry specific, but I will provide the key drivers and where you can typically find value. When you examine marketing it is sometimes best to simplify first, breaking the organization into five key elements:

1. Corporate marketing and communications: Corporate marketing is the segment of the marketing organization that controls the image and perception of the company in the public domain. This area typically will also have cognizance over corporate communications and press releases. For a single brand company, there will likely be overlap between corporate and brand marketing, as I have segmented them. Corporate marketing may also have budget and authority over special events or altruistic initiatives that help the community.

2. Brand marketing / brand management: Seeks to create a unique identity for a product that sets it apart from competitors and resonates with the target demographics. Brand marketing can have a number of functions including market research, messaging, brand development, and advertising. They are using these tools to drive a brand identity and inculcate a brand voice in the market that is unique to others. The purpose of the brand identity is to create a psychological destination for the consumer or buyer. This destination can drive value through willingness to pay (e.g., I want to be like Michael Jordan—do I buy Nike's product?). There is a point where brand marketing pivots into brand management. For multi-brand companies, it is common for the brand to actually be a business line. In these companies, a lot of the power in the company is resident in the brand. They will also typically be charged with product management, pricing, merchandising, and other functions.

3. Product / content marketing and demand generation marketing: In some industries, brand is not a major driver of value. For instance, for an electrical component manufacturer, they do not create value through the brand. They do so (largely) through engineering and delivering a

superior product at a lower cost point. For these types of companies, they focus on delivering marketing that educate and inform the market about the product or service. The content is typically designed to demonstrate the value that the product provides to their unique needs and interests. This creates demand for the product or service. There may also be market research profiles associated with the product or content marketing teams. They have to understand the voice of the customer and understand what their requirements are such that they can tailor the content about the product to meet that need.

For companies with highly complex products or high value products and services, the product marketing is more focused on demand generation. Through this marketing approach, the company can create a steady stream of leads. In more robust marketing and sales teams, there is a structured process associated with qualified leads that mark a transition point from marketing to sales management.

4. Channel marketing and channel management: focuses on promoting and selling products or services through a network of third-party partners or intermediaries, such as resellers, distributors, agents, or affiliates. The primary objective of channel marketing is to leverage these partner relationships and expertise to reach new customers and drive sales growth.

Channel marketing typically involves developing marketing programs and collateral that can be used by these partners to promote and sell the company's products or services. This may include training programs, sales incentives, co-marketing initiatives, and joint advertising campaigns, among others.

Channel marketing can be particularly effective for companies that operate in highly competitive or complex markets, where the partners' expertise and relationships can help the company reach new customers and differentiate itself from competitors. By leveraging the partners' reach and influence, channel marketing can help companies expand their market share, increase customer loyalty, and drive long-term growth and success.

A number of companies also go as far as a full channel management organization and channel management program with dedicated tiers. The type of program in place will vary tremendously by industry and company. Technical companies will typically have tiers and established tranches of support (e.g., Microsoft Gold Provider). For consumer companies, this organization will be more fluid and focus on discounts and driving demand for new products and ensuring collateral is provided to the partners.

5. Digital and social media marketing: Inclusion of digital marketing is not necessarily mutually exclusive, collectively exhaustive (MECE). I included this in this section to mention that I will cover this in totality in the digital section. It is more of a medium for the content developed. However, it is important and requires a different skillset than traditional marketing. When reviewing a marketing organization, it is important to segment these resources independent of the traditional marketing resources. Within this marketing subset, you will find community management, stakeholder engagement, and digital media management. The focus is to leverage the social platforms to entertain and engage your audience. This is of growing importance across industries, but indispensable for consumers product and retail companies. The platforms allow a continuous method of engagement and brand awareness. In addition, partnerships with influencers and celebrities can drive sales and awareness for the company. Companies that do this well can also leverage social media as a means to drive demand generation through active links from influencer content. The community management function will focus on managing the social media channels with an internal voice, communicating with the customer and stakeholders with the right brand or corporate voice. Stakeholder engagement is the development and attraction of influencers and others for your digital marketing platform. Digital media management is the process of deploying digital marketing dollars. For the majority of companies, this function can be given to an agency. For more mature processes, this may be brought in

house and can also be managed like a SOC/NOC to control revenue and cost.

I know that I provided a lot of information and it may not make sense in some of the mental models we each have. That is because each industry arranges their marketing teams to align with their unique value. Here are a few models and how they function.

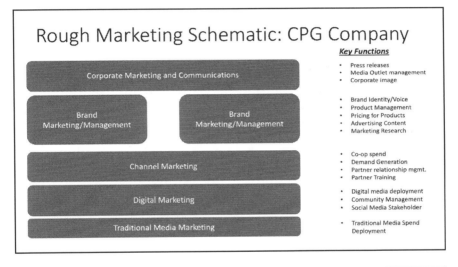

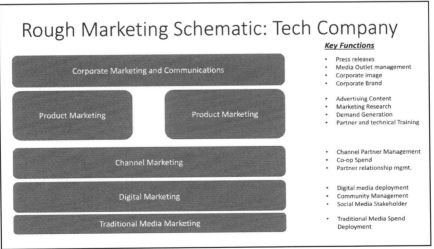

So with the varying models, how do you optimize the spend? To answer this, I segment this into two separate frameworks. We need to think of the world in two separate silos: brand-focused companies and product-focused companies. The key differentiator is that for brand-focused companies, marketing is the business. The value generated from the company is from the image of the brand. Typically in these industries, the product itself is commoditized. Consumers are then convinced to spend a disproportionate amount of money on the product versus what the company puts into it. For instance, a T-shirt is a great example of this willingness to pay. Here is the average price breakdown of a $15 T-shirt:[16]

Cost of Good	Cost
Materials (Cotton and Yarn)	$1.00
Labor/design	$2.15
Tax and duty	$0.25
Warehouse/storage	$1.72
Shipping and freight	$1.20
Total Cost	$6.32
Markup	$8.68
Price of product	$15.00

When you look at a channel pricing (what a retailer will pay the manufacturer for the product) you will typically reduce the listed price of $15 by between 50 to 60 percent. So if this shirt was sold at a retailer for $15, the company would be about breakeven with a selling cost to the retailer between $6 and $7.50. At $20 the shirt will have a positive profit margin. Now, for those that pay $50 for a T-shirt because it's a great brand, the input required by the company is not a commensurate increase in the cost of goods relative to the increase in price.

For product-focused companies, the focus is on driving value because of a differentiated product. Even in this situation, sometimes the product is not truly differentiated, but you compete in the market on the merits of the product itself.

---

16 "What Does a Shirt Really Cost?" Grain, August 22, 2017, graincreative.com/shirt-cost-break-down/#:~:text=For%20a%20shirt%20to%20be%20created%2C%20it%20needs,then%20sent%20to%20a%20wholesaler%20for%20further%20distribution.

Brand-Focused Companies

For brand-focused companies, there needs to be a significant amount of the P&L dedicated to marketing and enhancing brand image. For most industries, this investment will typically still be less than 6 percent of revenue. However, there are some sectors, specifically luxury or premium brands where this spend can easily be 15 to 25 percent of revenue. For instance, LVMH has a spend of 35.5 percent of revenue with their basket of brands—is all of that spend justified?[17] As brands grow, reposition, or ladder, the investment gets higher in the band.

Here are typical ways to optimize a brand focused marketing team:

Delayering and organizational hygiene: The organizations can become complicated with the mix of products, marketing teams, and teams focused on art/media design. Reviewing how the organization covers the required products is an initial first step. Often, you can find resources that are duplicative or in categories that are sufficiently similar that they can be covered by less resources. A review of the spans and layers will provide views into the organization where this may be effective.

Focus on positive ROAS and budgetary reduction: With improving tracked and multivariate analysis of marketing spend and return with customers, marketers have the data available to understand the actual return in their marketing investment. In one instance, when the analysis was conducted on the company's marketing spend, we quickly realized that they were losing 40 cents on every digital dollar that they spent. When made aware of information like this, the easiest response is to budgetarily reduce the spend. This forces the marketing teams to identify the key drivers of value and back those investments. In this instance, the marketing team had to change digital spend management agencies and improve targeting mechanisms. The other tool that is effective here is to reduce the amount of budget the company allocates to awareness media spend and shift those dollars down the funnel to more targeted investment in likely customers. In the past few years with changes to information tracking availability because of system changes on the iPhone, teams have found workarounds via APIs in Shopify platforms and other e-commerce site technologies.

Centralization of art, media, copywrite, and other services: Because the brand is responsible for the brand identity, it does not

---

17 "LVMH: 2022 Full Year Results," LVMH, January 26, 2023, www.lvmh.com/shareholders/agenda/2022-full-year-results/.

necessarily need its own art team. Instead, what you can do is maintain a single resource that is point on the brand identity and then centralize the art and media execution into a non-brand focused team. This works well for multi-brand companies. In addition, this service can potentially be outsourced or put into a back office onshore.

Centralize market research: Market research functions, likewise, can be centralized. The resources that are potentially spread across multiple teams can be aggregated into one pool of resources and then the leader of the function demand manages the talent and output of the team across the various marketing teams.

Improve content creation processes and improve reuse of content: Some marketing teams focus on fresh content when that is not neces-sary. Putting in place an enhanced content management system helps teams to re-utilize content that has already been produced. In addition, enhancing the process for content development can also serve to stream-line required resourcing and input into the process, improving efficiency. In addition, it also will directly reduce the amount of money spent on media development. A good general guideline is that you should spend between 5:1 up to 10:1 on media spend versus content development budgets. As a rapid analysis, you should look at the resonance of the media content in the market. Looking at YouTube and seeing views is one way. For some content that literally cost hundreds of thousands of dollars. One client was receiving maybe 10,000 impressions. However, you can quickly gain a view on this when you scan across the remainder of the social media sites.

Use of AI: With the advent of artificial intelligence and enhance language learning models like ChatGPT and Microsoft Copilot, manage-ment teams can reduce the need for copywriters and other junior staff. Senior resources can enhance their productivity and output.

Co-op spend: Co-op spend is spend that the company provides to the customer. It can be through training, guaranteed counter staffing, or other economic reductions that benefit the customer. It is difficult to reduce co-op spend with your customers. Typically, there is an all-in margin that the customer will aim for that will include co-op spend, rebates and others costs. The ability to improve this is typically tied with the brand and end-customer need for the product. Products in higher demand may be able to negotiate advantageous all-in economics. In addition, for companies with large retailer and distributor exposure, the rate of product returns is another consideration.

To extract value, you will need to benchmark the company and its contracts against the industry. The company will need to negotiate with the customer. This can be done, but may not yield the full benefit you desire—always be conservative if you seek to incorporate perceived co-op issues.

Consumer product companies with retail outlets: Companies should largely focus on their core. For companies that manufacture products, the core is in the design of the product. If vertical integration into manufacturing creates a competitive advantage, then that may also be part of the core. When this is extended into wholly owned retail outlets. Investors should seek to analyze the profitability of these outlets. There are some cases, such as Bonobos, where the strategy of the firm is largely online. These outlets do not carry inventory and serve to allow customers to try on the products and then order via online methods. These types of outlets become a form of marketing spend. If the investment is not profitable, then the company should seek to reduce its owned retail footprint.

Product-Focused Companies

For product-focused companies the ROI is more closely tracked with typical sales and marketing integration and management oversight of lead generation from the marketing teams. However, there are times that the marketing team can be ineffective. For product focused companies, typical marketing spend will be between 2 and 10 percent of revenue, depending on the company and whether they tend to focus on business or consumer end customers. Marketing media spend is typically well thought through. However, co-op, channel spend, and spending on events can be an issue. Also, you can find opportunities in the organization and process between sales and marketing. I will discuss these levers now.

Organization: Benchmarks are a key driver to identify opportunity in these types of organizations. It will highlight an organization that may have too many headcount. Eliminating the excess capacity is typically driven by a couple drivers:

1. High growth with limited oversight: This is typical in tech companies that begin to fall on slower growth. To reduce the

organization, you typically just have to show management
that there is a new reality and that the cost structure needs to
come down.

2.   Strategic Initiatives: Sometimes the organization is larger than
normal because of a strategic initiative or increased focus
on small to medium business. There are sometimes when
you examine a company, you have to overlay these strategic
initiatives against the opportunity.

With one company I examined, sales and marketing budgets
exceeded benchmarks. However, the company was in the middle of a
replatforming because the market technology has evolved. They had to
change their product set and go to market to focus more on marketing,
but still maintained its legacy sales force during the repositioning and
replatforming. When we discussed this with the private equity firm, we
did not eliminate the opportunity—we just changed the timeline for
optimization. If we did not take into account the strategic situation, we
would have estimated significant value accretion to the company about
two years before the management team could have effectively delivered
those dollars. This level of experienced decision making and advice is
what differentiates value creation advisors.

Organizational hygiene (spans and layers) can often be an opportunity for this type of function. The organization is typically simpler than
a brand focused marketing company. The majority of product focused
companies segment product management from marketing. It typically has
a product-focused team, a corporate focused marketing and communication team, marketing research/analytics, and some organizations will have
internal technical writers (e.g., people that make the manuals we all love).
Because of this simplicity and its removal from the actual management of
the business, the teams can be optimized. For potential reductions, you
need to work with the management teams on the product line coverage and
understand what is being done with each of the product lines.

Marketing spend: Marketing spend can be closely examined for
these companies. Comparison to benchmarks is usually a good starting
point, but the details and identifying line item edits to budgets is key to
deliver the value. One of the key areas that should be examined is trade
payables. These are incentives provided to channel providers or other

market partners. The management team should examine these relation-ships and ensure that they have a positive return on the investment. In addition, proper structuring of channel partnership arrangements helps to systemize the payments based on value provided to the company. Investment in this schema can pay dividends and ensure proper alloca-tion of value to key partners.

Advertising spend: For outsized advertising spend, you can bring that back in line with benchmarks. There is not as much concern for content and artistic focus of the content as the content tends to be more matter of fact. Use of an agency to manage spend is sometimes effec-tive to ensure you are optimizing internal resources. Use of marketing automation through agencies or others can also improve spend by up to 50 percent. Examination of processes and how dollars are allocated is critical. Marketing targeting can also be assessed.

Event spend and membership fees: The other major bucket of opportunity tends to be with event spend and Membership fees. For some, they tend to overspend for marketing events. Bringing these costs under control can be a source of value. Company sponsored member-ship fees should also be reviewed. In general, these are positive associa-tions for the company. However, putting in place level requirements can be helpful. For instance, does an individual contributor need to join the organization on the company's behalf or attend a conference? It may be more valuable for a manager level resource to do that.

Marketing consultants: Use of marketing consultants that dupli-cate the capabilities of your internal organization should be examined. Another source of spend is the use of temporary consultants in the marketing organization for an extended period of time. Oftentimes, these resources can be in an organization for a year or more. If the need is permanent, you should look to insource. This can typically save about one-third of the cost for the resource.

Marketing technology stack: The CRM system and marketing analysis stack can be a key driver of value for the marketing team. Assess-ment of its use should be made. Use of Salesforce for B2B companies tends to have a high ROI and enhances the company's ability to track sales through the funnel and manage customer information. However, work with the IT team to ensure you do not have extraneous modules. In one situation, we were able to eliminate an unused module that had been procured but never adopted. This saved hundreds of thousands of dollars.

CUSTOMER SERVICE

Customer service is a critical component of any successful company, regardless of the industry or size of the business. It is the process of ensuring that customers are satisfied with the products or services provided by a company. Customer service plays a vital role in a company for the following reasons:

Retention of customers: Good customer service helps to retain existing customers by addressing their concerns and problems promptly and efficiently.

Building a loyal customer base: Providing excellent customer service can create loyal customers who are more likely to recommend your business to others and continue to patronize your business.

Reputation management: Positive interactions with customers can help to build a positive reputation for the company, while negative interactions can damage the company's reputation.

Upselling and cross-selling: A positive customer service experience can lead to opportunities for upselling and cross-selling of products and services.

Competitive advantage: Excellent customer service can provide a competitive advantage by differentiating the company from competitors and enhancing the overall customer experience.

Getting customer right is critical to overall success, but you also want to ensure you seek to control and optimize cost in the center. Hitting the right balance is essential to company success and will impact customer satisfaction, customer retention, and the company's reputation. Here are some of the key elements that you can optimize to ensure you create a compelling, but cost optimized customer service experience.

Well-defined customer service policies and processes: Clear policies and processes that outline how customer service will be delivered, what the expectations are for customer service representatives, and how customer complaints will be handled. In addition, having clear limits of authority for what individual customer service representatives can give to various customers, typically developed in the CRM solutions, help support this.

Trained and competent customer service representatives: Customer service representatives should be well-trained and competent in their role, with the necessary skills to handle customer inquiries, complaints, and other interactions effectively. This needs to be balanced with the relatively high turnover rate for most customer service operations. For small businesses, use of outsourced providers can be helpful in managing this tension.

Efficient communication channels: Customers should be able to easily contact customer service representatives through multiple communication channels, such as phone, email, live chat, or social media. Use of the company's call routing system, typically an interactive voice response (IVR) system also allows companies to route the calls based on skills. For instance, it is very effective to have a billing question routed to the billing department versus a general customer service line. This helps to improve a contact centers first contact resolution rate (FCR). However, this level of automation can be made more granular and customized. The use of natural language processing (NLP) in some systems and integration with CRM feeds create breakthroughs for customer service. For instance, think about the improvements that can be made if you detect that a VIP customer is agitated—it may be helpful to route this person to a member of your team that is good at reducing tension and retaining a key customer. These types of insights can be generated with technology today with the CRM providing the input on customer history and NLP reviewing the customer's tone and wording that can create insight on the emotional state during the interaction.

Quick response times: Customers expect prompt responses to their inquiries or complaints, so customer service representatives should be able to respond quickly and efficiently. The increased use of automation and self-service also aids in this. The increased use of various communication channels, including use of chatbots and chat dialogues aid in optimizing staffing and time to resolution. For instance, a given agent may be able to handle up to four chats at the same time. This level of multitasking also relies on some machine-generated support including chat routing and automated responses. New agents without machine leverage typically can handle one or two chats at the same time.

Personalized customer interactions: Personalizing customer interactions by using the customer's name, understanding their unique needs, and offering tailored solutions can help to enhance the customer experience and build loyalty. In addition, integration of the systems with CRM can also reduce the need for customer validation, reducing overall time to resolution and customer frustration with the given agent.

Customer Service Optimization

Labor arbitrage through outsourcing and/or offshoring: Customer service is critical, but for most companies, it is a function that can be optimized. The biggest variable is the cost per resource in the contact center. Taking this function out of higher cost locations is critical. Depending on the customer and branding there is also the potential to offshore this to lower cost resources. Great operations can be found in low cost jurisdictions in the United States such as Phoenix, Salt Lake, Tulsa, Las Vegas, Kansas, and Tennessee and even in locations like the Philippines, El Salvador, and Bulgaria. Language availability and time zone alignment are critical to the success of the operation.

Because customer service call center operations are not core to most businesses. Finding a good partner that you can outsource this service to is typically a best practice. In addition, you can put in place provisions to profit share cost improvements. Through this, you can have an optimized system with a team that are professionals at managing these complex operations.

Optimized service level agreements (SLAs): Some companies require 24/7 support and white glove treatment for every call. This requires higher cost to maintain and if working with a partner, they will typically charge more because of the higher requirements. Companies can examine what they really need to succeed. Risk can be taken in some of the typical SLAs response time, resolution time, and availability have the largest impacts. These are largely industry specific, but a general guideline is that response times less than one hour improve customer satisfaction and longer than 24 hours degrade. Resolution times less than 24 hours tend to correlate with higher customer satisfaction and greater than 48 hours tends to degrade customer satisfaction.

The other variable is compliance allowance to the SLA. This allows the provider to take risk in delivering against the SLA. For response time, these can range from 80 to 99 percent. For resolution, it is typically 90 to 99 percent. For uptime during periods of availability, the typical standard for good uptime is 99.9 percent (three 9s) of the time with more critical applications and services being held to 99.99 percent (four 9s) uptime. To put this in perspective, at 99 percent for a 365 day, 24 hour year they can allow up to 3.65 days of downtime; at 99.9 percent this collapses to around nine hours; and at 99.99 percent, that allowance collapses to just under an hour. From a business perspective, the difference between four 9s and three 9s, may not be material. This is a risk that management can take, if desired.

The final variable is the actual time that services are available. Shifting from 24/7 coverage to a scheme within business hours can typically save between 10 to 30 percent of the cost of maintaining the 24/7 coverage. Depending on the economics and fixed cost structure of the operation, this opportunity could be more.

Decrease incoming call volume through effective IVR call handling: The goal of these changes is to reduce the call volume, reroute calls to self-service through website, or shift to a lower cost to serve channel. Here are the main techniques to do this:

Voicemail or callback: During peak volume times, offer the customer the opportunity to leave a voicemail or callback when there time in queue is available. This alleviates the need for them to wait during peak times and allows the call center to set a fixed capacity of resourcing.

Specialized knowledge routing: For unique issues or issues that would require immediate escalation, route the call to a specific department. This method improves FCR and potentially improving customer experience with specialized attention for critical issues.

Directing to a website and FAQs: Use secondary IVR menus and recorded messages that direct the caller to the website for self-service resolution. This should be considered when the customer has the ability to resolve on their own through the website. Investment to develop FAQs and make them easy to find are key. In addition, when developing your customer service page, ensure that FAQs is prominently displayed with volume ranked resolutions available to the customer.

Direct to a text chat: Offer to shift the call to a text chat with a customer service representative. This allows the call to be handled at a reduced cost to serve. Oftentimes, this also yields a higher customer satisfaction because the customer can do something else while getting the issue resolved.

Process improvement and improvements to handling time: For established and location optimized operations, the primary driver of value will be with process improvement and enhanced capability with system integration and improved data integration. The key is to continue to reduce average handling time. Handling times vary by industry, but here are global averages for a frame of reference:

Type of Interaction	Typical SLA / Handling Time
Email	1 hour to 24 hour response time, typical SLAs
Chat	5 minutes to up to 30 minutes per chat (handling time)
Phone Call	5 to 15 minutes (handling time)

Here are some areas to examine that aid in reducing handling time:

Provide clear process guidelines and streamline interaction process: The first step is to ensure that the handling process is clear and concise. In addition, ensure that the process itself is not cumbersome or gets bogged down when actually being applied. Ensure that all resources are trained on the process and that escalations required are reduced. This will help to reduce overall handling time. There are a number of technologies that help and aid the customer service representative. These prompts can also help them think through the problem with some of the most modern technologies using advanced algorithms and integration with data to provide the prompts.

System integration: The greatest improvements will come through automation and improving time to resolution with improved information for your customer service team. The key system integrations to consider are ones between the CRM and the IVR. This will enable the

IVR program to automate validation, optimize call routing, and leverage the data for further refinement through machine learning algorithms that most IVRs now provide. In addition, the CRM solution can be further integrated throughout the entire tech stack. There are some companies that have gone as far as integrating CRM into shipping applications, billing applications, order systems, etc. This enables the customer service representative to be fully informed when addressing potential needs of the customer reducing Handling and Resolution time and improving first time contact resolution. These integrations are becoming easier through API-led connectivity across its enterprise solutions.

Automated responses: Use of AI driven chatbots have helped to reduce overall issue handling. For instance, if you can provide automated responses through a chatbot you reduce that volume of issue handling, a direct saving of the resources that would be required to support this. To accomplish this, you can leverage natural language processing to identify and interpret key questions that a customer is asking. From there, you can provide tailored responses that will resolve the problems or offer automated economic resolution for common issues without input or control from a customer service representative. Please note chatbot implementation is long and can take time for the algorithms to bring significant value to the business.

Customer service is an area of the company that is critical, but there are a significant number of ways to reduce the cost structure to serve the customer. Calculated risks and close monitoring of customer satisfaction can enable management teams to achieve an optimized cost structure.

SALES

The sales department in a company is responsible for generating revenue by selling the company's products or services to customers. The sales department seeks to identify potential customers, establish relationships with them, persuade them to buy the company's products or services, and then with established customers convince them to continue buying the company's products and increase the amount they buy. I know that this is simple, but it is important to remember the purpose of the sales function relative to the other elements of the business. These are largely relationship people. Because selling can be relationship driven, there are some businesses where critical roles and personalities cannot be eliminated.

In general, sales people are also "coin operated." Essentially, these resources should be largely incented based on their sales in a given period of time. This provides a unique structure and is typically different in compensation than others in the company. Because of this, we will need to discuss sales operations and organization to understand how you can potentially optimize the function.

Regardless, most leaders are reticent to take on initiatives that reduce their salesforce. Typically, what you will see is the opportunity lies in allocation of sales territories, efficiency of the resources, allocation of the resources between new sales and account management, outsourcing non-core sales, and improved use of performance-based compensation.

Sales Organization

There are multiple types of sales people in an organization. In addition, there are people that are not really sales that can either influence or actually convert customers. We will discuss all of these as the business models will vary by industry.

Field sales: When people imagine a sales person, the majority immediately default to what I call the new sales resources. They can also be known as "hunters." These resources prospect new clients, establish relationships, and then persuade them to buy the company's product. These resources tend to be paid based on the revenue that they bring into the company. It is typically a percentage of the sale that they are responsible for. The prevent conflicts between these resources, companies typically allocate discrete "territories" to these resources. In practice, these territories can be physical (e.g., Northeast U.S., APAC), a list of clients, an industry or industry subsector. A smaller company typically has larger territories for the salespeople. As companies grow and increased infrastructure is present, the territories can become more discrete and focused. Their compensation is typically structured with a living wage as what they receive month to month and then they receive quarterly, semiannual, or annual bonuses based on the sales they are responsible for. For instance, in the advisory business, some firms managing directors receive a strait percentage for a referral. This can be up to 15 percent of the revenue the firm realizes. This can be a powerful incentive for some.

These resources can often be supported by new sales representatives. These tend to be junior resources that focus on generating leads or closing clients. These resources also receive a lot of training and on the job training from the more senior sales resources.

Account management: The other key overlay is account management. These resources work with established clients to understand their needs, maintain the relationship with them, and then seek methods to upsell the client based on their needs and the services the company can provide. Colloquially they are referred to as the "farmers." They work on established accounted and collect the benefits. Their pay model is most established for stability with some incentive for improved account performance. This improved performance can be focused on retention, revenue per account, and share of wallet for the customer. Some companies actually have these resources colocated with the client for very large accounts. The majority of these resources have coverage across a number of accounts, depending on the account size and their ability to manage. For extremely large accounts, account there may even be account management teams—multiple resources evaluating how the company can better serve its client. These roles can have idiosyncratic risk (e.g., a large account decides not to partner with your firm moving forward).

Technical sales or sales engineer: For highly technical products or products that require a special design for a given customer, these are the resources that cover this area of the sales cycle. These resources, typically called a sales engineer or technical sales representative will provide and act as the subject matter expert on the technical specifications of a product or for unique customer requirements they may serve as the key lead on the required solution or architecture. These roles will oftentimes work with solution architects or directly with the engineering teams to best understand the technical elements of the sale. If unique solutions are required, these teams will work with the clients' engineers or business teams to validate the design and technical elements of the contracts put in place between the two firms. These resources are typically shared across the new sales and account management teams. In addition, they are typically only allocated against validated leads.

Internal sales: Internal sales refers to typically junior resources that "call" out to potential customers. These resources are typically allocated against small or medium businesses with less complex or commoditized sales cycles. For instance, a company could market its SMB solution to a mom-and-pop grocery store. This store then submits an interest form online. The person reaching out to them would likely be an internal sales resource. These resources tend to be less expensive than new sales or account management resources. They can also be in lower cost locations and can cover hundreds if not thousands of smaller clients.

Some companies have also leveraged their customer service function for this role. Utilization during down time makes sense, but can cause sales to slow during peak periods when customer service demands peak. Use of CS representatives for upsell/cross-sell during routine customer service calls has increased, but requires a dedicated investment in training the resources.

Field representatives: These resources may or may not be part of the sales organization. However, these resources visit the customer and typically provide services or products to the customer. Through this service, they are also de factor sales representatives (or should be used as such) to help drive demand and also to enhance relationships throughout the customer organization. For consumer product companies, the merchandising function can often be part of this field representative organization. In addition, the technical field service organizations can also be part of this organization. Although their evaluations are largely based on efficiency of handling the technical issue of the customer, some opportunities present themselves for upselling. In these instances and in the right industries, these resources should have the tools to ensure they can best support the company's customer or direct them to someone that can.

Sales operations: Sales operations teams provide leverage to the field sales and account management teams. They can handle everything from meeting bookings, to client research, to support closing deals. In addition, there are resources that do sales analytics and that allocate the sales and sales credit to properly pay the sales teams. This is a critical function in the sales organization. Too little of these resources and the sales teams waste time doing administrative tasks. Too many and the sales overhead is too high and sales team members can feel like they have a dedicated assistant. Finding the right balance is key for a well functioning sales organization.

With all of these different types of resources, a typical sales organization is typically split between new sales and account management. The allocation of these resources between "hunters" and "farmers" is largely predicated on the maturity of the industry and of the maturity of the company. For instance, a large company like GE or Coca-Cola will largely have account management teams, as there are not a large number of new accounts ("logos") that a field sales team will prospect. However, a startup is largely all field sales and internal sales focused on generating revenue. As companies mature this structure should shift toward account management. For the same revenue, account management structures tend to be cheaper because there is less upside provided to account management leads.

Field sales organizations are typically given a "territory." Territories can be physical, industry-, or company-specific. Because of the incentives, territory allocation is a major concern of sales representatives. This process is a key outcome for the sales operations team. Development should be focused on splitting the territories into even slices of opportunity or setting quotas for the given resource different based on expected outcomes. A best practice is to review targets in the given territory and assess expected outcomes for a well performing sales resource, taking into account their ramp in to the company. Typically, it takes a sales resource about 12 to 18 months to reach full potential in a new company. The quota can then be set against the anticipated sales in the territory. The quota for a salesperson is the benchmark for their performance. This is a very serious negotiation for them.

Account management teams are set by a coverage model based on anticipated revenue for the customer. There is not a one-size-fits-all model for account management because it will depend on the company's circumstances and the specifics of a given industry. However, a key account executive may only have one or two accounts. For very critical clients, this may be one-to-one with a dedicated team. The majority of account executives, a layer down from a key account executive, may cover no more than 10 to 20 accounts, depending on the industry and complexity of the sales cycle. Account managers, can have account coverages in the dozens or even hundreds, depending on the industry and complexity of the sales cycle. In addition, for small and medium size businesses, internal sales can do both field sales and account management. The cover ratio for them may be in the thousands depending on the typical sale size.

What makes the latter possible is typically a highly standardized offering. Verizon or AT&T's mobile phone offerings are perfect for the internal sales teams. The small business can call into a call center or work through a website and sign their company up for the service with the number of resources needed. There is no complexity to the sale cycle. Typically, there is a tiered pricing structure that is published online, as well.

Managing the Sales Process

Management teams will conduct periodic reviews of the sales pipeline with key sales team leadership. The goal of the process is to ensure the sales team is developing a robust pipeline of new opportunities that will fuel growth in the company. For most companies, this process is standard and consists of:

Prospecting and lead generation: This stage involves identifying potential customers and generating leads. This can be done through various means such as networking, referrals, social media, email campaigns, or targeted advertising. Depending on the method used for lead generation, it is not uncommon to generate a list of several hundred or even thousands of leads. However, not all of these leads will be qualified or interested in the product or service being offered.

A key metric to track is the total number of leads. This can vary widely.

Outreach: In this stage, the sales team reaches out to the potential customers identified in the previous stage. This could be through email, phone calls, or other methods of communication. The number of potential customers who engage with the sales team at this stage can vary widely, depending on factors such as the quality of the lead list, the effectiveness of the outreach strategy, and the sales team's ability to connect with prospects. A common metric used at this stage is the "response rate," which measures the percentage of outreach attempts that result in a response from the prospect.

Typical response rates will vary by outreach channel. Here are the most common and some key drivers of average response rates:

Email: The average email response rate for sales outreach is around 23.9 percent, according to data from HubSpot. However, this can vary widely depending on factors such as the subject line, the content of the email, and the quality of the email list.

- **Phone:** The response rate for phone outreach can be more difficult to track, as it often involves leaving voicemails or scheduling callbacks. However, a good benchmark for phone outreach is to aim for a 10-15 percent callback rate, according to sales training company SalesHood.
- **LinkedIn:** The response rate for outreach through LinkedIn can also vary widely, but according to data from SalesHood, a good benchmark is to aim for a 5 to 10 percent response rate for LinkedIn InMail messages

Qualification: The qualification stage involves determining if the prospect is a good fit for the product or service being offered. This could include factors such as their budget, their needs, their authority to make purchasing decisions, and their timeline. The focus is on identifying those who are a good fit for the product or service being offered. The goal is to narrow down the list of leads to those who have a genuine interest in the product or service and are likely to move forward with a purchase.

A key metric to track is the conversion rate of a lead to a qualified lead. The typical benchmark is between 20 to 30 percent, however, this can vary significantly dependent on the quality of leads and the sales team effectiveness.

Discovery: In this stage, the sales team seeks to understand the prospect's needs, pain points, and goals. This is done through asking questions and actively listening to the prospect's responses. This stage is critical for building rapport and trust with the prospect, which can increase the likelihood of closing the deal.

This is a key step to ensure that the sales teams are identifying all of the critical needs of the client. When conducting solution selling, this can lead to increased average deal size by truly understanding what is needed by the client and then offering everything needed. Use of a la carte menus of options can also be beneficial to ensure the client can tailor the offering to what they truly need. Average Deal Size is a good measure of the effectiveness of the sales funnel. IT helps to ensure that your sales force is providing as much value to the client as possible.

Pitch/sales call: Based on the information gathered in the previous stages, the sales team develops a tailored pitch or presentation that highlights the benefits of the product or service being offered. This could be done through a sales call or an in-person meeting. At this stage, the number of potential customers is typically further narrowed down to those who have a genuine interest in the product or service and are ready to make a purchase decision. However, even at this stage, not all prospects will close, as some may have objections or concerns that cannot be addressed.

A key metric is the win rate. This measures the number of qualified leads that result in a closed deal. In general good is between 20 to 30 percent. That means that one-fifth of qualified leads will result in a sale. This is yet another strong indicator of the sales team effectiveness. However, it also measures the product fit the to marketplace. If win rates decrease precipitously, there may be need to examine the product offering as well as the individual sales team's performance.

Follow-up and close: After the pitch, the sales team follows up with the prospect to answer any remaining questions or concerns they may have. If the prospect is ready to move forward, the sales team will close the deal and finalize the sale. The goal is to provide any additional information or support needed to help the prospect make a confident purchase decision.

Who does what in each segment of the process will depend on the sales organization's structure and the specific roles and responsibilities of the sales team. Generally, the new sales representatives or field sales teams will handle the outreach, qualification, discovery, and pitch stages, while the sales manager may be involved in setting targets and overseeing the process. The sales operations team may assist with lead generation, data analysis, or providing additional resources to the sales team.

Following the sale, the team will typically follow up with the new client and check in within the first week, typically around three days after contract sign. This is just to ensure everything has been transitioned and that they are satisfied with their purchase. Depending on the product and relationship, another follows up around a month after is also a good practice to maintain the relationship and build rapport.

This process can be seamlessly tracked through the CRM tool like Salesforce. Despite its high cost, it is still a market leader to manage the sales funnel with enhanced diagnostics.

Another critical analysis is to understand the average sales cycle time. This is most germane for companies focused on B2B. This is measured from the time of initial outreach through to the final close of the deal. The length does vary by industry. However, on average three to six months is a typical range you will see in B2B sales.

The final metric I will highlight is the customer lifetime value. This is the amount of revenue generated from a given customer over the lifetime of the relationship with the company. The CLV can vary widely based on price of the product and typical retention rates. Some companies boil this down to a retention rate or churn rate. This is a critical metric for businesses as it is generally more cost effective to retain existing customers than to acquire new ones. So, you typically want to keep churn rate as low as possible. An annualized churn rate of over 20 to 30 percent makes it hard to maintain revenue growth. To grow sales, you first have to replace the lost sales. In month, a churn rate that approaches 5 percent is a trigger point and will warrant further investigation.

If the churn rate exceeds this threshold, sales teams may begin to investigate the reasons why customers are leaving and take steps to address any issues or concerns. This might involve improving the product or service, enhancing the customer experience, or providing additional resources or support to customers.

It's important to note that customer retention is not solely the responsibility of the sales team. It requires a cross-functional effort from the entire organization, including product development, customer support, and marketing teams. By working together to prioritize customer satisfaction and loyalty, businesses can improve retention rates and drive long-term growth

Sales Compensation Plans

I will spend a little bit of time on the typical structure of a sales compensation plan. They will vary by company, but providing a bit of context is helpful.

A standard sales compensation plan will have two major components: Base salary and commission. This is the most common compensation plan for sales resources. Here is what one could look like:

	Compensation
Base Salary	$100,000
Projected Sales	$1,000,000
Commission Start	$100,000
Commission Percent	11.1%
OTE Commission	$100,000
Commission Cap	$5,000,000
Commission Cap	$544,444
OTE Compensation	$200,000

This has a very aggressive split of 50/50 for fixed versus variable compensation. Typically, you will find sales compensation schemes ranging from 60/40 to 75/25. The more you need to instruct and teach, the less variable the compensation tends to become.

Both field sales and account management contracts can be structured this way. This ensures that the company's employees can live comfortably, but are also incented to perform.

Other schemas exist including:

Base plus bonus: This replaces the commission with a set bonus as long as certain KPIs and sales targets are hit. This plan may not incent sales reps to outperform, but may foster a very collegial environment.

Commission-only: "You keep what you kill." The only time a sales resource is paid is on the sale. Because of the implicit risk, the commissions tend to be higher, anywhere up to about 45 percent of the revenue value.

Set rate commission: A sales resource receives a base salary and then receives a certain amount for each new customer or a percent on an up-sell/cross-sell. These plans are very simple, easy to understand and provide incentives to the team to perform.

Gross margin commission: Sales reps are focused on gross margin only. For companies focused on profitability, this is a good plan. The downside is that representatives will focus on the highest margin products or services and may not care for expansionary opportunities, if they need to sacrifice margin to get the sale. Sometimes a better approach is putting in place a deals desk, which will prevent a sales rep from making a bad deal or require upper management approval for the sale to occur.

Variable commission plan: In this schema, the commission rate will vary based on percent of the quota attained. Often times the dividing line is at quota or 5 to 10 percent above or below. When at quota, they receive OTE. When below quota, they receive a commission that is less than target percent and if exceeding quota by more than a certain percent, they receive an outsized percentage commission.

Optimizing the Sales Function

The sales force is critical to company success. There is usually very little interest in optimizing the salesforce spend. However, this should not be a sacred cow. The sales team can and does tend to run inefficiently because people do not want to address it.

Here are some key areas that should be examined:

Maximizing salesforce selling time: One of the critical areas you want to maximize is the salesforce's time selling. In one instance, the company had overly burdened the sales force and caused them to only have about 30 percent of their time focused on selling. Typically, this number is reversed and we anticipate effective selling time to be about 70 percent of the salesforce time. A typical issue is that there are insufficient sales operations resources to support the sales force. Given that the sales operations resources is more cost effective than a sales resource, shifting those responsibilities are a way to improve efficiency of the organization. A typical ratio of salesforce to sales operations resources is anywhere from 6 to 1 to 10 to 1. Sales force resources do not need dedicated assistants, but leverage is critical. When the company does use new sales representatives, these count as sales operations people, as they are doing lead generation and scheduling versus actual selling. Similarly, the use of technical sales resources also help alleviate some of the burden. Typically this has a coverage ratio of about 5 or 6 to 1. For highly complex sales organizations, this ratio gets lower to about 4 to 1. With the productivity gains, the company gains operating leverage as it grows. Conversely, the sales resources can be reduced, if the company is cash constrained.

Use channel salesforce: In some business models, small to medium businesses or certain geographies can be seen as too high of a cost to serve, despite there being a product-need fit with the customers. When this is an issue, use of channel sales tends to allow access to the market with limited inputs from the company. If the company had a small to medium business salesforce, this can be a complement or a replacement, depending on the success of the model. Typically, the channel will want to be rewarded for its sales and will be paid a percentage of the revenue. For renewal contracts, it is common that the channel sales team will also get a portion of that revenue, as well. This remuneration is usually at least 10 percent and can be more, depending on the relationship and product you provide. This type of initiative is excellent for new territories or clientele for rapidly growing companies. In addition, there are some businesses and products that require a channel to provide the installation service and solution architecture. This is common when the solution is across different technologies or products (e.g., integration of products).

Implementation of CRM technology (Salesforce): For companies that have not implemented a CRM, this is a key step to improve oversight in the sales funnel. This leverage will typically improve the efficiency of the sales force through enhanced monitoring. It will also allow management to effectively manage out underperforming sales resources. Salesforce is a market leader in this segment of technology. Based on their experience set, company sales typically improve by up to 29 percent and salesforce efficiency improves by up to 34 percent. This is one of the major drivers of value for sales teams. Use of CRM solutions also improve forecast accuracy, as well, as they force discipline and rigor into the qualification process for the sales team.

Field sales versus account management: As companies mature, management teams will sometimes continue to try to "grow" sales throw new logo acquisition versus improving their retention rates. This is an experienced based decision, but often time needs to be identified to the management team. When you shift resources between field sales and account management, typically your cost structure reduces. The increased focus on customer satisfaction and customer retention also tends to slow revenue declines in more mature businesses and more mature industries. Opportunity can be identified by the number of resources you plan to shift between the two models and the difference in the average cost.

Sales performance and territory optimization: Other times the management team may not have identified all of its under-performing resources. For situations like this, looking at resources track record against aligned quotas, taking into account adequate ramp in time, is a key way to review the salesforce. Once you have an understanding of individual performance relative to the aligned bars, there are times when the decision may be made to reallocate territories and resources may no longer be required to support the new territory alignment. In other situations, specifically during mergers, there also can be excess capacity. Typically, you want to set quota target expectations to be at least about five times the salesforce earning. If not, then your sales team may not be sufficiently challenged or well trained. If the latter, then this can lend itself well to improving sales force effectiveness through training and investment.

Incentive changes: Companies can change sales incentive plans. If the compensation scheme is very generous, then it makes sense to review and change the model to make it in line with industry. Companies that do this will have some turnover and likely lose some key sales talent. This can be done, but companies should carefully consider the implementation. The messaging and how you transition are critical.

Deal desks: Another major issue with sales is that oftentimes, the sales resources are focused on topline and may reduce pricing to get the sale or provide other items of value for the sale. To minimize this leakage, companies that are experiencing a decline in profitability will institute a deals desk. This is a finance or sales finance resource that validates that the deal economics meet certain profitability hurdle rates to be approved by the field sales representative. For discounted deals, there is an escalation process for approval.

Organizational efficiency: Sales teams can also benefit from organizational hygiene in the management levels. Sales management should be able to effectively manage up to about eight more junior sales representatives. Above this, the manager begins to lose the ability to have adequate check-ins and reviews of funnels and pipelines. For more technical sales, the span may be lower down to about six resources.

Travel and expenses: A holistic review of company travel and expense can typically also improve the sales team's expenses. There is no good benchmark for travel for sales resources as each territory is different. It typically requires analysts to review an individual's Concur or expense management extract and review the types of hotels, airfares, and individual meal costs. This analysis can be subjective, but if you see people staying at the Ritz-Carlton versus the Courtyard Marriott, this may be an area to review.

Use of customer service to supplement internal sales: The customer service representatives and team can (and should) supplement the internal sales team. They are a central point of contact with the customers. If properly trained, you can leverage them for upsell and cross-sell opportunities. In addition, you can use them during low volume periods for outbound lead generation calls. Using an incentive structure like a fixed rate commission will also incent the customer service reps to help generate revenue and reduce the needed cost structure of the internal sales team.

PRODUCT LIFECYCLE AND SKU OPTIMIZATION

One of the biggest drivers for any company is the cost of their product. This cost will traverse both the cost of goods sold (COGS) and the SG&A line expense line items on the P&L. It is important for companies to effectively manage their product lifecycle. This is not just focused on research and development, but this is also ensuring that a company has a mature process that review product success, examines product failure, and manages out products and variants that are not accretive to the bottom-line.

Research and Product Lifecycle

First let's review what makes up the product lifecycle, regardless of industry, here are the major steps of the lifecycle:

Research: Research is what most consider phase 0 of any product. In the end the technology must exist and be mature and sufficiently stable to sell. In the military they have an entire technical readiness level (TRL) scale. This is a good framework just to think about technology, and even to some extent products. In the private sector, technology does not need to be fully mature. There are ways to rollout minimally viable products and then scale capability. In the military, when they deploy a weapon system, I think it has to work.

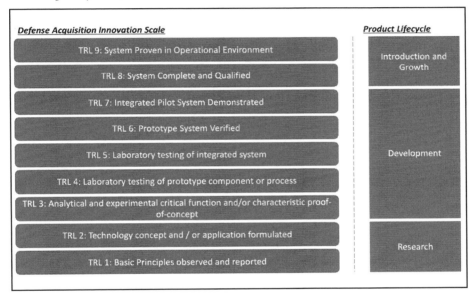

Research, in the product lifecycle, typically allows the company (or scientific research facility or entrepreneur) to conduct primary scientific research to crack a specific problem. This phase is not always correlated to a product—this is more focused on solving a problem or examining a physical phenomenon. The actual development of the solution into a product occurs in the development stage of the product lifecycle. Also, research tends to be lower ROI—you place a number of bets and one or two hit the mark. For private equity firms, they tend to de-emphasize the need for true blue ocean research and more focus on the development of new products. They often refer to this as "little r, big D."

Development: The product is conceptualized and developed. In the case of software, this involves planning, designing, coding, and testing.

For consumer or industrial products, this stage involves market research and developing the product concept, creating a prototype, and conducting market testing. There is clearly overlap between the research and development phase. Depending on the industry, the requirements and focus may be more highly allocated to research (e.g., life sciences). Whereas with Consumer of Industrial companies, the focus is more on productization and ensuring product-market fit and then iterating on the concept prior to moving it forward in the pipeline.

Introduction: The product is launched in the market. In the case of software, this involves releasing the product to the public and starting to market it. For consumer or industrial products, this stage involves launching the product, advertising it, and promoting it to generate consumer interest.

Growth: Sales of the product start to increase rapidly, and the product gains wider acceptance in the market. For software, this stage involves acquiring new customers and expanding the user base. For consumer or industrial products, this stage involves increasing production to meet demand and expanding distribution channels.

Maturity: Sales growth slows down as the product reaches its peak in the market. For software, this stage involves releasing updates and new versions to retain customers and compete with new products. For consumer or industrial products, this stage involves defending market share and maintaining profitability.

Decline: Sales start to decline as the product becomes outdated, loses market share, or faces competition from newer products. For software, this stage involves discontinuing the product or transitioning to a new product. For consumer or industrial products, this stage involves phasing out the product or introducing a new version with updated features.

The main difference between the product lifecycle of software and consumer/industrial products is that the pace of innovation and technological advancement is faster for software products. This means that the growth, maturity, and decline stages are often shorter for software products, as newer and more advanced products are constantly being introduced. Additionally, software products can be updated more easily and frequently than consumer/industrial products, which can help extend their lifespan and delay the decline stage. In addition, consumer products typically have longer development cycles and require more

extensive market research and testing, which can lead to a longer introduction stage.

Research

The primary driver of all research and development in the U.S.
economy is business. As of 2020, the total research and experimental
development spend was about $716 billion in the U.S. The majority
of the funding and execution of those dollars was all within the private
sector. The figure below shows the spend as presented by the National
Center for Science and Engineering Statistics.

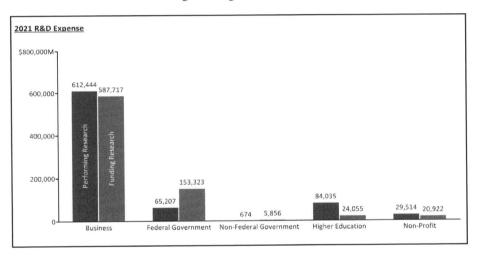

However, the allocation of these dollars for businesses is highly
concentrated on experimental development versus basic and applied
research. Across all industries, as of 2020, businesses had 78.8 percent of
their R&D focused on experimental development versus basic of applied
research. The better function and use of businesses is to commercialize
products. As you can see in the data set below, research is heavily focused
in higher education accounting for about 45 percent of the performance
of those dollars.

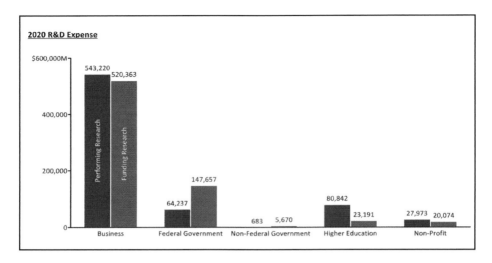

Now, the amount of research a company conducts is going to be heavily driven by the industry and whether the company is marketing or product led, but, in general, businesses should minimize the amount of research it conducts and focus its efforts on potentially applying research and definitely experimentally developing and commercializing the research.

With the exception of industries like the life sciences, where research is part of the company's value chain, the optimized company limits the amount of research that it conducts in house. Even for the larger life science companies, they have minimized the primary research they are conducting and buyout-promising technologies once they hit a mature stage that there company can profit from. The acquisition of technology is a better and higher ROI model for mature companies than developing it in house.

For companies that still need to conduct research, there are great models on how to manage engagement with research centers and ensure that you are keeping abreast of the research going on in the research centers. Some of the best and most economic models have an in-house scientist whose job it is to evangelize your company, and are also connected to all of the research centers. The key then is also to spend the research dollars backing talented researchers in these centers. When you use your research dollars in this manner, you have the ability to work with world-class talent in whatever primary research question you need answered versus maintaining in-house scientists. They may or may not be the best in the question you are trying to solve. A number of companies will have partnerships with universities and research centers that specialize in their key underlying sciences and technologies to also have those teams conduct research on their behalf.

There are some businesses that do have in-house research teams. In large, these are a cost centers for the company. Companies should have a discrete list of projects and let these researchers work those projects. These organizations can be managed down over time.

Product Lifecycle Management (PLM)

From hereon I will focus on the primary role of a business, developing and commercializing products to sell in the market.

Management of products will vary by industry, however there is a need to discuss an adequate level of oversight and control of the product design and lifecycle process. A number of companies have poor practices around PLM.

The innovation process (concept, design, prototype, and approval) is one of the segments of the company operations that can be a differentiator and somewhere where upper management reviews can help run a more streamlined company. The key areas of focus are the approval gates for the innovation process. The key approvals are going from concept to a formal project, which seeks to design the product then the design review and finally the product approval, which puts the product into production. When you begin to think through this process, it does require a lot of iteration. There are metrics and benchmarks of how many concepts to design, but are highly dependent on the industry.

What a number of companies need to focus on in this process is not just the design, but also integrating into this process value engineering. For instance, when you create a new product, does it need a brand new package? Or could the baseline package be the same as another product? A number of innovation processes do not incorporate this into the design. For luxury industries, this is something that may not always be necessary. However, it should be a consideration.

This process should never be too burdensome and should seek to streamline. This is the lifeblood of product-focused companies. The lifecycle of each product is a wave and every product will eventually wane to maturity. The only way to continue to grow the company is for the company to continue to product new innovation to drive revenue up on a fixed distribution schema. Obviously, sales and increased distribution is the other major driver.

Here is a conceptual way to think through adequate oversight and key elements of the process:

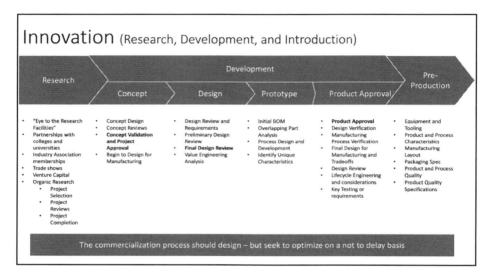

Here are some of the key elements and considerations of the innovation process. During the concept phase the company should also seek to evaluate whether the product is viable, assess the market demand, and estimate the cost of developing and manufacturing the product. The product and brand teams should also have a sense of total scale of the demand and the initial run they believe may be available. These metrics are critical to help the rest of the team gauge what is required and, if required, to begin to integrate partners into the development cycle.

For companies with significant contract manufacturing, the team will typically take the concept to the CMs. This is typically done in the form of a brief with the requirements of the product. From this point forward, typically a company will outsource the remainder of this up until the launch and go-to-market of the product.

For mature product and brand management teams, the concept phase may focus significantly on just updating the products that currently have in the portfolio (shade extensions, minor modifications).

The company then moves into design and prototyping. In this stage, the company creates the design of the product. This involves developing a prototype, testing the product's functionality, and evaluating its performance. This is where the "true" innovation occurs. It takes the design requirements and then works with the resources of the company or partners to develop the product. The product itself will come into reality. For software-based products, this is where the software development lifecycle (SDLC) comes into play.

Companies will also begin some of the testing required for the product. For FDA regulated products, for instance, they will also conduct the required testing to meet those requirements. They may also conduct testing for liability or other concerns that are made evident by other members of the development team. Finally, they will validate the product does what it says it does. This is critical because the claims that the marketing team make need to be based on these tests and outcomes.

There are key software packages that help the management of this process. The product lifecycle management (PLM) software packages will help manage the projects developing projects, but, also, they will keep track of the bill of material or ingredients, they can check them for compliance and other issues and also keep track of approved substitutes. The PLM software will also feed all of this information into most ERPs and can be the system of record for the bill of materials for the products.

Finally the company moves into product refinement and product approval. This is the stage where the product is refined and finally approved. The company finalizes the design, creates a manufacturing plan, and begins to build the initial run of the product. During this stage there may be tradeoffs in the design. When you try to mass produce the product, there are other anomalies that also can be introduced that were not observed in test or small batch sampling. Working with the manufacturing team or the CM partner you can typically negotiate all of these obstacles and issues.

Once approved, the product goes into pre-production. In this portion of the process, the manufacturing team has to ensure that you integrate the new product into the manufacturing location and schedule. They ensure they have the adequate quantity and the correct tooling needed to produce the product. Sometimes, this requires changes to the manufacturing layout. If so, this can cause delays as manufacturing layouts can be time consuming. The team will also develop the quality system to ensure that as the product is mass-produced, the company receives the product it needs at the end of the process. For trusted contract manufacturers, the quality system may be put in place by the CM, with final quality checks once it is in the possession of the company. We will discuss the full manufacturing process and optimization levers in the manufacturing section of this book.

In general, teams should try to create one or two large breakout innovations per year and a large number of lower tranche innovations, line expansions, and modifications. This allows the marketing teams to really focus on the winners and ensure that their initial launch and growth can be a primary focus.

Product Launch and Opportunities in Mature Products

The next stage of the innovation process is the control and oversight of the actual launch of the product and also the decision frameworks to eliminate products. When we look at the launch element of the business we think of this in four discrete steps:

1. Developing the launch strategy
2. Prelaunch preparations
3. Launch
4. Postlaunch reviews

This is an area of the company and cost structure that you need to get right. I have not seen effective schemes to reduce this cost structure except at the point of the initial budget and ambition setting for the product launch. The largest opportunity is to focus on the inventory build and to ensure you do not have to many overstock situations. Predicting inventory levels is the key and requires the marketing or product/brand management teams to be highly critical of their initial estimates and assessments. The other area for potential waste is large-scale changes of the product after the initial orders for raw or packaging materials have been submitted. This can leave a lot of stranded cost in the supply chain.

The final consideration is also to ensure that the marketing dollars are aligned with the projected incremental revenue. Allocation of marketing dollars to create creative assets or to market the product for lower value products in not value accretive.

Developing the Launch Strategy

Define your target audience: Before you can launch a product, you need to know who you're targeting. Determine the demographics and psychographics of your ideal customer, and understand what motivates them to buy.

Conduct market research: Gather insights about your target audience, competitors, and industry trends. Use this data to refine your product and marketing strategy.

Develop your positioning: Define what makes your product unique and different from your competitors. Create a value proposition that resonates with your target audience.

Set your goals and KPIs: Determine what you want to achieve with your launch, whether it's sales, brand awareness, or customer engagement. Set specific, measurable goals and key performance indicators to track your progress.

Plan the budget and timeline: Develop a budget for your launch, including all the expenses associated with production, marketing, and distribution. Set a timeline for each stage of the launch, and make sure all teams are aligned.

Budgets for launches should be allocated based on the projected increase in incremental sales. So, new innovations with breakout potential should receive larger dollars. Smaller innovations with lower projected revenues should receive less.

Develop initial launch and replenishment order quantities: This is a critical element and needs to be thought of up to a year in advance of the actual launch and marketing launch. The marketing team needs to range and then lock down the amount of product by SKU at this point. This ensures that the production teams or CMs can conduct the appropriate pre-orders.

When a company launches a product a general guideline is to order sufficient quantity for a conservative estimate of sales during the lead-time of the product with a potential buffer for unexpected demand or supply chain issues. Generally, the company may want to order up to about 75 percent of the anticipated volume during the lead-time. Adding an additional 10 to 20 percent buffer may be appropriate. Doing this helps to ensure that the company will have sufficient stock to meet the initial demand, but not enough to overstock.

Pre-Launch Preparations

Build buzz and excitement: Create a teaser campaign that generates interest in your product before launch. Leverage social media, influencer marketing, and PR to build buzz.

Develop creative assets: Create a strong brand identity and develop creative assets such as packaging, product photos, and videos. Make sure all assets are aligned with your brand positioning and messaging.

Test and optimize: Conduct beta testing and user feedback sessions to refine your product and marketing strategy. Use data to optimize your launch plan.

Launch

Execute the marketing plan: Launch your product with a multi-channel marketing campaign that includes digital, social, and traditional media. Leverage influencers, email marketing, and paid advertising to drive sales and awareness.

Monitor performance: Track your KPIs and adjust your marketing strategy as needed. Continuously optimize your campaigns based on data and user feedback.

Post-Launch Reviews

Evaluate performance: Review your launch results and compare them to your goals and KPIs. Analyze data and user feedback to identify areas for improvement. Most companies will conduct reviews at post 90 days, 180 days, and a year out from product launch. This helps the business to ensure it is keeping winning products and holding the brand or product managers accountable for their estimates. In addition, it allows the business to identify bad products that can be eliminated or not reordered.

Refine your strategy: Use insights from your post-launch review to refine your product and marketing strategy. Adjust your budget, timeline, planned buys, and KPIs as needed.

Plan for the future: Use your launch experience to inform your long-term product roadmap and marketing strategy.

Monitor inventory levels: Track your inventory levels and adjust production as needed to meet demand. Because of the lead times involved, you will typically receive orders based on the success of the launch. Having that additional quantum at launch (around 75 percent of lead time volume) will allow you to understand initial market demand of the product prior to launch and then adjust the reorders needed. This allows the business to minimize excess inventory levels while ensuring it meets the majority of demand.

Product maturity: As the product shifts to maturity sales growth will slow. Teams should begin to focus their efforts on maintaining profitability and market share. Depending on the industry, this can take many forms. One of the easiest areas to focus on here is the product margin. With more produced, the unit cost should come down. Ensure that you have contracts with manufacturers where you both share in the upside associated with longer production runs. In addition, additional rounds of value engineering typically creates significant value in products.

As you mature the product, you also begin to look at new features and fixing quality concerns. When you do so, you should also look at opportunities to design the product for value, further reducing your unit cost. Firms like McKinsey and Kearney and specialized firms in each industry typically have robust practices that help identify opportunities for enhanced margin generation. These practices can identify everything from small changes like changing out the eyelet of a bag from metal to plastic all the way up to large process or structural level changes to the product with larger impact. These practices can typically identify anywhere between 2 and 10 percent improvement in margins on a given product. These improvements need to be done on a product by product basis so the best answer is to develop this skill in-house and have teams of your engineers continue to evolve product design, independent of external support.

Another method to improve margin is to change the amount of product (bulk fill) provided to the customer. This is most prevalent in the food industry but can be done elsewhere. The idea is to, over time, increase the price per unit of bulk fill and reduce the amount of product the end customer receives. Initially, you start with the same size container, but you reduce the amount of potato chips the end customer receives. They typically do not notice the reduction in the amount from 10 to eight ounces. Over time, you develop new packaging. You can increase or decrease the size of the packaging, it does not matter. However, what you then do is to maintain the per-ounce pricing with a larger size. This allows you to over time improve margins on these products. This technique is called price laddering. You will see it used extensively in industries and when the company is trying to take price to improve margins.

Sunsetting Products

Eventually, all products leave the market. They become outdated, they lose market share, or become disrupted from competition or new technology. Sometimes, the company may proactively eliminate products from the market that are becoming too expensive to maintain.

The decision can be emotional for some companies. However, companies that are efficient and effective will make these decisions based on a few different criteria. Here are a few of them:

Sales and profitability: Profit is a priority. In this framework the company analyzes the sales and fully burdened costs of the product and determine whether it's generating enough margin to justify its continuation. When products are not generating profit, they should likely be removed from the product catalog. There are exceptions to this—specifically, when they are complementary products that are needed for basket effect issues with a customer.

Market demand and competition: This is a forward-looking framework. For instance, if you are in the buggy whip business and you just saw the Ford plant startup, you may want to reevaluate. In this instance the company should, evaluate the demand for its current product in the market, and determine whether there are any changes in customer preferences or competitive pressures that may affect its future growth potential. Analyze the competitive landscape and determine whether the product can compete effectively against other offerings in the market. Often times when companies use this lens, it is really one that results in lower forecasts and then sunsetting once the profitability trigger is reached is when the product is finally sunset.

Resource allocation: Sometimes the company makes a decision that they do not have sufficient resources to stay in a given product. In this instance, the company makes a determination that the resources required to maintain and support the product are better allocated to other products or initiatives that have higher growth potential or strategic importance. In this instance, there is always an implied profitability issue with the product. If the product was highly profitable, then the company could increase the number of resources.

Customer conversion: In some instances, a company has a better product. Usually, it also has higher margins. In this instance, the company will try to convert its current customers over to this new platform or product. The key analysis that the company has to believe is that it can capture those customers on its new platform that will offset the loss in revenue and profit from the older variant. I once oversaw the analysis of this type of improvement. The conversion decision for that company was very easy. The other product had a five times higher profit margin than the older product. In addition, there were significant upcoming costs to maintain the older product. The decision to sunset was made rapidly.

Regulatory and legal considerations: Consider any regulatory or legal requirements that may impact the decision to sunset the product, such as contractual obligations or intellectual property rights. In my prior discussion, the largest driver of the impending cost was a regulatory update that was required on the software package.

Brand reputation: Evaluate the impact of sunsetting the product on the company's brand reputation, and determine whether there are any steps that can be taken to mitigate any negative effects.

Once the decision is made to sunset the product, the company then needs to inform its existing customer base. When it does, they will typically have another product offering that they are trying to convert them to. Use of incentives and other marketing techniques is critical to try to retain the customer base. In one instance, I oversaw the elimination of a fleet of retail outlets. We used a number of methods to retain the customers. In some situations, we converted them to near-by outlets that also sold the company's product. In others, we shifted them to an online channel that had higher margins. In general, we were able to retain up to about 30 percent of our customers in this manner. Typically, companies will retain 15 to 20 percent of their customer base.

One special consideration is the timeline to sunset an application. When you sunset an application or software package, the timeline is typically at least six months to multiple years. The more critical to business operations, typically, the longer it will take. Even when you do, there have been instances of companies working with their prior providers to elongate the technology and then pay them more than in the past to maintain the product. I have seen this occur with an ERP-like solution. In short, the customer would lose their business and cause large reputational damage to the company if it had not agreed to extend the support. The understanding in those situations is that the customer is on a short timeline to replace the solution.

Product Roadmaps and Update Release Schedules

Product roadmaps are a great tool for companies to understand their future development needs and requirements. For highly-engineered companies, the need for technology development or interlacing development streams, make product and technology roadmaps even more important.

An example of a product roadmap is the aviation science and technology program for the U.S. Army. This is a great example as it is publicly disclosable and shows the major elements that need to be discussed. In addition, for companies in the aerospace and defense sector, during this time period, there were unique revenue generation opportunities in all of these boxes. The technology development for the military also coincides with the technology development for private sector firms like Northrop Grumman or Raytheon.

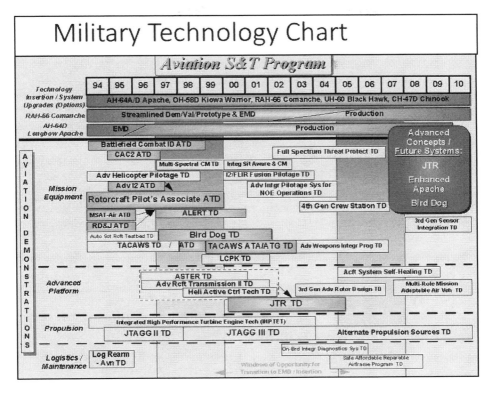

In this product roadmap, you can see the development timeline and projected delivery of each of the capabilities. In addition, they have even thought about when the various technologies can be inserted into the critical platforms (dark vertical segments). Another thing to look at is the sequential development of ASTER TD, Adv RCFT Transmission II TD, and Heli Active Ctrl Tech TD that appear to be required in order to support the main technology of JTR TD. As a businessperson, you do not need to know the scientific intricacies of each of these programs, you just need to understand what the technologists and product managers need to deliver the required product or capability.

To optimize a roadmap and to optimize the engineering teams, you actually need to remove work from the system. To remove work, you actually need to work with the technologists to remove development and engineering programs or delay them. One of the critical elements of the transformation toolkit is to review the actual technology priorities. Eliminating or elongating development programs to be in line with market requirements is key. Oftentimes, technologists may want to anticipate the market. In general that is not a good thing. Instead, what can be better is to ensure your technology meets the market requirements when the market wants them. This then allows you to reduce the overall workload of a team and thereby the resources needed. These resources do not need to be exited from the company. Instead, they can be reallocated to higher value projects.

Similar to product roadmaps, software release schedules are also a driver of trapped team potential. The optimal solution is to shift to a continuous delivery model. This means that when a solution is ready, it is rolled out to the implementations. This requires a cloud-based product. It also requires a software-based solution that is not a monolith engineering architecture, but one that is service oriented and modular in nature (you may hear the term micro-service architecture). With continuous delivery, there are no expectations of when improvements will be made. For major reissues or items that will change the user experience, the company will typically treat this like an actual software release with the appropriate change management materials. For these, it makes sense to bundle large changes into these releases. One or two major re-issues per year is usually sufficient for most applications.

For solutions that are still on-prem, all changes require a release or patch update. Reducing the need and frequency of these is a key efficiency improvement. Most teams prefer to have an update at most every six months. If you see a company outputting an update every quarter, that may be in efficient and cause a higher than necessary cost structure. There are some spaces that may require this frequent of an update.

Elongation to either the product roadmap of the release schedule reduces the needs for the engineering teams to support them. In addition, it also reduced the required support from production, marketing, and new product introduction, technical writing, and others that support these releases. Any changes to the product release timing also need to be weighed against the improvements to revenue projected from each of them.

Software Development Lifecycle (SDLC)

For software-based companies, it is important to provide at least an overview of the SDLC. This is a key element of how they do product development. Just like a tangible product, software has a corollary.

However, given that software engineering is kind of a subset of other potential products, I have treated it separate and distinct from the full product lifecycle management. For larger technology companies, the SDLC is often times integrated into PLM.

This is a standard framework and the company specifics will depend on whether their individual development style is waterfall, agile, or DevOps.

The standard SDLC consists of several stages that a software project goes through from inception to retirement. While there are variations depending on the specific methodology or framework used, the sequential steps in the software development lifecycle generally include:

Requirements definition and planning: In this stage, the project is defined, and the project scope is established. The team identifies the requirements and goals for the software project, and creates a plan to achieve them. This stage involves defining the project scope, creating a project plan, and estimating the project's budget and timeline.

Analysis: In this stage, the team analyzes the requirements gathered in the planning stage to create a detailed functional specification document. The team may also identify any technical constraints or risks that need to be addressed during the development process.

Design: In this stage, the team creates a detailed design specification document that outlines the software architecture, database design, user interface design, and other technical details. The design should align with the functional specification and address any technical constraints or risks identified in the analysis stage.

Development: In this stage, the software is developed based on the design specification. The development stage involves coding, testing, and debugging the software to ensure it meets the functional and technical specifications.

Testing: In this stage, the software is tested to ensure it meets the quality and performance requirements. The testing process may include functional testing, performance testing, security testing, and user acceptance testing.

Deployment: In this stage, the software is deployed to the production environment, and users can start using it. The deployment process may involve configuration management, release management, and user training.

Maintenance: In this stage, the software is monitored and maintained to ensure it continues to meet the business requirements and is secure and reliable. This stage involves identifying and fixing any bugs or issues, updating the software to meet changing needs, and providing ongoing support to users.

SDLC Methodologies

Waterfall, agile, and DevOps are three of the main methodologies used in software development. Each of these methodologies has its own unique approach and philosophy towards software development.

Waterfall methodology is a linear approach that follows a sequential process in which each phase of development is completed before moving on to the next phase. It typically includes the following phases: requirements gathering and analysis, design, implementation, testing, and maintenance. This methodology is suitable for projects with well-defined and stable requirements and a fixed scope, as it requires extensive planning and documentation.

Agile methodology, on the other hand, is an iterative approach that emphasizes collaboration, flexibility, and rapid delivery. It involves breaking down the project into smaller, more manageable chunks, known as sprints, and each sprint involves a series of activities, including planning, designing, developing, testing, and delivery. Agile methodology allows for constant feedback and adjustment throughout the development process, which makes it ideal for projects that require flexibility and adaptability to change. Scrum is a subset of agile that is a lightweight framework that emphasizes teamwork, accountability, and iterative progress towards a well-defined goal.

DevOps methodology is a combination of development and operations, with a focus on automating the entire software delivery process. DevOps methodology emphasizes collaboration and communication between developers, operations, and other stakeholders. It involves continuous integration, continuous delivery, and continuous deployment, where each phase of development is closely integrated with operations to ensure that the software is delivered rapidly and reliably. This methodology is suitable for organizations that need to deliver software quickly and efficiently, with a focus on speed, quality, and scalability.

Here are some others that you may also hear about:

Lean: A methodology that focuses on eliminating waste, maximizing value, and continuous improvement.

Kanban: A lean approach that emphasizes visualizing work, limiting work in progress, and optimizing flow.

Spiral: An iterative approach that combines elements of waterfall and agile methodologies.

Rapid application development (RAD): A methodology that emphasizes rapid prototyping and iterative development.

Extreme programming (XP): A methodology that emphasizes customer satisfaction, teamwork, and continuous improvement.

Crystal: A family of methodologies that emphasize communication, simplicity, and reflective improvement.

Feature-driven development (FDD): A methodology that emphasizes creating a model of the system and building features iteratively.

Dynamic systems development method (DSDM): An Agile methodology that emphasizes collaboration, frequent delivery, and continuous testing.

From an efficiency perspective, the use of agile with scrums tends to be one of the more efficient methods from a cost structure perspective for most situations and teams.

However, waterfall can be more productive when the project requirements are stable and well-defined, and the team has a clear understanding of what they need to do. Agile methodologies, such as scrum or kanban, can be more productive when there is a need for flexibility and adaptability to change throughout the development process. DevOps can be more productive when the goal is to deliver software quickly and reliably, with a focus on automation and continuous delivery.

There are several methods to understand developer productivity. The five I am most used to seeing are:

Lines of committed code: this measures the number of lines of code from the developer that are committed to the program. By using lines of committed code, you eliminate quality issues. It also helps understand and account for experience levels. The one subjective that remains is the complexity of the programming problems being addressed. For instance, a devops engineer may be committing code every week, but a breakthrough developer working on a new product feature may not publish until the end of the year because the problem is harder. Some firms will continue to use lines of code as a metric for productivity—just remember the biggest issue is quality.

Another growing metric is cycle time—the time it takes a developer to complete a task from start to finish. This may be a good metric when paired with a quality assessment.

Code review feedback: This is a good measure and helps you understand the strengths and weaknesses of a given programmer.

Number of bugs: This is another measure. When paired with lines of committed code, lines of code, or cycle time, it begins to give a full assessment of the quality and speed of a given developer.

Business value delivered: This is another growing metric (albeit subjective in design). It is a rubric that can include things like revenue generated, customer satisfaction, time saved, or other. This helps tie the developer's incentives to the end state business.

Using these tools as a benchmark can help you gauge the help and productivity of a given development team. The fixes tend to focus on the process and then also up-leveling or training talent. With the right investment, increasing the development teams productivity can yield significant upside opportunity for the company.

Product Management Organization

Product management organizations have to be product or category focused. Depending on the size of the company and level of complexity and similarity of the products. For small to mid-market companies, you will often see product managers allocated across multiple products or categories. For instance, in a highly engineered technology company, the product management team was organized around technologies. One focused on cloud solutions, another on the integration with the ecosystem. For larger or less complex companies, you may find the product management team allocated with an individual product owner for each product. In general, a product needs between $5 to $10 million in annual sales to justify an entry-level product owner. A product owner may also be warranted for strategically important products. Although that number is a general guideline, it is not a sizing tool for a product management team. There are some exceptionally successful, large products that do not require a product owner because the product is relatively simple or has low strategic value.

In order to optimize a product management organization, you also need to incorporate some strategic analysis of the company and judgment of the company's management team. Use of a spans and layers approach may not yield any benefit. Typically, you will need to ensure full coverage of the portfolio of products and adequate coverage of expansionary elements of the portfolio. Use of benchmarks, can also support the analysis and justification for reduced resourcing of the function. The optimal structure is to typically focus the product team along category lines. This allows the team to optimize across technologies and typical customer base.

In software companies, you typically want to have a ratio of about one product manager for every eight to 10 developers. For venture-backed companies with a large amount of development needs, it can be closer to eight. For more mature companies, it is closer to 10.

In addition, with development teams moving further to lower cost jurisdictions, it also allows the product owners to also have a split distribution. There are no firm ratios to think about on this, but should be used in the judgment of the management team.

Development Organization

The organizational structure of the development team is less of a concern, as they tend to operate in ad hoc teams. The larger issue you think about is to ensure you have an adequate number of programmers for front end and back end development, UI/UX, and lower cost resources to support testing. In addition, there will also be project and program managers. The other major issue is the "fungibility" of the development talent. It is important to understand what programming languages are required to support the company and which elements of the organization specialize in that element of the code base. There are significant differences in the capability and architecture requirements between a C#, Python, and Java programmers. There is value in replatforming companies to more dominate languages for instance conducting a program to eliminate all of the C# code and replace it with Python.

Assuming the same code base, there are some typical ratios that are helpful to keep the organization healthy and proportionate to needed workload. Typically, you want about three to four developers to every one QA resource. This can be reduced with improved testing methodologies that include regression testing and programs that automate code patent searches.

Additionally, the use of UI/UX can vary significantly, dependent on the focus of the development. If it requires heavy user interaction, UI/UX can be up to 10 to 20 percent of an engineering organization. Typically, you should have one UI/UX developer for every five to 10 developers. This can also be pushed lower if customer satisfaction is high, focusing on maintaining that advantage and monetizing it for the company.

Use of low cost countries can and should be leveraged for any development team—even emerging technologies can benefit from some offshore leverage. For the majority of healthy, mature companies you should seek about 50 to 65 percent of the population to be in a lower-cost jurisdiction. This approach is not per category. This is in aggregate across the teams. In general the QA teams tend to be more disproportionately offshore. The UI/UX tend to be more onshore. The development teams are more highly split between onshore and offshore. For new, emerging products, the teams tend to be onshore. For mature products with more break/fix issues and limited new development, these product teams tend to be offshore.

Development organizations should focus on development resources. In general, the organization should seek to keep its R&D density to about 80 percent within the organization. This means limiting the management, PMs, and QA to about 20 percent of the organization.

The biggest driver of software development teams is the need for solving product problems through code. You can and should treat this as a capacity constrained funnel. What does that mean—you don't need to hire more and more developers to meet the ever growing backlog of projects. A healthy backlog of projects is between six to 12 months. This ensures you have sufficient projects or tests for the developers to continue to work through whilst the product management team goes through and reprioritizes and adds to the list. It also allows your product and program management teams to do the adequate planning and fine tuning of requirements to make the work once in flight to be worth the effort. If you only have about one to two sprints worth of backlog, then you should seek to reduce the organization, as you have a significant amount of capacity in the organization.

If required, you can also increase the backlog further. I would not push the backlog past about 15 months, as you begin to be less and less effective in the marketplace. In addition, it becomes hard to prioritize the issues.

There are limited options to improve the productivity of the actual development resources. Typical paths are focused on improving the workflow and project management of the projects. Typically, the use of scrum team coaching can be helpful to ensure the process is seamless. In addition, the use of tools and repositories like bitbucket help to reduce time for the engineers to solve problems that may already have been solved before. The use of wiki's has also helped to improve efficacy of the individual programmers. These are helpful to ensure teams share the knowledge that they create. Teams should also leverage ChatGPT and other AI tools. This can help them resolve coding issues quickly.

Engineering Organization

Some people use engineers and developers interchangeably. However, I have found it easier to refer to people that code software as developers. All other people that develop technologies or that solve problems through technologies as engineers. So in this section, we will discuss the business of solving physical problems. Please note that in today's world, even these engineers will typically work with hardware or machine level coding to interface the physical world with the electronic world. It is easier and cheaper to process the information through a microchip than through an analog circuit in most instances.

These organizations will be managed similar to a software development organization. There will be certain products of technologies. The organization will have technology leads for each of the major components. From there, they will have engineers for all of the major equipment in that technology or product, depending on the company and purpose. The other key team or partnership that needs to be considered is the use of your manufacturing and suppliers. These teams will have resources and can be resources as the teams develop the new technologies or products.

During development or to solve problems, the businesses should use integrated product development teams (IPDTs). These are cross-functional teams that help develop the next product and also help to provide views on how the technology being developed can be cost optimized and improved for stability and other purposes. This usage requires multi-functional staffing processes and systems. In the most mature organizations, these behaviors are incented. For less mature organizations, you may find reticence to share resources across functional lines.

Here is a summary matrix to improve the cost structure for product engineering teams:

Reduction Strategies	Levers
Work Reduction	• Eliminate Projects • Eliminate low-value added features, functions, and options • Leverage Supplier design support • Use common parts across products • Use Design platforms
Improve Productivity	• Performance Improvement Reviews and Programs • Streamline workflow, meetings, and reports • Manage change control • Frontload design to minimize alternatives later in the process • Develop standards and guidelines that engineers can use to minimize variance
Labor Rate Reduction	• Use of Low Cost Countries • Enhanced use of outside vendors • Reduce supplier cost through negotiation, guaranteed minimums, and bundled offerings

FRAMEWORKS FOR OPERATIONS AND SERVICE DELIVERY

Operations is a pretty vague term and highly dependent on which industry, what company, and what the operating model is for the firm. In general, operations refers to the client delivery element of the business. To be more specific (and risk sounding like a dictionary), operations refers to the day-to-day activities the company conducts to product goods and services, manage resources, and deliver those goods and services to their end point client.

For an industrial company, the inbound and outbound logistics, the manufacturing of the product, and the distribution of the product are likely all elements of the operations of the company. For a consulting firm, the contracting, recruiting, staffing, and service delivery of advisement to the end client are the operations of the company. For an e-commerce company with logistics outsourced, the operations of the company might be advertising, website management, product procurement, and customer service might be the operations of the company.

Important to Understand the Goal of the Next Section

With this much variation, I discuss the potential elements that I have not already covered. I believe there are nine core operational frameworks that the majority of businesses will follow—well, 11 when you include software delivery—which was already covered in the section on innovation and manufacturing, which will be covered in a subsequent chapter. The goal of this next section is not to be exhaustive or comprehensive. The goal is to put in your mind what I consider the nine (or 11) basic frameworks of operations in a company. It is meant, in true Naval Ravikant fashion, to give the key basics—understand them at a fundamental level—then you apply those frameworks to other situations or operational paradigms you encounter. You will just see it as "another one of those." From these building blocks, you can piece together other organizations as you may find them.

Here is my list of key frameworks—if you feel strongly that another should be added, feel free to send it my way. Please note that software service delivery is covered in the Innovation section under SDLC. When writing the book, I did try to create a dedicated line item for it, but it was literally a few paragraphs. For any other topics, I'll incorporate them into the next edition of this book.

1. Retail and point of sale operations
2. Website service delivery and e-commerce merchandise delivery
3. Coverage based services and on-site service delivery models
4. Talent-based services
5. Consumer/industrial fulfillment
6. Capital construction, infrastructure, and leasing
7. Commodity extraction

8. Financial services and investing
9. Creative services and IP management
10. Software delivery (already covered)
11. Manufacturing (to be covered the manufacturing section of the book)

I cover manufacturing separately, as it is a major element of value in a company and deserves its own section of the book. End state distribution for industrials is through logistics and this will be covered in an independent section as well.

I'll give you a very basic example of a very common business model that would bridge across these categories. If you think about a restaurant, it has some elements of retail and point of sale operations, but then another element of coverage-based services where the on-hand staff will deliver a meal to that customer. So, there will be times where the basic frameworks work well and others were you may need to leverage a few of the chapters and derive what is needed for the applicable situation.

When you begin to think about the core of the business's operations, these may be good starting points for any further analysis.

Retail and Point of Sale Operations

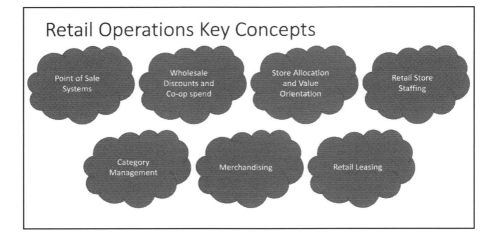

Store operations are not that complex. The majority of us have a fairly good understanding of how retail operations work. In general, the retailer will buy the goods from the wholesaler with anywhere between a 10 to 60 percent discount. The more commoditized the industry, the lower the discount. For instance, a grocery chain will typically buy from the wholesaler with a 10 to 20 percent discount off retail, while the fashion industry will typically discount by 50 to 60 percent. This is highly variable and subject to negotiation. For instance, if you are a smaller company and negotiating with Walmart or Target, those terms may seem exceptionally favorable versus what they may actually be transacting upon.

In addition to the wholesale discount, there are other co-op spends that can typically be provided. These include sharing the cost of counter staff for boutiques in the retailer—for instance the fragrance counter at Macy's. In addition, there are some others that you may encounter. Contractually obliged coadvertising, reimbursing the retailer for returns, improved discounts for end of season or clearance products. In return, you will also see some elements of contracts that discuss reporting requirements, reimbursement terms, and level of exclusivity. In addition, there can be specific promotional activities called out in these documents. Normally, with a retailer, consumer companies will enter into a selective distribution agreement. For new or declining markets, you may also see the company enter into exclusive distribution agreements. These should be avoided unless the strategy is to leverage the distributor as your extension in that region.

The assortment for the business is purchased by "buyers" or category management. These are people that are responsible for specific categories that the retailer will sell. For instance, Target has a fragrance buyer. Their job is to build relationships with the various established consumer product companies and look for new brands that could meet the needs of the end customer. In fashion, they need to be on trend. In other categories, it is more about ensuring you have the brands that consumers desire and need. There is a lot of information to support these resources including NielsenIQ and Kantar data. These services provide retail intelligence on the key brands and consumer buying patterns. In highly advanced companies, they can tie specific consumer data to perceived buying patterns through proprietary data elements. To get even more *1984* on everyone, there is now technology that is being developed to understand what products you are shopping for and who you are. They can then see items you may have liked in the past and make recommendations on what you should or should not buy all while in store. This multi-channel integration is just beginning.[18] However, this is also helpful data for the buyers, to ensure they have product assortments that will entice you to buy.

In store presentation of the products and also allocation of the products are key. The merchandising, presentation of the product, and the visual merchandising displays tell a story of the product and the brand. It is one of the last opportunities for that company and brand to interact with the potential customer prior to the purchase decision. The storytelling and appearance can be a point of differentiation for the company. These assets are typically wholly provided by the consumer product company versus the retailer. Typically, the retailer is just responsible for the standard shelf and racking in the store. However, everything is negotiable and there are likely instances where these have been procured by the store themselves. Merchandising is typically an area that can be optimized in most companies. At a minimum, review the types of displays used and costing. Oftentimes, the companies create displays without thinking about sustainability. When you create displays that can be reused, and with displays with interchangeable inserts, you can greatly reduce the temporary visual merchandising cost structure. In addition, it is better for the environment, something everyone can align with.

Shelf allocation of the various products is also key. Advisory firms can review this for you and determine what products or what categories should receive the highest amount of space on the shelf. In addition, placement on the shelf and within the store also matters. In general, the front of the store is always the most desired. For stores with dedicated aisles, end caps are always highly sought after, as they receive the highest traffic volume. Then you should look at the flow of the traffic. The middle aisles tend to receive more flow than the outer aisles, making them higher value. Then, on the actual shelves, placement about eye level is a higher value than the bottom shelf. The goal being to put your highest value, highly sought after items in the highest flow with the most eyes on them.

---

18   Vered Levy-Ron, "The Future of Shopping: What Retail Will Look Like in 2030," Syte, April 18, 2022, www.syte.ai/blog/retail-innovation/the-future-of-shopping/.

Staffing of retail operations is seasonal and temporal within a day. Good store operations leverage temporary resources during these peak periods. In addition, looking at the staffing and store hours can help eliminate additional resourcing needs. Looking at transactional data, you should also see when you need resources and when you do not—pending requirements to maintain stores open—often there are specific store hour requirements when the retail outlet is associated with a mall or some other locations.

Retail store contracts can be entered into easily, but they are very hard to exit. If the retailer is financially healthy, there is usually no reason for the retail store landlord to break the lease. When they do, they will typically want a prepayment of some portion of the rent. This is highly dependent on the location of the real estate and the likelihood of them having another renter lined up. When they do, they are more than happy to take the additional payment and then allow you to exit the lease early. When you think about this – you will typically see a recoupment over the total cost of the leases of about 40 to 60 percent. So, if your 10-year outstanding liability is $10 million then you may have to pay about $4 to $6 million in prepayment to extinguish the leases. Usually, your recoupment is closer to only 40 percent of the value—and this is not constant across all of your leases. Some will be 100 percent, others close to 0 percent, depending on contractual terms and the landlord you are working with. A great firm to work with on this is A&G Real Estate Partners. They specialize in working with landlords to optimize their clients' retail real estate portfolio.

Point of sale systems will oftentimes interact with the ERP. There is usually a data exchange on the point of sales data. In addition, there are sometimes exchanges that support inventory management, the CRM system, and other systems for analytics. The point-of-sale system can also be integrated with the HRIS to ensure that only valid employees are using the system. This can be a dedicated exchange or a daily upload. Typically, the stores will also keep cash on-hand (there are some retailers that no longer do). Because of this, there is typically a safe in the store manager's office. In addition, there are usually armored cars that will take the cash to the bank for you.

So where are opportunities in retail operations?

In general, if a company produces products, it should try to avoid own store retail. This is helpful when the company is trying to educate customers and provide a service to them. However, this is an area that should be minimized. The reason to avoid retail is the larger working capital requirements. Some CP companies have fixed this like Bonobos. They have a store where you can try on their product and then order online. In addition, it removes the need for special merchandising and reduces a significant cost footprint to maintain the retail operations.

In the same vein, there are opportunities to reduce your overall store footprint as a retailer. When looking at how to do so, you will need to look at the fully burdened cost of maintaining the store. Stores that are not profitably should be reduced. Now, there are some caveats. First, the biggest concern for retailers is overhead allocation. When you reduce stores, there is an assumption that the overhead can also be reduced. If it can't, when you reduce the stores, you can actually put the company into a further downward spiral, as the company now does not have profit to manage the full business and pay for the required overhead for the business. When you close down the business, it does not necessarily mean you lose all of the revenue. There are methods to try to recapture those dollars. Trained Retail Operations teams have dealt with this in the past and typically will have a playbook to convert those customers to your e-commerce channel or nearby stores.

Staffing is another major area of opportunity. The use of enhanced schedules that reduce the need for an additional shift or use of temporary or part-time employees can add in efficiency targets. Enhanced staffing can be effective when you work with the store level leadership to implement the right programs and give them the proper framework.

Inventory management is another key element of retail operations. Automated inventory tracking through the use of RFID and improved inventory tracking software helps maintain levels in real time. This helps to ensure you are adequately stocked and replenish when required, minimizing inefficiency. This combined with improved replenishment strategies focused on economic order quantity (EOQ) or just-in-time (JIT) methodology. EOQ takes into account cost to order and cost to hold to inform how much you should order. JIT relies on the availability of the merchandise when needed in each order cycle. Another key lever in enhanced inventory management is improved analytics to understand

and better predict seasonality and other occurrences that can impact retailers.

For certain companies, they can also outsource their merchandising function. There are a number of players that work across brands and other retailers and CP companies that service stores. This allows the company to not maintain a large number of merchandisers or field representatives across the country. Instead, they can outsource this service—typically, this is a significant cost reduction over maintaining those resources for themselves. In addition, there is a significant efficiency gain, largely eliminating the window time of the drivers.

Similar to other organizations the buyer and retail operations teams can be optimized. For the buyers, they have an important job, so the categories still need to be covered. For the retail operations team, this is largely a cost center. It should be optimized. You can look to also reduce workload within retail operations as a mechanism to reduce the required resourcing.

Website Service Delivery and E-Commerce Merchandise Delivery

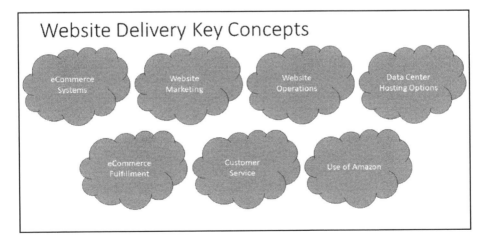

The core of e-commerce operations revolves around attracting the consumer to the website, keeping the website open for business, fulfilling the user's need, and optimizing the user's experience while on the website. To tell this story, we will start with the inbound leads and end with the discussion of how to optimize the user experience (and also improve your chances for a sale!).

Typical e-commerce configurations will leverage a commerce-focused platform to host their website. The two dominant technologies in the market right now are Shopify and Salesforce Commerce Cloud. These technologies host the e-commerce experience and interconnect with a large amount of other platforms and technology to enhance the website experience and improve revenue capture. This ecosystem is still evolving and has a large number of players. One of the critical interactions in the system is with the customer data platform. The CDP is a platform that collects and unified data about the customer. This is a critical element of the user experience that provides the user personalized experiences and aids in improving customer engagement. The other critical interaction is to the ERP. This interaction is what sends the fulfillment data to the logistics provider and dispatches the purchases or other fulfillment requirements. There is also typically an interaction with the company's CRM software, specifically to support customer service. Zendesk and Salesforce's Service Cloud are two typical interactions. This feed provides all of the required information for the company's orders to customer service. In the event there are issues, this is how the CS team knows about the order and can help the customer service experience. There are a number of other interactions. It would be important to review each of those interactions with the team to understand how they are leveraged. There are times when the utility of some of these programs has diminished, but the team is still using it. In those, instances, it may make sense to eliminate the spend.

There are a number of methods to attract customers to your website. In general, there are seven distinct methods to attract people to the website:

1. **Direct visit:** These are "free visits" to the company's website. In general, we would want a large amount of their web traffic to come from free visits to the website. In order to drive this volume, companies will use offline marketing tactics such as billboards, radio ads, or TV commercials to increase brand awareness and drive people to your website. In addition, use of word of mouth and excellent interaction with the company

and brand can drive initial and repeat direct visits to the company's online presence. For smaller companies, the use of memorable brand and domain names can support direct visits. In addition, depending on the scope and scale of the enterprise, they may also use business cards, flyers, brochures, and other hard copy promotional material to try to drive direct visits to the website.

2. **Search engine optimization:** To optimize the website for search engines, the company will conduct research and identify high traffic, relevant keywords that can drive traffic to the website. The company then creates content on the website that matches those keywords. It can also leverage meta tags and include a title, description, and header that also draw additional hits for key searches. Another key element of search engine optimization is the use of high-quality backlinks to authoritative websites in the industry. This helps boost the website in the rankings. These seem simple, but businesses have to ensure they are relevant and continually appear at the top of search queries to drive traffic.

3. **Pay-per-click:** These are the paid advertising links at the top of a search query on Google and Bing. For these, companies create targeted ads that appear in search engine results or on social media platforms, and bid on relevant keywords. To win these bids, some firms are paying anywhere from less than $1 to over $8 per click depending on industry and platform. For instance, google is typically more expensive than social media platforms.

To enhance ROI, the use of companies like Mightyhive and others also helps companies improve their return. These firms leverage user provided data in companies CDP for very targeted advertising and retargeting of users that previously visited or engaged with the brand. This helps ensure that the clicks you do pay for have a higher conversion rate on the e-commerce site. Typically, the conversion rate once on a shopping website if around 3 to 4 percent, fashion jewelry, and capital purchases like furniture tend to be lower, around 1 to 2 percent. Specific services like doctors, dentists, auto tend to have higher conversions between 5 to 10 percent.

Google and other platforms also are using and deploying location-based targeting to show ads to people in specific geographic locations. These services may cost more given a higher likelihood of conversion.

4. **Targeted marketing:** Using a prior interaction, e-commerce teams use email and/or text messages with personalized content to potential customers. Typically, the emails and texts will have personalized messages to those potential consumers and also may include promotional offers and new product updates.

   The key for marketers is to create a compelling call to action for the user to have the highest conversion rates. If the email is opened, there appears to be a high correlation for the user to at least visit the site with about one in five converting after that point. Here is what the funnel looks like for this marketing channel, on average:

   For email:
   Open rates: 18 to 20 percent of emails sent
   Response Rates: 10 to 15 percent of emails sent
   Conversion rate: 2 to 3 percent
   For SMS:
   Open Rates: 98 percent of texts are opened
   Response Rate: 45 percent
   Conversion Rate: 20 percent

   SMS is a very successful channel for this type of marketing. There is a large cost difference between the two. For example, using an email marketing platform like MailChimp or Constant Contact, the cost of sending 10,000 targeted emails per month is typically between $200 and $400. For SMS using platforms like Twilio or SimpleTexting, the cost per 10,000 SMS messages will typically cost between $500 and $2000 depending on your plan and other variables.

5. **Social media and influencer:** Companies are now improving their use of community management on social media and leveraging micro and celebrity influencers to significant

effect for their companies. Social media now allows the brand storytellers and company storytellers to have a near continuous dialogue with their community and key stakeholders. Companies that effectively use social and influencer can create an incredibly loyal user base. Social Media is used as an engagement tool and also captive marketing platform. Influencers can be used for information and brand building, but they can also be used for targeted campaigns for various products or other key elements. Some of the most effective launches in marketing leverage influencer marketing to ensure that the company's message reaches all of the potential target audiences.

A subset of this is referral marketing. It could be considered unique, but it relies on existing customers to influence their network to visit your website. When you do, you can provide incentives to those people for the references they provide to you.

6. **Content marketing:** Some companies may also create high-quality, engaging, and informative content that attracts and engages your target audience. These companies use that content to bring more potential consumers to their websites. The content can vary between academic articles, research reports, blog posts, videos, infographics, white papers, case studies, or more.

7. **Promotions, discounts, and incentive-based:** Finally, there is the use of discounts to potential customers. I think we all have seen the 10 to 20 percent discount that websites will provide. These are enticing offers and may end up tipping us into the decision to purchase.

In addition, companies may also use loyalty programs to reward repeat customers with exclusive discounts, freebies, or early access to new products. The final mechanism is the use contests and giveaways to encourage people to visit your website and engage with your content. I know that this category, in particular, can also be leveraged in the types of communication above. However, I specifically call it out because some marketing teams, especially when a brand is in relative decline, will leverage discounting as the primary driver of website traffic. When that happens your average basket size and average price-per-unit also declines.

Once a customer lands on the website, it is the role of the product management team and the website engineers to streamline their path to purchase. I think we have all had negative experiences where we tried to check out with a product that we wanted, but the website itself blocked us from doing so.

The teams that I have seen are much more advanced than those basic issues. At the high end of website operations, teams will conduct A/B testing to evaluate features and what enhancements yield the highest benefit to the consumer and the company. These teams will work in a continuous development schema to develop, test, and, if successful, deploy changes to websites all with an aim to improve the customer journey.

From there, website operations can become more mundane. The remainder of the operations is to ensure that the website stays up. When companies use Shopify, I believe their uptime is about 99.98 percent, based on their latest public statistics. If the company maintains their own sites, then they will typically have a large datacenter. A large number of companies leverage co-location facilities. Companies like Equinix will basically run the datacenter for the company versus managing it themselves. Others pride themselves in running their own. Others are beginning to leverage the cloud. All of these are acceptable. Depending on the required functionality of the website, the company may have concerns with latency. If so, they will deploy content across multiple larger datacenters or some have also begun to leverage edge servers—essentially micro datacenters in major municipalities that reduce latency to enhance consumer experience. In addition to the required infrastructure, these companies may also leverage a website operations center to ensure that all of the operations are up and running and streamlined. Depending on the maturity of the company, the use of advertising spend can also be a major driver of volume. Some companies deploy 24/7 management of the advertising spend to turn on the spend when needed to maintain website traffic at a constant volume or drive increased revenue. The main determinant on this spend is to ensure that the company is maintaining a positive ROI on the investment. In one company I assessed, the company was losing about $0.40 for every dollar it was spending on online advertising. The near immediate response was to reduce the spend until we could get our hands around the problem.

The variability in the capability and complexity in website operations will depend on the size and maturity of the company. Simplifying these operations is critical, as any additional expense, that is not required for the operations is a loss in profit.

The fulfillment of e-commerce can largely be outsourced. The majority of smaller companies can leverage capabilities provided through their e-commerce platform. For medium to large-scale operations, they will typically partner with a third party logistics company. There are a large number of these providers. From there, these companies will house your product and be responsible for shipping the product when the company providers a valid order to them. Distribution across the United States from one location will typically allow for four-day shipping. If the company wants better than that, then they may need to invest in two locations (e.g., Memphis and Reno). Configurations with two hubs for e-commerce fulfillment will typically be able to deliver products within two days.

For online businesses, customer service is a critical part of the brand and company experience. To ensure you have an excellent experience, the integrations between your CRM, CDP, and e-commerce solution with Zendesk or other customer service platform are important to ensure you empower the CS team with information that allows for a personalized experience that addresses the customer's issues. This is also one of the only touchpoints that customers will have with the company. Positive impressions are helpful to continue to grow the brand.

The final element to discuss is Amazon. The majority of companies, even if they have their own online presence, may decide to list their products on Amazon. If they do, they should have a dedicated team review the plans. To ensure you are at the top of the Amazon lists, the initial increment of product needs to be successful. In addition, there are some unique packaging requirements, use of a partner, if this is the company's first venture into Amazon may be warranted. If so, the company will treat the partner like a retailer. They will have a specific discount they provide to the partner and the partner will be responsible for growing sales on Amazon.

So where are the opportunities?

The majority of spend with e-commerce operations is in the advertising spend. Optimizing the advertising spend will be one of the major value creation levers. The enhanced use of the CDP and use of consumer data integration to drive targeting of advertising and improving downstream funnel conversion are critical. The use of agencies to manage the data and conduct the targeted campaigns and ensure the advertising is optimized is important.

The other area of opportunity is in the organization. In more mature companies, these organizations tend to focus on hierarchy. For younger companies, they tend to be more scrappy and aggressive. In the age of social media and voluminous data, the organizations that I have seen perform the best tend to be more scrappy and aggressive. The main focus is engagement and targeted investment. There should be two distinct sides to the organization: one focused on engagement of your stakeholders. This has a community management function and group focused on the social media presence. The second is more analytical and focused on investment of the firm's resources and operations of the website. There are partners that you can outsource both of these elements to. There are firms like Kubbco who manage a firm's social media presence and content. There are also firms that will manage the website and all of its operations (e.g., Shopify). The investment made by the company in this organization should focus on experienced professionals that can optimize the advertising spend whilst attracting as many customers to the website as possible.

The final area is on website operations. There are a lot of tactical ways to reduce this cost. The main driver is going to be the company's choice on how to host the website. As we have discussed, there are multiple options. The cloud is typically a lower cost alternative and will have all of the functionality required. For companies that want to maintain their own infrastructure, the use of colocation facilities also optimize the companies financial results. The final option is to use your own data centers. This is typically a higher cost alternative, but may be a required operating condition for some companies. If not, the other two options are preferred. It also allows management to focus on what is important in the business.

Increasing Margins through Increased Percent Sales in Direct to Consumer

This is technically a commercial excellence mechanism. However, growing your e-commerce presence and sales will improve your channel margin. The typical fully-burdened e-commerce channel margin is typically higher than that of its brick and mortar counterpart. You will typically see an increase in overall operating margin when your sales mix shifts to e-commerce. Investment to grow the organic direct-to-consumer channel typically pays dividends to the end consumer. In addition, for brands with limited reach or penetration, the use of the e-commerce channel with direct and targeted marketing can cause sales to increase exponentially.

An added benefit is that the direct-to-consumer channel allows the company to capture user data and maintain closer control over its brand, product distribution, and customer experience. With the improved data capture and advanced analytics mapped with demographic and consumer data, you can effectively target your customers and identify the highest value customers. This improved consumer understanding then allows you to improve your digital media spend return on investment enabling better targeting for down funnel (closer to actual sale) prospects and consumers.

Increasing the use of social media influencers can also improve your reach. There is a debate on whether to use brand names or a number of microinfluencers. From a cost efficiency perspective, the micro-influencers are more effective and can generate as much, if not more, pop in sales. Larger personalities are more expensive and may not be as effective. The other concern with large personalities lifting brands is the linkage of the brand with the person. People can fail or have a bad day. These public relation issues can sink a brand. There is nothing that can bankrupt a company quicker than a celebrity brand where the celebrity gets caught in a scandal or a company that has a CEO with a #Metoo issue.

Coverage Based Services and On-Site Service Delivery Models (Typically Consumer)

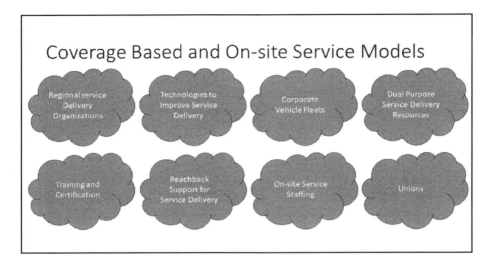

The next two sections focus on service delivery. I have segmented these across an axis focused on the price point of the resourcing to support the service delivery. The reason why is that from a business operations framework perspective, in one category you are dealing with a coverage and replacement issue. On the other, you are focused on finding, improving, and retaining key talent and capabilities to service the client. This view will become clearer as we dive into these next two sections.

For coverage and on-site services, the goal is to provide adequate service to the identified coverage areas or sites with as few resources as needed. In addition, these businesses typically provide services that require physical labor. To support, the company will typically have a training infrastructure, a regional or coverage based management structure, systems or teams to maximize scheduling and routing, and backend dedicated technical support for the service specialists. In this section, I will also discuss unions and some specific considerations when working with companies in heavily unionized industries, like service industries. For on-site service industries, you can leverage a lot of this framework for everything from hospitality and restaurants to hospitals. For services that require large geographic coverage, the firms will also typically have a fleet of vehicles and the associated infrastructure to support them.

One thing you will notice is that I did not highlight a specific need for a highly specialized HR department or specific recruitment requirements. This is one of the main differentiators to the talent-based services model. In this model, there is typically some turnover in the service personnel, but these tend to be steady jobs that should be focused on the delivery of value to the end customer. In some jurisdictions these roles are highly unionized. Because of the limitations with union resources, you may also see a large number of contractors that service some of the demand.

These resources and the contractor supplements are typically organized in a highly scaled organization. The average manager will manage somewhere between 15 and 25 independent service delivery resources. The need for management in this is more about the fair allocation of work packages amongst the team. Oftentimes, there is discrepancy in the allocation of jobs amongst the various team members. Typically there is a preference for easier schedules given to the resources with higher tenure. One system that I have seen work well is for the various jobs to be numerically rated on a scale of complexity. With the easiest installation being a 1 and a highly complex troubleshoot and repair being a 4. In order to ensure equal distribution of the jobs, each employee had to receive a certain number of credits each day—let's say that the quota each day was six. Therefore a team member could do six easy installs or they would have one troubleshoot and repair and two easy installs. The allocation would still be up to the manager to leverage those with the best skills for each task.

The service delivery team has reporting metrics and also monitors customer satisfaction. These are typically easy data manipulations or automated dashboards based on systems utilized by the business. In addition, the service delivery management team will typically have a software package that helps efficiently route their resources between the various jobs. UPS uses a proprietary system called On-Road Integrated Optimization and Navigation (ORION). From this system, UPS drivers are directed to each of their delivery with a high level of precision and only taking right turns. There are a number of route optimization packages that firms will use. These packages are highly valuable as it improves the windshield efficiency of the service delivery professional and when integrated with CRM and others can provide an excellent customer experience to know when professionals will be at a given service delivery location.

Because of the geographic nature of service delivery, these businesses will also typically maintain a fleet of vehicles. Companies will make an economic decision on whether to lease or buy the vehicles for their fleet. As a note, when the company buys the vehicles, on average, they can achieve a more efficient cost structure over time versus the leased vehicles. The company would also need to invest to ensure that the vehicles are properly maintained. Each of these services can easily be outsourced with partners in the company's geography. The benefit for leasing vehicles is to maintain a newer fleet and allow for variety. If you are seeking an efficient cost structure this may not be the best option. If the company decided to own its own garage to service the vehicles, this can be a cost-effective measure with sufficient volume in a small enough geographic area.

For instance, Verizon's fleet is managed by a dedicated team of fleet managers and technicians who oversee vehicle maintenance, repair, and replacement, as well as driver training and safety programs. The company uses advanced technology and data analytics to optimize its fleet operations, including route planning and scheduling, fuel management, and vehicle performance monitoring. With sufficient size, this can be a significant cost saver and creator of value for a given company. If run inefficiently or without sufficient aggregated demand, the company may be better served outsourcing this service.

In some situations these field resources also perform some elements of the sales for the company. For instance, field reps in the cosmetics industry engage with store level representatives to help drum up demand in the given store and inform store employees about the merits of their newest products. In addition, they also ensure Presentation quantities are in place and in some instances will aid in the sale to customers while they are in the store. Their goal being to upsell and cross-sell the customer on their product portfolio. When the service resources serve a dual purpose, like sales, their compensation, or other incentives that management puts in place should also ensure that they are rewarded for that secondary behavior.

These resources also need to be trained and have the appropriate certifications to conduct the required work. HR will typically have an onboarding training plan for these professionals to ensure they are trained on the latest systems and configurations. When there is new technology, they are also trained on those new systems and technologies to ensure they are properly prepared and efficient in the execution of their assignments. The results of this training and their certifications are typically aggregated in an HR system. These systems can and should be integrated into the work management software and control systems. This ensures that you have the right professionals with the right training doing jobs they are qualified to perform.

Also, with large distributed systems that are being maintained, these companies may have a prompt, service deliver professional dedicated support team. For instance, in the telecommunications space, there is typically an operational network infrastructure team. Some elements of that team work in a centralized office that helps oversee network operations. Their job is to take calls from service personnel to activate circuits and support field troubleshooting efforts. These resources improve the efficiency of the field team and are a required element of the larger operations delivery team to support a large dispersed service network.

On-site operations are similar in a lot of regards to this model. The biggest difference is that the customer typically comes to you for an experience. These teams are likely more robustly staffed and focused on customer care – for instance in the hospitality sector. In general, the problem is still the same. You need adequate team members to support the operation of the facility and deliver the services required. In general, the staffing will be highly dependent on the services being delivered. Typical managerial cover ratios can easily be 15 to 25 people per manager, similar to the field. If highly focused customer care, those ratios may need to be closer to 15 to 1.

Similar to retail, the largest variable for on-site services will be staffing levels. For some, like an amusement park, the staffing needs may be seasonal, similar to the retail example. In either of these situations the scheduling and staffing will likely fall onto the manager of the given function or area of coverage within the operation.

Finally, we will discuss unions. Unions are a great service to the economy. They help the common worker, through collective bargaining, achieve more than fair outcomes with company management teams. When dealing with unions, all communications should be managed through a lawyer. In addition, you cannot discuss or plan major force reductions of union employees without the cognizance of the union leadership. As such, it is important that all discussions regarding unions be handled appropriately. All union contracts are different and it is best to have your legal team or legal advisors actively involved in any discussions associated with them.

A study by the Economic Policy Institute indicated that Union employees wage rate is typically 13.2 percent higher than a non-union employee.[19] In addition, they typically have better access to healthcare and retirement benefits. To put this in perspective, 94 percent of union employees have retirement and healthcare benefits. Whereas only about 68 percent of non-union workers have the same benefits according to the Bureau of Labor Statistics. In practice, I have seen a difference in the total resource burden of about 25 to 40 percent in the United States between a union and non-union resource.

So how we optimize service delivery?

The largest driver of value is the utilization of the individual resources. Typically, you want your utilization of these resources, when you remove their vacation time to be about 85 to 90 percent. This includes time for training and other administrative tasks. When you see other items impinging on their ability to hit this number, then they you should seek to remove them. In addition, if you see too many staff, then there is opportunity to reduce the total number of resources. Because of potential union implications, you would need to closely review any collective bargaining agreements.

Another efficacy measure is to minimize the amount of windshield time of distributed service teams. This can be done in several methods. First, for hard-to-reach service destinations, you can establish extended partner networks that allow you to prevent having one of your team

19   Valerie Wilson and William M. Rodgers III, "Black-White Wage Gaps Expand with Rising Wage Inequality," Economic Policy Institute, September 20, 2016, www.epi.org/publication/black-white-wage-gaps-expand-with-rising-wage-inequality/.

members' travel to those locations. We have already discussed the use of route optimization and other technologies that improve the downtime between jobs for your teams.

Another method is to try to make some of the basic services DIY for the consumers. For instance, installing a new router can be done by the consumer in most instances. This eliminates some of the need for the service resources and allows you to utilize them for the requirements that require someone to actually be present. Another method is to also better leverage independent contractors. These resources may be more cost effective than some of the internal resources. If so, then using them for some of the lower value jobs or what may be allowed by your collective bargaining contracts may add value to your company.

Optimal staffing for on-site operations typically involves some element of service level changes. Some of the most common involve changes in hours of operation for the venue and demand based staffing. For instance, for a breakfast restaurant, you still do not need a full staff after 2:00 p.m. In that situation, there may be the ability to reduce staffing after a certain point in the morning when the demand wanes. For other companies, it may also be possible to adjust business hours—for instance, shutting down the restaurant after noon or 2:00 p.m. for a breakfast restaurant.

For fleet based services, contract negotiations with leased vehicle providers can sometimes yield benefits and reduced costing for the same service. Also, you should look at how long the company is holding the leased vehicles. Typical contract length is between 24 and 48 months. However, these contracts can go out to about five years. At the tail end of the contract, there may be maintenance obligations the company incurs. As such, you need to assess the types of vehicles and the typical cost to extend the lease any further.

Typically, owned vehicle fleets are the most cost effective when the company provides a car. To be cost effective, you typically need to own the vehicle for at least four to five years. However, if properly maintained, vehicles can remain in service for between 10 and 15 years, allowing the company to profit on the value of the car outside of year five. In the U.S., the average age of an owned vehicle is about seven to eight years.

If the company does need to provide a car, but the job still requires frequent travel in local regions, a monthly stipend for the car and payment for gas associated with business travel is also a cost effective method.

Training costs can also be optimized. Depending on the volume of the training, there are times where it may be beneficial to outsource the training versus maintaining in-house training resources. These options will typically allow you to develop the content, but then have professional trainers deliver the training. In addition, I have seen effective use of prior employees to do this where they are no longer at the company, but can provide these services on an ad hoc basis. They will often have some following at the company, as well, and be a credible source for the training.

Talent Based Services (Typically B2B)

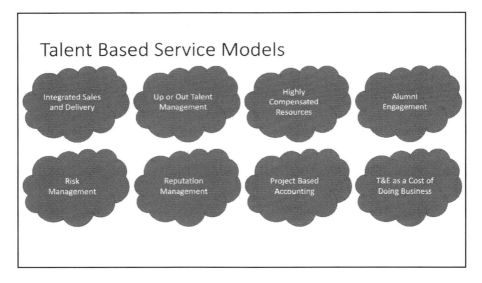

Unlike coverage based service models, talent based service models are focused on selecting the right person with the best talent at senior levels and growing more trained professionals at lower tiers. In addition, its sales force is largely its service delivery arm—e.g., its partners or managing directors are typically responsible for driving business and then delivering the service to the end client. Other unique elements tend to be an increased focus on risk management, reputation management, talent management to include training, up or out progression (typically), and travel and expense management, and risk sharing compensation models. In addition, because of the unique nature of the firms, these firms will also maintain active alumni engagement models.

To support this model, the company's main product is human capital. The majority of their "product" will be developed in house through an apprenticeship and training regime. These companies will typically have a very robust talent selection process. Some of the top programs will walk potential candidates through simulated cases and test their technical knowledge. In addition, cultural fit and external relationships will also often times dictate outcomes for the talent selection.

Once people are selected for these organizations, there is a rigorous talent review process and training curriculum. These programs review the quality of the performance and also ensure that the talent is ready for the next task that the company can ask them to do. These resources are critical and often times a draw for the talent that often times seeks additional development. The on-the-job training that they receive from their leadership teams is also pivotal to their long-term success in this industry.

The talent, as it grows in the organization is typically subjected to an up or out policy at the top tier firms. Other firms in the industry may or may not leverage similar policies. This ensures that the talent that reaches the top is the best performers in the organization. An up or out policy is where a firm puts its professionals in a review system where they need to be promoted every two to three years. If they do not reach that next milestone or promotion, then they have them leave the firm. Typically, these structure off-ramps are assisted exits and the firms actually help the employees land another opportunity.

Another element of these firms is the typically have an active alumni engagement function. This is a critical element of their success. Maintaining an active alumni engagement network serves several purposes such as serving as a low cost business development opportunity, act as a known pool of talent that could reassimilate into the firm, leverage the extended knowledge base for collaboration and sharing, leverage the success of their alumni as enhancements to their brand perception, and leverage it to improve professional development for the firm. Although the ROI can be hard to quantify, the use of these networks and their benefits can be tangibly felt in the companies that deploy them.

These leaders are also the sales force in this industry. Typically, the sales process is based on relationships and knowing certain individuals and their capabilities. Because of the nature of the sale, it requires investment in the people and marketing to ensure that the market understands a given person's capabilities and what they offer to their clients.

Additionally, retention and higher than average pay is a key element of the business model. The professionals in these businesses are typically compensated more than their corporate peers. For instance, it is not uncommon for partners at larger talent-based service companies to make more than $1 million per year. The average cost per resource can vary wildly based on skillset. On average, the these companies have a profit margin before bonuses and benefits of about 90 percent based on publicly available information on the Big Four.

Seniority	Base Salary	Base Fee	Profit Margin (before Bonuses and Burden)
Junior Consultant	$60 to 80k	$400k to $1m ($200 to 500 per hour)	85% to 92%
Experienced Consultant	$80 to 120k	$600k to $1.6m ($300 to $800 per hour)	87% to 92.5%
Senior Consultants	$100 to 180k	$1m to $2.4m ($500 to $1,200 per hour)	90% to 92.5%
Directors/Partners	$200 to 500k	$1.6m to $4.0m ($800 to $2,000 per hour)	~87%
Assumes a 2,000 hr work year – 40 hrs @50 weeks; Estimates based on public information for Big-4 firms			

In the delivery of the service, the key to profitability is the utilization of the resources. In general, these resources, net of their annual leave and training, should be close to 100 percent utilized. The staffing management team in these industries should ensure that to be the case. The other consideration for the staffing members is to ensure that the resource is receiving adequate diversity or concentration of experience as is appropriate for their role and tenure.

These businesses rely on reputation, perception and managing the risk associated with their service delivery. This requires them to have larger than typical risk management departments. In particular, the audit-based firms will have a large risk management department to ensure they meet the requirements of the regulated elements of their business and ensure they do not have conflicts of interest.

These firms will also typically have highly empowered contract management teams to ensure that the firm does not enter into engagements with significant risk. For instance, a top tier strategy firm had a few recent incidents where their contract and risk management processes failed.

Here are two of them and the ramifications:

Opioid crisis involvement: The advisory firm faced scrutiny for its work with Purdue Pharma, the maker of OxyContin, which has been widely blamed for its role in the opioid crisis in the United States. The firm's consulting services were alleged to have helped Purdue Pharma boost sales of OxyContin, even as the opioid epidemic worsened. In response to the backlash, They reached a $573 million settlement with 47 U.S. states, the District of Columbia, and five territories in February 2021.

Saudi Arabia's crackdown on dissidents: Several firms were criticized for a 2018 report that identified influential critics of the Saudi government's policies on social media. The *New York Times* reported that at least one person named in the report was later arrested, raising concerns about the firms' role in the Saudi government's crackdown on dissent.[20]

These are major issues for advisory firms as it begins to erode client's confidence in the credibility of the platform. A proper review of risk would allow firms to avoid issues like this by not taking on the project or limiting their involvement.

The marketing function and reputation management for the firm is also critical. The modern talent services firm is now also a printing press. These firms publish and create knowledge for the world to consume. These publications and productions are part of enhancing the firm's reach and serve as content marketing to draw in potential buyers.

The last unique element of these firms is that they typically have a lot of travel and other expenses associated with them. To ensure that this is covered, the organizations will typically have larger than anticipated travel and expense teams that oversee the use of company funds and the reimbursement of their employees. They will also have established discounts with all of the major providers such as the various airlines, hotel chains, and rental car purveyors.

Another unique element is that their profitability is project based. The ERPs that they leverage will track a lot of the work through project codes. This is a unique element and something to consider as you review firm or business line profitability. In addition, the sales executives have different value propositions. Some are more successful at full margin than others, when assessing

---

20 Michael Forsythe, Mark Mazzetti, Ben Hubbard, and Walt Bogdanich, "Consulting Firms Keep Lucrative Saudi Alliance, Shaping Crown Prince's Vision," *New York Times*, November 4, 2018, www.nytimes.com/2018/11/04/world/middleeast/mckinsey-bcg-booz-allen-saudi-khashoggi.html; Michael Forsythe and Walt Bodganich, "McKinsey Settles for Nearly $600 Million Over Role in Opioid Crisis," *New York Times*, February 3, 2021, www.nytimes.com/2021/02/03/business/mckinsey-opioids-settlement.html.

performance total sales and profit margin per project are both important.

So where are the opportunities?

Utilization is the largest driver of opportunity in these companies. The company is in the business of human capital, maintaining a utilization rate above 90 percent on the resources (net of vacation and training) is in the best interest of the company. If lower, enhanced use of staffing software and other improvements can be considered. If you find utilization exceptionally low, the other option is to reduce the workforce size.

There are times when the back office gets too large for these organizations. Reductions in the back office typically have limited impact on the operations of the company.

Because of the heavy reliance on human capital, the majority of spend for talent based services are on people. This typically requires the companies to focus on the organization to improve efficacy.

Consumer/Industrial Fulfillment

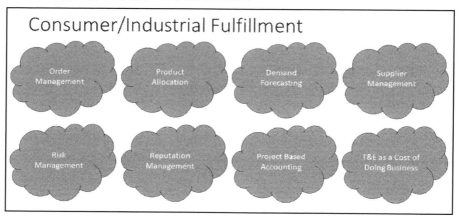

The consumer and industrial fulfillment is a relatively light chapter on unique elements of the process. In large part this was covered in the OTC process in the Accounting section of this book. So, there really is nothing truly unique, but I am covering it to be collectively exhaustive for business models.

The order to delivery process requires the consumer or industrial teams to have their customers place orders. From there, the teams will need to allocate available product to the customer. The company then partners with the end customer to deliver the product. The unique systems and processes you need to consider are the order management function, the allocation process, and the delivery of the goods. On the front-end, these companies also need excellent demand forecasting, distribution channel engagement, channel marketing, and supplier relationships to ensure that their goods continuously flow to the end consumer.

For order management, there will be a team of resources, typically a centrally managed team or automated module in the ERP with exception processing, that will process, review, update, and accept orders from the various clients. In some companies, this service is provided by the salesforce. However, it is typically most efficient when it is managed centrally. With a centrally-managed function, the order team and supply chain team can review and allocate products effectively amongst the various distribution channels and geographies.

These resources do not need to be in a high cost location. Instead, depending on the industry, these can even potentially be offshored. At a minimum, they should be in a lower cost center of excellence to improve efficacy.

The core of this process is a precalculated allocation matrix by customer. This allocation matrix provided to the centrally managed team at a SKU level shows how many of each product can be provided to each customer. To conduct this calculation, the finance or supply team will take into account the on hand inventory and any potential freshness or quality hold issues. As long as the customer asks for quantity within the limits of the allocation matrix, the order goes through. If not, then the order needs to be handled as an exception with the customer potentially receiving less than they requested. This process needs to be communicated with the sales team and the end customer.

Typically, these companies will also have an external operations or manufacturing oversight function. These resources have deep relationships with the supplier base. When issues arise or there are production issues, these resources work with the supplier in question to resolve the issues. In emergencies, they will also negotiate with the supplier to get the products into production when the space on the line has already been booked.

Quality assurance checks also need to occur on the product. This can happen in two different ways (or some hybrid approach). The most cost-efficient way is for the suppliers to conduct the QA. This requires the external operations team and the QA team to also provide oversight over the quality of the products once in receipt. They also need to qualify the suppliers to conduct the QA on the company's behalf. The second option is to have the internal teams do the QA upon receipt. This is burdensome, but it is the typical solution companies deploy when they want to have the highest levels of quality assurance. This policy requires internal teams to conduct a sample or 100 percent audit of the product upon receipt in your warehouse. If deficiencies are noted, the product needs to be placed in a QI hold pending resolution. This can take hours, weeks, or months, depending on the issue, the company's processes, and the speed by which the company can make decisions.

Following this, the orders are sent or (if internal) released to the distribution warehouse. I will cover logistics operations in detail in the logistics section of the book. The ERP from the company will interface with a warehouse management system (WMS). The WMS will take the orders from the ERP and create pick tickets for the warehouse. The warehouse will then fill the order and prepare for pickup or ship the product to the end customer. Various companies and industries will have a different methodology for who is responsible for what.

With increasing cross border, the other key elements to consider are the international commercial terms (INCOTERMS). Within the given commercial contract, this dictates where the goods will transfer custody (and risk) and who will be responsible for what elements of the delivery costs. The chart below from the Nigerian Economic Promotion Council provides a summary of the various terms:[21]

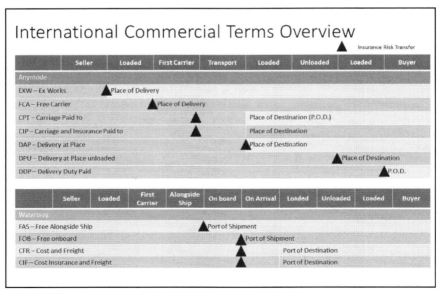

21 "The International Export Trade Terms," INCOTERMS—Basis for a Successful Export Contract, January 24, 2022, nepc.gov.ng/cms/wp-content/uploads/2022/01/INCOTERMS-II.pdf.

The two most common is Ex Works and delivered at place (DAP). In Ex Works, risk and custody transfers once the seller delivers it to the loading dock. For Delivered at Place, the risk and custody never transfers until it is received by the customer. If you are selling, you typically want to maintain contracts Ex Works. For buyers, it is better for DAP. Please note, DAP just shifts the cost burden to the seller, but likely also increases your price of acquisition. In general, this cost difference can be between 4 and 10% of the value of the good. Please note INCOTERMS change from time to time. At the time of writing this book, the most up to date terms were aligned in 2020. The concepts of incoterms (although not really applicable are also used in domestic discussions. For instance, a shipment from Florida to Pennsylvania may still be discussed as Ex Works or DAP, depending on who pays for what portion of the shipment and when custody transfers.

For forecasting, consumer forecasting is highly variable and is a complex, cross-functional process. There are inputs from marketing, supply chain, and finance, with each sometimes creating their own independent forecast. Below I have provided a high level example of the key functions and roles that they play in developing the demand forecast. The individual steps and responsible parties may vary based on the company and specific needs of the organization.

Description	Key Meetings	Key Outcomes
Collect data	The finance team gathers historical sales data, market trends, and other relevant information.	Finance team meeting
Analyze data	The marketing team analyzes the data to identify trends, patterns, and other insights that can be used to forecast future demand.	Marketing team meeting
Develop forecasts	The sales and supply chain teams use the insights and data provided by the marketing team to develop demand forecasts for each product and SKU.	Sales and supply chain team meeting

Review forecasts	The finance team reviews the forecasts to ensure they are financially feasible and aligned with the company's overall financial goals.	Finance team meeting
Finalize forecasts	The sales and supply chain teams finalize the demand forecasts, incorporating any feedback or revisions from other teams.	Cross-functional team meeting
Initiate ordering and production	The supply chain team uses the demand forecasts to plan production, inventory levels, and distribution to ensure that the company is able to meet. demand.	Supply chain team meeting
Monthly performance monitoring	The finance, marketing, sales, and supply chain teams monitor actual sales performance against the forecasts and adjust plans as needed.	Cross-functional team meeting

For industrial fulfillment, the primary difference is the availability of the product at time of order. For industrial fulfillment, typically the orders are taken by the salesforce. The order complexity tends to be higher and may involve significant customization. If so, then it may also be a consultative sale. From there, the product is manufactured. It is then sent to the customer based on the aligned delivery terms.

Industrial forecasting is similar to the consumer products chart above. One benefit for industrial companies is that the sales cycle is typically longer and can provide better visibility into the potential purchases. For more in-demand products, industrial companies may also have a production backlog. In these instances, the forecasting process above looks at that and takes that into account as well.

So where are the opportunities?

The largest opportunity is in demand forecasting in most of these companies. Demand forecasts are highly variable. Experienced teams do not always predict required product volumes consistently. You will want to understand inventory turns to understand more about this. The use of enhanced MRP systems such as Blue Yonder are helpful. These programs apply some elements of machine learning to determine optimal demand and ordering volumes. Incorporating them into the future state design of the process is beneficial.

For allocation, you can also improve this depending on your ability to fill. Typical fill is never 100 percent of the demand. If there are accounts that are strategic priorities, always ensure those are filled. For the next tranche, you should also seek to ensure that you fill the highest margin customers next With the lowest margin customers (net of strategic priority customers) to be filled with the lowest priority.

Another area of opportunity can potentially be the not-for-sale/demo quantities in a company. The company should seek to limit the amount of inventory that is provided at a discounted price point for demonstration or for promotional activity. The volume should definitely be less than 10 percent of the overall quantity and as close to zero as reasonably practicable. The discount on these items can range from 100 percent (given free) or close to cost of production, typically a 10 to 30 percent discount off of wholesale, depending on initial wholesale discount and cost of production.

Another area to review is incoterms. Incoterms tend to be driven by industry norms and benchmarks. These are also regional. When reviewing distribution contracts, the management teams should seek to remove as much risk from the operations and economics as possible. Typically shipping can be around 4 to 10 percent of the price of the product for a scaled business. Shifting to Ex Works has the ability to shift that cost to the customer. If your contracts are all currently DAP/DDP, I would not expect discussions with establish customers to shift to Ex Works overnight without some offset. However, when you are establishing new relationships, this is a key point to consider. The other are FX rates. Sometimes, you can gain advantage in FX. However, you are betting that you understand the foreign currency markets than your customer or supplier.

In quality assurance, you can also seek to shift more of that burden to the suppliers. This can reduce internal staffing requirements. You do have to monitor the potential for increased costs. If you seek to do this, there may or may not be a positive impact on the P&L if negotiated poorly.

Another key area to review is the order management team. Ensuring that the teams are adequately staffed and in a lower cost jurisdiction are beneficial to gaining operating leverage for the enterprise. Depending on the complexity and required customer experience, they can also be offshored.

External operations team can be in an on-shore lower cost jurisdiction, or even remote. The key is that they are able to visit and work with your key suppliers. These resources should be able to visit each of the suppliers on a routine basis and discuss the status of the work in flight.

Capital Construction, Infrastructure, and Leasing

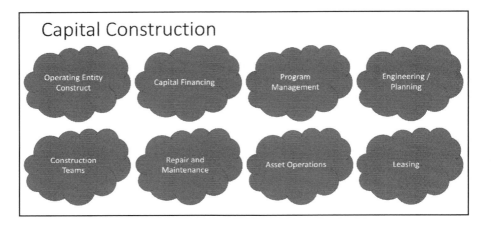

Capital construction and infrastructure are a project and discrete asset business model. The company is typically structured with a holding company and the various assets having a separate legal entity. Companies may choose to group assets, but often times there are specific incentives associated with the various assets.

A typical construct in the electricity production space is to have an operating generation company (an OpGenCo) for each of their assets. These companies will typically house the assets and operations of each of the facilities that produce electricity. The main reasons to have these assets set aside in this manner is that:

1. It ensures focus on the proper operation and profitability of each of the assets. This creates a level of transparency and accountability that can be masked in other constructs.

2. It creates tremendous flexibility in the management of the overall portfolio management for the holding company. The sale of these assets is much easier when you have a dedicated legal entity with all of the IP and assets already captured in the entity.

3. By separating them, there is also a method to reduce the cross asset and parent company liability. These same rationales apply across the majority of large capital asset programs and the industry.

Some of the organizational constructs will be applicable for other companies. The best example will be the program or project management construct. This is vital to the success of the capital construction element of these businesses. The same philosophies and constructs will be applicable. However, in this industry success and leadership is based on being able to profitability deliver programs and projects. The aerospace and defense business also has this program delivery mindset. A large number of their senior corporate leaders come from line management of the individual programs.

So, what are the unique capabilities in these industries? Here are the unique and high focus areas of these businesses: capital financing, program management and delivery, engineering/construction planning, construction teams, repair and maintenance teams, and decommissioning withhold and expense management.

Capital financing: This function, typically kept in the holding company or investor level focuses on approving and funding the capital projects. They will maintain relationships within the government, investment community, and with financiers. There main focus is to assess the financial feasibility of the project, work with management and knowledgeable resources to develop budgets, and then work with the pool of investors to secure the required funding. Because of the long-term nature of these assets, the investors focus on a very tight operational budget. They also take into account the demographic and macro shifts that may occur to best understand the value that this long-lived asset can bring.

Funding for these large, cash flow negative projects during the build period carry a unique profile and may vary in concept depending on the type of investment it is. The key here is that the investors are betting on the delivery of the project and the long-term payback of the capital asset. Some of these assets have long duration loans because of the nature of the asset.

Financing capital assets during the construction period can involve a combination of loans and bonds, equity financing through investor contributions, and government grants or subsidies. During the construction phase, projects are typically financed through construction loans, which are interest-only loans that convert to long-term loans upon completion. These loans are usually disbursed in stages, based on the progress of the project.

In public-private partnerships (PPPs), private companies may take on some or all of the financing, construction, and operational responsibilities in exchange for a share of the revenues generated by the project. In these cases, the public sector may provide financial support in the form of grants or subsidies, or by guaranteeing a minimum revenue stream for the project.

During the operational phase of the asset, the asset generates revenue through leasing or other income streams, which are used to repay the loans and provide returns to equity investors. The cost of ongoing maintenance and repairs is typically borne by the asset owner, while tenants may be responsible for some maintenance costs, depending on the terms of their lease agreements.

Engineering/planning: The other unique element you will typically find in these businesses is a dedicated engineering and planning function. This function conducts the design, planning, and supports gaining approval for the design through any regulatory agency. They develop detailed plans, blueprints, and specifications that the construction teams will implement. The team will also need to ensure that their plans meet all relevant codes, standards, and regulations. Depending on the nature of the capital asset, the teams will typically consist of architects, civil engineers, and other professionals. For instance, for the telecommunications industry, the team may rely more heavily on electrical and signal engineers where the civil or mechanical engineering elements of the business may be more commoditized. Some of the capabilities of this team can be offshore. In addition, it can also be outsourced or the team can leverage a vast network of partners. It is critical to get the detailed plans on capital assets right.

A failed example is the Hubble Space Telescope. When it was launched in 1990, the telescope was initially plagued by a design flaw in its primary mirror, which resulted in distorted images. This required the first of several servicing missions by NASA, involving astronauts performing repairs and maintenance in space. Although not a typical infrastructure project, the Hubble Space Telescope serves as an example of how design flaws can lead to extensive shutdowns and expensive repairs. In addition, it also highlights that some elements of the design are so critical that additional layers of oversight and even external validation may be warranted before final design acceptance.

Because of the longevity of the assets, the engineers and planners will also focus on engineering down the lifetime cost of ownership (LTC). Minor changes to the design can reduce overall cost significantly. When designing long lived assets, the cost of the construction and cost of the lifetime gets locked in relatively quickly with about 70 percent of the lifetime cost locked in at the conceptual design phase and about 95 percent locked in at the completion of the detailed design. Being able to influence and make changes that do not impact the operational attributes is important to ensure longer term profitability.

The Washington, D.C. Metrorail system is a great example of poor lifetime engineering. The system began operation in 1976 and has been faced with numerous safety and maintenance issues due to design flaws and poor planning. Chief among the issues include inadequate ventilation, water infiltration, and electrical system issues that have led to several accidents and service disruptions. In 2016, the entire Metrorail system was shut down for 29 hours for emergency safety inspections, and the subsequent "SafeTrack" program required extensive partial shutdowns and single-tracking to address maintenance backlogs.

The engineering and planning team will also be a key resource to the program management team when issues arise with the plans as designed. Often in construction and capital asset construction, there will be issues or changes that are required. These teams will support the program delivery by identifying what is or is not acceptable and issuing approved changes during the construction phase. During operations, these teams will also be the central point for the repair and maintenance teams when there are key issues that cannot be resolved in the field.

Program management: Once a program is approved, the company will typically appoint a lead program manager. This function is responsible across the entirety of the lifecycle of the program for the delivery of the capital asset or other key deliverable. Typically, a program management office will be established. On average, companies will have a PM resource for every $5 million to $15 million in capital outlay. For instance a $50 million program may have anywhere between about four and 10 dedicated program management resources. This large variance is driven by the complexity of the project. For instance, a highly technical program with expensive equipment with limited schedule interlocks may only require one program resource. However, a program of the same size may need more if the complexity is significantly higher or the program is on an exceptionally tight timeline.

These resources manage and are responsible for the budget, timeline, and quality delivery of the program. On a day-to-day basis, they will also manage the resources, schedule, and coordinate issue resolution with the required elements of the larger construction team. Given the central and critical role these resources have, the team is highly empowered to ensure the company can deliver the asset as designed.

Construction teams: These are the resources that actually conduct the work to construct or implement the capital assets. Depending on the capabilities of the firm, this function may be fully outsourced or done through partnerships. For companies that operate capital assets, you will typically find some internal construction teams for minor or routine projects. However, it is often better to outsource this capability to companies that regularly construct the capital assets like Gilbane Company, J.E. Dunn, or others. These businesses can be global, but also regionally focused given the equipment and relationships they require to construct the assets.

These teams or partners will conduct site preparation, procure materials, and conduct the assembly of the infrastructure or capital asset. They work closely with engineering and program management to ensure the project is built according to plans and specifications. Picking the right partner and ensuring appropriate quality inspection points is critical. If not monitored, it can cause significant issues upon delivery.

An example of poor execution is San Francisco-Oakland Bay Bridge. The eastern span of the Bay Bridge in California, completed in 2013, suffered from several design and construction issues, including faulty welds and corrosion-prone steel rods. As a result, the bridge required multiple closures for inspection and repairs, causing disruptions to traffic and increasing maintenance costs.

Once the program is delivered, it will go through required testing or quality review. It will then have a grand opening and then enter operations. That is a key shift as the program is delivered and then is shifted into operation. Once in operation, the main teams will be the in house construction team, the repair and maintenance teams, and the asset operations and leasing function. Once in place, the asset is not likely to undergo major overhauls for some time. The majority of the other functions are not required, with the exception of some of the engineers and planners that are familiar with the program.

Asset operations and leasing: This function manages the operation of the completed infrastructure or capital asset. The main function is the oversight of the asset. This will be a smaller and efficient team that coordinates the monitoring of the asset, the operational availability of the asset, manages and schedules the repair and maintenance of the asset, collects the revenue from the asset, and conducts the operations of the asset. The operations of the asset will vary based on the asset itself. A ship needs to be driven, a space telescope needs to be targeted, a telecommunications network needs to be monitored. Because these assets tend to be in service 24/7, the operations also tend to be 24/7 in nature with rotating shifts of people. In general three shifts are used: mornings, swing, and mids. Mornings (6:00 a.m. to 2:00 p.m.), swings (2:00 p.m. to 10:00 p.m.), and mids (10:00 p.m. to 6:00 a.m.). The actual times may vary, but in general each shift is eight hours. There are times when resources are asked to stay later or work earlier for overtime pay.

The other critical function is the revenue collection. Because of the nature of the assets, these are typically a tolling or leasing arrangement. However, they can also be used in a pay-per-use or volumetric mechanism. For instance in the oil and gas industry pipelines use a volumetric allocation system with their customers. However, a toll road uses a toll collected from each vehicle using the asset.

Because of the longevity of the asset, the companies tend to maintain an operational excellence culture. This culture results in a number of minor fact-findings to ensure there is understanding of the root causes of the issues when things do not go well. These fact-findings help the management team discuss the issue or incident and then work with the teams to gain a better understanding of why the issues arose. Sometimes these issues can be because of the asset itself and those issues need to be corrected through repairs. Other times, the issues are with the operational teams. When this is the case, it may make sense to ensure that the operational team is properly trained on the issue to prevent recurrence.

Another element of these operational teams is that they tend to be large and hierarchical. The nature of the shift work will typically cause the teams to have shift level leadership controlling the operations of the asset and then functional leadership that helps them grow in their specific job capability. For larger field service organizations, the organization and levers for optimization will be similar to that of the coverage based service model.

Repair and maintenance teams: Because of the longevity of the assets, the proper repair and maintenance of the asset is critical. There are two types of maintenance: preventative or prophylactic, and maintenance or corrective. Preventative maintenance focuses on inspections and routine, minor measures that elongate the lifespan of the capital asset. In consumer terms, changing out the oil in your car is preventative maintenance. Similarly, the clean and inspect of an oil filter on a large mechanical device is a required preventative maintenance item.

The other type of maintenance is repair or corrective maintenance. This is done when something on the capital asset needs to be fixed or replaced. In addition, there are some repairs or engineering updates that are required. In these situations, the engineers or planners have identified something that should be fixed proactively to prevent further issue. Depending on the severity of the issue, the issue may need to be corrected immediately. Often times, immediate corrective issues involve personnel safety or ineffective operation. Here are two examples:

1. Philadelphia Amtrak derailment (2015): After the fatal derailment of Amtrak Train 188 in Philadelphia in May 2015, the Federal Railroad Administration (FRA) required Amtrak and other railroads to implement safety measures, including installing automatic train control (ATC) or positive train control (PTC) systems. PTC systems automatically slow down or stop

trains to prevent collisions, derailments, and other accidents. Amtrak accelerated its PTC implementation schedule and completed installation throughout the Northeast Corridor by December 2015.

2. Colonial pipeline leak (2016): In September 2016, a leak in the Colonial Pipeline in Alabama resulted in the release of approximately 336,000 gallons of gasoline. The pipeline was temporarily shut down for repairs and inspections, and the company implemented corrective measures, including improvements in leak detection, pipeline integrity management, and emergency response.

However, a number of these issues do not need to be corrected immediately. They can be managed through a maintenance backlog and then worked through when conditions permit or when resources are available to conduct the maintenance. By maintaining a maintenance backlog, you can optimize the size of your R&M teams. The amount on the backlog for physical assets is less relevant than the issues actually on the backlog. Several critical issues can be a major issue whereas a large number of minor repairs like a broken light bulb may not be critical to the operation of the asset.

Depending on the type of asset, the asset may also need to conduct repair availabilities. Contrary to the name, this is when the company will specifically take down an operational asset or element of an operational asset to allow for significant maintenance events to occur. Often, these RAs are supported through a centralized large repair team or outsourced repair partners. For instance, ships will go to a shipyard where teams of trained mechanics and shipwrights will support the company's resources to repair the ship and conduct the deeper maintenance items.

The final element to consider is the decommissioning of the asset. Depending on the nature of the asset, the costs for the decommissioning are often set aside into a fund as part of the operations of the asset. For instance a nuclear facility will set aside those funds as the environmental clean up will be significant. A telecommunication asset may not need to consider a decommissioning fund because it will not likely be decommissioned just updated with newer technology and reused.

So where are the opportunities?

Use of organizational hygiene is always helpful. It usually identifies some opportunities that the management team can consider to streamline the organization. Because these are largely industrial type of operations, the spans of control—except for capital financing, engineering, and program management—can be larger with eight to 10 people per manager. For the more professional functions, they will be closer to standard at six to eight.

In the construction phase, use of outsourced planning a construction teams can create value, depending on the value proposition of the company. For a company that focuses on the operation of an asset, it would make sense to outsource as much of the upfront construction as possible, Conversely for companies focused on the construction and then sale of the capital asset.

The management of the asset itself, including maintenance, is a core function once the asset is operational. The decisions on when and which maintenance to conduct is required by the management team. Streamlining repair and maintenance can be done, but it will depend on the maintenance backlog and typical maintenance workload. Assessing job completion and relative level of complexity with the management team can yield some benefit. If the company retains a large number of resources for complex maintenance or availabilities, it may be more efficient to outsource the maintenance. Almost all maintenance activities for capital assets can be outsourced. (I caveat this because there is always a corner case). However, in general, all maintenance or technical capabilities can be done by a partner or external service provider. However, at sufficient scale, you can also insource all of these capabilities. The economic assessment for the utilization of the resource is really the litmus test. If the management can estimate that they have sufficient volume and workload to keep a permanent resource occupied and that offsets the number of maintenance items conducted by external service providers, then the permanent resource should be retained. Please remember that given the disparate locations, it is likely that the person will also need T&E to support their service model.

The maintenance backlog can also be managed for any given asset. In general, this is a management lever to manage the number of routine maintenance resources the asset needs to keep on staff.

Putting in place new improvements for the assets also works well.

There are times when new technologies will create a distinct advantage for an older asset. For instance, there are a number of new technology companies that are helping to improve waste processing operations. AMP Robotics is one such company. They are applying AI technology to improve recycling and waste processing with positive economic outcomes such as enhanced value material recapture.

The other area to assess is the operations of the asset. There are some opportunities to streamline some requirements. This allows you to reduce the required manning. Additionally, for routine monitoring there may also be the opportunity to centralize this across a number of assets or shift routine monitoring to a lower cost jurisdiction.

Land Use and Commodity Extraction

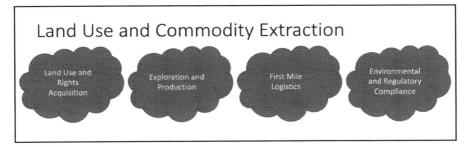

Commodity extraction businesses require several unique elements to function well. These are somewhat separate and distinct from an industrial because of the nature of the production. In general, you will find unique organizational capabilities supporting access to the resources, the organization that identifies the areas where deposits are likely, the organization that actually explores and extracts the commodity, the infrastructure to transport the commodity to the long line transportation mode, and a larger regulatory compliance organization, which is required to maintain the licensing and permission to extract from the various locales.

In general these companies are very hierarchical. They require a large amount of hands on work in person at the site of extraction. In addition, they are capital intensive. Based on industry estimates, a deepwater oil well can cost between $100 to $300 million. A deepwater well drilled to a depth of 7,000 feet in the Gulf of Mexico can cost up to about $200 million to drill and complete. To mitigate this level of investment risk, the oil companies undertake extensive geological and geophysical surveys to identify potential reservoirs and reduce the risk of a dry or unproductive well. Mineral extraction on shore investment is typically normally between a million dollars to start to tens of millions depending on the scope, scale, site and specific handling requirements.

To support these operations, there are three unique teams and capabilities that you will find in these businesses:

1. Land use rights team: These teams work with the operations team (E&P) to acquire the rights for the company to use the land for passage (right of way) or extraction based objectives. These teams will typically consist of land acquisition managers—these are the professionals that work with landowners and negotiate access to the land or acquire leases as needed to support business operations. They will be supported by legal counsel, environmental specialists, community relationship managers, and supporting systems like geospatial information systems (GIS). These systems help to manage the land use data, map land use activities, and identify potential land use conflicts.

2. Exploration and production team: This is the technical operations of the extraction company. Companies making these large capital investments go through a rigorous cross-functional process to find, test, and finally extract the commodity they seek.

    Here are the high level steps you will likely encounter when discussing these operations with companies. For this, I will leverage oil as an example commodity.

Exploration:

Geological surveys: The first step is conducting geological surveys to identify areas that may have potential for oil reserves. This can include mapping rock formations, analyzing satellite images, and studying the geology of the area. The companies will have teams of geologists and scientists that understand these formations in detail and support these operations.

Seismic surveys: Once a potential area is identified, seismic surveys are conducted to gather detailed data about the subsurface geology. This involves using sound waves to create images of the rock formations and structures deep beneath the Earth's surface. For instance for potential reservoirs in the ocean, the companies will use air guns and streamers that they tow behind seismic survey vessels. This in conjunction with ocean bottom seismometers can give a good depiction of the ocean floor geology. Use of multiple points of reference can create a 3D version of the geology and longitudinal studies create a time lapsed, 4D view of the geology providing detailed information to the exploration teams.

Exploratory drilling: If the seismic surveys indicate the presence of oil reserves, exploratory drilling is conducted to confirm the existence and quality of the oil. This involves drilling an exploratory well to extract rock samples and analyze the oil content.

Analysis and Confirmation of the Business Case

Reservoir modeling: Once the oil reserves are confirmed, reservoir modeling is conducted to estimate the size and potential production of the reserves. This involves analyzing data from the exploratory wells to build a 3D model of the subsurface reservoir.

Reservoir engineering: Reservoir engineering is used to determine the optimal methods for extracting the oil. This involves analyzing the physical properties of the reservoir, such as porosity and permeability, to develop a production plan that maximizes oil recovery.

Production

Drilling and completion: Once the production plan is developed, drilling and completion operations are conducted to construct the production wells. This involves drilling a hole into the reservoir and installing production equipment such as casing, tubing, and pumps.

Oil production: Once the production wells are completed, oil production can begin. This involves extracting the oil from the reservoir and transporting it to the surface for processing and refinement.

Production optimization: The production process is optimized over time to maximize oil recovery and reduce production costs. This can involve using advanced technologies such as hydraulic fracturing or secondary recovery techniques like water flooding.

Logistics team: This team is responsible for obtaining the necessary equipment, materials, and supplies needed to support the operations. It also manages transportation and logistics to ensure that the extracted resources are transported safely and efficiently. Some commodities such as natural gas require dedicated pipelines from the site. These pipelines can be aggregated across an entire geography simplifying logistics for the company.

Environmental and regulatory team: Another team is the environmental and regulatory team. This team is responsible for ensuring compliance with environmental and regulatory requirements. It includes environmental scientists, lawyers, and regulatory affairs personnel.

So where are the opportunities? In general, industrial and extractive businesses run relatively lean overhead structures. There are some exceptions to this such as with aerospace and defense companies, but on average are relatively lean for back office. Organizational excess typically sits in the near adjacent fields to operations such as Engineering, purchasing, procurement, field support and logistical overhead.

For operational resources, typical levers focus on optimizing the utilization of the resources. This incudes improved work planning to reduce overtime usage, improved crew manning to support operations. These methods will typically also review in totality the management of personnel for the operations of the business and labor cost management. For instance, shifting resources to a lower cost onshore location may be beneficial for some of the back office operations. In addition, use of contract personnel for some elements of the operations is beneficial to minimize management overhead and reduce overall cost burden.

The typical improvement levers are operationally focused and require knowledge of the extraction business and the operations associated with the core operation. I will discuss the methodology of how those reductions and efficiency gains occur. There are too many "eachs" to adequately represent.

Improvements in operational efficiency is one of the major drivers of value for extractive businesses, typical improvement is focused on streamlining workflows, improving equipment maintenance, reducing downtime. These reductions tend to be highly technical and require in-depth knowledge of the process. To support these types of efficiency gains, leadership will typically have external observers review operations and come to the table with a number of areas they identify. They will then work with the existing teams to workshop and refine the ideas. The initial concept stage can take two to four weeks to develop with execution and implementation over the course of three to six months. The use of lean methodologies with emphasis on maximizing asset utilization is critical. The teams will drive out downtime from the systems in place.

Analysis of the company's logistics network and routing can enhance understanding of margins and improvements to routing flows. This can yield some upside. Companies can also improve routing criteria to capture maximum margin per molecule. In addition, it can also indicate some elements of the infrastructure network that may no longer be of profitable value.

When reviewing operations, there are often times to optimize maintenance planning practices. This can reduce the overall repair and maintenance (R&M) budget.

Because of the large amount of capital spend, teams may be able to identify significant opportunity to improve margin through contract negotiations. Contracts for third party spend are a key area of improvement.

Financial Services, Credit Cards, and Investing

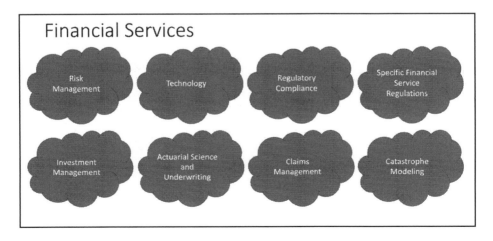

I grouped the "money" businesses into one category. The structures in each of these businesses will vary based on the final financial service being provided—accepting deposits, lending, investing, or insurance. However, there is sufficient commonality that I went with a single category of company. When you think about why this can make sense, the average bank will have the lending and investing elements under one roof with sufficient synergies that it is financially viable.

Insurance typically is not part of these company portfolios. However there are notable exceptions like USAA, PNC Bank, BB&T, and Fifth Third. The others typically use partnerships to provide these services. There are different regulations and requirements for insurance providers that can potentially create conflicts of interest with the banks. Because of this the large banks like Bank of America, Wells Fargo, and Citibank offer insurance services through partners. PNC, BB&T, and Fifth Third offer the services through a subsidiary. There are a number of reasons why this occurs. One of the largest reasons is that capital requirements for insurance companies tend to be higher than banks. This can potentially make a bank less competitive than its competitors with the same deposits if its insurance aim prevents it from deploying capital. In addition, there are differences in regulatory requirements that can cause issues with compliance.

In general, a financial services company makes its money on the spread between what it pays its depositors and what it makes on its loans, net of any defaults. What makes a financial services company successful is its ability to manage risk and to manage this risk is a reliable, systematic way. To create those systems, there are some key capabilities that are required of the business.

Risk management: Financial service companies need to be able to identify, measure, and manage different types of risks. The three major risks that need to be managed are:

1. **Credit risk:** Credit risk is the risk that a borrower will default on a loan or fail to make payments as agreed. Banks typically have credit risk management processes in place to assess the creditworthiness of borrowers, set appropriate credit limits, and monitor loan performance. These processes may involve credit scoring, financial statement analysis, and ongoing credit monitoring. For smaller banks and community banks, some of

this also leverages knowledge of the people. This, however, is not scalable and something to consider when looking at smaller banks versus larger. Can systems and processes be scaled without significant investment.

2. **Market risk:** Market risk is the risk of losses due to fluctuations in market prices or other market factors. Banks typically have market risk management processes in place to identify, measure, and manage market risk exposures. These processes may involve the use of modeling and simulation techniques to assess the potential impact of market fluctuations on the bank's portfolio.

3. **Operational risk:** Operational risk is the risk of losses due to internal processes, systems, or human error. Banks typically have operational risk management processes in place to identify, assess, and manage operational risk exposures. These processes may involve the use of internal controls, process mapping, and scenario analysis to identify potential risks and mitigate them.

To manage these and other risks within the company, the bank or financial service institution will establish risk committees that are made up of senior management and experts of the various risk concerns. These committees will ensure that issues are within the financial service firms risk tolerance. A great example of this is an investment committee. This is a committee that approves or disapproves potential investments with the bank's capital.

To support these risk assessments, the bank will employ and manage a large number of financial and risk analysts. These resources will typically be highly compensated and retained in the headquarters of the company, given the value and focus on the core of the business. The banks will also typically maintain a full complement of economists to evaluate and understand macro- and microeconomic trends that could drive the market.

To ensure objectivity, the bank will also typically maintain an internal audit department. This department reviews internal controls, risk management practices, and compliance.

Technology and data analytics: Because of the size and scale of today's financial service companies the use of a comprehensive technology stack to meet the majority of the customers needs is needed to maintain efficiency and productivity. These systems are supplemented with larger onshore and offshore teams to support the full needs of the business. The majority of the backbone of the world's commerce flows across these interconnected technology stacks. They are important for a number of reasons.

To understand the scale of just one company, in 2019, Visa's network connected 61 million merchants with 3.4 billion Visa-branded cardholders. They have a card for half of the people in the world. In addition, in 2019, the company's network processed $9 trillion in sales – equivalent to about a tenth of the world's economy.[22] Because of this scale, the networks and technology backbones need to be technically sound and handle large volumes across the globe.

In addition to the base processing of the business, the large reams of data also can provide significant insight to the needs of the consumer. The technology pared with the data and analytics of the data can lead product management teams to offer innovative products and services that better serve the customer than their competitors.

With the shift of a lot of banking online, you will also find banks having increasing numbers of product managers and larger technology teams. These resources and capabilities are building the digital products that consumers will use. In addition, the IT backbone technology also requires talented technology teams.

Regulatory compliance: Financial service companies are subject to a range of regulatory requirements, and they need to be able to comply with these requirements to avoid fines and other penalties. They need to have a strong understanding of regulatory requirements and a robust compliance program to ensure that they are operating within the rules.

Here are some of the most significant:

Capital adequacy requirements: Capital adequacy requirements are designed to ensure that banks have enough capital to absorb losses and remain solvent. Banks are required to maintain a minimum amount of capital relative to their risk-weighted assets. Banks that fail to meet

---

22 "How Visa became the Top Dog in Global Finance," *The Economist*, March 21, 2020, www. economist.com/business/2020/03/21/how-visa-became-the-top-dog-in-global-finance.

these requirements may be subject to sanctions or even forced to close down.

Liquidity requirements: Liquidity requirements are intended to ensure that banks have sufficient cash or liquid assets to meet their obligations as they become due. Banks must maintain a minimum amount of liquidity to be able to handle unforeseen events such as deposit withdrawals or market disruptions.

Anti-money laundering (AML) regulations: AML regulations are designed to prevent the use of the financial system for money laundering and terrorist financing. Banks are required to have robust AML programs in place to detect and report suspicious activity. Failure to comply with AML regulations can result in significant fines and reputational damage.

A key element of AML requirements require the banks to know your customer (KYC). This is a process that banks and other financial institutions use to verify the identity of their customer and assess the potential risk of doing business with them. KYC is a key element of the bank's anti-money laundering and counter-terrorism financing framework to prevent crimes like money laundering and the finance of terrorism.

Consumer protection regulations: Consumer protection regulations are intended to protect consumers from abusive or fraudulent practices by financial institutions. These regulations govern areas such as disclosure, marketing, and complaints handling. Non-compliance with these regulations can result in legal action, fines, and reputational damage.

Cybersecurity requirements: Cybersecurity requirements are designed to ensure that banks have adequate measures in place to protect against cyber threats. Banks must have strong cybersecurity policies and procedures, as well as a comprehensive incident response plan. Failure to comply with cybersecurity regulations can result in significant financial losses and reputational damage.

Fraud detection: Is a critical operational process in financial service companies. The capability is delivered through automated systems and manual processes and reviews. The main vehicle is through transaction monitoring. The system will automatically flag and potentially block suspicious activity. To support this, the company will create unique customer profiles based on transaction history, demographics, and other factors. These are used to identify typical behavioral patterns. That help the company identify when fraudulent activity may be occurring. In addition, manual reviews do occur to investigate suspicious activity. This may involve review of the transaction details, contacting the customer, and conducting investigations that identify the source of the fraudulent activity.

Investment management: Financial service companies that offer investment products, such as mutual funds and exchange-traded funds (ETFs), need to be able to manage investments effectively and deliver strong investment returns. They need to have strong investment management teams and processes in place to ensure that they are making informed investment decisions.

The bank itself will also have internal money managers to allocate their capital in the highest grossing securities. The capability to advise others will consist of teams of money managers. Increasingly, this capability is being automated for smaller capital investors. This will be similar to a talent based service industry.

Insurance companies need to be able to manage their investment portfolios effectively to ensure that they are generating sufficient returns to meet their obligations to policyholders. They need to have strong investment management teams and processes in place to ensure that they are making informed investment decisions.

Insurance Unique Capabilities

Insurance companies will also need some special unique capabilities dealing with the actual underwriting process for various insurance policies. Some of which may contain esoteric risks that need to be captured. In addition, Insurance companies need to look at each of the policies individually, but it also needs to assess its risk across various regions in the event of a catastrophe.

Actuarial science: Insurance companies need to have strong actuarial capabilities to assess risk, price policies, and manage claims. Actuaries use statistical modeling and data analysis to assess risk and predict future claims.

Underwriting: Insurance companies need to be able to underwrite policies effectively to ensure that they are pricing policies appropriately and minimizing the risk of claims. Underwriters assess the risk of insuring a particular individual or entity and determine the appropriate premium to charge.

Claims management: Insurance companies need to be able to manage claims effectively to ensure that they are paying claims accurately and efficiently. Claims adjusters assess claims and determine the appropriate payout based on the terms of the policy.

Catastrophe modeling: Insurance companies need to be able to assess the potential impact of natural disasters and other catastrophic events on their business. Catastrophe modelers use data and modeling to predict the potential losses that could result from a catastrophic event.

Hurricane Katrina resulted in damages of $125 billion and over 1,800 deaths in a narrowly-focused region. Exacerbating the issues with the insurance issues was that damage exceeded what was anticipated and modeled. A number of insurance companies including AIG, Allstate, State Farm, and Travelers posted significant losses due to the disaster. Subsequent to Hurricane Katrina, additional emphasis has been put on the analysis of fully burdened risk for the enterprise in the number of policies they have in a given region that could face a catastrophic event.

So where are the opportunities? The majority of these functions have highly compensated resources. Because of this, the largest opportunities will be in the organization. Typical levers such as offshore centers and lower cost onshore hubs are typical methods to create sustainable value. Additional value can be created through streamlining the organization. Organizational hygiene will trim the organization.

Process optimization is another lever in financial services. However, this is true in every organization. Looking outside in, it is hard to determine with any certainty how much value lies in process optimization.

Reviews of coverage models for customer facing roles are beneficial. There are a large number of products that can now be done wholly online with the right information systems in place to support. Digital transformation to improve methods of service delivery have been another key lever of value creation in the financial services industry. Other elements of the business that can be automated can and should given the scale of the business. Digital transformation continues to be a major source of value. Automation of document collection, archiving, and signatures are other key drivers of value, reducing the need for field resources.

Another area being deployed is robotic process automation for routine processes such as AR and AP. The use of AI, machine learning, and advanced technologies such as optical character recognition are aiding in the processing of the volume of documents required by the financial service business.

Review and elimination of brick and mortar bank branches has proved beneficial for some. With some banks being solely or almost only online. Ally Bank, Chime, USAA, Marcus by Goldman Sachs, Simple, and Varo Bank are shifting to a lighter physical footprint while still delivering the needed services to the end customer. McKinsey has estimated that the cost to serve a customer through online/digital channels can be up to 80 percent lower than serving customers through a traditional branch.

On the operational side, given the volume, even small changes to key assumptions and adjustments to risk profiles can yield significant improvements (or deterioration) in profitability. Because of the nature of the business, advanced analytics and statistical analysis are key to driving this value. Capital One has been a winner in this area with a cadre of analytic professionals driving value for their business.

Creative Businesses and IP Management

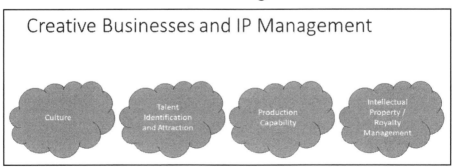

Creative companies are mainly focused on the generation of intellectual property (IP). The IP can be anything from music, art, books, or advertisements. The monetization of these assets will vary. For some, the monetization is to sell the service of production to a company that is required to market. For others, the monetization is to collect royalties off of its IP or leverage the intellectual property of others.

To support this business there are some critical capabilities required that include culture, talent identification and attraction, production capability, and intellectual property/royalty management.

Creative companies require a unique culture that promotes creativity and innovation. These types of organizations encourage employees to bring their whole selves to work enabling a culture of risk taking and sharing. This type of culture also promotes and values diversity and inclusivity. It values intellectual disagreement and constructive discussion to drive better decision-making. In addition, there is a need to promote collaboration and open communication. This allows for sharing of ideas and constructive feedback.

This is a different ethos and culture than most private equity or industry settings. Because of this, there is special care needed to drive this type of organization and culture. These cultures also work well in a very decentralized and non-hierarchical organization.

These companies also need to attract talent that provides a differentiated outcome for the various intellectual property that it needs to maintain its business. For music businesses, they need to have an organization that identifies up and coming talent. This is conducted through the artists and repertoire (A&R) department. This department leads the scouting, signing, and development of new talent, as well as managing relationships with existing artists. The team will typically consist of a number of managers and scouts that discover the new artists. They will attend live shows and build the needed relationships with musicians, producers, and other industry professionals.

Once the artists or others are onboarded there is also typically a talent management organization. The talent management organization works closely with artists to develop their careers, offering guidance and support in areas such as touring, merchandising, and branding. These representatives also act as a liaison between the artist and other industry professionals, such as booking agents, promoters, and publicists. For talent representation companies, these resources would also negotiate deals and contracts on behalf of the artist. On average, you will see companies retain one talent manager per 10 to 15 artists. However, this is a general guideline and will depend on the demands of the independent artists.

Companies will also need to develop the creative concepts and ideas. This occurs through the creative department. This is typically a cross-functional team of copywriters, designers, art directors, and creative directors that work to develop the creative concepts that meet the client or company's objectives. They will conduct brainstorming, workshops, and other ideation activities to generate breakthrough concepts. This work will be backed by research and refinement from senior management. Although this may seem unstructured, the easiest way to think of it from an analytical perspective is a block of time needed to develop the concept. For some minor concepts, it can take a few hours. For others it may take weeks or even months when a lot of refinement is required. The key is to establish a structured and efficient creative process that includes project scoping, timelines, and milestones. The management (the creative and art directors) should have a strong sense of the required timing.

Once the creative ideation process is complete, the team will leverage the various mediums needed to develop and product high quality creative assets that meet the needs of a client or the company. This process is broken down into production and post-production. During the production phase, the company develops the raw creative assets. For photography, it will go to a studio or set and take the required photographs. For a book publisher, this is the creative time for the author to write and develop their book or manuscript.

Following the production phase, there is post-production. In this phase, the company will refine the raw product. For a book, they will go through editorial review. For photography, there may be touchups and selection of the final images. The post-production phase may lead to reshoots, if absolutely necessary. Production is expensive and typically requires use of studios and photographers, which cost the company additional money.

Once developed, the company will launch the product. This is similar to the launch of a product in a CPG company. From there, the company will need to track and manage the intellectual property. In addition, it will also need to have a system in place to track the key metrics and then pay royalties to the artists.

To support this, the company will have a system that tracks and manages intellectual property rights, including copyright, trademarks, and licenses that it uses. Based on the contract, it will then pay per use or a percentage of revenue to the talent. For instance, a book author typically receives somewhere between 5 to 15 percent of gross sales of hardcover books and between 25 and 50 percent of ebooks. (Please buy my ebook.) However, if the talent is in high demand, the royalty percentages may be higher. For instance, there are some authors that have received up to about 30 percent of book sales. Per usage models are different and typically charge a nominal fee. Some radio stations have also entered into contracts with music producers that provide a share of the station's revenue for access to their music catalog.

The key is to ensure that you have clear contracts in place between the producers, publishers, and the authors, illustrators, and other content creators to outline terms and royalty payment structures.

So where are the opportunities? There are some areas that immediately can be addressed in this model that create a sustainable structural impact to the cost structure.

For talent identification, this is a function that can be accomplished through partnerships. The use of industry professionals that can identify the talent and bring them to you allows you to minimize the structural overhead for the company. This allows you to focus on the selection of the talent that meets the needs of the company.

Another area of opportunity is to assess the workload and requirements of the talent management organization. Can you increase the workload to minimize the required staffing?

For the creative direction and ideation elements, some elements of this can be outsourced. This allows the company to focus on the creative and artistic direction. The execution can potentially be contracted out to talented individuals and organizations for delivery. You can also leverage an agency that works directly with your company for the execution of the concept. This depends on the number of efforts you have running at any given point in time. In general, you just need to maintain a base level of capacity within the company and maintain relationships with a few external providers to support the remainder of your needs. When you deploy this, you will need to cap the external spend budget or the creative team will create flowback that offsets your efficiency gains. The critical element is minimizing the overhead for this function.

The other element to monitor is the director's ability to adequately assess timing for conceptual ideation and the quality of the output when delivered. This is a capacity constrained funnel, so you need to think of it similar to the backlog for product management. These teams should have a highly repeatable process to deliver consistent quality of thought on the creative concept. If not, then assessment of the process and refinement should be conducted.

Pre- and post-production are areas for the average creative service company that can be outsourced. Everything from the facility to the post-production execution can be outsourced. What some companies have done that is still highly efficient is to leverage a room or some elements of their corporate offices as a place for quick or rapid photo shoots. They will have a dedicated space with the right lighting. This helps to minimize the cost structure for shoots that do not require significant backdrops or other accoutrement. For post-production, there are a number of companies that you can outsource this process to.

For royalty management, the key metrics and sales should be tracked systematically and largely through a system that automatically calculates the royalty payments to the relevant content owners. There are a number of providers for these services and software solutions. Royalties can become very complicated to calculate if the company also packages content together, e.g., bundles. To minimize risk of incorrect calculations, a system is preferred. The goal is to always pay the author appropriately for the work they produce.

Another method to structurally reduce cost is through content buyouts. For a given author's piece of work, you can buy out the remainder of their rights to royalties. Typically, this costs somewhere between three to eight times the annual royalty fee. This can make sense depending on the type of company and provided valuation on free cash flow.

For the long-term, you should also shift your method of content acquisition to work for hire. This is where you pay the author upfront for their work on the product. The author then is not entitled for any royalties because the IP is an asset of the company. For small pieces of content, this can work. However, it may not always be best. This is something your product and talent teams can best assess.

MANUFACTURING AND SUPPLY CHAIN

The manufacturing function for a company is responsible for producing the physical good that the company markets and/or distributes. These goods can be manufactured in house or through your supply chain and contract manufacturing relationships. Because of this interplay, to speak of manufacturing without a larger discussion on supply chain is inadequate. Manufacturing itself can also be optimized, but the larger value items come from looking at the totality of how the product is delivered.

For the average company, there is not a significant amount of waste in the manufacturing processes. If a PE firm is able to get an additional 5 percent out of the manufacturing cost for the same manufactured product, that is good. Getting to 10 percent cost out for just the manufacturing operations requires there to be significant inefficiencies in the company or working to structurally improve how the products are made. To support this, we will discuss the key drivers of value for the manufacturing operations and supply chain of a company, the typical organization that supports production in a company, and the core processes to manage manufacturing.

To best understand manufacturing, you also need to start at the demand signal and controlling process for the company—the sales and operation planning (S&OP) process. I have covered some of this when we discussed consumer and industrial fulfillment, but we will re-review because it is a critical element of the

Sales and Operation Planning (S&OP)

The S&OP process is a crucial process and framework within the company to determine how much demand for the product is in the marketplace and how much supply the company can generate through its supply chain. For this, we will look at the totality of the process here— the three key elements are the demand planning process, the supply planning process, and the S&OP alignment to determine what products will be delivered and when.

As a review, here are the key steps of the demand planning process. This was covered initially in the consumer and industrial fulfillment section of the book.

Description	Key Meetings	Key Outcomes
Collect data	The finance team gathers historical sales data, market trends, and other relevant information.	Finance team meeting
Analyze data	The marketing team analyzes the data to identify trends, patterns, and other insights that can be used to forecast future demand.	Marketing team meeting
Develop forecasts	The sales and supply chain teams use the insights and data provided by the marketing team to develop demand forecasts for each product and SKU.	Sales and supply chain team meeting
Review forecasts	The finance team reviews the forecasts to ensure they are financially feasible and aligned with the company's overall financial goals.	Finance team meeting
Finalize forecasts	The sales and supply chain teams finalize the demand forecasts, incorporating any feedback or revisions from other teams.	Cross-functional team meeting
Initiate ordering and production	The supply chain team uses the demand forecasts to plan production, inventory levels, and distribution to ensure that the company is able to meet demand.	Supply chain team meeting
Monthly performance monitoring	The finance, marketing, sales, and supply chain teams monitor actual sales performance against the forecasts and adjust plans as needed.	Cross-functional team meeting

In this process, demand should be the major driver. The company needs to spend a significant amount of time to ensure that the demand signal is as accurate as possible. More advanced companies are leveraging AI and machine learning to also improve their outcomes. Please note that implementing a system with these technologies takes time for the system to recognize and learn. The more previous year data you can supply the better, but it takes time for the model and the algorithm to be refined.

The next element is an evaluation of the on-hand inventory and then to determine how much additional inventory is required. The majority of this is done within the supply chain with some support from finance when additional money is required. If choices need to be made when capacity or money is constrained the decision is typically elevated to a product management or brand management team with consultation from the various business and P&L owners.

These decisions need to be made outside of the lead times of the supply chain. This usually requires a forecast for demand up to about a year out. Typically, the longer lead times for production (e.g., aerospace) typically operate on an order backlog. Lead times will vary by industry. Here are some sample lead times:

Industry	Typical Lead Time	Rationale for Lead Time
Sporting Goods	1 - 3 months	Depends on complexity and customization. Handmade or customized goods take longer
Chemicals	1 - 6 months	Production processes can be complex and have regulatory requirements
Machined Goods	1 - 3 months	Depends on the complexity of the product and the production process. Customized goods take longer
Aerospace	1 - 2 years	Highly complex products with long production cycles and rigorous testing and certification processes
Luxury Fashion	2 - 8 months	Handmade goods and high-quality materials often sourced globally. Seasonal collections also influence lead times
Cosmetics	1 - 6 months	Product testing, regulatory compliance, and sourcing of specific ingredients can add to lead times
Apparel	1 - 6 months	Depending on the complexity of design, sourcing materials, and manufacturing location. Fast-fashion has shorter lead times
Food	Days to weeks	Highly perishable, often with a focus on reducing lead times as much as possible
Building Materials	1 - 3 months	Dependent on the type of material. Custom orders and large quantities can increase lead times
Home Goods	1 - 3 months	Depends on complexity and customization. Handmade or customized goods take longer

Please note, for the typical contract manufacturer the lead time will be on the longer end of this timeline. CMs will typically buy the raw materials and order the packaging materials once your order is placed. This allows them to minimize working capital. If you want to reduce your lead times and still use contract manufacturing capacity, you will typically need to arrange to maintain safety stock for your key raw materials and packaging material with them. In addition, during times of limited capacity, you can also work with the Contract Manufacturers to reserve line capacity. This will sometimes come at a premium to the typical cost.

Internal production can be managed as desired and re-prioritized relatively quickly. The company owns that. With that level of control and reduction in lead time, it is beneficial for the companies with sufficient scale to reduce its overall working capital cost and eliminate potential margin for the CM. However, the company has to have sufficient scale to manage a full production plant and ensure it has sufficient volume to absorb the overhead. If the company cannot maintain high utilization and efficiency, then sale of the asset (production plant) may be warranted to a partner that is incented to do so. In one instance, I saw a wholly owned plant with about 70 percent capacity unused and high levels of inefficient, highly manual operations. This results in higher than antici-pated per unit costs in the factory.

Once the orders are placed, the management and delivery of the product falls into the supply chain management team. The team will review and manage the orders both to the internal production facility and the external contract manufacturers.

As a routine practice, the supply chain will manage a monthly production meeting. The purpose of the monthly production meeting is to review the performance of the production facilities during the previous month including fulfillment, efficiency, and quality issues. It will also review the upcoming production plan. It will review the planned produc-tion and readiness to deliver on the next month's volume. During this meeting, the company will typically lock in the planned production for the next month and line commits. During the session it will also review its resources for the plant and facilities, and risks that management needs to be concerned about, and the key KPIs for the production facilities. It will also review the upcoming planned production and inbound shipments from the contract manufacturers as part of the total production of the company. In addition, it will review the on-time delivery and quality concerns of the various CMs.

If the company only leverages CMs, then this meeting will focus more on the management of the CMs and the input of a team of external operations resources. These resources will more closely manage the network of contract manufacturing providers and monitor for on-time production. These resources are retained to ensure on-time and on-quality delivery of the products from the CMs. The CMs should be liaising with these resources to let them know if any schedules might slip, any quality issues they are experiencing, or any other concerns that need to be addressed between the CMs and the company.

With the on-time and on-quality delivery, it will then meet the required demand projected by the business leaders, fulfilling the S&OP process.

When capacity or money is constrained, this is when business teams will need to provide guidance to the supply chain. In these instances, the management of the production is required and should focus on profitability and strategic needs of the company. For instance, is it better to take risk with customers that represent 80 percent of the business or is it better to send products to the most profitable channel? Strategic prioritization of production and allocation of product is critical.

Development of relationships with the vendor base is critical to supporting the company.

Supply Chain

I once Googled the phrase supply chain, and every website I saw had a different definition for the phrase. Since there are so many differing opinions, here is how I think about supply chain. A company's supply chain is the group of external partners, internal capabilities, and internal resources that ensure that a company's products are produced, inspected, housed, and delivered to the end customer. In this definition, this would also include the logistic function—the housing and delivery of materials and products.

The modern company has a number of critical decisions around how it addresses its total supply chain. Supply chains do not need to be complex. In fact, the majority of companies have very simple supply chains. For small companies, they can partner with a small number of contract manufacturers and a 3PL and then are able to meet the needs of their supply chain. This level of complexity can be maintained in perpetuity as a company scales. The major difference between a $10,000 company and a $500 million company is the scale of the operations, the number of contract manufacturers, the number of resources in the company managing the scale, and the systems and processes to deliver on the scale. That seems like a long list of "yeah but's." However, as a company scales, these are more evolutionary versus revolutionary.

For instance, as a company grows, it will start with no dedicated supply chain resources. When it hits $500,000 in sales, it may then decide to add a dedicated resource to manage the demand and supply to meet the next level of growth. As the scale and complexity grows, there may need to be a dedicated demand resource and a supply resource. Once you shift from one CM to four, you may need a dedicated external operations resource. Then the scale becomes so large when the company passes $15 million in sales that you need a dedicated person to focus on supply chain and another to manage the marketing and so on. Always remember that the management team and the structure of a company will need to evolve as the company grows.

Modern value chains, the process and sources to create a given product, are typically global to ensure the products are produced at the lowest possible price for the company and its size. Even if the company itself does not directly interact with a company in China, their suppliers may. So, although the company's supply chain is simple (e.g., single interaction with a CM), the value chain for the company's product may remain complex, depending on the choices of its partners. In one company I worked with, the packaging material was produced in China, the labels were produced in New York, and the raw materials were sourced throughout Asia to be manufactured in the United States. This all occurred through a single contract with a CM in the United States. However, the company should be aware of the sourcing of its raw and packaging materials to understand if or when it could run into problems with potential geopolitical issues.

The other thing to consider in this analysis is where the materials are being sourced and whether that is necessary. For instance, if you are getting a commodity product from a non-local product does that make sense? In one situation, I encountered a company that was buying an industry commodity from Japan when the same chemical could be bought in the U.S. for about 20 percent less. This pricing difference is an outlier. With commoditized offerings, you will not typically find a significant variance.

When a company reaches sufficient scale, there are choices it will need to make about whether to take production in house or maintain it through a contract manufacturing partner. The fundamental driver should be economic. However, there are some strategic considerations that could over-rule economics to support long-term health of a business or brand (e.g., perception, quality issues increasing, intellectual property protection).

The second choice is also what it maintains in house versus outsourced. There can be significant value to outsourcing major components of the value chain for a given product. For instance, one aerospace provider shifted some elements of their assemblies to production in China while maintaining the remainder of the build and final assembly at their facility onshore. This saved some production costs for that section of the aircraft. For this decision, there were economics involved, but the larger consideration in the decision was whether to shift a relatively significant portion of the construction to an external vendor. What finally convinced them this was okay was that the final certification would be based on their final assembly.

For a company of sufficient scale, it helps to ensure there is a dedicated function reviewing the cost of production and making recommendations to management on how to streamline these processes and cost structures. This continuous improvement function should be held to a KPI on cost per unit. This unit should be a profit center in that it is saving the company more year-over-year than what it costs the company to maintain. This function will likely be a combination of transformation or lean professionals and support from the finance function.

This continuous improvement function should not just focus on the tactical projects, but also work to inculcate a culture of continuous improvement. The line employees and all else involved with the operations of the team should be looking for ways to make the supply chain function more efficient.

Another key element of the supply chain organization is the oversight and control of the contract manufacturing and external partners and vendors. There is typically an organization focused on quality assurance. This organization sets the standards and qualifies suppliers. They will also be responsible for conducting all of the inbound inspections on your finished goods and some of your input materials for any manufacturing operations.

Supply Chain Organization

The supply chain organization is a middle office function and ties the elements of the Sales teams to the means of production and procurement of goods. The key elements of the organization and a brief description are provided below.

Demand planning: This function is responsible for forecasting customer demand for products and services, developing and executing demand plans, and collaborating with other functions to ensure timely and accurate delivery of products and services. For the majority of consumer product companies, this is the nerve center of the supply chain. It ties it in with the remainder of the business functions. This function should be responsible for finalizing the consensus demand estimates from all of the functions. They then coordinate with the supply planning function to get those items ordered through the supply chain.

Sizing for this organization will depend on the required interactions within the company. With the right systems in place, one or two demand planners can manage an entire brand with thousands of SKUs and the product launches. The key driver of additional resources is complexity and stage of the company. If you are adding new products or nascent in ability to forecast demand, then you may need additional resources to supplement the existing workforce. Depending on longevity of the need, these can be temporary or permanent resources.

Supply planning: This function is responsible for ensuring that the organization has the necessary resources, including raw materials, finished goods, and capacity, to meet customer demand. Supply planners work with demand planners, suppliers, and other stakeholders to optimize inventory levels and production schedules. Depending on the company, they will work with demand planning on what the supply chain can deliver and then input those orders into the applicable vendors.

This is a fairly mechanical function you can have a relatively small team to service all of the needs. Typically, you will have about 60 to 80 percent of the number of demand planners to manage supply and inventory. For very simple supply chains, it may be less. This also includes the inventory management function. In times of supply constraint, you may need to supplement with additional resources.

Inventory management: This function is responsible for managing inventory levels and ensuring that the organization has the right amount of stock to meet customer demand. Inventory managers work with supply planners, logistics teams, and other stakeholders to optimize inventory levels and minimize stockouts and excess inventory.

External operations: This function is responsible for managing relationships with external partners, such as suppliers, contract manufacturers, and logistics providers. External operations teams negotiate contracts, monitor performance, and ensure that partners meet quality and delivery standards.

External operations staffing will be driven by the number of suppliers and the number of issues that need to be addressed. This is a function where you can compress the number of resources and then demand manage the engagement with the suppliers. Just realize that this introduces risk into the operation and supervision of the external providers.

Quality assurance: This function is responsible for ensuring that products and services meet customer requirements and quality standards. Quality assurance teams develop and implement quality control processes, conduct audits and inspections, and manage customer complaints and feedback.

The size is dependent on the operating model of the company. If the model is to shift the quality control onto the suppliers and quality checks to a 3PL, then this function is relatively small. It can be less than five people for a company up to about $1 billion, depending on complexity. For smaller companies with less complex supply chains and limited suppliers, this function can be even smaller.

If the operating model is to have all of quality control in house, this can be a significant size. This would have to include the resources to set policy, conduct quality inspections upon receipt, qualify vendors, track down and process quality issues, manage complaints and reporting to government authorities (if applicable), and a few other categories.

Program management: This function is responsible for overseeing new product launch, large-scale projects and initiatives within the supply chain organization. Program managers ensure that projects are completed on time, within budget, and to the required quality standards. This is an area that can be compressed or eliminated, depending on the quality of oversight in external operations and volume of projects.

Continuous improvement: This function is responsible for identifying and implementing process improvements within the supply chain. Continuous improvement teams use data analytics and other tools to identify areas for improvement and implement changes to improve efficiency, reduce costs, and enhance customer satisfaction. This is another area that can be compressed or consolidated to a centralized function within the total enterprise.

Logistics: This function is responsible for managing the physical movement of goods from suppliers to customers. Logistics teams oversee transportation, warehousing, and distribution activities, and they work to optimize transportation routes, inventory levels, and delivery times. We will discuss more of this in the section dedicated to logistics.

I have only provided the description of the functions. The allocation of the resources into various elements of the organization will be determined by the lead of the supply chain team. Some leaders like to have an integrated demand and supply planning team. This creates a very powerful number two in the organization. Others like a flatter organizational structure. Others will layer other functions such as external operations. It will depend on what best serves the interests of the company.

In general, layering is discouraged within any organization, unless this also results in lower cost resources.

Manufacturing Operations Overview

Manufacturing operations are relatively simple. For this exercise, we will follow the flow of goods. The complexity comes in the actual manufacturing process, which will be unique to each industry and each company.

In general, there will be a receiving dock at the manufacturing facility. The inbound goods will be received and then inspected by the receiving department. They will conduct the required inspections for the given materials. Sometimes this is as simple as counting to ensure receipt. Other times they will need to do a quality inspection or testing, for more advanced components. Once accepted, the product will go into the on-site warehouse. This is setup to support queuing of goods for production. Typically, quantities are ordered per a safety stock concept, but the goal is to minimize this WIP inventory.

For any given build there are either manufacturing procedure cards or work packages developed, which tell the operators of the plant what components and equipment is needed. In addition, it will specify the required quality assurance checks and quality standards that need to be maintained during production. The machine operator will then conduct the production. During the production, there will be in process quality inspections. This will also be done by the line operators themselves or their supervisor. The goal is to catch quality issues while manufacturing versus catching it during post-production quality inspections, or even worse, have a quality escapement where the quality defect leaves the factory and is caught by the customer. Escapements are a major issue for capital equipment production. Oftentimes, there are penalties in contracts associated with escapements and can risk damaging customer relationships.

Following the in process production and quality inspections, the team will conduct post production quality assessments. These may be periodic or for some core safety items, a dedicated 100 percent inspection. For a number of products, a technique of sampling is sufficient. The lot will then be held pending release from quality. Some of these tests can take weeks. For instance microbiologic testing takes about a week before any potential release. If it passes the required tests, then it can be released.

Once released, it will then flow to an outbound logistics center. Depending on the incoterms, the customer will either pick up at the location or the supplier will need to ship the product to the customers required location.

For ready reference, here is a quick table on the major steps and who is responsible for what elements:

Operation	Description	Typical Resources Responsible
Receiving	This stage involves the physical receipt of raw materials that will be used in the production process. It includes inspecting and verifying the quantity and quality of the raw materials received against the purchase order.	Receiving clerk, quality control inspector
Inbound material storage	This stage involves the physical storage of received materials. These materials will be stored, typically on a safety stock basis until requested through a work order. The control and release is typically through an MRP solution.	Warehouse manager, inventory control specialist
Work scheduling and work order/ manufacturing card	This stage involves the scheduling of work and the development (or distribution) of a detailed work order package that outlines the specific steps involved in the production process. It includes identifying the materials and equipment needed, determining the sequence of operations, and establishing quality standards.	Production planner, manufacturing engineer
Component and raw material checkout	This stage involves verifying that all necessary components and raw materials are available and in good condition. It includes checking for any defects or damage that could impact the production process.	Materials handler, quality control inspector
Production	This stage involves the actual manufacturing of the product according to the work order package. It includes the assembly, testing, and inspection of the product to ensure it meets the required specifications.	Line/machine operator, assembler, quality control inspector

In-production quality assurance	This stage involves monitoring the production process to ensure that the product is being manufactured to the required quality standards. It includes performing periodic inspections and tests to identify any defects or issues that could impact the final product.	Quality control inspector, manufacturing engineer
Post-production testing and sampling	This stage involves testing and sampling the finished product to ensure it meets the required specifications. It includes performing various tests such as functionality, durability, and reliability testing.	Quality control inspector, test engineer
Housing of finished products	This stage involves storing the finished products in a safe and secure location until they are ready to be shipped to customers. It includes managing inventory levels and ensuring that the products are properly labeled and identified.	Warehouse manager, inventory control specialist
Outbound logistics of finished goods	This stage involves coordinating the shipment of the finished products to customers. It includes managing transportation logistics, preparing shipping documents, and tracking the shipment to ensure timely delivery.	Shipping clerk, logistics coordinator

The efficiency of a manufacturing operation is measured in overall equipment effectiveness (OEE). Although originally conceived to think about the effectiveness of a piece of equipment, this has been embraced as a concept to also think about the overall effectiveness of a production line. OEE takes into account three key factors: availability (how much time the machine or production line is available), performance, and quality. It then provides a percent effectiveness based on a full year that shows the amount of time that the machine or process is producing quality products at full rated throughput.

$$\text{OEE} = \text{Availability x Performance x Quality}$$

Availability measures the percentage of time that a machine or process is available for production. It takes into account factors like breakdowns, changeovers, and other events that cause downtime. The formula for availability is:

Availability = (Operating Time - Downtime) / Operating Time

Where operating time is the total time that the equipment should have been available for production, and Downtime is the total time that the equipment was not available due to planned or unplanned events.

Performance measures the efficiency of the equipment or process by comparing the actual production rate to the maximum possible production rate. The formula for performance is:

Performance = (Actual Production Rate / Maximum Production Rate) x 100

Where actual production rate is the amount of product produced during the operating time, and Maximum Production Rate is the theoretical maximum amount of product that could have been produced during the same time.

Quality measures the percentage of good quality products that are produced by the equipment or process. The formula for quality is:

Quality = (Good Quality Products / Total Products Produced) x 100

Once you have calculated each of these factors, you can multiply them together to get the OEE. For example, if a machine has an availability of 90 percent, a performance of 80 percent, and a quality of 95 percent, the OEE would be:

OEE = 90% x 80% x 95% = 68.4%

Generally, a good OEE is above 85 percent and a bad OEE is less than 60 percent. However, this can vary depending on the industry. Different industries and processes have different levels of complexity and variability, which can affect what is considered a good or bad OEE. For example, a high-speed production line with a lot of changeovers and setups may have a lower OEE than a slower production line with fewer changeovers and setups, even if both lines are considered efficient for their specific circumstances.

Manufacturing Labor

There are a large number of functions within the plant that make the manufacturing operations process run seamlessly. Here are the typical functions and how they typically contribute to the manufacturing operations. The other key consideration is how the resources are allocated—whether they are considered direct or indirect labor. In general, direct labor is associated with the actual production of the product. Other functions that support production are typically considered indirect labor. Below is an outline of the typical players in a production plant.

Function	Direct/Indirect Labor	Description	Organization
Production operators / line operators / machine operators	Direct labor	These are the individuals responsible for the actual production of goods, including operating machinery and assembling products.	Typically organized in production teams or on individual production lines.
Quality control inspectors	Direct labor	These individuals are responsible for ensuring that products meet quality standards and specifications. They inspect products at various stages of the production process to identify defects or issues.	Typically organized within the production process but may also have a separate quality control department.w

Maintenance technicians	Direct labor	These individuals are responsible for maintaining and repairing machinery and equipment. They perform regular maintenance tasks and troubleshoot issues to minimize downtime.	Typically organized within the maintenance department.
Receiving	Direct labor	This function is responsible for physically receiving and inspecting raw materials and supplies. They verify the quantity and quality of the received materials against purchase orders and ensure that they are properly labeled and identified.	Typically organized within the receiving department.

Inventory control / warehouse personnel	Direct labor	These individuals are responsible for managing the inventory and storage of raw materials, supplies, and finished goods. They ensure that materials are stored in the appropriate locations and that inventory levels are accurate.	Typically organized within the warehouse department.
Logistics personnel	Direct labor	These individuals are responsible for coordinating the shipment of finished goods to customers. They manage transportation logistics, prepare shipping documents, and track shipments to ensure timely delivery.	Shipping department.

Engineers	Indirect labor	These individuals are responsible for designing and developing new products, as well as improving existing processes and products. They work closely with production teams to ensure that designs are practical and can be manufactured efficiently.	A separate engineering or part of the planning department.
Production planners	Indirect labor	These individuals are responsible for developing production schedules, allocating resources, and coordinating the flow of materials and goods through the production process. They work closely with supervisors and managers to ensure that production goals are met efficiently.	Production planning department.

Human resources	Indirect labor	This function is responsible for managing personnel-related activities, including hiring, training, and compensation.	HR department.
Accounting and finance	Indirect labor	This function is responsible for managing financial activities, including budgeting, forecasting, and financial reporting.	Accounting and finance department.
Purchasing / procurement	Indirect labor	This function is responsible for managing the procurement of raw materials and supplies needed for the production process.	Procurement or purchasing department.
Management	Indirect labor	These individuals are responsible for overseeing the production process, receiving, warehousing, and logistics functions, and ensuring that they run smoothly. They manage production teams, allocate resources, and make decisions to improve efficiency and productivity.	Typically organized in a separate management structure overseeing the production process, receiving, warehousing, and logistics functions.

Because there are so many different elements of labor, you can now see generally how the operations are structured. In some sense, a plant is its own miniature company with a separate back office. The nature of the production requires that to be duplicated as the operations tend to be remote from a centralized office and the hiring needs are varied. Human resources is a great example for the reason why. For an industry with seasonal variations, they may hire more resources leading into a peak season, requiring on-site talent acquisition and support. There are usually more personnel problems and higher levels of attrition at production facilities among blue-collar workers than with white-collar equivalents.

One item to monitor is to ensure you do not have too much overhead at any given site. A good general guideline is that the ratio of hourly to salaried employees on site should be more than 10 to 1. Ideally, this should be closer to 15 to 1. Another general guideline is to keep the indirect labor to about 25 to 30 percent of the total labor population. This will help to ensure that the focus of the effort is on production versus administration functions in support of the actual production.

Key Elements of a Contract Manufacturer Contract

A contract manufacturer (CM) contract is an agreement between two companies where one agrees to produce parts, components, or products for the other. This kind of agreement is widely used in industries such as electronics, pharmaceuticals, food and beverage, and consumer products, to name a few. Here are some key elements of a CM contract and how value can be lost for the buyer:

Scope of work: The scope of work defines what the CM is supposed to produce, often with explicit specifications and tolerances. This includes manufacturing, assembly, testing, packaging, and shipping. Poor definition or communication of the scope of work can lead to a significant loss in value for the buying company. This is because the company may receive products that don't meet their expectations or requirements, leading to a potential product rejection or customer dissatisfaction.

Quality assurance: Quality assurance outlines the standards the CM must meet in manufacturing the product, often involving regular inspections and audits, testing processes, and certifications. Failure to enforce these quality standards can lead to the production of inferior products, which can harm the buying company's reputation, increase product returns, and incur additional costs for reworking or replacing faulty products.

Pricing and payment terms: These are the terms outlining how much the buyer will pay, when, and under what conditions. It may include details on unit pricing, minimum orders, payment schedules, and any potential penalties or late fees. Value can be lost if pricing isn't negotiated properly or if the market price for materials decreases, as the buyer might end up overpaying. In addition, late payment penalties can add to the cost and reduce the overall value gained from the contract.

Product forecasting and integration into the production schedule: This element refers to the buyer's responsibility to provide accurate product demand forecasts and the CM's obligation to integrate these forecasts into their production schedule. There may also be specific clauses about participation in the CM's production planning meetings. Accurate forecasts allow the CM to plan production, resource allocation, and inventory management effectively. If the buyer provides inaccurate or untimely forecasts, it can lead to several value-loss scenarios. Overestimating demand can result in excess inventory, increased storage costs, and potential product waste, especially for perishable items. Underestimating demand, on the other hand, can cause stockouts, missed sales opportunities, and customer dissatisfaction due to delayed deliveries. Thus, the value derived from the contract significantly depends on the accuracy and effectiveness of product forecasting and its integration into the CM's production schedule.

Delivery schedule: This element covers when and how the CM will deliver the product, including frequency, logistics, and any penalties for late or early deliveries. If the delivery schedule isn't adhered to, it can disrupt the buyer's operations, particularly if they run a just-in-time inventory system. This disruption can lead to stockouts or excess inventory, both of which can be costly, resulting in a loss of value for the buyer.

Intellectual property (IP) rights: This specifies who owns the IP (such as patents, designs, and trade secrets) used or created in the manufacturing process. Unclear definition and protection of IP rights can cause the buyer to lose exclusive control over their IP. This could potentially be exploited by the CM or a third party, leading to lost sales or even legal disputes, thereby eroding the value the buyer gets from the contract.

Liability and indemnification: This element outlines who is responsible if something goes wrong, such as a product defect or delay, and who would pay for associated costs. If this element isn't properly stipulated in the contract, the buyer might end up being liable for issues caused by the CM, potentially leading to significant financial losses and reduction in value gained from the contract.

Termination clauses: This part of the contract details the conditions under which either party can end the contract, including notice periods and any associated fees. Improperly outlined termination clauses can cause the buyer to find themselves locked into an unfavorable contract or face hefty penalties for ending the contract early. This could lead to value loss for the buyer, reducing the benefits they derive from the contract.

It's essential for the company buying from the contract manufacturer to ensure that all these elements are clearly defined and agreed upon in the contract. They should also monitor the CM's performance regularly to ensure compliance with the contract.

Repair, Maintenance, and Availability

Repairs and maintenance are inevitable for mechanical equipment. The majority of maintenance and repair does not require the machine to be down a significant period of time or can, if scheduled well, be conducted during scheduled off time for the machine or when the production plant is not in operation.

There are really three types of maintenance:

1. **Preventive maintenance (PM):** Preventive maintenance involves regularly scheduled inspections and maintenance tasks that are performed on equipment to prevent breakdowns and prolong the equipment's life. PM tasks can include things like cleaning, lubrication, calibration, and replacement of worn parts.

2. **Corrective maintenance (CM):** Corrective maintenance involves repairs that are performed after a piece of equipment has broken down or is not functioning properly. CM tasks

can include things like replacing broken parts, fixing leaks, and addressing other issues that are identified during routine inspections.

3. **Predictive maintenance (PdM):** Predictive maintenance involves using data and analytics to predict when equipment is likely to fail, and then performing maintenance tasks to prevent the failure from occurring. PdM tasks can include things like vibration analysis, oil analysis, and thermography, among others.

The last of these categories relies on analytics and pre-failure analysis of similar machines. However, with predictive maintenance, external vendors can, with high probability, predict when a smaller piece of the equipment might fail—let's say a pump impeller. The problem is that when the pump impeller wipes out, it usually causes other bits of damage to the casing, motor shaft, etc. With the predictive maintenance, you can get signals that indicate that the pump impeller may fail. At which point, you can shut down the pump and inspect or preemptively replace the pump impeller before it fails. At one point in my career, I had a pump impeller catastrophically fail during number operations. We had a backup process and began to use that. However, the shaft bent and the casing had to be replaced as well. If we had other sensors that could potentially have prevented this. Sometimes machine operators can catch this, but with limited manning these minor changes in the machine before failure may not be caught.

With the right support in place, you may be able to also refurbish and reuse that pump impeller on another machine. In general, companies can save as much as eight to 12 percent of corrective maintenance costs implementing a predictive maintenance program. However, the bigger impacts are for the production plant itself. This also leads to reduced downtime, lower maintenance costs, and longer equipment life—all of these things typically outweigh the monetary savings for the maintenance.

To measure the effectiveness of preventive and corrective maintenance, there are several key KPIs to consider:

Planned maintenance percentage: This is a gross measure of if the preventative maintenance program is effective. As a percent of maintenance actions, it indicates what percent are pre-planned and which are emergent. A good planned maintenance percentage is to have more than 70 to 80 percent of the actions be preplanned. If lower, that indicates that the R&M team is more reactive and the PMs are not effective in managing the equipment. Another gross measure of this effectiveness is mean time between failure (MTBF) this measures the time between equipment failures. In general, this should be in excess of 10,000 machine run hours, but is highly dependent on the type of machine used.

Equipment availability is the measure, net of planned availabilities for maintenance, of the time the machine is available for operation. In general, this should be more than 95 percent of the time. If not, then that indicates a potential issue with the machine or the programs to maintain the equipment.

Mean time to repair is another key metric that measures the time it takes the R&M team to repair a machine and restore it to operation. In general, this should be about four to eight hours. This is highly dependent on the industry and type of equipment. If the equipment is highly complex, this can result in longer times to troubleshoot and resolve the issues.

The goal whenever assessing repair and maintenance is to improve the availability of the asset or production line. Preventative maintenance schedules should generally be adhered to. Longer periodicity items or items that will reduce the availability of the production line will typically be scheduled or approved to occur during a longer maintenance availability.

However, not every corrective issue needs to be addressed immediately. Maintaining an active backlog and having the correct engineering judgment of what issues need to be addressed immediately and which do not is critical. These judgments require experience and understanding of the impacts of the maintenance not being conducted.

Savings in procurement of the supplies also helps in efficiency. Reuse of capital equipment after refurbishment also tends to keep costs down.

Repair, maintenance, and availability are a cost of doing business. Risk can be taken in times of crisis. However, you should have engineering judgment associated with decisions on not conducting any type of maintenance. Efficiency comes from the amount of maintenance required, properly maintaining and reviewing your CM backlog, and the appropriate staffing, and use of external vendors to get the tasks completed. Please note, staffing for maintenance departments can be reduced. However, you have to understand exactly what your tradeoffs are. In addition, there is likely to be flowback in the form of reduced uptime on the equipment, increased CM, or increased external vendor spend. In general, this is not always a sustainable method to reduce cost structure.

Quality

The systems and practices for product quality will vary by industry. For instance, the focus on quality and the quality control system for a healthcare company are going to be different than a plywood manufacturer. The main objective of any quality program is to deliver a consistent product and ensure safety for the end customer of the company. They also should seek to do so in the lowest cost possible to the company.

The cost of poor quality (COPQ) can be debilitating to a company. In general, experts estimate that a good company will suffer about 10 to 15 percent impact in cost due to poor quality through rework, disposal, material, and recall costs. In companies that do not get quality right, it can be even higher often about 15 to 20 percent. The other major driver of concern is reputational. When there are quality issues present in the product, the company needs to make an economic decision whether to launch or not—weighing revenue, customer relationships with perception of their brand in the market.

So, how can you tell if a company is having quality issues? The main measures are to measure defect rate, first pass yield, rework rates, and customer complaints.

Defect rates are highly variable by industry, but an acceptable defect rate for most industries is between 1 and 5 percent. However, for industries like aerospace, defense, and medical equipment the defect rate may be as low as 0.1 percent.

First pass yields typically range between 90 and 99 percent, depending on the industry, processes deployed, and product complexity.

Rework rates are typically between 1 and 10 percent. The costs of rework are high—typically increasing cost of production by between 10 and 40 percent of the original. Putting in place measures that eliminate the need for rework has positive paybacks.

Customer complaints is another method to understand when quality issues. In general, payouts for customer complaints should be about 1 percent of revenue. However, this will vary by industry.

Mechanically, quality control will be portrayed as a system of interlocking activities. However, the true breakthroughs on quality come from the systems and methods becoming cultural where the average line operator and team members will not let quality issues exist in their product and in the engineering or planning to ensure safety and quality are elements designed for and thought through in advance.

Typically, operationally-focused companies focused on improvement and quality will have a root cause and corrective actions program. This helps the company to understand what the true issues are that generated the defect or quality issue. Once identified, they will put in place corrective actions that should address the issue and minimize likelihood for reoccurrence. They will typically keep a record of these issues and track completion of these corrective actions. In manufacturing, the typical default is for issues in production to be addressed on the spot and remove and replace the damaged component or item of issue. This works as long as there is someone that looks over the total impact to see if there is recurrence of issues.

In general, here are the key areas that quality seeks to maintain a standard outcome for each product:

Performance: This will vary by the type of product. Does the product do everything we say it can? These specifications can vary but can range from the appropriate electrical resistance for a resistor to the flight envelope for a commercial airplane.

Reliability: Can the product maintain this performance, without (or with known) degradation throughout the life of the asset?

Stability: Does the product remain in the same condition over time?

Durability: Does it meet the required toughness standards and normal wear and tear?

Aesthetics: Does it meet the visual criteria asked for by the product owner?

Safety: Are there any concerns with safety from the product?

Every company will have a policy and objective for their quality system. The main elements of the program and interlocking systems and approval schema will typically be captured in a quality manual and other various documents like standard operating procedures, testing protocols, and other operational processes.

The costs associated with quality typically stem from the commitments required in the quality manual which is what the contract manufacturers will need to agree to and what your manufacturing facility will need to manage to. The quality manual should be a central book for any product-oriented company. In it and any other associated books (e.g., standard operating procedures), it will contain an overview of the quality management system, including its structure, who is responsible for what elements of the quality control system, and procedures in place to maintain quality. It will also outline organizational elements that include management and oversight responsibilities and resource management. Finally, it will also discuss required elements of how the product or services are delivered to include key elements of design criteria, development, purchasing, production, and delivery. Finally, it will also discuss methods for monitoring quality, reporting and record documentation, and how corrective actions will be implemented. It may also include typical forms or templates that can be used to support the fulfillment of the quality control system requirements.

For contract manufacturing based customers, in general, it is more efficient to have the contract manufacturer manage as much of the quality control as possible. This will still require some sampling done upon receipt and active quality inspections of the contract manufacturing site. This will reduce the required overhead for your company and ensure that the CMs are meeting their requirements. If quality is a major driver of the product value, then additional inspections and sampling may be required, or the company may determine it best to manage the quality receipt in house. This does require a large amount of overhead and tracking.

The other major cost of quality is the returns from customers for defective products. I will address this in the next section on material, scrap, and returns. However, the cost of returns is a cost of doing business. The goal of the quality system is to reduce the number of these returns. In capital programs these are also called escapements, which typically have penalties in the contracts.

When an issue is found, the items will be placed on a quality hold.

This prevents these items from being released for the end customer or to the production line. Once the quality issue is resolved, then the items can be put back into the normal inventory stacks and be distributed.

Quality teams are typically small, relative to the supply chain or manufacturing teams they are a part of. Some people believe that QA should be part of the supply chain/manufacturing team. There is another view where the QA team should be separate and distinct from the supply chain/manufacturing team. In general, you want these individuals to have autonomy and be able to escalate issues to the appropriate level of the organization. Whatever organizational construct that centralizes the QA team and leadership and allows those escalations to occur should be considered.

Safety

Safety is a critical element of any operations. Maintaining a strong safety culture is important for the people that work for the company and also enhances the company's image in the industry. I am not certain of anyone who would want to work for a company that did not take safety seriously as it is there life and body that could potentially be in jeopardy.

All operational companies have a safety program. This outlines the policies, procedures, and guidelines to ensure worker and plant safety. The program should also have measures that are proactive and identify hazards and risks, equipment issues, training gaps, and preplanned emergency responses.

Safety also manifests itself in direct costs to the company through a number of mechanisms that include medical expenses, legal expenses, fines and penalties, and property damage. Worker's compensation premiums, which are typically about 0.5 to 1.0 percent of payroll, could be increased with poor safety as well. The largest variable is industry and the setting in which business is conducted.

To assess whether or not safety is a concern within a company you can typically review a company's safety audit (if they do not want you to see it, that is potentially an issue). There are also some key metrics to review, as well. These include incident rate, severity rate, near-miss reporting rate, and employee sentiment.

Incident rate is typically measured over a year's time and is the number of incidents per 100 workers. This number should be as close to zero as possible. For a safety conscientious company, this rate can be less than 1 percent. Above 2 percent and it is worth investigating, as there may be an issue. However, if you see a company with higher than 5 percent, there is likely a significant issue. This means that 5 out of 100 workers have an incident each year.

Severity rate measures the impact of the incident that results in lost days of work. Ideally, this should be less than or close to one day per incident. However, large or serious incidents can skew this data set. The bigger element is the trend. If you see a number of significant incidents each year, then there is likely an opportunity to improve safety in the company. Doing so will also likely improve bottom line.

The final number that helps you gauge the actual culture of safety in the company is the near misreporting rate. Ideally the near misreporting rate should be at least 50 percent of the actual incident rates. Higher rates here mean that the employees are engaged and trying to report issues that they see so it can be addressed. A higher rate can also indicate that there are significant safety issues that have been unaddressed by management. Small investment can go a long way to improve those conditions. For instance, in one factory I toured, they had a rash of incidents or near misses where employees were almost hit by forklifts when negotiating the stacks in the onsite warehouse. They installed gates with flashing lights to prevent pedestrians from going into the forklift lanes without signals warning the forklift operators that the person was present in the crosswalk.

The last metric is employee sentiment. Some of this can be captured in the near-miss rate as discussed, but hearing from the employees is also important and tells you how the management team actually behaves. From outside of the company, you can check websites like Glassdoor and Indeed to understand employee sentiment. There are a number of other operational insights from current or prior employees. Inside of the company, you can conduct employee sentiment surveys. These surveys can yield a lot of insight both with the culture of safety and other elements.

Getting safety right is a priority. Amazon, a leading internet retailer, announced in 2021 that it was investing up to $300 million through 2025 to reduce its incident rate by 50 percent. Fifty percent seems high, but is doable. OSHA has stated that companies that put in place effective safety programs have seen incident rates reduce by between 40 to 50 percent. One of the facilities initially in the pilot program has taken an incident rate of about 12 percent down to close to zero in the course of just two years. If you think about that on the scale of Amazon's operations, that is impressive and also reduces the cost of doing business.[23]

And safety is just that—it's a cost of doing business. This is not an area to really save money. However, there are some things that help contain cost. For instance, use of vending machines for PPE helps companies manage and control usage of PPE. These are standard now in most operational settings.

If you do see a company with poor safety, improving its safety program and results has a double bottom line impact, where you improve the safety for the employees and there are typically cost efficiencies that you gain through reduced medical expenses, insurance costs, and lost productivity.

Footprint Analysis and Offshore Manufacturing

Two evaluations of your manufacturing should occur. The first is an analysis of the productivity of the plant. This can be a high level assessment on productivity of the plant on a revenue per square foot basis. You can then benchmark that against others in the industry. This will be a gauge of the productivity of the plant. Here are some typical benchmarks for select industries:

Industry	Revenue/sq ft to be profitable
Food and beverage	$300 to $500
Pharmaceutical manufacturing	$800 to $1,000
Automotive manufacturing	$600 to $700
Electronics manufacturing	$1,000 to $1,200

You can also look at this on a return on fixed assets basis. ROFA is equal to net income/total fixed asset. Typically, you want to see this above 8 percent.

23 Eric Rosenbaum, "Amazon has a new plan to cut worker injuries by 50%," CNBC, May 17, 2021, www.cnbc.com/2021/05/17/relentless-amazon-has-new-plan-to-cut-worker-injuries-by-50percent-.html#:~:text=While%20it%20may%20seem%20like%20a,52%25%20reduction%20in%20the%20injury%20rate.&text=While%20it%20may%20seem,in%20the%20injury%20rate.&text=may%20seem%20like%20a,52%25%20reduction%20in%20the.

Fixed Costs and Absorption

There are a large number of fixed costs in a production plant. The typical driver is the amortization of the plant equipment, the building lease or amortization for an owned building, taxes, and service spend.

These costs are usually amortized across the products produced in the plant called absorption. The method of absorption is typically through a quantitative allocation process. This can impact a plant's profitability and inability to hit cost per unit targets if you have low utilization of the plant, itself. In some situations, some companies have actually conducted sub-contract work for other near peer competitors with their equipment.

For efficiency, if the company cannot load the plant such that it can absorb the overhead and maintain profitability, there may be a reason to explore the sale of the plant to a contract manufacturer or other. Doing so can allow another company to more efficiently run the plant and allow for the company to regain profitable per unit economics.

Scrap

Scrap is an often-overlooked element of cost efficiency in manufac-turing operations. Scrap is the residual material that remains after production. This material is often not usable for any additional work. To be efficient, the company should seek to reduce its scrap rates.

In general, a good scrap rate is less than 1 or 2 percent, depending on the industry. To get scrap rates lower with the management team, you need to conduct workshops as it will typically be an issue within the manufacturing processes or some element of quality system issues.

LOGISTICS AND WAREHOUSING

The ability to physically deliver products is a required capability of any company that delivers a physical product to its end customer.

The specific focus of this section of the book is the operations in the logistics chain, the value chain of solutions and organizations that enable a company to handle its products and ship between locations and the key elements to consider.

There are three major components to this capability: first is the ability to receive, store, pick, and process the product or other materials; second is the ability to manage the inventory and integrate that management into the sales, order management, and supply chain function; and, finally, the ability to ship that product to another location, whether an internal location or external to customers or vendors.

With the exception of actual logistics companies (e.g., FedEx, UPS, DHL, and Amazon), logistics is not typically a differentiator. Because of this the majority of product companies will outsource their operations to 3PL providers. 3PLs are a key strategic enabler for modern business. Because logistics is not typically core to a company, the ability to outsource this to an entity where it is there core business has proven to be a successful model time and again. Despite this, we will review the inner workings of the operation and what functions go into the logistics chain and how the service can be optimized. We will also discuss return processing and also the handling of excess, obsolete, and expired goods.

Distribution Footprint

The specific location for distribution centers is usually dictated by a study of the companies operations. The key inputs are the locations of their suppliers, cost of shipment, cost of the location, and the location of their end customers.

Conceptually, this is pretty easy to understand—when I take a good I need to store it and I need to ship it. At a certain frequency it will go to a customer in another location. Based on this, I can put together a rough model of the flows of product volumes for a company and the associated costs. Typically, the analysts will use one of three models: a transportation cost model, a location and transportation cost model, or a complex total supply chain optimization model. The last model maps raw material flows, finished good flows, and total cost for the locations given typical economics. The amazing part of all of this analysis is that depending on the country and region, the answers are usually similar.

In the United States, there is a small region between Ohio, Kentucky, Indiana, and Tennessee that is one of the optimal locations for distribution when you have to serve clients across the country. Texas, can also be a good base of operation, depending on Northern or Southern reach for your customer base. If you have a significant amount of flows that go to Europe, that expands eastward out to New Jersey, Philadelphia, and parts of Maryland to provide better access to the eastern seaports, while still maintaining a lower cost base. If you largely serve the west coast, the best places are typically in California and Nevada because of lower costs and access to key population points in California.

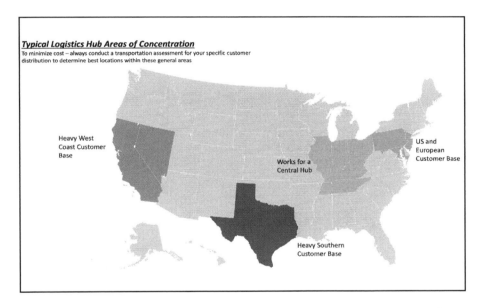

In the UK, there is a golden triangle in the Western Midlands of the United Kingdom centered around Birmingham. This was an area that allows access to 90 percent of the British population within a four-hour drive. This has been the primary locus of logistics operations in the UK. However, they are now seeing some expansion out to the Humber and with some additional operations going up toward Yorkshire.[24]

---

24 "The Rise of the UK Warehouse and the 'Golden Logistics Triangle'," Office for National Statis-tics, April 11, 2022, www.ons.gov.uk/businessindustryandtrade/business/activitysizeandlocation/articles/theriseoftheukwarehouseandthegoldenlogisticstriangle/2022-04-11.

In Europe, there is the blue banana. The blue banana of logistics runs from London to Belgium, Netherlands, Germany, Switzerland, and then into Italy. It largely follows the route of the Rhine River in Europe and provides excellent access to the infrastructure of Europe. This is largely where the majority of company central European distribution centers reside. However, depending on your markets and customers, there are a number of other hubs and concentration areas emerging around the large metropolitan areas in the European Union. The other key consideration in Europe is the business environment in each country. There are pros and cons with Belgium and the Netherlands actually being relatively attractive from a tax and business environment perspective. However, transportation costs and cost of the distribution centers will trump the majority of these other concerns.

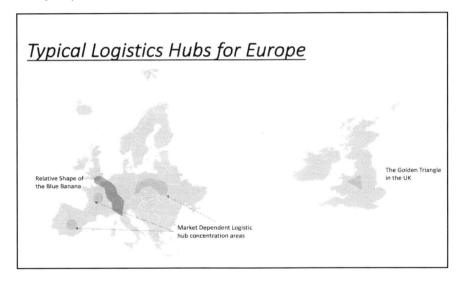

Typical Logistics Hubs for Europe

Relative Shape of
the Blue Banana

The Golden Triangle
in the UK

Market Dependent Logistic
hub concentration areas

In Asia, the bigger concern is not necessarily access to road infrastructure. The key element is access to port infrastructure. The other key driver is that a large number of countries need to be accessed from a centralized point. This makes tax and tariff implications a major driver of value for a distribution hub in Asia. This drives a number of companies to leverage select locations when expanding operations into Asia. Below I have listed some of the frequent logistics hubs and some of the advantageous relationships that can be explored for companies seeking to expand in Asia, depending on their situation and needs in the region.

Location	Tax and Tariff Advantage	Unique Advantages and Trade Zones
Singapore	No value-added tax (VAT) or goods and services tax (GST) on most exports; preferential trade agreements with numerous countries.	Jurong Port: one of the world's leading multipurpose ports; Tuas Port: set to be the largest fully automated container terminal in the world.
Hong Kong	No VAT or GST on most exports; free port status; low corporate tax rate; well-established logistics and financial infrastructure.	Hong Kong International Airport: one of the busiest cargo airports in the world; Hong Kong-Zhuhai-Macau Bridge: connects Hong Kong with mainland China; Hong Kong: mainland China Closer Economic Partnership Arrangement (CEPA): eliminates tariffs and barriers on certain goods traded between Hong Kong and mainland China.
Shanghai, China	Free trade zone (FTZ): offers tax incentives, simplified customs procedures, and streamlined administrative procedures for businesses; proximity to major markets in China and Southeast Asia.	Shanghai Pudong International Airport: one of the busiest airports in China; Port of Shanghai: the world's busiest container port; Yangshan Free Trade Port Zone: located on an island off the coast of Shanghai, with facilities for logistics, manufacturing, and trade.

Dubai, UAE	No corporate tax or personal income tax; free zones— offer 100 percent foreign ownership, no customs duties, and no restrictions on repatriation of capital.	Jebel Ali Free Zone: one of the largest and most comprehensive free zones in the world; Dubai South: located near Dubai World Central Airport, with facilities for logistics, manufacturing, and trade; Dubai Multi Commodities Centre (DMCC): specializes in the trading of commodities.
Tokyo, Japan	Bilateral trade agreements with numerous countries; strategic location near major markets in Asia.	Yokohama Port: one of the busiest ports in Japan; Narita International Airport: one of the busiest airports in Japan; Keiyo Industrial Zone: located on the coast near Tokyo, with facilities for logistics and manufacturing.
Kuala Lumpur, Malaysia	Free industrial zones: offer tax incentives, streamlined procedures, and access to infrastructure and services.	Port Klang: one of the busiest ports in Malaysia; Kuala Lumpur International Airport: one of the busiest airports in Malaysia; Malaysia-China Kuantan Industrial Park: joint venture between Malaysia and China, with facilities for logistics and manufacturing.
Bangkok, Thailand	Free trade zone: offers tax incentives, streamlined customs procedures, and access to infrastructure and services.	Laem Chabang Port: one of the busiest ports in Thailand; Suvarnabhumi Airport: one of the busiest airports in Thailand; Eastern Economic Corridor (EEC): located near Bangkok, with facilities for logistics, manufacturing, and trade.
Seoul, South Korea	Bilateral trade agreements with numerous countries; proximity to major markets in Asia.	Incheon International Airport: one of the busiest airports.

In South America, logistics can be a little more difficult because of the limitations on reliable infrastructure for business. Use of a centralized hub in a tax optimized location like Panama or Mexico near a transportation hub where you can leverage a combination of land, sea, and air transportation may be best suited to those operations.

There are also a number of trade agreements between the countries in Central and South America such as the Mercosur trade bloc. The Mercosur trade bloc, the Southern Market in English, and Mercosul in Portuguese consist of a free trade and customs union between Brazil, Argentina, Paraguay, and Uruguay. In addition, Bolivia, Chile, Colombia, Ecuador, Guyana, Peru, and Suriname are associate members of the trading bloc. If you are trading into the Mercosur, then it may make sense to ensure that your logistics are focused there. In this region there is a Common external tariff except for countries or regions that have an enhanced trade agreement with the Southern market. The EU is one of those regions. Exploring shipments from the EU versus other geographies may be beneficial to a company with interests in that region.

Distribution Centers, Automation, and Warehouses

In any logistics operation, there is an element of inventory management and storage. To support the storage of a company's products the company will typically use a series of warehouses and distribution centers (DC). A warehouse is typically used for the storage of goods and materials, whereas a DC is focused on the distribution of goods. A warehouse may be used for long-term storage of inventory or for consolidation of shipments, while a DC is typically used for the sorting, packing, and shipping of goods to customers or retail stores.

Think of a warehouse as a place to queue material or products. They are typically near production facilities and the contents are typically in bulk packaging or palletized. DCs tend to have smaller quantities, but move the product quickly. In addition, the placement of DCs is typically strategic (see the preceding section).

For companies with slower moving material or that store materials needed for their operations, they may just have a warehouse. It is simply a place to store material until it is needed. This is typical in a capital-intensive industry when there are long lead times on products needed for operation. For instance, a telecommunications company may have 100 telephone poles queued for when they need to replace a telephone pole. This type of good would typically be in a warehouse. Typically the storage facility adjacent to a production facility will also typically be called a warehouse. When you walk into them, you will see a large amount of palletized materials that will need to be broken down and set up per the production schedule. There is an inventory management and check out process from a warehouse. When a good is needed, an order will be placed and the product will be retrieved, typically with a person going to do the pick of the good. The delivery will be into a staging area, to a technician, or to a loading dock if the product is being shipped elsewhere.

The operations of a warehouse are relatively basic and because of that, the metrics on performance are relatively tight. To assess the operation, the analyst can look at inventory accuracy, order accuracy, turnaround time, space utilization, and labor productivity.

Inventory accuracy for a warehouse should be at least 98 to 99 percent with minimal discrepancies between the physical inventory and the recorded inventory

Order accuracy should be north of 99 percent with 99.5 to 99.9 percent accuracy indicating a well-run operation. Please note that these metrics can suffer from the law of small numbers.

Turnaround time should be within SLA. This can vary based on the company's design for the warehouse. Typically, this is somewhere between 24 and 48 hours. However, the company can adjust this if needed.

Space utilization is another major driver of efficiency but can be assessed visually when you see that there is not a lot of open or empty storage locations. Typically you want the utilization to be above 80 percent. However, you do want some room for growth, keeping utilization below 90 to 95 percent is okay to allow for flex space needed for the business.

Labor productivity is the final key metric to think through. Typically, you want the resources efficiently managed and productive. Typically, you are looking for a labor productivity metric of about 85 to 95 percent utilization.

For small operations such as a warehouse to store materials needed for the company, the key to efficiency in a warehouse is to shift these operations to low cost areas that still give access to the needed elements of the business and reduce the costs for the lease of the property and typically a lower cost for the resourcing. Also, ensure that the space is appropriately sized for the need. Sometimes, companies will buy larger warehouses than needed. Additional upfront time to size the need for the operation is helpful to ensure that you are efficiently using the space. Reduction in staffing to as low as practicable is advised, as well. The nature of non-production located facilities is that the goods are in storage and will need to be delivered when needed. Taking additional risk in the SLA for turnaround time may be beneficial. If owned, then the occasional urgent request may offset the need for additional overhead to maintain a shorter standard SLA.

For larger warehouse operation, if at all possible, shift the operation to a 3PL. Even in a production facility, everything from the receipt of the good to the deliver to the production line can be done by a 3PL.

A distribution center is more focused on moving products versus storing them. For small and medium size operations, they may use a portion of their DC as a warehouse as well for certain materials needed for the business. However, the main line of a DC is the ability to receive products, store them, pick the products for the order, and pack them for shipment, typically to an end customer. Depending on the volume and requirements of the product, the DC will use some elements of mechanical systems for movement of the orders or automation to move pick, pack, and ship the product.

The engineering of a DC is conducted by a solution engineer. The solution engineer will develop a solution that will work for the product and industry. For the apparel industry, they need special handling of the garments as they are being picked because if they are exposed to an industrial environment, the end customer may receive a garment that is soiled. The bulk foods industry only ships products by the box. This allows them to have a highly automated solution that takes products from their stowage location and route via a mechanical system to the loading dock. For an internet wine seller, they have a number of each picks. This requires a conveyor belt with the order and a series of manual workers to scan the order and then go and pick the bottles required and place them in the consolidated order box with a conveyor belt that is automated to route to the appropriate "fingers" of the operation to get the full complement of bottles ordered. In other operations, they have robots that can go to the stacks and pick the boxes or requirements for the order.

In others, they have robotic trolleys that assist the DC worker in picking the goods and carrying the goods for them.

This is just a light touch of the various technologies available for use in distribution centers. The technology is constantly evolving and something that dedicated logistics professionals continue to monitor. The actual solution deployed will need to engineered and negotiated. These solutions are large capital investments with conveyor belts and storage racks easily entering into costs of millions of dollars.

As you can see, depending on the operation, it can range from highly manual to fully-automated. It just depends on the requirements of the business and size and scale of the operation and what the business is willing to invest. Additionally, the operation will not be static. The team managing the operation should continue to seek operational efficiencies and improvements that drops the cost of product handling year over year. This will require continued investment, but typically is required for the business to grow and scale with operational leverage (e.g., becoming more profitable as you grow). The handling of the product is ideally about 2 to 3 percent of revenue for each touch in a distribution center. Because of the cost, it is important to optimize the operation.

To ensure the operation is being run efficiently, here are four of the key metrics and good/target values:

1. Order fulfillment accuracy should be at least 96 to 98 percent. However, companies should strive to have a accuracy rate as close to 100 percent as possible. When a company falls below 95 percent you are operating at a disadvantage to your competitors.

2. Turnaround time: the time from receiving the order to delivery to the loading dock is typically within 24 to 48 hours. Most SLAs are for 24 hours. A good operation can also support expedited orders, if you need something less than 24 hours.

3. A well run DC should have a high inventory turnover rate, typically indicating efficient inventory management. The target value for inventory turnover will depend on the specific operation and the type of products being stored, but a turnover rate of at least six to eight times per year is considered good.

4. On time, in full measures the percentage of orders that are delivered on time and with all of the products ordered are delivered in the quantity requested. A well-run DC should have a high OTIF rate, typically 95 percent or higher. This metric also can be a barometer for the total supply chain, indicating whether or not the end customer is getting what it needs.

The operation of a distribution center is a cost of doing business. The two largest costs are the upfront CAPEX and the labor used to pick, pack, and ship (PPS) the product. To optimize the operation, there are typically methods to improve the productivity of the labor or to automate elements of the pick, pack, and ship operation. These will be the largest drivers of savings.

The methods to do this will vary, depending on the current state of the operation. It can be anything from implementing a conveyor system (if currently fully manual) to implementing a fully automated system. It all depends on what the next level of break through for efficiency.

The other opportunity is the choice of location and labor rate differences. For instance, Memphis is one of the lowest cost places to operate a distribution center in the U.S.—I have seen rate differences up to about 30 percent. However, the quality of labor and ability to establish an efficient and well-run operation is something that needs to be balanced.

Another major cost of labor is the turnover of the resources. The average across the U.S., according to the Bureau of Labor Statistics, indicates 36 percent in 2020.[25] This is a full 20 percent higher than average private sector turnover of 15.5 percent in 2019. Because of this, it is critical to think about the staffing and how to maintain consistency in your operation. In addition, most industries are seasonal. The staffing of distribution centers needs to flex up to that seasonal peak with temporary associates. There are a large number of seasoned logistics executives that have managed this paradigm before. When looking at standing up an operation or improving outcomes, leveraging that expertise may be critical. Because of these dynamics, it is often advisable to shift these operations to a 3PL. 3PLs have these resources and often are well

25 "Warehousing and Storage: NAICS 493," U.S. Bureau of Labor Statistics, July 7, 2023, www.bls.gov/iag/tgs/iag493.htm.

established in a given market or geography to better manage the needs of the business and operation. Some 3PLs have shown consistent ability to maintain turnover of associates to less than 15 percent through various programs including some use of a probationary, temporary employment period with the company and other mechanisms that incent the employees for longer tenures. When the 3PL has an established presence in a region, they can also flex their resources across multiple operations that helps to mitigate some of the seasonal variance with known and trusted resources.

Active management of productivity is a central element of management of a DC. The day-to-day metrics and KPIs are actively tracked and shown to employees. This culture of performance should also be active in the management of resources. The resources should be able to maintain the level of operations of the business.

To avoid the upfront capital expenditure, the use of a 3PL can help to offset that cost. The 3PL will typically fund the upfront expenditure and then charge the company on a monthly basis for the capex burn down with a nominal financing charge.

With 3PLs, it is also common to work with them to share in the improvements in the operation. For instance, if the 3PL puts in place a performance improvement initiative that improves cost by $100,000 per year, there may be a system in place that allows the 3PL to capture 50 percent of that upside the first year and then 25 percent the next year and then nothing the following. These arrangements can be negotiated between the company and a 3PL provider.

The 3PL model is very mature. It is common to rebid the work and changeover operations. The goal is to ensure that you start those processes early enough when your contract is coming due. Beginning at least six to 12 months before the end of the contract is about right. However, if you are looking at a significant expansion or a situation where you need to change facilities or locations, the bid out should start sooner with the average build time for an operation being between six to 18 months. The more manual the operation, the closer to six months. With automation and required lead times for various elements of needed equipment, those installs will be closer to 18 months.

Inventory Accuracy and Warehouse Management Systems

Companies maintain accuracy of their inventory through a warehouse management system (WMS). This system tracks inventories and locations. It is also the main controlling system for the receipt and pick, pack, and ship operations within the warehouse. It has to be integrated into any engineered solution in the warehouse. This system, in conjunction with the ERP, is one of the main methods for the company to maintain accurate and up to date inventory levels and help to prevent stock-outs, overstocks, and discrepancies.

Some advanced operations will also include other technologies such as barcodes and radio frequency identification (RFID) tagging to maintain even tighter control over the product and location. With these technologies, it allows the system to have real time understanding of the location and inventory levels for the products or materials in the warehouse or distribution center.

To maintain inventory, the company will typically have a system of periodic cycle counts and annual inventory counts.

Cycle counts are a system where in a given periodicity (can be daily weekly, or monthly) a select number of the products or materials in the distribution center or warehouse are counted. The products rotate to ensure full coverage of the SKUs in the system. Those counts are then validated against the warehouse management system or ERP inventory counts. This system helps the team identify discrepancies in a timely manner and then correct any major issues without major disruptions to the business.

Once each year, the company will conduct a full inventory count in the distribution center or warehouse. This evolution can be burdensome to operations and should be limited to when necessary. This may also occur if the cycle counts have significant discrepancies or other unique situations for instance upon sale of a company or other reason to review the stock quantities.

Leakage is a common phenomenon in product storage facilities. Logistics operations and 3PLs typically install security control points when the goods are small and valuable (e.g., a watch distribution facility).

Methods to reduce leakage are critical and help to improve the company's bottom line.

Return Processing

Returns need to be processed by the company. These can be direct-to-consumer returns or returns from retail customers. In general, the return process has to record receipt of the product and who it is from and then provide them credits or refunds, depending on the contractual arrangements. In addition, a well-run company will seek to return unused product to stock to be resold at full price.

For corporate retail customers, this return processing will typically take in full boxes of merchandise. When that occurs, the company can take the unused volumes and return it to the stock shelf. For opened boxes, the materials have to be inspected. This will often lead to some loss because it no longer meets the standards for resale. The other issue is that it takes a long time to reissue the product into inventory. When that occurs, it increases the likelihood for the product to hit expiration dates or become obsolete. Because of those issues, the prompt processing of returns is critical to reduce losses in the process.

For direct-to-consumer volumes being returned, for consumable products they are typically discarded unless there is an external packaging that has not been tampered. This is why Amazon has another layer of wrapping around a number of products. If unopened, you know that the product can be safe to reissue. For other products, they will be inspected and then reissued.

There are no valid general guidelines as every industry will be different and every company will view returns differently. However, if you see a lot of the merchandise being discarded, an assessment of methods to improve the return processing should be conducted.

Inventory Write-Downs: Excess, Obsolete, Damaged, and Expired Goods

Inventory is written down when the value of the product is less than that recorded by accounting. This typically occurs through one of four mechanisms.

When inventory is not selling as fast as anticipated and results in an overstock situation, the resulting overstocked inventory is considered excess. Excess inventory ties up working capital and storage space and may eventually become obsolete if not sold. Writing down excess inventory allows companies to adjust the inventory's recorded value to its actual worth. The actual timing of the write-down will vary by the company's accounting policies. In general, the write-down occurs when the inventory is no longer expected to sell at its recorded value, and it will not recover that value in the future. These policies can be changed. Because of that, caution is required whenever a company tells you that it has excess inventory provisions.

When inventory is no longer in demand or useful this is considered obsolete inventory. One of the main drivers of obsolete inventory is when the product changes or is discontinued. Obsolete inventory can also occur due to changes in market demand and technology. Writing down obsolete inventory helps to clear out the inventory and prevent further storage costs.

Despite best efforts, inventory can be damaged in handling or from environmental factors. Damaged inventory may be unsellable or may require repairs, and can tie up working capital and storage space. In one situation, a company I worked with had to write-down close to $2 million in inventory due to a fire at a consigned inventory location. This was inventory that we still technically owned, but was being managed and sold by a third party. It was still our inventory and when it was damaged, we had to write that inventory down.

When inventory reaches an expiration date, this is expired inventory. The inventory can no longer be sold and needs to be written down. For some goods, there are freshness requirements. Freshness is different than an expiration date. Freshness is typically measured from the date of manufacture and for some customers they prefer goods to be received when they are still relatively new. Contractually, they can require the company to provide only products that are within their freshness tolerance. Another method some customers will employ is to only buy merchandise that has a certain amount of time left before expiration (e.g., six to 12 months). This allows them to provide an adequate window to sell the merchandise without the potential for it to expire while on their balance sheet.

Companies have to write down its inventory from time to time. Typically, a company will have a provision of less than 5 percent of revenue across all of these categories. However, best in class typically keeps inventory write-downs to less than 2 percent with improved demand forecasting. When in excess of 5 percent, investigation is needed to understand what can be improved.

Although the inventory is written down, there is still an intrinsic value to the product. This intrinsic value can potentially be monetized for excess and obsolete (E&O) inventory. For consumer companies, there are businesses that will buy the E&O inventory. These products can also be sold to discount merchants known as Channel 2. The typical discount on retail for both of these methods can be as high as 80 percent. However, it allows the company to monetize the inventory versus destruction. Other companies will provide this inventory to their employees and others will establish a company store at the distribution center and sell the E&O to the distribution center team at steeply discounted prices. The key watch out for is that these products can turn into a gray market where the products are sold at a steep discount and then sold in normal channels or via the internet. This also occurs in other geographies on merchandise provided to merchants as Not for Sale or Demonstration purposes. Some firms are also partnering with non-profits to provide these goods to them as an act of charity and provide a double bottom line benefit to the company.

If not sold through these channels, then the final disposition is for the merchandise to be disposed of to eliminate the carrying cost of the inventory. The typical mechanism is to have the items destroyed so they are not sellable and then discarded. This process in itself costs money, so it is always better to try to monetize the inventory. Some firms are also exploring other methods to improve the amount that can be recycled to maintain a more green posture.

Transportation: Freight and International Freight

The transportation function is responsible for arranging and scheduling shipments on behalf of the company. This can be done in bulk through trucks, rail, and shipping, or it can be done direct-to-consumer via postal service, FedEx, UPS, and similar services.

There is typically a dedicated team that does this for the company. For International shipping, you do need expertise on customer clearance and requirements. Alternatively, a large number of companies leverage freight forwarding services and customs brokers to manage this element of the business. This is typically easier than trying to hire the right talent for these roles. A number of 3PL providers will also host this service for the company.

A well-run transportation department should be able to contain expenses to less than 7 percent of revenue. An exceptional transportation department will be closer to 4 percent. The target value for transportation costs will depend on the specific operation and the type of products being shipped. This cost structure will include the actual cost of shipping, the freight forwarders and customs brokers, all required costs in order to move goods from vendor to end customer.

Most companies will have a transportation management system that will help optimize costs by automating processes, improving visibility into shipments, and optimizing routing and scheduling of shipments. The main methods to improve efficiency for transportation are the consolidation of shipments, improving the routing, and negotiating for price.

Consolidating multiple smaller shipments into fewer, larger shipments, companies can reduce transportation costs by taking advantage of economies of scale. The counterbalance is the time to do so. This can be done by combining orders from different customers, or by coordinating with suppliers to consolidate inbound shipments. For shipments that are less than a truckload (LTL), there are times that freight brokers can book those shipments at a cheaper price on trucks routing between locations appropriate for your shipment. Consolidation of shipments can yield up to about 30 percent improvement in costing.

For companies operating a fleet of vehicles, optimizing routing and scheduling can reduce transportation costs by minimizing the distance traveled and maximizing the capacity of each shipment. This can be achieved by using route planning software, considering traffic patterns and congestion, and coordinating with carriers to optimize scheduling. Companies that have optimized routing have been able to save up to about 20 percent in transportation costs.

Depending on where your shipments need to go, it may make more sense to use multiple modes of transportation. For instance, if you need to ship from NYC to L.A., does it make more sense to use a truck or a combination of trucks and rail? By using a combination of different modes of transportation, such as truck, rail, and ships, companies have been able improve transportation costs by up to 25 percent.

Rate negotiation can yield some benefits. However, you are typically experiencing a potential improvement of up to about 10 percent, if you have sufficient size and volume to get better rates with the freight providers.

For direct-to-consumer, FedEx and UPS rates are typically published. If a company or vendor of sufficient size is able to negotiate, they have been able to achieve rate reductions in the neighborhood of between 10 and 15 percent. Larger companies or companies of strategic importance to those carriers have seen discounts off of published rates up to 40 percent. This high of a discount requires significant volume and deep understanding of shipping patterns that are advantageous to both parties.

THIRD PARTY SPEND

There are no good numbers for total spend on salary and benefits, however, a good estimate is to take GDP in 2019 of $87.7 trillion and multiple by 50 percent (global average for compensation of employees as a percent of GDP, according to the World Bank) and that is about $44 trillion.

In total, companies across the globe spend approximately $30 trillion each year on third party spend. The external spend for a company is a major element of the cost structure. With so much spend it makes sense to ensure it is spent wisely. Just like the need for a HR manager, there is a general need for a head of procurement and purchasing to ensure the company's third party spend is managed properly.

A well-run company of sufficient size has a dedicated procurement team that is a value added component of the business team. In general, you need one procurement member for every $15 million to $50 million in spend. The difference in coverage is if the spend is on highly complex contracts or items or whether it is on simpler procurement initiatives. For large enough enterprises these organizations will likely be arranged with specialty commodity managers (e.g., type of component, common in industrials) or spend-type managers (e.g., IT, G&A, marketing).

In a number of businesses, the spend is not carefully managed or reviewed. In some situations, the company has a procurement team, but the team is not really delivering as much value as is achievable. A good procurement team should be able to drive negative purchase price variance year after year, including insourcing and other initiatives. In addition, they are acting as an advisor to the business on a routine basis to look at the decision on whether to spend dollars or in-source at a lower overall cost structure. In some functions, the procurement team should also be working with the team to systematically look for inefficiencies like where the business has too many licenses for a software platform or have over scoped the buy and are not using elements of what has been procured. These seem like small areas, but it can be the death of 1,000 cuts.

To be successful, the procurement leader needs to be empowered within the company. An effective way to do this is to require their approval for any purchase over $25,000 or once spend hits the $25,000 threshold. For companies over $1 billion it may make more sense to have this threshold at $250,000 to minimize administrative burden. These values may seem low, but it ensures that as much of the spend as practicable is being reviewed and consolidated. For instance, there are companies that will "buy" a temporary service for $10,000, but two years later that service is still being used. A process like this allows the total spend to be reviewed and if no longer required to be stopped.

The easiest method to insert a process like this is when the purchase is being requisitioned. Involving procurement at that stage can allow them to review the buy and, if necessary, leverage existing contracts or relationships to reduce the overall cost of the buy. If of sufficient importance, they can launch an RFP or other initiative in coordination with the business team to seek the lowest cost achievable.

Through this, it provides the procurement team sufficient influence in the organization to maintain and reduce spend year over year. For some business leaders, they will not like this approach. They will feel that their power is being reduced. It is.

However, the healthier way to think about this situation is that the experts should focus on their individual area of expertise. The business is responsible for identifying that it has a requirement for a capability or need. It is up to the procurement team to buy that capability at the lowest cost within acceptable parameters of the business. Those parameters should be mutually aligned with the business leaders and the procurement team. This is a best practice and prevents sweetheart deals from being made from unwitting management teams. Also, when you better empower the procurement team, they can also work with the business functions to understand flexibility in requirements that can unlock additional savings when in contract negotiation.

Spend Analysis

To understand what a company is spending its money on, a best practice is to establish a spend cube or spend analysis. The end state of the spend cube is to have all of the third party spend categorized such that you can see the typical vendors and the total spend with each and as a whole in a category.

To conduct the analysis, the company will have to provide you with an extract of their accounts payable transactional ledger. You are most interested in the cash payments. Please note that when you get the cash payments this can also serve as your cost baseline for spend.

This is a common approach where an analyst works with the last twelve months of spend from a company. They will take a transactional extract of the company's AP ledger and then through various methods and proprietary databases categorize the spend into understandable categories based initially on the typical spend with a company. The analytical process will also typically involve members of the management team reviewing the spend cube and helping to better understand the transactions and what transactions were being made to ensure appropriate categorization.

In some of the AP dumps you will receive, there will be a large amount of intercompany payables. For these, you want to eliminate them from the analysis. They are not beneficial as there is no cash flow impact to the overall entity, they are typically just record keeping and book transactions for P&L purposes. To boot, these transactions should zero out. If they do not zero out, it is something to discuss with the Finance team. There may be some accruals (the difference between actual cash spend and the booked expense or revenue in a given time period) that you need to be aware of.

The proprietary databases that support categorization are not that fancy. On average, they will have names of companies and the typical categories that they provide to a company. The more advanced databases may also have some subcategories, if appropriate and can be determined from the company's data. So, for instance, Microsoft would typically be a software provider. The database would have that relationship. However, the company may in fact be buying its computers from Microsoft in the form of the Surface tablets. This latter fact would be established in the discussion with management. These issues are typically minor. From an outside-in perspective, this analysis stands well to about 80 to 90 percent of the spend. Meaning that the analysis should still be valid for investment purposes.

There are now automated software programs that companies use that can digest the spend information directly from the ERP and provide the company with the analysis typically available via spend cube. In addition, tools like Coupa, Ariba, and Zycus and others can also help to provide some procurement recommendations on what may be beneficial. You may also be able to leverage a tool like this with the native ERP advanced analytics solutions. The key is to have these reviews and be able to drill into transaction level details when and if necessary.

The transaction level details can also shed some light on your purchasing practices and how the company is buying its goods. Is it the most effective to buy smaller quantities just in time or to buy larger bulk buys with larger per transaction discounts. Some of these decisions may also help to optimize working capital and other decisions.

Key Spend Cube Categories

Spend Cube

Document No.	Invoice Date	Vendor	Amount (USD)	Amount (Local)	Remark	Bill to Account	Category	Sub Category
1	11/2/22	Cintas	$100	$100	Cleaning	73500	Services	Consumable
2	11/3/22	Car Mgmt Services	$15000	$15000	Fleet Repairs	65400	Transportation	Repair
3	11/3/23	Dupont Chem	1,500,000	1,500,000	Bulk HDPE	33450	Raw Materials	HDPE Resin
4	11/3/23	Dow Chem	250,000	250,000	Bulk LDPE	33460	Raw Materials	LDPE Resin

With the spend categorized, a procurement professional can then estimate per commodity category what they believe they can achieve through typical levers. The typical levers include rate negotiation, consolidation of spend, reduction in scope, and elimination of need. In general, they will just estimate a percentage range of the category spend. So for raw materials HDPE and LDPE resin, they may have seen buying between DuPont and Dow. If so, consolidation with a larger corporate contract that takes into account full volume for discount or directed buys from your suppliers may yield additional efficiency in the spend. To have this level of insight, you need to have informed players in the various commodity or spend categories. This is not likely to be achieved by your in-house teams.

There are a number of external procurement resources available to a company. They can be everything from an individual contributor to a large shop like an AlixPartners or Alvarez and Marsal. Those two organizations have some of the best practitioners in procurement in the private equity performance improvement industry. However, for industry specific knowledge, there are other providers that can yield even greater insight and benefit to a company.

In some situations, once you identify the issue, all you need to do is send a letter and ask for the reductions to be in line with market. These letters, although simple, often will yield results. Or at a minimum, they will spark a response from the vendor teams that warrant a discussion and resolution.

Oftentimes, the company will need to negotiate for the benefit. It is not likely to just be given to you. The professionals from Alvarez and Marsal and AlixPartners can help to supplement your in house team to support them and negotiate the rates and achieve the consolidation discounts you desire. If internal, then your internal teams should work to develop the objectives, strategy, and the negotiating levers to support the asks.

Methods to Extract Value

With third party spend, there are only four real ways to reduce the spend-rate negotiation, consolidation of spend, reduction in scope or number, and elimination of need.

Negotiation: For rate negotiation, this is the most intuitive for most people when they think about procurement. In general, procurement teams will look at how much a company is spending per unit or quantum of a given resource, service, or material and then negotiate for a better price. This is a common element for the role of procurement.

To realize this value, there is typically a negotiation. There are some great books on effective negotiation. I am not trying to replicate the content or give you my own framework—one thing you learn is that if the work is already done, then don't do it again. To that end, my favorite book is *Getting to Yes* by Roger Fisher and William Ury. The book is easy to read and provides the best framework for a great mutual outcome focused on finding the right solution for everyone. Their approach that focuses on trying to understand the other person's position versus demanding your point of view has proven most successful in my interactions and negotiations to date. It is worse when you have achieved an outcome and the contract does not really meet the needs of either party or worse one of the parties feels like it has been screwed. In those instances, likelihood that the full contract will be complied with is low, which is an even worse outcome than not reaching an agreement. When this occurs, the relationship can break down. In addition, it can cause the other elements of the contract, even ones that are material to you, to be not fully upheld by the other side. This can cause massive issues and if a critical agreement to the business, can cause significant work delays or other issues that could jeopardize the business.

In general, negotiations consist of five stages: preparation, establishing the relationship, present proposal and areas of concern, collaboratively problem solve, bargain and compromise, and agreement and closure.

Preparation: Preparation is a critical element of the negotiation process. It helps align everyone on your side of the table to your objectives and ensures that you identify the desired outcomes and prioritize your must haves and must not allows. Understanding what your best alternative to a negotiated agreement (BATNA) is critical. This is the line where you walk away from the table. This helps you understand your strength for negotiation at the table and also what you are not willing to accept.

During this phase, you will also research the other party and try to understand their drivers, priorities, and constraints. You should also seek to understand the power dynamics between all members of their party and who the ultimate decision maker is. To the extent possible, you want to conduct these discussions with the decision maker. On your side, you obviously want the end point decision maker removed from the day-to-day discussions. Why? So no one becomes overly attached to one way of resolving the problem.

Build rapport and relationships: Trust and rapport go a long way in a negotiation. For protracted negotiations, taking time to develop this is critical. The easiest way to do that is to always demonstrate integrity and reliability to ensure that you have a stable foundation to discuss the key topics and resolutions. If the other side believes you are just telling them what they want to hear, then that will not help in the process.

I once had a boss that I could not trust. Everything he said was not the full truth or tilted in a way that made it uneasy to work with him. Any time we discussed something, I always made sure there were two people in the room. In addition, I documented as much as practicable via email communication. Doing this helps in situations when there cannot be trust established with you and the other side of the table.

Next, you should seek during this period to align on what I always call "motherhood and apple pie." It is an American saying that really just means ideas and concepts that everyone can agree upon. In some situations, it is as simple as, "We would like to continue our relationship and keep terms as close to they are now." This can easily be a win-win. Or, you may know that they have been giving discounts to other customers. Maybe that changes to, "We have had a great relationship, but we want to see how we can work together to get our contractual rates in line with like companies such as X. Otherwise, you may be inadvertently giving them a competitive advantage." I think most people would agree that unless they are acting maliciously, a supplier should never seek to create an advantage for one like customer versus another, unless there are drivers. In the next stage, we will layout the issues and then try to understand the drivers.

Exchange information: At this point, you should make your case whether pitching or receiving. This should be done to clearly articulate your key interests in the discussions, your priorities and, to the extent they can be shared, your constraints. It goes without saying that some of these you may keep to yourself for the time being—for instance, "Here is how much I can spend." That may be a bad idea.

When they present their case or concerns, you should also be an active listener. At this point, you want to try to be an active problem solver. You and your counterpart should be seeking to solve each others' problems such that you can get to a negotiated settlement. The active listening will help you really hear what the other party is saying. In addition, it will help to identify any underlying interests that they may have. At the end of the day, you are negotiating with a person. That person has incentives and must dos. Because of this, the closer you listen, the more likely you are to hear them and help solve for those issues – breaking down the barrier to getting to a negotiated answer.

Collaboratively problem solve, bargain, and compromise: During this phase, which can potentially occur in parallel with the exchange of information, you will need to work together to solve the problems that may be impeding the negotiated settlement. You should try to work collaboratively with the other side to solve these issues, within the constraints that you have. The goal is to try to see the issues from their side, empathizing with them. This will help you to understand some of the alternatives that might be present and that they themselves may not have thought about. At the end, the goal is really to seek the win-win solutions and aim to improve their outcome in line with your own.

In one negotiation, a client was constrained with an ERP implementation in a certain region. To execute the deal, we needed to finish our IT suite within 12 months to accommodate that ask. This was a tall ask, but something we had to solve for. If not, no deal. We then engineered a solution that could fit within that window, changing one of our constraints, but getting to a win-win solution for all. However, we also did not budge on the need for continued access to markets all the way out past that date—this was somewhat of an offset to us having to assume more risk to meet their timelines.

When you have to compromise, try to offer those that are lower cost to you, but higher value to them. This sounds great when written, but typically it does not happen that way. Usually, both sides understand the value levers. When that is the case, they will understand what they are getting versus what you are giving. To achieve this, asymmetry, you need to do one of a few things. Two of which are to look for those areas that matter to the individual and might not actually matter to the outcome on your end. For instance, the person negotiating on their end needs to close this deal to get their bonus. Guess what? You know that this deal is getting done. Ask for the concessions you really want. However, there are times when you need to "grow the pie" or "bundle" to get there. For instance, you know that there is a $15 million pricing non-linearity that they are trying to get away with. Asking for the $15 million may be a non-starter, because there is some uncertainty to the analysis or whatever they identify. However, if you package that $15 million with another $5 million offset and ask for $17.5 million, they think they are getting a deal and you are happy to compromise with a net benefit of $17.5 million.

Agreement and closure: When everything is said and done and everyone is aligned with the value, then you should take the time to clearly outline the agreed upon terms and conditions and confirm the commitments with the other party. This ensures that the other party will be committed to fulfilling their obligations. Finally, you will be able to monitor implementation of the agreement and then hold the other side accountable when or if needed.

Consolidation of spend: Consolidation of spend is a special form of negotiation and is typically something that requires the company to commit to additional volume with a given supplier for tiered discounts or rebates. A number of consultancies will immediately say this is achievable just by looking at the pareto of spend and suppliers. Yes, but the typical consolidation of spend analysis requires a number of critical buy offs or buy-ins from the team. The first is that there is a supplier that you can aggregate the spend with. Typically you can. However, there are key tradeoffs. The biggest of which is the capability quality. There are differences in quality between various vendors. In addition, there may be specific machining processes that need to be in place. Can the vendor overcome them? Yes. However, it may take time. It may take requalifying the vendor or a new process to manufacture the product. This could then impact customer experience or perception of the product. The easiest products to do this with are commodity products. However, when you get to other goods, there is typically a tradeoff and you need to ensure everyone is bought into it.

Actualizing the volume can sometimes be difficult. So, a great practice is to have a tiered structure where there is no harm with the as is volumes. However, the more you give to them, the better. Another key lesson is to ensure you use total volume and not just commodity specific. This allows for the greatest discount and ensures you are both incented to grow the relationship. The final call out is for the customer. There are often ways when you are tolling your production to do directed buys. Ensure that all of your contracts can allow for directed buys or already allow for them.

Reduction in scope or number: Oftentimes, companies that do not have an active and empowered procurement team will be buying more capability than is required or acquiring more licenses. The biggest issue is typically in IT. To assess the number of licenses, the procurement team should be working with IT to see the average number of daily users for all of the capabilities needed and the periodicity for when others truly need to see the system. There are a number of times you can reduce a significant number of the licenses because people are only accessing the system maybe once every month or every three months. In those instances, working with the business to change the workflow may be a way to avoid maintaining the various licenses.

Another way is the scope of the license. There are a number of modules in each of the new IT systems. There are times when the company has procured four modules when it really just needed three for the capability it is using the system for. This can be identified with a survey or discussion with management on how the system is used and what capabilities are currently present on the system. Other times, a company may have needed the capability in a prior system configuration. However it is no longer used. In those situations work with your account manager and have the company stop billing for the capability that is no longer being used.

Elimination of need: The final way to reduce third party spend is to eliminate the need for the third party spend. This can vary from just no longer procuring something to changing company policy to in-sourcing to eliminate certain spends.

Coming out of the excesses of Silicon Valley in the mid 2010s, the majority of firms bought their staff lunch every day or on select days each week. When we moved forward and some of the Silicon Valley companies began to have trouble and issues, then the company began to cut back. Nowadays there are a very limited number of companies that offer lunch for free every day. A large number have decided to move completely away from that trend. Because of that choice, the spend has gone away. Decisions like this can occur for other areas of spend and the spend can be eliminated.

In another situation, the company changed its policy from the company buying and paying for the resources cell phone. The new policy eliminated these accounts sponsored by the company and instead shifted to a bring your own device (BYOD). In this situation, they now would reimburse their people for up to $80 per month for the employee's line. This eliminated the need for a tech refresh spend and also eliminated the company paying for the total bill for its employees.

The final method to eliminate third party spend is through initiatives that in-source the work. In this instance, there was a company in a high cost location that was using consultants in lieu of permanent employees. It was costing them about $200,000 per employee per year. The company had recently opened a new facility in North Carolina. The management team immediately saw that if they in-sourced those roles to the North Carolina office, then they could save up to $66,000 (about 33 percent) per person. They quickly made a decision to hire the required resources in North Carolina and transition all of those capabilities from the high-cost location to the low cost in-house option.

REAL ESTATE

Real estate is an often-overlooked driver of value for a company. The reality is that most management teams want a beautiful glittery office. However, when you digest this and look at the true drivers of value, it is not what most employees want. The employees focus on the working environment (what they will be living in for eight to 12 hours a day) and the office location (driver of their commute time). Following the abrupt change to working patterns in 2020 due to the coronavirus, we also need to consider maintaining some element of the hybrid and remote work arrangements (or at a minimum flexibility). By focusing on the primary drivers of satisfaction, you can likely reduce your spend and develop a global real estate strategy that works for the company.

The office environment is one of the most important elements. This will drive workplace productivity. In general, the major drivers employees are looking for fall into three major buckets:

1. **Well-being of the person:** It sounds odd to say it, but indoor air quality and temperature control are a primary driver of employee satisfaction. This is an item that most business people overlook. However, those that have managed facilities or have been employed by a company that does not have a facility with adequate ventilation can attest that these are critical drivers of value and productivity. When you look at the warehousing industry, the biggest driver of satisfaction is to have a warehouse that is climate controlled. Otherwise, during the summer months the worker is exposed to 100° temperatures while conducting a physically-strenuous activity.

   Another factor is the ergonomics of the individual workstation. Taking into account the workspace and furniture that is selected is critical. Picking furniture that provides good posture and prevents strain reduces the risk of injury and boost productivity. When you think of an office worker, paying the additional $100 per chair may make sense, if it provides more comfort than the cheaper option.

2. **Cleanliness and lighting:** The cleanliness of the space is also a critical element of satisfaction. The office environment just needs to be well maintained and clean. That is it. Light switches need to be replaced if malfunctioning and minor cosmetic issues addressed.

   Lighting in the space is a differentiator. When you work in a dimly lit space, it creates a negative sentiment within the population. Whatever you may save in electricity you lose in productivity. Always remember, the rule of 10s: One person costs $1,000, the space costs about a tenth of that, so $100, and the electricity and other spend for the space costs about a tenth of that, or $10. This is a very rough general guideline, but helps you prioritize the value. Don't prioritize saving a small percentage on a $10 expenditure if you reduce the effectiveness of something 100 times the value.

3. **Acoustics and workplace design:** The final area is to create a space that enables the required work for the company. This does not require elegant solutions. In the end, the employee needs a place where they can control noise or soundproof if needed to minimize distractions. This is for employees that need an area where they can focus.

The second element is to create the necessary space that can flex between open and private spaces. Employee productivity improves with those more flexible and adaptive workspace solutions.

Please note that there are some other needs. For instance, there is the need for some places where executives or others can conduct confidential conversations. This typically requires some dedicated conference rooms or offices. An office per executive is not required.

The average executive wants a corner suite or a room with a view. However, how much value does that provide to the company? What an executive needs is a space to hold confidential information, this can be done with a foot pedestal under the desk in an open plan workspace, and they also need access to a place to hold confidential meetings, if needed. This can be done in a communal conference room. To the extent that the executive is in confidential meetings all day long, then he or she may warrant a dedicated office. Otherwise, the office is just an ego boost and of little to no value to the company itself.

The second key consideration (and the largest driver of value for the company) is access to employees. We have already discussed the strategic location of your offices. However, within the chosen geography, you should seek to find the optimal location that gives you access to the most talent. The best way to do that is through an employee mapping and commute analysis. This allows the company to understand the current layout of where their employee's live, where desired employee populations live, and then through algorithms identify how long of a commute a given office location will generate for the current and desired employee population.

In general, employees prefer a commute less than 30 minutes one way. Multiple studies indicate that 30 minutes is where preference shifts.[26]

---

26   Alois Stutzer and Bruno Frey, "Stress That Doesn't Pay: The Commuting Paradox," *The Scandinavian Journal of Economics* 110, no. 2, June 2008; Hilary Osbourne, "Commuting Makes you 'Unhappy and Anxious', Says ONS," *The Guardian*, February 12, 2014, www.theguardian.com/money/2014/feb/12/commuting-unhappy-anxious-ons.

Furthering that, the UK study also indicates that employee well-being decreases and their anxiety increases with each additional minute of a commute beyond 30 minutes.

Because of this selecting a location in the geography that gives you access to the right populations is critical. If you want to access artists in New York, it may make sense to keep your location in Brooklyn versus putting the studio or office in Manhattan. However, if you are trying to attract a general population set, it may make sense to put your location close to a subway and within walking distance of Grand Central Station, access to the commuter lines going North and east and access to New York Moynihan Station, commuter lines going West and South. Doing so, will give you maximize access to employees.

The other key element is access to amenities. It is great for quality of life if your employees have access to unique experiences they can readily use from the office. For some locations, it may just be access to restaurants or a gym. For others, keeping an office near a location that is a draw (e.g., an outdoor park, a concert venue, or a stadium).

The final element is safety. Everyone wants to be safe in their work environment and going to and from their work location. At the location level, ensure that the location has access control. This is typically done through the use of magnetic card technologies and the use of a receptionist or security control center for larger installations. In one situation, an office ended up near a bar and a large entertainment venue. It was a great location with the appropriate access to top talent. The management team quickly recognized that during entertainment events additional security was needed. The goal was to leverage a security professional to ensure staff was protected and they had someone that they could rely on to get them to their cars regardless of events going on near the location.

When you drill down to these key drivers, it allows you a lot more flexibility in where you place your locations. When you do, you will also find a lot more value in the commercial space market. For instance, when you look at the office market in New York in 2023 the cost per square foot is expensive. It can average at $82.50 per square foot. When you look at micromarkets, Central Park can average around $112, while Midtown East is about $71.68. When you look at this from a value driver perspective, you will find the two offices equal. So why pay a $40 per square foot premium?

Evaluation of Footprint

So, how much space do you need? Well, this is actually very easy from an analytical perspective. But requires some thinking to understand. In general, in the United States, you need at least 150 square feet per person to maintain an adequate work environment. You will find a large number of companies operating somewhere between 200 and 300 square feet per person. This is an opportunity for improvement. In Asia and EMEA, space requirements can decrease to about 100 square feet per person.

Functionally, only about 40 to 60 percent of that requirement is the true workspace for the employee. This includes the individual workstations and the offices. However, you also need to account for the common areas, which is another 20 to 30 percent of the footprint, hallways and aisles (10 to 20 percent), storage and unique equipment needs (5 to 15 percent), and some room for growth (5 to 10 percent). When you try to operationalize the 150 square feet per person, there are times when the layout of the space or requirements of the company only allow you to get down to about 175 to 200 square feet per person.

Strategies to Reduce Real Estate Cost

The implementation timeline for real estate cost savings tends to be long. To realize the efficiencies, you typically need to align the initiative with the end of the current lease to capture the full savings. The leasing company typically structures the contract such that the company signs up for the total lease liability that is due in the event of a lease break. Or that the allowance for tenant improvement (TI) is due, either prorated or in full. This tends to be a large sum provided to a company to make improvements to the property as a benefit for signing the lease. The net result is that the cost to achieve becomes exceptionally high, and typically negative NPV. The majority of companies typically wait out the lease, unless there is a significant value that can be achieved.

There are a number of companies that know there is value in the real estate portfolio and before they put themselves up for sale, they will lock in a long duration lease. This is done to ensure that the company is able to retain its current location. This is smart, but does not prevent the realization of value.

When the initiative lines up with the end of the lease, the manifestation of value is relatively simple. First, the company notifies the landlord that they are vacating the premise. There is a notification time horizon for the tenant to notify the landlord. Ensure that this timeline is met. There is typically a notification and response that needs to be captured. In coordination, the company will have already started a search for a new location. In general, in the U.S., this process takes about six months to one year. It will be about three months to search for the location. Depending on the required improvements, it can take anywhere between three months to nine months to complete the space per the company's requirements.

This timeline needs to be completed about one to two months before the end of your current lease end. This builds in a buffer, but also allows for the facilities team to transfer all of the personal goods and desk equipment to the new facility, unless you are using all new furnishings in the space.

At that point, the new location is available and then you can exit the other lease. There are usually some dilapidation costs that need to be paid. In lieu, you can have your contracts fix those issues and the costs are typically waived.

In the event you need to exit the space before the end of the lease, the best answer is to sublet the space. There is a significant cost to do so. Typically, a company that sublets a space has a value recapture of about 50 to 70 percent of the lease value. This typically makes sense when you are no longer using the space.

There was one client where the company made a decision to reduce overall staffing by about 20 to 25 percent of the overall employee population. On a five floor building, this allowed one to two floors of their current space to be open for sublet. Please note that they also had inefficiencies in the allocation of space. Because of that, the company was able to market two of the five floors for sublet. For sublets, the longer your current contract the better. When the company has a long duration contract, it may allow them to sublet the property at close to market rates and even provide the tenant with a TI allowance. Typically, the leases are shorter duration and you discount the pricing off of market to attract buyers. This gap is typically about 10 to 20 percent, however it can be as high as 40 percent, with heavier discounts typically for shorter lease durations, limited to no customization or improvement allowances, and high financial stability of the tenant. This method has risks, typically on the financial stability of the sub-tenant. The other major risk is whether or not the original landlord allows subtenants to exist. Oftentimes, they may have prohibited that in the original lease, require permission from the original landlord, or may require the original lease to share any upside if market conditions have caused the market rate to increase.

The other stakeholder that also benefits from the lease is the leasing agent. These resources will typically charge about 7 to 10 percent of the lease cost to manage the property.

Shared Space Supplement

There is increased use of shared spaces for smaller office locations or unique situations for investors. WeWork, Regus, Industrious, and others have variable sized office locations in high demand locations at reasonable pricing. In addition, the service typically provides all of the amenities typically required such as coffee, security support, internet access, among others.

When the company needs to establish a smaller scale operation (anything less than about 100 to 150 employees), the company can evaluate the use of these types of facilities. They can quickly scale up and down a location on your behalf. In one situation, I needed a facility that could hold (initially) about 250 people. We knew that we would reduce the population by about 100 resources, requiring us to just need one floor. We structured the contract with one of these providers to have a one year lease for one floor and a longer term five year lease on the main floor. This level of flexibility and ability to scale up or down was highly beneficial for the needs that that deal had. The final element of value with these contracts is that if the company grows, these companies can allow you to transfer to a new location in their network, transferring the remaining lease liability for the newer location that may have more seats or space as required. These features are also beneficial for remote sales teams and also for companies as they navigate the final disposition of offices and the decisions on remote versus in-office presence of resources.

INSURANCE

Insurance is another area of value that companies typically overlook. The best answer when assessing insurance needs for a company is to get a top-notch insurance broker and advisor such as Marsh McLennan for large companies. For smaller companies, there are a large number of providers. If you are looking at a company to buy, these companies can do a diligence on the company and provide estimates of what coverages they actually need.

Please note that anything I have in this section is a directional and rough guide to where insurance coverages typically land. This has been sourced through various methods on the internet and should not be relied on to inform or make your decisions on insurance coverage for your company.

In general, a company will typically spend between 1 and 4 percent of revenue on insurance premiums. For companies in high-risk industries or with a history of claims will tend to be higher than ones in lower risk industries and with less claims.

Types of Insurance Companies Use (Not Exhaustive)

Insurance companies can underwrite a large number of risks. This list will capture the primary ones you will likely encounter when speaking with a company. The list below providers a quick understanding of what the policy generally covers.

Workers' compensation: This insurance provides coverage for medical expenses, rehabilitation costs, and lost wages for employees who suffer from work-related injuries or illnesses.

Umbrella liability: This insurance provides additional liability coverage beyond the limits of underlying policies (such as general liability, auto liability, and employers liability). It can protect businesses from large claims that could potentially exhaust their primary insurance coverages.

Employers liability: This coverage protects employers from lawsuits filed by employees for work-related injuries or illnesses that are not covered under workers' compensation insurance.

General liability: This insurance provides coverage for bodily injury, property damage, and personal injury claims resulting from the business's operations, products, or services.

Auto liability: This coverage protects businesses from financial losses arising from accidents involving company-owned, leased, or hired vehicles.

Foreign liability: This insurance covers businesses for liability claims arising from their operations in foreign countries.

Property insurance: This coverage protects businesses from financial losses due to damage to their physical assets, such as buildings, equipment, and inventory, caused by events like fire, theft, or natural disasters.

Marine insurance: This insurance covers the transportation of goods, both domestically and internationally, and provides coverage for losses due to damage, theft, or other risks during transit.

Directors and officers (D&O) insurance: This coverage protects the personal assets of a company's directors and officers from lawsuits alleging wrongful acts, such as mismanagement or breach of fiduciary duty, in their capacity as corporate executives.

Cyber insurance: This insurance covers businesses for financial losses resulting from cyberattacks, data breaches, and other technology-related incidents.

Professional liability insurance: Also known as errors and omissions (E&O) insurance, this coverage protects businesses from financial losses due to negligence, errors, or omissions in the provision of professional services.

Crime insurance: This insurance covers businesses from financial losses resulting from theft, fraud, or other criminal acts committed by employees or third parties.

Business interruption insurance: This coverage compensates businesses for lost income and extra expenses incurred due to the temporary shutdown of operations resulting from a covered event, such as a fire or natural disaster.

In addition to the core policies, there can be riders and exclusions. These will be outlined in the actual insurance policy.

A rider is an additional coverage or modification to the insurance policy that alters the terms or coverages. Here are some typical riders:

Additional insured: This rider extends coverage to other parties, such as subcontractors, vendors, or landlords, as specified in the policy.

Waiver of subrogation: This rider prevents the insurance company from seeking recovery from a third party after paying a claim on behalf of the policyholder.

Cyber liability: This rider extends coverage to include losses resulting from data breaches, cyberattacks, and other technology-related incidents.

Employment practices liability: This rider provides coverage for claims related to employment practices, such as discrimination, harassment, and wrongful termination.

An exclusion is basically the opposite. An exclusion is a specific situation, event, or type of loss that is not covered by the insurance policy. Exclusions help insurance companies manage their risk by limiting the types of claims they are willing to pay for.

Here are some examples of exclusions that can be applied to insurance policies:

Intentional acts: Losses resulting from deliberate or malicious actions taken by the insured or their employees.

War and terrorism: Losses resulting from acts of war, terrorism, or insurrection.

Nuclear hazards: Losses caused by nuclear reactions, radiation, or radioactive contamination.

Pollution: Losses related to environmental pollution, such as the release of hazardous substances into the air, water, or soil.

Contractual liability: Losses arising from liability assumed under a contract or agreement unless the liability exists in the absence of the contract.

I have provided some general estimates for typical insurance coverage below. Please note that these estimates should only be used as a starting point for your own research and should not be considered as specific recommendations. It is important to consult with an insurance professional to determine the appropriate coverage for your company.

Rough Orders of Magnitude for Typical Insurance Coverages

Always consult an insurance expert to assess your unique risks and determine the appropriate coverage.

Insurance Rough Orders of Magnitude

Industry	Worker's Compensation	Umbrella Liability	Employer's Liability	General Liability	Auto Liability	Foreign	Property
Industrial	0.5-1.5%	1.0-2.5%	0.1-0.5%	0.3-0.8%	0.2-0.5%	0.1-0.3%	0.3-1.5%
Consumer	0.3-1.0%	0.5-1.5%	0.05-0.3%	0.2-0.6%	0.1-0.4%	0.05-0.2%	0.2-1.0%
Technology	0.2-0.6%	0.5-2.0%	0.05-0.3%	0.1-0.4%	0.1-0.3%	0.05-0.2%	0.1-0.5%
Service	0.3-1.0%	0.5-1.5%	0.05-0.3%	0.2-0.6%	0.1-0.4%	0.05-0.2%	0.1-0.7%

Industry	Marine Property	D&O	Cyber	Professional Liability	Crime	Business Interruption
Industrial	0.05-0.2%	0.2-0.5%	0.1-0.4%	0.1-0.5%	0.05-0.2%	0.2-0.8%
Consumer	0.03-0.1%	0.1-0.4%	0.1-0.3%	0.05-0.3%	0.03-0.1%	0.1-0.5%
Technology	0.02-0.1%	0.2-0.8%	0.2-0.8%	0.2-0.8%	0.05-0.2%	0.1-0.4%
Service	0.02-0.1%	0.1-0.4%	0.1-0.4%	0.1-0.6%	0.03-0.1%	0.1-0.5%

These percentages represent an estimated range of umbrella liability coverage per $100 million in revenue. For example, an industrial company with $100 million in revenue may need umbrella liability coverage between 1.0 and 2.5 percent of its revenue (i.e., between $1 million and $2.5 million).

Methods to Reduce Insurance Spend

The method to reduce insurance spend should never be at the expense of adequate coverage as defined by you and the insurance broker you are working with. The primary driver of value is to get a highly qualified insurance broker. The insurance broker understands the insurance markets and can even help you with timing of your placements to reduce your overall cost.

In addition, the insurance broker can work with you to regularly review your insurance coverages and sculpt the insurance coverages needed to support your company. The other benefit is that they will shop your coverage requirements out to the market. This allows you to find the best coverages for your business. In addition, you can likely negotiate with the broker or the agent to secure better terms or discounts. You can also work to bundle some of the coverages through the broker and that may help to lower your total premium cost structure.

Better analysis of your operations and risk is always a benefit. The biggest lever will always be around the level of coverage and knowing how much risk the company can assume. This is an experiential call, but if you see a significant difference in the insurance coverage and where you assess the risk to actually be, then adjust the level. For instance, if you routinely have $4 million of merchandise on transports, do you need $10 million of coverage? This is something the company can measure and monitor to ensure that the coverage levels are correct.

Second, if your company is financially stable, then you can look at other methods to finance the risk. There is the ability to self-insure for some of the risks to reduce some of the insurance costs. This is something where you will want to understand your own financial stability, but also your risk exposure. If you do not want to self-insure, you can still increase your deductibles to lower your premiums. Over time, you can also look at your claims history. Those with fewer claims typically can drive lower rates.

PUBLIC TO PRIVATE TRANSITIONS

When a company is taken private, there are some costs that are eliminated. In general, it is about 1 to 2 percent of the company's revenue. Some estimates for these costs have been as high as 5 percent. Some of these costs have already been discussed as a potentially redundant resource in a private setting. However, I plan to show this in full so you know the main drivers of the value. In general, the largest costs removed will be with regulatory compliance and reporting.

Typical Costs Removed During the Transition to Private Holding

Below I have provided the typical list of areas where costs are removed once a company shifts from public to private.

Regulatory compliance and public disclosures: The Sarbanes-Oxley Act requires a high level of financial transparency. Going into a private setting reduces these requirements to what is needed to satisfy the private equity holder's needs. This reduction in need for transparency, in and of itself, reduces cost structure. However, going private also reduces the need for periodic reports to the Securities and Exchange Commission. This workload is reduced, but is replaced with filling the needs of the new owner of the firm. Depending on those requirements, the company may or may not see a reduction in headcount to support the reporting. However, the legal, accounting, and other costs and time burden of the reporting and draw of management attention is removed.

Investor relations: The Investor Relations team is removed from the organization in total. The private equity team essentially becomes your IR department. The workload associated with this, which could include investor communications, roadshows, analyst meetings, and shareholder relationships, is all shifted to the PE firm. This eliminates the cost of the resources, but also the marketing costs, and travel expenses for the function.

Board of directors: The cost for the board of directors is greatly reduced. The board is usually replaced with one put forward by the private equity firm. This is not a 100 percent cost reduction—typically somewhere between 40 and 50 percent reduction is achievable, as a number of the board seats will be held by the PE firm. Second, there will be tangible reductions in the amount of time the management team is involved in board committees and compliance and reporting to the board. This is not a "hard" number, but realize that there are efficiencies in the new paradigm.

Listing fees: Depending on the market and market capitalization of the entity, the publicly traded company will pay listing fees to the stock exchanges where their shares are traded.

Market	Initial Listing Fees	Annual Fees
NASDAQ	Fees can range from around $50,000 to several hundred thousand dollars. The actual amount depends on the market value of the company's listed securities.	Fees can range from approximately $25,000 to $300,000 or more, depending on the company's market capitalization.
NYSE	The initial listing fees for the NYSE vary based on the market capitalization of the company. The fees can range from tens of thousands of dollars to several hundred thousand dollars or more.	Depending on the company's market capitalization, annual fees can range from approximately $5,000 to $300,000 or more.
Tokyo Stock Exchange	The initial listing fees for the TSE can range from approximately ¥1 million to several million yen.	Annual fees ranging from several hundred thousand yen to several million yen.
Shanghai Stock Exchange	Initial listing fees for companies on the SSE can range from several hundred thousand yuan to several million yuan.	Annual fees are typically a percentage of the company's market capitalization and can vary.

Hong Kong Stock Exchange	The listing fees for the main board and the growth enterprise market (GEM) can vary. Initial listing fees for the main board are based on market capitalization and can range from several hundred thousand Hong Kong dollars to several million Hong Kong dollars. The GEM has a separate fee structure, and the fees are generally lower.	Annual fees for both main board and GEM listings are based on market capitalization.
Euronext	Euronext operates multiple stock exchanges across several countries, including France, Belgium, Netherlands, Portugal, and others. The listing fees on Euronext can vary depending on the specific country and market segment. Fees are typically based on market capitalization and other factors, and it's advisable to consult directly with Euronext for accurate and up-to-date information.	
London Stock Exchange	The LSE has a complex formula, but they have an easy to access online calculator—use that here: www.londonstockexchange.com/raise-finance/equity/how-list-equity/calculating-fees	

Corporate development: In general, the corporate development function can be eliminated. However, there are times where the company's investment thesis relies on active portfolio management including acquisitions and divestitures. When that is the case, they will typically retain the corporate development function to allow for someone to actively manage those elements of the investment thesis.

PE firm costs to the company: This is an offset to these costs. There are a number of other costs that the PE firm will saddle the company with. Typically, there is a management fee that they will charge the company. This includes costs for certain advisors and time for some of their staff supporting the company. They may also charge the company a general management fee. This is dependent on the PE firm. However, it is not uncommon to see a charge for a million or more each quarter from the PE firm to their companies. When doing any pre-acquisition analysis, it is better to leave this off as some of it may also include elements of advisory spend.

CHAPTER 5

Growing Topline and Commercial Excellence

The growth of the portfolio asset is a key driver of exit multiples and economic valuation. Growing top line shows that the company is economically thriving. The majority of companies sold into private equity are not typically the darlings of an industry. The companies they buy tend to be past prime or a company that is not focused solely on growth. From a rational actor perspective, it would not make sense to sell an asset to a PE buyer if there are significant strategic tailwinds and significant room to continue growing. You would be leaving easy money on the table. Whereas a short quantum of years later from that point, when the market believes there may still be some growth, but you know it is short-lived—that would be the time to sell—maximizing your economic profit and shifting the downside risk to the investor. Further, for the companies with a very strong market and high growth estimate, they can just as easily be absorbed into a near competitor, receiving a potentially higher buy multiple, and not entering into privately owned hands with larger risk profiles for leadership teams.

All of the PE investment firms I have worked with do a deep diligence on the strategic position of the asset and the tailwind of the industry. They pay top dollar to the likes of Bain or McKinsey to do a commercial diligence on the asset. These assessments will review the strategic headwind or tailwind of the asset's core and adjacent markets, the strategic position of the asset in the market, the brand reputation of the asset, and the consumer sentiment. This diligence validates that the companies' strategy and the segment are not heading into a significant area of uncertainty. In short, it will typically eliminate (or at least identify) any potential strategic issue with the company, its brands, and its market.

These analyses will even pick up on external exogenous factors. For instance, there was one company I analyzed that could be impacted by legislative changes. There was potential legislation in Congress where, if passed, it would shutdown a revenue stream for about 5 percent of their revenue. We pulled together an assessment of the likelihood of that legislation passing. We conducted 10 or 15 expert interview phone calls, culled a number of research reports, articles and other primary and secondary sources on the topic. It got distilled into a 15 slide report out on what the legislation was, who were the backers, and what were the upside and downside implications for the potential asset. However, for the core answer they were looking for—would this legislation be passed—in true consulting form we said maybe. And that is the beauty of strategy and growth estimates. There is always a caveat and a maybe.

Although growth is critical to the investment, why did I save it for last? Growth is decremented in any pre-acquisition analysis to the investment by any external party providing funding. Why? There are three main reasons:

1. People can always be optimistic on growth and revenue synergy assessments. When things do not go as predicted, they can point to a number of other counterparties that prevented it from happening. Growth is a con artist's dream—they can make promises and not deliver and, unless you hold them accountable, they will tell you a million reasons why it was not their fault.

2. Growth takes time. The market needs to buy in to the changes and then respond. This can take time. When you try to push this sooner, it may not take hold. There is a confluence of initiatives and relationships that typically need to occur or mature in order to drive topline higher. For instance, when you re-position a brand. You typically need to also improve the customer experience. To achieve that might take a year or more and then you will start to see topline grow. When you are expanding your geographic reach, there are a number of relationships that need to be fostered to gain access to the right venues in a new market.

3. Topline growth does not always equate to profitability growth. This is not well understood. However, when you really start getting into a five-year plan you will see it in the numbers presented. You need to understand where your margin growth is actually coming from. The short answer is that it does not come from selling more! You need to continue to force discipline and improve back office efficiency. For that to be true, you need to create a back office that creates operating leverage first—that was the first element of this book. The second thing is that just by selling more, even with operating leverage that does not mean you have maximized your commercial potential. Focusing on commercial excellence does. That is what the second element of this book is focused on.

Some have asked, why aren't you talking about strategy versus commercial excellence? I always tell them, "Excellent question!" Here's why: In short, it is timeline for implementation and results.

However, here is the longer discussion: Strategy refers to the overall plan or approach that a company adopts to achieve its long-term goals and objectives. Strategy can take five to 10 years to achieve and realize. Think about Netflix, Proctor & Gamble, General Electric, and Microsoft.

Netflix: Netflix is a prime example of a company that transformed its strategy over time. Initially, Netflix operated as a DVD-by-mail rental service, but it recognized the shift towards digital streaming and made a bold strategic decision to transition into an online streaming platform. This involved negotiating content licensing agreements, investing in streaming technology, and building a vast library of digital content. Over the course of several years, Netflix successfully executed its strategy and became a dominant force in the streaming industry, eventually phasing out its DVD rental business altogether.

Procter & Gamble: P&G, a multinational consumer goods company, embarked on a significant strategy shift known as "P&G 2020" under the leadership of former CEO A.G. Lafley. The company aimed to focus on its core brands and categories, streamline operations, and enhance productivity. P&G divested more than 100 non-core brands and reduced its product portfolio to focus on its most profitable and strategic brands. This involved restructuring the organization, implementing cost-saving measures, and investing in innovation and marketing for key brands. The strategy overhaul took several years to implement and aimed to drive sustainable growth and profitability for the company.

General Electric: GE, a renowned industrial conglomerate, underwent a strategic transformation under former CEO Jeffrey Immelt. The company shifted its focus from traditional industrial sectors, such as appliances and lighting, to high-growth areas such as renewable energy, healthcare technology, and aviation. GE divested various business units and acquired companies in emerging sectors to reshape its portfolio. This strategy required significant investments in research and development, partnerships, and new product development. The transformation aimed to position GE as a leading digital industrial company and took several years to execute.

Microsoft: Microsoft, originally known for its dominance in the personal computer software market, underwent a significant strategic shift under the leadership of CEO Satya Nadella. Nadella introduced a "cloud-first, mobile-first" strategy, recognizing the shift towards cloud computing and the growing importance of mobile devices. Over the course of several years, Microsoft shifted its focus from packaged software to cloud-based services and platforms, such as Microsoft Azure and Office 365. This transformation required substantial investments, organizational restructuring, and changes in product development and distribution. It took Microsoft several years to implement this strategy and successfully establish itself as a major player in the cloud computing market.

Strategy requires making informed decisions about how the company will allocate its resources, compete in the market, and create value for its stakeholders in the next five to 10 years. Strategy focuses on the big picture and involves analyzing the external environment, identifying opportunities and risks, and formulating a plan to position the company for success. It encompasses aspects such as target markets, product or service offerings, competitive advantage, and differentiation. With that long of a time horizon, unless existential to the company and investment, it will not likely prompt a PE firm to invest in something that does not pay off within the investment hold period. However, commercial excellence does.

Commercial excellence is a specific focus within a company's operations that aims to optimize its commercial performance and maximize profitable revenue generation. It involves implementing strategies and practices that enhance the company's effectiveness in areas such as sales, SKU/portfolio rationalization, marketing, branding, customer relationship management, go-to-market, and pricing. Commercial excellence aims to improve customer acquisition, retention, and satisfaction, as well as increase profitability and market share. It often involves analyzing market trends, customer preferences, and competitive dynamics to identify areas for improvement and develop targeted initiatives.

Commercial excellence, combined with cost cutting and containment are drivers of rapid value. Here are a few examples:

Walmart: Walmart, the multinational retail corporation, implemented a series of initiatives to improve its commercial performance and drive profitability. The company focused on optimizing its supply chain, enhancing inventory management, and leveraging data analytics to improve pricing and promotions. Walmart also invested in e-commerce capabilities and expanded its online presence. These efforts, combined with cost control measures, resulted in significant EBITDA margin improvements within a two-year timeframe.

Ford: Ford, the American automotive manufacturer, embarked on a comprehensive turnaround plan called "The Way Forward" to enhance its commercial performance. The company focused on streamlining its product lineup, reducing costs, and improving manufacturing efficiency. Ford also implemented pricing strategies to enhance margins and increased its emphasis on higher-margin vehicles, such as trucks and SUVs. These initiatives led to EBITDA margin improvements within a relatively short period.

Adobe: Adobe, the software and technology company, underwent a strategic shift to a subscription-based business model with its Creative Cloud platform. By transitioning from perpetual licensing to a subscription model, Adobe achieved improved revenue predictability, customer retention, and upselling opportunities. The company's commercial excellence efforts, including targeted marketing campaigns and improved customer engagement, resulted in significant EBITDA margin improvements within a two-year timeframe.

Marriott International: Marriott International, the global hospitality company, focused on commercial excellence initiatives to drive revenue growth and margin improvement. The company implemented revenue management strategies to optimize pricing and maximize room occupancy. Marriott also enhanced its loyalty program and invested in digital marketing and distribution channels to improve customer acquisition and retention. These efforts contributed to EBITDA margin improvements within a relatively short timeframe.

The Coca-Cola Company: The Coca-Cola Company, the multinational beverage corporation, pursued commercial excellence initiatives to drive revenue growth and improve profitability. The company focused on portfolio optimization by divesting non-core brands and expanding its offerings in higher-margin product categories. Coca-Cola also implemented pricing and revenue management strategies to enhance margins and invested in marketing campaigns to drive consumer demand. These efforts resulted in EBITDA margin improvements within a two-year period.

Because these initiatives are critical, I will now discuss some focused elements of commercial excellence that you may see play out and what it typically takes to achieve them. This is not meant to be a graduate course in pricing analysis or SKU rationalization. Instead, this will focus on the basic quantifications and how the initiatives are implemented in the company. This will allow you to better understand how the company will go and realize the initiative versus analyze the initiative.

PRICING IMPROVEMENT

Pricing improvement is a major driver of commercial excellence. This should always be one of the first levers that a company attempts to pull. Why? Because any improvement in revenue, net of impacts from reduced volumes from demand reductions, flows directly to the bottom line. However, how do you know there is an opportunity?

Consumer Facing Companies

From outside of the company, you can see some evidence of it online and in other forums. These forums are typically available for all products in today's era of ubiquitous knowledge. In general, I always look for a site that has a large number of competitive brands in a given segment. For instance, for semiconductors, Digikey is a great platform to understand pricing. You can look at the components and the pricing on a per unit and tiered basis. In one instance, I identified almost the exact same product that had a 20 percent improvement in pricing driven by marketing—one had marketed itself to the automotive industry. The other, with the exact same technical specifications, was 20 percent cheaper and was focused on the technology. This was a near immediate pricing opportunity or arbitrage if you are buying.

Another great site for consumer sentiment is Reddit. With the right data analytics team, they can download and analyze the sentiment of the forum on a given topic. From there, you can typically understand the majority of the issues with a product versus its competitors.

One of the best pages available online for typical consumer products is the Amazon Best Sellers page for a given category for a quick assessment. I just took a snapshot of the top sellers on sandals. I highlighted three sets of sandals that are similar in design. For instance, take a look at the pricing discrepancy between the regular sandal examples. There is anywhere between a 33 and 66 percent difference in pricing for sandals that have similar ratings on Amazon. We can immediately identify that there is a brand differentiator between the options, but is that sufficient to cause a significant decline in demand for the lower cost options? This is similar to orthopedic examples, with a 42 percent increase over the other option. However, on the good side take a look at the limited pricing discrepancy between the women's options. Does this irrefutably say there is opportunity? No, but it indicates there is a potential pricing discrepancy and worth investigation. If not, for that one SKU, the top middle regular flip flop company could be missing out on a potential increase of up to 66 percent. You can also go onto more specialized forums and gain a similar level of insight.

To be clear, this gives you a signal that there may be an opportunity, However, the only way to then confirm if there is a profitable opportunity is to then estimate elasticity in a given marketplace. Given the nature of some of the wholesale relationships if you increase price, the true impact of a bad decision may not be felt for up to one year as unbought merchandise languishes on the shelf awaiting return.

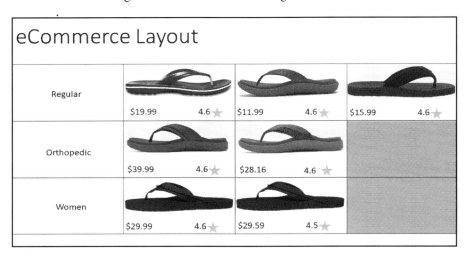

eCommerce Layout

Regular	$19.99 4.6 ★	$11.99 4.6 ★	$15.99 4.6 ★
Orthopedic	$39.99 4.6 ★	$28.16 4.6 ★	
Women	$29.99 4.6 ★	$29.59 4.5 ★	

Pricing elasticity is the measure of demand reduction with a given increase of pricing (typically $1). To establish pricing elasticity, you need to conduct a consumer survey. In general, a pricing elasticity survey will focus on a few core elements that will provide a broad survey of consumer preferences, but then also conduct price testing. The typical method it will assess this is through an A/B test where it will show the consumer a number of products across a number of categories and ask which they would buy at what price points. This allows you to get a very good quantitative perspective, taking into account the appropriate competitive set, how a change in pricing will change the demand relative to their peer products. This same outcome can be seen with pricing experiments, if you have the ability to rapidly and with low friction adjust your pricing. Typically, companies, in a competitive market, experience a high level of frictional cost that make the survey a better option than a price experiment.

Following the actual "test," analysts will take the data and leverage a few methods including a demand curve analysis and regression analysis to assess the actual elasticity of the pricing. Please note, that elasticity acts linearly on a narrow band of pricing. There are sometimes price cliffs that need to be understood and those price cliffs can significantly alter elasticities or willingness for a consumer to buy a given product.

For one consumer brand I worked with, one of the major products was up against a price cliff. When we looked at elasticities, it jumped from just under -1 to -3 once it went above a certain threshold. If we were priced at the threshold, then we could not push that price any further. If our price was less than the threshold, then we could continue to increase given the elasticity.

Once the pricing elasticity is understood, then you can solve for margin improvement based on projected decrease in demand versus uplift in revenue taking into account gross margin. This provides a view on the total impact. Then the goal is to increase pricing such that it maximizes your overall profit.

Please note that this needs to be done on every product, as each product will have a different elasticity. However, what I have found is that this type of analysis is key on the largest volume products. Others with less volume will have less of a rigorous need for analysis to validate the pricing impact.

Also, the optimal outcome is for the company to have in place a continual system monitoring pricing on channels like this and making routine pricing adjustments or conscientious decisions not to update pricing. These systems are typically a group of professionals that monitor pricing and at a quarterly or more frequent cadence to make recommendations to the executives that determine pricing. Additional analysis can be conducted including demand and forecasts through this group. So, the investment is not wasted.

Purchase Price Architecture

Purchase price architecture is a specific pricing and margin accretion mechanism is the use of purchase price architecture to improve per unit economics for large bulk consumer companies. In this, the company uses the same pricing, but lowers the per unit economics through either larger packaging with equal or lower fill and charging more. Or it keeps similar packaging and lowers bulk fill in line with other competitors. From there, they will evolve the product for the next iteration with the new per unit economics of the bulk fill either through smaller packaging or new packaging at a higher value with the same amount of product, locking in the new pricing and improved margin. This is a method to improve outcomes when the consumer does not, through quantitative elasticity analysis, indicate that they would be willing to except per purchase unit price increases. This evolution requires a full company approach as it will require new product design for some approaches and may take up to about 18 months to implement, depending on the packaging redesign.

Implementing Consumer Pricing Changes

There is always a lag between when a manufacturer raises wholesale prices and when those price increases are reflected in the channel. The timing will depend on the specific agreements and contractual terms between the manufacturer and channel.

Here are a few typical contractual arrangements that manufacturers will have with their channel partners. This will be the main guiding principle on how long it takes to actually implement the changes.

Some agreements might allow for immediate price changes. In this case, as soon as the manufacturer raises the wholesale price, the retailer would start paying the increased price for any new orders placed after the change.

Other contracts between manufacturers and retailers will stipulate a certain notice period for price changes and potentially an option to reject the pricing changes. The notification period could be anywhere from 30 days to several months. For example, if the notice period is 30 days and the manufacturer notifies the retailer of a price increase on June 1st, the new price would take effect on July 1st. Sometimes, this could be a full quarter and may depend on when the retailer typically adjusts prices or visual merchandising in its stores.

In other contracts, wholesale prices might be fixed for certain periods of time, such as a quarter or a year. In this case, even if the manufacturer decides to raise prices on June 1st, the new price wouldn't take effect until the start of the next pricing period.

Other agreements might include price protection clauses that prevent the wholesale price from changing for a certain period of time, even if the manufacturer raises prices. This could be designed to give the retailer time to adjust their own pricing and marketing strategies.

For most brands whether by contract or to maintain relationships, the ability to change pricing requires a discussion and might require the business to "sell" the pricing increase to the channel partners. This process will be done through your channel sales team or leadership higher up in the sales organization. The main elements that the customer will be looking for is the quantum of the price increase and the rationale on why. They may also want to understand the company's analysis that underlies the changes. They may want to evaluate themselves and may push back or recommend against the change.

If they push back, it may require you to re-evaluate why you are making this decision, depending on the importance of that outlet to your overall sales volume. The outlet always has a choice to de-list the product, if they do not agree with the pricing changes.

For some brands, they may need a process to update all of the required collateral and visual merchandising, if required. This element can take up to six months if design and delivery of the content is required. If simple design changes are needed, it will likely be closer to three months. This means that even once the decision is made to change pricing, you could see somewhere between a three and six month lag. For bulk and high volume manufacturers, the pricing changes may just require updates by the channel on the small stickers on the shelf, which does not require much additional effort.

For DTC, the pricing changes are largely approved by the company and implementation is to ensure the item master and catalog on the website is up to date.

Industrial and B2B

To begin to understand pricing discrepancies you need to hear it from your customers. Your salesforce will be attuned to what they are hearing. Having a good connection with that front line is highly beneficial. A number of companies have an active quarterly (or more frequent) check in with sales leadership and the strategy or finance function to validate pricing and other key elements of commercial contracts.

For some B2B, there will be access to large pricing depositories typically through a distribution channel like a Digikey or Grainger's catalogs. However, this just provides the re-seller's pricing and may not disclose the wholesale discount.

The lack of transparency on final pricing and wholesale for most industrial or B2B arrangements is what creates a slightly harder ask when it comes to pricing. For instance, FedEx does discount off of its list price. How much is up to the final negotiated price between FedEx and its partners. Even harder would be to understand the average price imposed across all of their customer base.

For large volume B2B, the pricing analysis will be similar to that of B2C. You would use a source like Digikey or Grainger to determine pricing inefficiency and move from them.

For industrial or low volume pricing, this is where you would need to look at other mechanisms. The salesforce will likely sense or know there is a pricing issue. You can also analytically see it in the win/loss analysis that a company or you can pull together. Often times customers will be able to straightaway tell you that you lost due to price. When this occurs, you have to examine why. Is it actually an underlying manufacturing or service costing issue? Are you charging too much for allocations? In this, you will need to go through and understand competitive cost to deliver relative to your own, similar to the benchmarking conducted by Xerox in the 1970s and 1980s.

If you do not find underlying costing issues, then you may need to review how you price. One method to do this is through a "deals desk." By including and ensuring finance reviews the deal submission, you can likely get the cost structure down while also ensuring profitability of the business. One of the primary ways is through improved bundled pricing to eliminate duplicate costs in the initial pricing. The other element is you can also reduce or add additional low cost and value added services to improve the perception of what is being provided.

In line with this, is the ability for you and your team to develop a higher willingness to pay for your service. This can be done through a complete review of your current offering and putting in place bundled value offerings. You will see this quite often in the telecommunications space. There is not much differentiation between two internet connection services. However, one provider might add free messaging applications,

SD-WAN, or another high perceived value, low cost to serve service to the package.

I will leave any discussion of brand and driving willingness to pay through emotion or brand loyalty to the chapter on brand repositioning.

IMPROVING LEAD TO CASH AND CUSTOMER EXPERIENCE

Another issue you will see in companies is an inability to scale or grow because of issues with their lead to cash cycle. These issues tend to trap cash in the system, create a negative perception of the company and dissuade customers from using the service because of long lead times to implement or deliver a product, or generally creates a structural inability to scale and grow with operating leverage because of minor organizational or process issues. There are times that investments to streamline the lead to cash cycle can change the growth trajectory of the company. In addition, there is an efficiency play that can be made that makes the company more efficient and thereby frees up resourcing.

These issues are most pronounced for companies that deliver high, value customized solutions or companies with an engineered solution. For other companies where the solution is not customized, I will show some investments that those companies may find beneficial to improve their lead to cash cycle. These companies typically do not see issues in the process limiting growth. Rather, they tend to have issues with exceptions to the process (e.g., discounts, credits to customers).

First, let's review the lead to cash cycle. When the process is streamlined, not only does it remove blockers for scale, it also unlocks trapped cash, but it also improves customer satisfaction (net of collection calls). This last impact has a number of knock on effects. If the improvements here improve your ability to deliver solutions by weeks, that may be the competitive advantage that the company needs to be a market leading solution and win more business.

Lead to Cash Cycle Improvements (Complex Sales)

Let's focus first on the more complex contract to cash cycle. The major difference between this and a typical order to cash cycle we will discuss later is the engineering or design phase and the longer implementation period prior to the actual order being processed for the larger disbursements of cash.

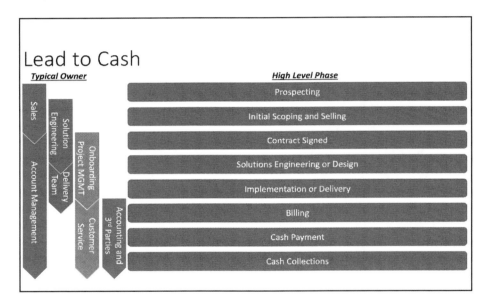

Here are all of the key phases of this process:

Prospecting: This is the process of identifying clients and selling them on the services.

Initial scoping and selling: This phase of the process typically introduces a solution selling team to identify any technical elements of the sale, begin to price out the key elements, and discuss at a technical or design level the solution that is being bought by the end customer. For non-technical complex sales, these are typically design professionals or in the services industry, they can potentially be managing directors identifying how their teams will conduct the work.

Contract signed: Once terms are aligned for the implementation and long-term revenue stream, the contract is signed. The solution design is usually close to locked in at that point and the teams shift to project implementation.

Implementation or delivery: The teams deliver the key long-term infrastructure or deliverable to the end client. This typically shifts the company to a long-term recurring bill or a large payment for the deliverable, depending on the company and nature of the product. For instance, in a telecommunications company, this phase might indicate that the SD-WAN has been configured and the company or team is using the SD-WAN for daily operations. This shifts billing to a recurring phase. For other companies like a capital equipment manufacturer, this might indicate that the specially designed equipment has been produced, tested, and received by the customer. This then requires final payment resolution.

Billing: This is typically conducted by accounting or an order management team. The bill should be taken from the accounting team and sent through either the account management team or the customer service team to the client. However, with automated systems this now can be done through the automated billing system.

Cash payment: This is where the client pays the company. The company has to have a system, largely automated, to identify the payment to the bill. This process of cash reconciliation is a critical step. It can also be highly manual if automated solutions are not capturing a large share of the volume properly, this will cause excesses in your general accounting cost structure.

Collections: Finally, if a customer does not pay. This requires collections and follow-up. Depending on the customer and situation, this can be handled internally. This can be done through the account management team, the accounts receivable team, or through external parties where the past dues collections are turned over to a collection agency.

On the left hand side of the diagram are the typical organizations that manage this process. One thing to note are the key handoffs that are conducted across multiple value elements to the end customer. There are typically at least three to four critical handoffs within the first increment of time with a new customer. One of the first is typically, the shift of the sales representative to the account management team. This is a well-practiced transition and typically expected. On the technical side, it shifts from a solutions sales engineer to a delivery team lead and also a long-term engineering team lead for tech support. The other layer of change is at the working level. There is typically introduction of either a project manager to solve major issues during delivery or the delivery team lead, as previously mentioned. The final transition or introduction is to the billing team.

I have never seen a company perfect this. These handoffs are typically a large cause of consternation for the customer. The best you can typically do is provide overlay resources that make some of this transparent to the end customer through use of account management or an onboarding project manager. These methods stabilize and reduce the need for the customer to interact with four or five different leads and have a centralized point of contact as you enter them into the longer-term contract post implementation.

So, where do the delays come in? Here are some of the most common areas where this cycle becomes delayed. Remember, any delays once the contract is signed typically traps cash in the process. Methods to streamline this reduce the time for the company to get paid and reduce the amount of work in progress inventory or CAPEX outlay prior to payment. The key element is that the timing only matters after the contract is signed. So, how do you relieve the trapped cash?

1. Monitor what you want to manage. The majority of companies do not monitor this process with any rigor. Because they do not have a good understanding of their lead to cash timelines and pain points, they will sometimes just accept it. This process is one of the key processes you have to simplify and correct to scale the business. The post sale experience of the customer is their first real experience in your relationship. Paying attention to this through typical management frameworks helps to understand what they are experiencing and allows management to improve the outcomes.

2. Improve the initial scoping and integration between sales teams and solution engineering. Diligence on the requirements and getting to the final solution prior to locking down the contract is helpful. This requires early and

concentrated involvement of the solutions engineers and even some of the design engineers prior to contract signature. For less technical products this may or may not be required as the design may be part of the post contract process and will need to occur post transaction.

3. Reduce the implementation timeline by reducing the ability to make changes to the scope after contract sign. There are some elements that will need to be some changes that occur after contract sign, but reducing this to as little as practical is important. Putting in place specific change provisions and penalizing changes outside of normal course may be beneficial depending on the customer and company dynamics. Significant changes can cause delays. Some are warranted, others are not.

4. Ensure you have adequate capacity to support the design. Another team I worked with became capacity constrained with experts that could support the design element. As the business began to scale, they needed to add additional resourcing. Often, this may be limiting with the technologies at play. One solution is to reallocate resources between divisions. Sometimes, there are organizations that have a good enough understanding of the technologies or systems. When that is the case, they can be flexed into this positions with some oversight. When the company needs to scale or improve, these resources can be a ready supply of talent that can be trained quickly.

5. Ensure you can flex your teams to support implementation at scale. There are some teams where the true bog down occurs in the delivery. The delivery team should be a capacity constrained funnel by which you push these projects through. Managing a month long backlog for internal teams may be okay. However, delivery is usually also commoditized. One company I worked with that needed to scale their business began qualifying external partners and contractors to support them on these deliveries. Even if you outsource the simpler jobs, it eliminates the work from the internal team. This allowed them to flex the funnel up and down to reduce backlog.

6.   Another element are handoff delays. These occur when the teams are not in sync. Some of this can be mitigated with excellent program management teams. Their role should be to keep these handoffs seamless and ensure the project or program remains on schedule. When they are not able to, there is typically an issue of misaligned incentives that lead to resourcing issues. These issues typically occur when responsibilities cross some organizational seam (e.g., reporting lines change higher up in the organization—for instance sales to operations). The receiving party may not have their incentives aligned to the needs of the giving organization. There are usually a few methods to eliminate these types of issues: 1) Upper management needs to align the incentives such that the receiving manager provides sufficient resources to keep the process moving seamlessly. 2) This truly is a resourcing issue. This is common when the company begins to scale rapidly without foresight. The other element of the company may not be aware of the need for more resources or their budgets may not support it. These issues can typically be resolved between the two executives and maybe some cajoling from a layer above. 3) These issues sometimes require organizational changes to remove the seam that is impacting the customer. For instance, you may make a decision that all delivery teams are to be in their own organization or they may roll up under the head of Sales. This may not be ideal, but may eliminate some of the issues.

Another area that can be an issue is the billing. However, this is more of an efficiency play. Billing should largely be automated. To support this, you should strive to standardize contracts to support entry into your systems that automate the billing process. There are some companies with non-standardized contracts that result in large levels of effort by the billing team to calculate the invoice. The other thing to watch out for is non-standard methods for discounts or ones that the systems cannot automatically process. This then requires the billing team to handle that invoice by exception. Alignment of the sales team and the accounting team on how to handle the discounts is a critical element to streamline the business. When this occurs, and the contractual discounting mechanisms match the system methods of discounting, then the billing is automated. This reduces the need for additional resourcing to process exceptions. This resourcing can then be reapplied to areas of the process that can benefit and support business scaling.

Invoicing through systems like Ariba help businesses better manage expectations on cash receipt. They provide transparency on invoice processing. But also can provide some transparency on advice of payment. Linkage of this with your systems is beneficial as it provides clarity into when cash disbursements are likely to occur. The key is to select a few of these key systems. The selection should not be based on what your preferences are, but rather what systems your customers have. When you structure your invoicing system to support the customer and then conduct the necessary integrations to your system, you will find much larger adoption of your new process. There was one facility service provider that had a very small AR organization. They focused their system selection to align their future system with that of the corpus of their major customers. They were able to process over $1 billion in revenue with about five accounts receivable resources.

Contract to Cash (Simple Orders)

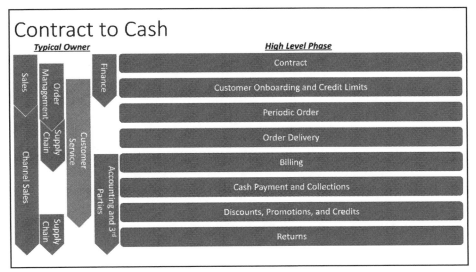

Here is what a typical contract to cash process looks like for companies that manage standardized products. They key difference is that there is limited customization this limits the value of the pre-signing phase to mitigate the impact of the cash and scalability of the process post sign. However, what I will also add in here is the returns and credit processing. For the other process, you typically do not see a capital good just returned. Usually, it fails a test and then the delivery team repairs the issue, so it is largely embedded in the process. There are times that credits are applied when an issue arises. These are infrequent and not something you will focus design on. However, for simpler products, it may make sense.

Here is what this process looks like:

First let's describe each of these elements:

Contracting: This is the initial step where a legally binding agreement is made between the customer and the supplier. This contract specifies the products or services to be provided, their quantities, the price, payment terms, and other necessary details. These contracts can either be one-time or recurring.

Customer onboarding and credit check: Once the contract is in place, the customer is onboarded into the supplier's system. To streamline, the customer details can begin to be collected during the sales process and entered into the CRM tool. When the contract is signed, the data is then ported over to any other systems required. This creates a customer account and populates it with relevant details like contact information, billing address, shipping address, etc. A credit check is usually performed at this stage to assess the creditworthiness of the customer, especially if the contract involves credit terms. If the contract involves credit, that step and credit limits may be established prior to the contract being signed.

Periodic order: This stage is where the customer places orders periodically based on the contract. The supplier needs to ensure that the order matches the contract terms and any discrepancies are resolved. They also need to validate that the items ordered and quantities are available for purchase and shipment.

Order delivery: This stage involves fulfilling the order by delivering the products or services. The supplier needs to ensure the order is correctly picked, packed, and shipped to the customer's specified location. For services, it could mean the execution of the agreed-upon tasks.

Billing: Once the order is fulfilled, an invoice is generated and sent to the customer. The invoice should match the order in terms of quantity, price, and other contract terms.

Cash payment and cash collection: After the invoice is sent, the customer makes the payment based on the agreed-upon payment terms. The supplier's responsibility is to track these payments, apply them to the correct invoices, and update the customer's account.

Discounts or credits: Sometimes, discounts or credits may be applied to the invoice as per the contract. For example, there could be an early payment discount, or a volume-based discount, or credits issued for defective products or services.

Returns: This is the last step in the cycle. If a customer is not satisfied with the products or services, they might return the products or ask for a service correction. The supplier needs to manage these returns, inspect the returned goods, process refunds or replacements, and adjust the customer's account accordingly.

The machinations of this process are simpler and more process focused versus focused on customization, design, and delivery of the unique solution required by the customer.

So where are the opportunities to improve scale and revenue generation? For this process, the majority of companies leverage an ERP and CRM solution to manage these processes following the contract. The largest efficiency gain is through the streamlined integration of those two core systems. There have been numerous clients I have worked with where they will tell you the delays that have with onboarding customers because the CRM system does not communicate with the ERP. This process efficiency results in significant delays to onboard clients, reduces customer satisfaction, and delays revenue generation. From an efficiency perspective, the companies typically generate a large shadow organization just to support this process or there are multiple organizations that are taking data and inputting it into multiple systems.

The issuance of credit can be a blocker. There should be a risk-managed approach. The use of Dun & Bradstreet and others to understand the credit worthiness of a company is important. That service is important. However, common sense also applies. To get the process and orders started, what is the limit to which all companies can be authorized? Sometimes, companies will immediately allow the customer to use a purchasing or credit card to secure the purchases as credit limits are validated with finance.

The onboarding of customers can also be streamlined. For small and medium businesses, it makes sense to have online portals where they can enter their information and credit card information and you can begin shipping product to them. Use of large-scale marketing campaigns targeted at these smaller companies can be and are effective. They are efficiency and allow the business to scale. The other nice part is that it reduces the cost to serve for these smaller accounts, making the business highly profitable. The other element is that you have little to no downside exposure as the company charges the clients preexisting credit card with about two day payment terms to the company.

The majority of the delivery has already been discussed in previous chapters. However there are times where there is a breakdown in communication between the order management and accounting teams for billing. If the systems and contracts are not streamlined, there can be a lot of exception processing that needs to be managed by either the Accounting team or order management team. In one situation, we had to leverage an ad hoc offshore team just to manage the exceptions that were generated. There are great services for situations where you need to spin up a rapid operation offshore. Firms like ContinuServe and others can rapidly provide these types of services. In one situation, a firm like this was able to spin up a few HR resources in less than 24 hours to meet some emergent needs a client had.

For cash payment, you can still use solutions like Ariba. However, you really need to ensure that the customers are using these systems. Otherwise, it may complicate the invoicing. The reconciliation and exception handling is the burdensome point that limits scalability. With more commoditized products, the customers are more likely to just withhold payment for credits they believe they are owed. This complicates the cash application and reconciliation element of the accounts receivable process. There are RPA technologies and bots that can help streamline this process. They will auto match the reconciled invoices and cash receipts. This then leaves just the exceptions to be manually managed and resolved. However, you can automate this routine as well and send the short payment or non-payment lists to both AR and account management teams. This can then be resolved in a more rapid fashion with transparency of what is occurring. For the payment disputes that require resolution, you can quickly determine what the best course of action is for the company, which may include challenging the customer's assertions or concerns. However, the majority of the time, you are likely to accept the issue and move on with the relationship.

AR aging analysis is another key focus to eliminate trapped cash in the system. This is one area where companies may not have sufficient discipline or rigor to analyze on a continual basis. However, when you begin to assess this and make the simple follow-ups, the majority of customers will pay what is needed. There are arrangements that company can make for situations where the account goes into default, typically 60 to 90 days post due. For those accounts, there are collections agencies. These agencies are not friendly and may be an issue for your reputation. The decision to use them is on the company. For some situations it is advisable, for others, it is not.

The process for approval and application for credits and discounts is challenging and requires both finance and operational teams to approve them. Typically, this is a rubber stamp as the customer is asking for it. However, it allows the management team to evaluate which customers may be overly leveraging that generosity and discuss relationship level methods to manage this leakage or address system shipment or other issues that result in the damaged goods or discounts needed for that particular customer. However, to generate more value, the teams can begin to gently question the customers or seek those larger resolution discussions. This has been effective in some scenarios where you identify that the trade accounts appear to be higher than normal.

The final area is returns. This can trap a lot of cash unless the process is streamlined. For product base companies, the expedition processing and disposal or return to saleable product is critical. Teams tend to outsource this service and when they do, they put it in a centralized location for the third party supporting it. This traps inventory (cash) in the system. The better answer is to collocate this process with your 3PL facility. This allows products to be returned to saleable more quickly and allow the bulk waste to be aggregated. The same 3PL can continue to service your operation. The other element to consider is the use of intermediate packaging. This allows more of your product, specifically

DTC returns to be returned to saleable. This can save millions of dollars, depending on the product, volumes, and price points.

All of these elements cause the company to lose or trap cash. It also prevents the company from scaling with operating leverage. Each situation will be slightly different—the goal is to provide the typical hunting grounds for where the problem typically exists. When you fix the underlying issues, streamlining these processes can create a better customer experience and a better commercial outcome for the company.

SALESFORCE EFFECTIVENESS

A number of careers in consulting have been made from salesforce effectiveness consulting and training. Entire organizations and consulting enterprises were built off this trend over the past 15 to 20 years. Sales teams are a large expense in the organization typically costing about (roughly) 10 to 15 percent of the cost structure of a given company. This tends closer to 20 to 25 percent when you look at sales and marketing together. With that much expense of a company, you want to ensure that the teams are as sharp, structured, and enabled as possible.

We measure salesforce effectiveness through a number of key performance indicators. Here is a sampling of them:

Sales volume and sales growth: The primary drivers of salesforce effectiveness. How much did the team sell? This is typically tied to budget and revenue and profitability estimates. It is a high level barometer of the effectiveness of the team, but can also be a result of product, go-to-market, brand, or other underlying issues.

The items listed below are better indicators of the underlying issues.

Hit rate or conversion rate: This tells you how effective the team is at selling. It takes the number of sales converted as a percentage of the qualified leads within the organization. Generally, a conversion rate of 20 to 25 percent is considered good in many B2B industries. This also requires your qualified lead process to be solid and actually provide solid leads to the sales teams.

Sales cycle length: This measures the amount of time it takes for a prospect to go from the initial contact to a final sale. Sales cycles need to be benchmarked against near competitors. There are some technologies that require a long sales cycle to teach and then convert the qualified lead. There are other products and industries where this cycle can be minutes based on the simplicity of the product. However, by streamlining this process (just like with lead to cash) you can accelerate revenue and capture additional cash from the company.

Average deal size: This is the average value of the deals closed by the sales team. The goal is to see this increase over time. There are only a few mechanisms by which to increase the deal size—sell more or increase price. You need to correct this for price increases. The goal of measuring this should be to help your team understand and hopefully begin to cross-sell and up-sell the existing customer base on other services or products your company provides.

Sales per rep: There is typically sufficient data through the CRM system to identify the efficiency of each of the sales reps. The use of this level of information is more important and tells more about the efficacy of the sales team, as it can take into account ramp up time and individual performance. Understanding the regression based analysis of sales team ramp up and performance based on tenure in the company can help understand how effect the management team is in onboarding and scaling the team.

Quota attainment: This is the percentage of salespeople who meet or exceed their sales quota. A higher percentage indicates a more effective salesforce. For well performing teams, you should see at least 60 percent of the team hitting their quota.

Customer retention rate: This measures the number of customers that continue to buy from the company over a given period. This is a good measure for the account management elements of the team. A higher retention rate suggests the sales team is not only good at making sales, but also at maintaining relationships. For recurring revenue businesses, if this begins to slip, it can cause a rapid reduction in the base revenue of the firm.

Win/loss analysis: Reviewing the company's win/loss analysis to understand the major drivers of why a sale was won or loss also sheds a lot of light onto the issues underlying positive or negative performance. There are times when the company does not do well telling the story or does not relay the product/market fit well to the customer.

Discounting and gross margin per rep: Another issue that can be diagnosed is the loss of margin because of the representatives. In order to meet quota, some reps will need to discount heavily. Salesforce effectiveness measures tend to assist these members of the team by providing them the tools and techniques to make the sale at full value versus at discount. A company that does this well is Broadcom. Their sales teams are well disciplined to not discount their products. This yields excellent margins that Broadcom than uses to redeploy and capture new markets through acquisition of key semiconductor lines of business.

The efficacy of the company's salesforce is also a good barometer of the overall health of the company and the go-to-market strategy for the company. The majority of the diagnosis of the real issues comes in at the operational level when you look at the process from marketing, lead generation, sales, the actual selling, and the utilization of the sales resources time.

Examination of the process can also unpack a lot of what is seen in the analysis of the KPIs. For instance, there was a client that had awful conversion rates, in the 5 to 10 percent range. When we looked further into this, we found the client's marketing team was using a shotgun blast approach to marketing with a customer segmentation as broad as the upper end of the U.S. economy—literally, any company with more than $200 million in revenue. How do you prepare a sales team for that meeting based on the lead qualification being any company greater than $200 million. The better answer is to focus the team on various industry verticals with defined use cases. This allows the sales team to be concentrated and focused and likely improve their conversion.

Oftentimes, when you look into salesforce issues, it is more complicated and typically requires a cross-functional resolution. However, there are still levers that can and should be used to support the sales team. In general, you will hear quotes of about 20 percent improvement in salesforce effectiveness. Most companies that make this investment do see some uplift. However, they typically improve a number of levers at the same time and it would be hard to allocate that value amongst all of them.

In one situation, we were brought in to help a company that had been growing well over 20 percent per year with a highly effective channel sales strategy. However, the company changed strategies and began to lose sales and fell to about 10 percent growth. We quickly identified the issues with the sales team and attempts to go direct versus continue to maintain the channel strategy. However, personnel changes had begun to occur.

It required some new hires focused on channel sales, retraining existing resources, and improvement to their channel management program to improve their reputation. When I last checked, they began growing again at or above 20 percent. However, I could not attribute any one of those actions to the success or failure. It was all of the program that resulted in these improvements.

When issues with the salesforce are diagnosed, there are a number of typical solutions that can be put into place. Some are more effective than others. Here are the majority of solutions used to improve salesforce performance:

Sales training and coaching: This is one of the most fundamental ways of improving salesforce effectiveness. This could involve product training, tailored sales technique training, negotiation skills, communication skills, and more. The professionals that conduct this training are typically experienced and successful sales people. They work with your team in an objective manner to get them to perfect their pitch or any other areas where they may result in under performance. Regular coaching sessions can help to address individual issues and improve performance. This is one of the more effective programs as it can tailor to the company and focuses on maximizing each sales reps performance. They also can serve as an experienced coach to your sales management team. Oftentimes, they can help identify top talent from less well performing talent to support talent management and attention from the management team.

Sales process optimization: Advisory firms often work with companies to streamline their sales processes. This can involve identifying bottlenecks or inefficiencies and developing strategies to overcome them. It could also involve implementing a more structured sales methodology or improving sales automation and CRM use. This effort will typically be cross-functional. It also may interact with the marketing teams and the marketing process.

Sales and incentive compensation planning: Compensation and incentive structures can have a huge impact on salesforce effectiveness. When unwanted behaviors are observed in the sales team, redesigning the compensation plans that motivate salespeople can better align those behaviors with the desired outcomes. This process takes a long time to implement. It is usually at least six to nine months. With that knowledge, what you typically want to do is to implement this when the quota and geographies reset naturally—typically the fiscal year. Sales people are largely coin operated. So, the biggest hurdle is your ability to sell them that if they did what they did last year, then you will get the target compensation. This may or may not be true. However, it needs to appear to be in line with it. Or you need to show the specific ways it is changing and show them you are making investments or training to ensure they are able to adjust to the new paradigm.

Sales territory management and improved targeting: Effective sales territory management can ensure that sales resources are being utilized in the most productive manner. This might involve adjusting territory assignments, setting appropriate sales targets for each territory, or improving the way sales visits are planned and managed. The effective establishment of territories is a critical element of the sales operations or revenue operations teams. They need to design the territories such that the team member assigned is likely to hit their quota. For every lead or target, the company and the sales operations team should be thinking about it with a probability of sale. They should probability weight the territory such that sales people are likely to be successful. In addition, they should have some thoughts on priority versus non-priority targets within a given territory.

Sales analytics and reporting: In grade school, report cards drove my performance. The same is true for professionals. The ability to see your success in a quantitative rubric is helpful. It also allows everyone to see where they are on the playing field.

Sales technology utilization: Oftentimes, companies will have made the investment into a solution like Salesforce or another CRM technology, but the use is not improving outcomes. Simple questions reveal that the teams are not utilizing the service or the existing process bogs down or over burdens the sales team. When these issues arise, having a team come in to streamline the process or train the team how to use the system to reduce burden can be beneficial and improve sales outcomes.

Customer segmentation: Different stories need to be told to different customers for the same product. Think about the use of the 737 fuselage for Boeing. The 737 fuselage has been used for both a U.S. Navy P-8 Poseidon aircraft and commercial aircraft from almost every commercial airline. The story and modifications for the military are a bit different. The outfitting of the fuselage will likely have a lot more technology, sonar, and other equipment, whereas the commercial airline will focus on customer comfort. The story can be told and customized for each. At the end of the day, the sale of the fuselage for Boeing is the same. The same is true in the private sector. A product has multiple uses, all of which are true. For instance, this book can be used by multiple people for multiple reasons. For an investor, they could use it as a guide to operations. For someone in a business, they could use it as a reference on how to prevent a PE firm from getting value out of their company prior to a sale. The messaging is different. To be effective, a sales team needs to know the use case and value drivers for each customer segment. They then should be able to deliver a talk track on the solution that each customer will find compelling. The marketing and sales leadership should help to define and support these talk tracks and solutions for each market.

Salesforce effectiveness investment can be a critical method to unlock the growth potential of the company. However, it is not a panacea. The best outcomes typically scan the entirety of the marketing to selling process. They then identify key issues and address each. Through this holistic process, you typically have better outcomes than just targeted investment in coaching or trying to improve selling effectiveness.

Using Authorized Agents

Another method to improve sales is through an authorized agent model. There are a number of companies that limit their growth because they attempt to do everything through an internal salesforce. When a company is trying to grow, there are times that it may make sense to use an authorized agent or distributor model to sell the product in high cost to serve areas. This model is highly effective in locations where people can be remote relative to centralized offices. The benefit of these authorized agents is that they will typically know the people of businesses better than an internal salesforce. It also allows you to penetrate a market that you would not be able to access otherwise. The economics typically take a 10 to 15 percent commission for all sales and recurring sales. These economics just have to be baked into the pricing to serve these markets or price lists provided to the authorized agents. However, they can act as an accelerant to your growth. To keep these agents energized, you also need to have a channel management program where they can continue to be recognized or given additional opportunities to grow their business. There is no one size fits all model, but use of outsourced resources and proper programs to keep them incented to supplement your own teams can be highly beneficial.

PRODUCT LIFECYCLE OPTIMIZATION AND SKU RATIONALIZATION

A well-run company will have an effective product lifecycle management system in place. The key tenets of the process have been described in prior chapters of this book. When the product lifecycle management process is effective, it actually improves the commercial excellence of the company. It focuses the efforts of the brand, product, and marketing teams on the right products and services that the company views as a going concern. When the system is ineffective and kills products too soon or does not kill products (the more likely situation), then the company begins to lose focus. It begins to divert resources, which could be used for higher gain on new or higher margin products on products with lower viability.

For optimal commercial performance, a review of this process should occur. This can yield a number of unexpected benefits that allows the company to grow more effectively. There are three key processes in the product lifecycle management system that help improve the commercial excellence of the company:

1. Approval of new product development
2. New product launch oversight
3. Elimination of existing product lines

When you focus on these three processes at the management and executive level, it allows you to make rapid decisions on which products you will continue to invest in and with appropriate decision making while reviewing new product launches, allows you to rapidly deploy more resourcing to products that have unexpected traction.

Here are the lessons I have from this.

1. Implementing a proactive process for allocation of investment dollars against new product development allows proper oversight of the investment. It also allows the company and leadership to weigh in and ensure that the teams are developing the products needed for the market. If market conditions change, then the leadership team can shift resourcing as appropriate.

2. Effective oversight of the launch helps the leadership team hold the marketing team and new product development team accountable for the success and estimates for the new product. The effective system is to review the launch at a periodicity that makes sense for the market— typically 90-day, 180-day, and 365-day reviews. During these intervals, you can help the product team make the product successful at the early stage of the process. There may need to be more marketing dollars to make the product successful. For products that are exceptionally successful, the management team might double down or explore additional use cases to market, accelerating growth of a hero product.

3. The launch oversight also helps hone the skills of the marketing and product teams to truly understand the dynamics of the product during launch and how they can improve the success of the products and what makes a product successful and what does not.

4. The final area is the use of a forum that reviews profitability, sales, and sales growth for existing product lines. The forum should look to eliminate underperforming product lines rapidly. To make room for managerial attention for core products. Companies that do this well focus their execution on the core product lines and limit their losses on non-performing product lines. A number of companies are afraid to take this action because it typically causes a reduction in revenue. However, if executed well, then the profitability should increase. To execute well, you have to reduce the associated allocation and direct spends associated with those products that are eliminated. Often times, the resources are just reallocated to what is perceived to be a higher opportunity

product. This is a decision by management, but does not allow for the capture of the profitability.

SKU Rationalization

SKU rationalization is a tool of inventory management and commercial excellence. It is typically a mechanism used when the product lifecycle management process at a company has failed to proactively sculpt the product lines. When the commercial teams do not do the necessary sculpting this causes cost inefficiency in the supply chain, but also in the product management and marketing teams. The unnecessary product complexity also can complicate sales and diverts resourcing from product development to quality assurance on the maintenance of these non-core, and potentially nonprofitable product lines.

To identify if the company has an issue, you typically can review the product catalog. You will see a number of products that appear to serve the same function or use case, potentially with minor nuance difference. If you are confused about the differences - so is the customer. To be effective, you will need to also evaluate the burdened cost structure of each product. This would include the gross margin, but also the cost it requires to be maintained by product development, the inventory carrying cost in the warehouse, and the marketing budget that product utilizes. Some of these costs will need to be allocated across a number of other products. For instance, a resin product management team may be split across multiple products. When this occurs, you will need to identify the best allocation method. The most defensible is always revenue. However, cost does not always follow revenue. Better drivers of allocation for a product may be required substitution changes or total order volume, or an average inventory hold volume for inventory carrying costs.

When you have identified those costs and have allocated them appropriately, you put together a fully burdened profitability for each product. The easiest answer is to just to reduce the negative profitability products. In most situations, that should be the target and the max opportunity.

Most companies and the product teams will defend products because of strategic rationale. Sometimes this is true. Management experience does have a say in this outcome. However, I have often seen those product lines retained, but never made successful because the overlap is so large or the use case so narrow that it never gains mass-market appeal.

The mechanisms by which you improve efficiency are the allocated methods. The exercise for SKU rationalization obviously reduces the complexity of the product portfolio. However, you also need to reduce the support people for the product lines, the marketing teams, the additional supply chain resources supporting those additional SKUs and the orders associated with them, and budgets for the products. On the supply chain side, you also need to have a sufficiently variable cost structure that you see the reduction in costing. The best SKU rationalizations are when you can strategically exit entire product lines. For instance, you realize a company is not successful in hair dryers. This then allows you to remove the engineering teams, the marketing teams, the marketing budgets, the product managers, and the management team for the hair dryer line. The carrying costs are typically a fraction of this larger eliminated cost structure.

For product exits, they should be fully structured to ensure that you try to capture and convert your current user base to the complementary product line that you may have kept.

When you do this, you are essentially eliminating all of your nonprofitable products. If, in addition, to reducing the complexity, you also eliminate the overhead associated with that complexity, then you will see profitability improve with a lower revenue base.

In the next chapter, we will discuss the opposite side of the coin. Focus on eliminating customers that cost a lot to serve.

CHOOSING YOUR CUSTOMERS

For B2B companies, the equation is flipped from a product focus to a customer focus. The cost to serve some customers is just too expensive relative to the profit that they are providing you. This element of commercial excellence tells you to: Fire your customers!

Some of the methods I am discussing are counter intuitive to people that have spent their entire careers in a public market company. Companies live and die by revenue and revenue estimates from the market. The thought of giving up revenue to improve earnings may not make sense. As you will recall, public markets are not always rationale with respect to cash generation of companies—the true strategic value of a company.

There is a significant amount of speculation in the public market about future growth potential. The purpose of that future potential used to focus on someday extracting cash from the operations of an entity to fund other things that the investor considers important.

However, for mature companies, they will likely have thousands of customers. The customers will have varying products or services that they are using. This will yield a final gross profit for the customer. Based on dynamics we have discussed, those margins can be all over the place for B2B businesses. In addition, there are direct services and corporate overhead that needs to be allocated to each of these accounts. When done well, you get a very good picture of the fully burdened profitability of each of the customers you are currently serving.

For consulting firms, they will routinely look at the profit and loss of a given client and most specifically a client engagement. This is a good way to ensure that your management team for the engagement is effective. In addition, it ensures that the resources selling the given project are effective and provide sufficient margin to the company. If not, their discounting practices should be reviewed. Ideally, their bonuses are tied not just to the revenue dollar, but also to the profitability of the projects they sell.

Reviewing customer profitability is a similar tool that can be used to improve commercial excellence. It is a framework that allows you to assess the efficiency of your account management teams. The goal is to develop an accurate picture of which of your clients are adding to your bottom line and which are not. The goal is not always to actually fire your customer. Sometimes, the goal is to actually review the practices and what is driving the loss of profitability and then address it. There are a large number of clients that will appear profitable on paper.

However, the additional overhead and burden they cause make them less desirable. For instance, you have a company that used to spend $50 million with your company, they now spend $20 million, but they are a long-standing customer. You have a dedicated account manager for the client. However, as they reduced their spend bad decisions were made and the margin on a number of your products deteriorated relative to others. In addition, you have a fixed overhead with the account management team for this client. With all of this, if you then assess the fully burdened P&L for the client you realize its negative as a combination of everything that has occurred. What do you do? The management team should then evaluate what it can do. It doesn't mean you eliminate the client. Instead, you can have a discussion with the client and let them know that you are removing the dedicated account management team. Conversely, you can talk to them about the need to increase the cost and show them the data that indicates that you are losing money serving the account. These discussions and measures are important to maintain the business and improve profitability.

This analysis is most sensitive to the allocations made for the burden beyond the direct product expenses. You need to ensure that all people are aligned with those assumptions on how to allocate the values. This will have the largest impact.

Also, if decisions are made to eliminate a customer, you have to ensure that the overhead burden can also "come out of the system." The issue with trying to optimize the commercial elements of an organization with reducing topline is that you also need to reduce the cost burden. If not, your assumptions will fall short of the anticipated opportunities.

For instance, you have made a decision to eliminate the longstanding client I mentioned above. The account management team is easily managed and is reduced. However, the accounting resources required to support that is a fraction of a person. You still need the other "fraction." This is a stranded cost that will cause you to not hit your profitability improvement from the action.

The other key thing to watch out for is that when you exit a customer or product line, you have to do so in a deliberate manner for reputational concern. For customer exits, you should have the discussion. However, they may not budge on pricing or demand the account management team. At that point, you let them know you do not plan to renew the upcoming contract for support. You should have a plan for them and help them through the transition of services. This is an additional cost, but should be viewed as a cost to achieve to ensure your client base does not have a negative reputation of your organization following these actions.

BRAND VALUE AND REPOSITIONING

When buying companies that profit from a brand, the majority of the focus should be on buying a brand that has a strong sentiment in the market with drivers that create loyalty. These drivers can be emotional, product based, or mission focused. When assessing companies to buy, the majority of PE firms will conduct consumer surveys to understand the company, brand position, and the drivers of the brand value. The goal is to find a brand that is strong, but may not be fully penetrated in markets were they can be successful or with the ability to grow through line extensions and other topline accretive measures.

Take Yeti, for example. Yeti was only selling $300 to $400 coolers in the early 2000s. However, they gained a cult following with the hook and bullet crowd of fishers and hunters. There success with this crowd then spilled into oil fields and other places were their product's reputation of durability (being able to withstand a grizzly bear) and the performance (so cold, it can keep your beer chilled in the Texas oil fields). These strong drivers compelled a small private equity firm to make a $67 million investment in the company.

Leveraging their reputation, the investor worked with management to pivot from that strength into a premium outdoor brand known for durability and performance now expanded its product line to include drinkware, bags, and other outdoor accessories. Now, the brand built for the hook and bullet crowd is seen at high-end events and also in its roots in the back of a hunter's truck or the oil fields of West Texas. The key driver of value was the image and reputation that Yeti had built on durability and performance. When Yeti conducted its IPO in 2016, that small $67 million investment had a book value of $3.3 billion with a total valuation of the company at $5 billion. That is a good day for the investors and the founders.

Another example is Under Armour. Founded in 1996 by Kevin Plank, the company began with a novel product based on Kevin's experiences as a football player at the University of Maryland. He was tired of being in a sweat-soaked T-shirt. He was one of the first to market and sell moisture wicking fabrics for their products. This, combined with his connections, allowed his brand to build by being worn by numerous athletes in the late 1990s and early 2000s. As he wanted to scale, he received investment from a private equity company for about $12 million. This allowed him to continue to scale the business based on the strength of the brand and products. In 2005, he conducted an IPO and raised about $153 million to further grow the business. When he did, leveraging the reputation for quality and innovation, the company has since pivoted into footwear, accessories, and connected technologies.

Another example is when you can expand internationally. Dunkin' Brands, the parent company of Dunkin' Donuts and Baskin-Robbins, was acquired by a consortium of private equity firms in 2006. The investors recognized the potential for global expansion of the brand and embarked on an international growth strategy. They successfully expanded Dunkin' Donuts and Baskin-Robbins into various countries, including China, India, and Brazil.

When they did, they leveraged cultural affinity to the U.S. and product localization to drive adoption. Dunkin' Brands leveraged the strength of the brand and its reputation in America to expand. However, to supplement, they conducted analysis of the markets to identify countries with strong coffee cultures to enter. They also adapted the brand to local preferences and used the country's recognition of the brand as a trusted American icon to drive business.

Capitalizing on the growing coffee culture in markets like China, India, and Brazil, the brand positioned itself as a provider of quality coffee beverages alongside its donuts and other baked goods. With the rising popularity of coffee consumption in these countries, Dunkin' Donuts' coffee offerings and its emphasis on providing a convenient and affordable coffee experience appealed to consumers. This leveraged the brand reputation and strategic tailwinds in the markets to capture the value.

In markets where consumers had a positive perception of American brands, the teams reinforced Dunkin' Donuts' association with quality, consistency, and reliability. This played a significant role in attracting customers in those geographies.

Despite this reputation, they also recognized the importance of adapting its brand to suit local preferences and cultural nuances. In each country, the brand made efforts to incorporate local flavors, ingredients, and menu items. For example, in China, Dunkin' Donuts introduced pork floss and green tea donuts to cater to local tastes. This localization strategy helped the brand connect with consumers and differentiate itself from competitors.

In 2012, Dunkin' Brands went public, and the private equity investors made significant returns on their investment, with one of the primary investors alone reportedly making billions of dollars upon the sale of its stake.

These are three examples of why the brand reputation and the drivers of that sentiment are critical for the investors to gain a full understanding of before making an investment. It allows the investors and the company to look for brand pivots and brand extensions that accelerate topline growth.

Brand Repositioning

Trying to turn around a brand that has been deteriorated, has a very low probability of success. However, when they are successful, it still relies on the strength of the brand to do so. These strengths create natural pivot points for the brand to reinvent itself. Most investors will not bet on a deteriorated brand. At the end of the day, you are betting with lots of money that you can turn around a failing brand. That feat would not get even odds in Vegas.

When these investments occur and the investor is successful, the investment returns significant value. Hunter Boot Limited is a British heritage brand known for its iconic Wellington boots, which are commonly referred to as Hunter boots. In April of 2006, Hunter went into administration (UK equivalent of bankruptcy) and was bought out by a group of independent investors led by Jonathan Marland, a conservative politico, Peter Mullen, the founder of Thomas Pink, Julian Taylor, and the Pentland Group.

Under the new ownership and leveraging their heritage and the strength of their products, Hunter underwent a significant revitalization effort. The new team focused on making the old company into a global fashion brand and expanded its product range, enhancing brand image, and targeting new consumer segments.

The brand's turnaround gained momentum in the late 2000s when it experienced a surge in popularity, particularly among fashion-forward consumers. Hunter boots became a sought-after fashion item, as they were embraced by celebrities, influencers, and the fashion industry at large. The brand successfully transitioned from being solely functional outdoor footwear to a fashion statement, capitalizing on the growing demand for stylish and durable rain boots.

In 2011, an investor acquired a majority stake in Hunter. This partnership provided additional financial resources and strategic guidance to further accelerate Hunter's growth trajectory. The brand continued to expand its product offerings beyond boots, introducing new lines such as outerwear, accessories, and collaborations with renowned designers and focusing on international expansion.

Hunter focused on international expansion. The brand expanded its presence in key markets, including the United States, Europe, and Asia. Furthermore, Hunter capitalized on its British heritage and associations with outdoor pursuits, nature, and country lifestyle to create a distinct brand identity that resonated with consumers worldwide.

This vignette points to what investors are capable of when the brand has strength. The key is not necessarily revenue trajectory. It is the brand value drivers, sentiment, and the loyalty it can create with users. Investment in how to go above a standard wellie and pivot the company into a global fashion brand was built on the strength of the initial product and its reputation in the market. Never underestimate the ability for reputational perception to enable brand extension and expansion.

In this situation, there was significant investment in the brand. They also had to make difficult operational decisions, exiting all of their manufacturing operations in Scotland. They shifted all of their production to Serbia, China, and Brazil as it was no longer economically viable to produce the product in Scotland.[27]

In a failed example, Eddie Bauer is an iconic American outdoor clothing and gear brand that was founded in the 1920s. It came to notoriety in the 1930s when its founder, Eddie Bauer, after nearly freezing to death on a hunting trip, designed and patented the quilted goose down jacket. These jackets were a success and propelled Eddie

27 "Boot Firm to End Scots Production," BBC News, May 2, 2008, news.bbc.co.uk/2/hi/uk_news/scotland/south_of_scotland/7379713.stm; "Buyer Found for Famous Boot Firm," BBC News, April 28, 2006, news.bbc.co.uk/2/hi/uk_news/scotland/south_of_scotland/4955454.stm.

Bauer into an iconic brand, outfitting expeditions to Mount Everest, as well as fashionable Americans.

In 2003, it was spun out of Spiegel Companies with a heavy debt load because of Spiegel's bankruptcy process. However, in 2004, the management team of Eddie Bauer attempted to pivot the brand into becoming a women's casual apparel chain, like a Talbots or J. Jill. It brought in more color and tried to target the younger elements of its typical demographic. The consumer response was poor. As you can tell, it did not leverage the strength of the brand, known for its roots in the outdoors.

This appears to have been a bad decision and resulted in the company not turning a profit for over three years. A new management team was brought in, but the changes may have been too late. That combined with a recession that occurred between 2007 and 2010 brought the iconic brand into insolvency.

Unfortunately for the iconic brand, it went into bankruptcy in 2009, despite what appeared to be the right direction. The company was acquired by an investor out of bankruptcy. The investor finally sold Eddie Bauer in 2021. The terms of the sale were not disclosed, but the company had successfully transformed back to its roots in the outdoors, recognizing its one-hundred-plus years of legacy and success in that arena.[28]

For product-dominated businesses, the turnaround or transformation of the company can be executed with a focus on product. In one instance, an investor that I worked with bought infrastructure assets from a larger national player. This segment of the business had been underinvested causing less than stellar customer service, and lack of the latest technology to all of its customers. The investor saw this as an opportunity to change the company's trajectory.

They leveraged key, targeted investment in the infrastructure and some new point-to-point infrastructure. These investments improved overall service levels. They also made targeted, but efficient upgrades to the customer experience. Improving customer satisfaction, the two key drivers of a poor brand in the market they were facing.

With the acquisition, they rebranded the company and noted the key improvements in the customer experience and investment to expand access across the region. When conducting a rebranding campaign, it is

---

28 "Eddie Bauer to Be Sold to Authentic Brands and Simon," SBG Media, May 8, 2021, sgbonline.com/eddie-bauer-to-be-sold-to-authentic-brands-and-simon/.

typical that a company will use an additional (supernumerary to typical marketing budgets) an additional three to six months worth of spend during the new brand launch. This strategy proved exceptionally strong and despite economic headwinds performed well.

You will notice that the key for all of these transformations or turnarounds is to always pivot from the core of your company or product set. In each example, the private equity firms or investors took the strength and used that strength to enter adjacent products or to enter new markets. Nothing was ever too far afield—that is the key to a strategic pivot. In the one instance where this was not true with Eddie Bauer, it ended in insolvency and bankruptcy. The investments can be sizable, which is why it pays to understand the value of the brand up front.

Even in the most radical of transformations, the key to success are the pivots off of strength with several large bets placed. Even with the large bets, it still needs to derive from the strength of the company. For instance, Under Armour entering into shoes was a relatively large bet. However, it was related and it was based on their innovation and relationships, which is why it succeeded. The infrastructure investor also made a large bet. However, they had identified an asset with underlying infrastructure that was not fully utilized. It leveraged its last mile strength with some core investment to improve customer outcomes and increase market share.

Large-scale pivots and rebranding have occurred, but they can take years or decades to execute. One of the best examples is IBM. It took IBM decades to pivot from a hardware manufacturer into an enterprise service and software enterprise. This was a fundamental strategy pivot because of the emerging changes in the technology market. A private equity Investor would have likely avoided IBM in the 1990s because the market headwinds that would likely have been identified.

Beginning in the early 1990s, and spanning decades, it required substantial investments from IBM in research and development, serial acquisitions, key partnerships, and focused talent development. To execute the planned pivot, the company underwent organizational restructuring, divested certain businesses, and realigned its resources to align with its new strategic direction toward software and services.

Over time, IBM successfully positioned itself as a leader in enterprise software and services, offering solutions across various industries.

By diversifying its offerings and focusing on high-value services, IBM was able to adapt to the evolving technology landscape and meet the changing needs of its customers.

Large-scale transformations of this nature are complex and multi-faceted. They require a comprehensive strategy, strong leadership, significant investments, and a clear vision for the future. The transformation of IBM spanned multiple decades and was an ongoing process, such fundamental shifts in a company's identity and business model will take a considerable amount of time to fully materialize. However, even this pivot still leveraged the strength of IBM's brand in computer science and software solutions to execute.

Based on the strength of the brand, investors can make a significant return. This is magnified both up and down when those key drivers are misunderstood. Brands are never fully turned around. Brands leverage their strength and re-position. This is why the success of brand turnarounds and brand expansion has a relatively low rate of success. However, when done properly with the right foresight prior to the investment, the returns can be compelling.

MARKET ENTRY AND MARKET EXPANSION

One of the key mechanisms of topline expansion is through international expansion. The ability to expand your current product into other markets is a key enabler of growth and can be done rapidly with the right team and targeted engagements from the investors and management team.

Investors typically look for a company that has the capability to expand into adjacencies. We covered the product adjacencies through some examples in the last section. The focus here will be on international markets expansion.

The International Organization

Depending on the size of the company and complexity dictates the strategy of how you build the international team. There tends to be a spectrum from domestic to regional to global and matrixed. This is largely based on how large the company is, how complex the company's

international operations are, number of business lines, and how specialized the company plans to be for delivery in each region. Here is a good
initial framework to understand this spectrum:

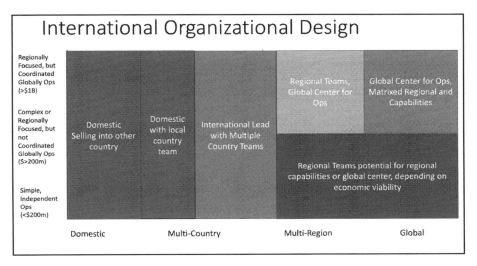

You will notice there are key transition points between a domestic
organization selling into other countries, into an international organization, and then regional teams, and finally the regional teams with a global
coordination layer (global, matrixed organization). These transitions
tend to occur organically within a company. Think about a small business
expanding from the U.S. Typically, one of the first countries they expand
to is Canada. It has a close cultural affinity, treaties are in place to limit
tariffs and maintain similar legal protections. At first, it is the current
sales teams with a relationship at a major Canadian retailer or outlet.
However, operations grow large enough that the company invests in a
team in Canada.

That success leads to multiple countries, maybe still being served
through the same sales team. At a certain point, International Expansion becomes a priority, and the company appoints an international
lead, which has all of the country teams report into them. At a certain
point, one region gets large enough that you put in place someone that
can manage that region, independent of the others. You typically do not
see a head of International after this point, as the regions control their
individual outcomes. This International layer at this point essentially

replicates the global center and adds an unnecessary cost structure to the company.

The company has a choice at this point. Keep all of the back office resources centralized (cost-efficient and levered growth) or replicate functionality at the regional level (highest cost). There is no solid middle ground where some functionality is shifted to the region. There still needs to be a center that audits and consolidates. I have seen the highest leverage in the global center model. This then allows the transition into the global matrixed organization with expansion of additional resources into the region, controlled centrally.

On the converse, companies that do not have solid execution discipline and that allow the regions to make these decisions typically end up with bloated cost structures. Depending on the needs of the business, there are times when it makes sense to replicate all of the centralized functions of the global center in each region. However, most of the time you can work from the global center and then put in place elements into the regions reporting into the global center, which is cost controlled.

Key Functions

For global operations, there are a few functions, which need to be thought through and in place. First, you need a global regulatory compliance operation. The goal of the compliance operation is to ensure that all local requirements and regulations are met for you to serve that market. This can be met several ways. Sometimes the partners that you have in the new country or region will support you. Other times, you will need to develop the required infrastructure yourself. I do not recommend outsourcing this function in its entirety—you should have someone that is an employee responsible for it. However, the specific country elements will likely require a partner, given some of the eccentricities of the local laws for various products or services.

The second is international trade for transportation and tariff management. This can and should be outsourced. However, you need to ensure it is stood up and covered in the organization. This is capability in the company that ensures all of the appropriate paperwork for each shipment is developed.

Market Determination

Target markets typically happen through one of a few mechanisms:

1. They occur organically. The company is solicited by an outlet or importer in a market. This interest spurs the company to explore the potential for success in a given market. They select that provider or another and enter into an agreement for import and begins importing the product to the new geography.

2. For some, they see a potential market opportunity in a specific country and try to exploit it. China has been a country that many companies have continued to try to develop to varying outcomes. Because the market is so large with a growing middle class with discretionary spend, the cost to enter the market has increased and may be a deterrent for some companies.

3. Some companies have a focused strategy for international expansion. This is where the company takes time and plans a strategy for international expansion. They identify countries that have a strong cultural affinity for their product or service (e.g., coffee culture for Dunkin' Brands). The expansion is controlled and reported to management. For each country they develop relationships and identify the best possible partners for their products and services. They work with those partners to develop the expansion plans and projected growth. For some key regions or countries, the company will make investments in people and resources to improve sales and direct selling capabilities.

The preferred method would be option 3 where everything is planned out. However, in reality it is likely a mix of 1, 2, and 3. Where there are some markets that are entered with lack of intentionally, some markets that everyone believes can and should be exploited and others where you make conscious decisions to develop and plan for entry. The biggest determinant of success is the cultural affinity of the market for your product or service. There are some notable examples of failure to understand the local market and your product or services fit within that rubric.

In 2012, Home Depot shut down all of its stores in China. One of the key reasons for this failure was a lack of understanding and adaptation to the Chinese market's cultural context. In the U.S., the concept of do-it-yourself (DIY) is very popular and drives Home Depot's business model. However, in China, where labor is cheap, the DIY concept isn't common. Most Chinese people prefer do-it-for-me (DIFM), hiring someone else to do the work, making Home Depot's core business model a mismatch with local customs and habits.

Barbie, the iconic American doll, has struggled in Middle-Eastern markets where the doll is seen as promoting Western ideals and values that conflict with the more conservative societal norms and religious beliefs in the region. Local products like Fulla, a doll that wears a hijab and abaya, are more popular and culturally appropriate alternatives.

However, when you get that element right there can be tremendous success and value created.

Coca-Cola has been extremely successful in Mexico and has a large market share. This success is partly due to the Mexican culture's strong affinity for soda and sweet beverages. Coca-Cola also adapted to the market by offering their product in glass bottles, which are preferred by many consumers in Mexico due to the perception of better taste compared to plastic bottles. Their understanding and alignment with local cultural preferences have helped establish Coca-Cola as a leading beverage brand in Mexico.

IKEA's first venture into the Japanese market from 1974 to 1986 failed due to the Japanese audience's unwillingness to embrace the concept of self-service and do-it-yourself assembling. When they reentered Japan in 2006, they adjusted their product offerings and store operations to cater to Japanese customers. They offered furniture with sizes suitable for smaller Japanese homes and provided delivery and assembly services as Japanese customers weren't keen on the "do-it-yourself" approach. Their understanding and adoption of local cultural preferences led to their successful reentry into the Japanese market.

The second largest determinant of success is your partner and the relationships you have in the market. Building strong relationships with local partners, customers, and authorities can be a key to success. This element requires significant investment of time and resources from the company.

Local partners provide valuable insights about the market, help navigate the legal and regulatory environment, and provide access to local resources and commercial outlets. Having good relationships with authorities can facilitate smoother operations and reduce regulatory hurdles.

If you or the organic team does not have connections in a given market, there are typically relationship brokers that you can leverage. These businesses make a market providing introductions between firms seeking international expansion and local businesses that can partner with them. This is critical for markets that have prohibitions on foreign entities—the majority of these laws and regulations are sector specific. Some of the markets that have these requirements are countries like India, Saudi Arabia, Indonesia, Vietnam, UAE (outside free trade zones), and Thailand. China was notorious for this type of limitation on foreign direct investment, but has slowly liberalized its policies.

Before working with businesses or businessmen in various locales, it is always helpful to do some diligence and ensure they are entities that you can see working and that you are willing to place some of your company's reputation at risk with. Be on the lookout for potential ethical risks with these partners.

How to Enter Markets

When entering a market, the company needs to make a few strategic decisions. One of the primary is whether to enter the market on its own, to leverage joint ventures or partnerships, or finally enter through a distributor. I have simplified this into a pros and cons chart for your thoughts. There is no right way. However, the economics should dictate what the company does. In general, with overhead for the country included, you typically need between $5 to $10 million in annual sales to make direct entry profitable (depends on gross margin, team size, industry, and investments to the market).

Pros and Cons

Entry Method	Pros	Cons	Typical Economics
Direct entry (entering on your own)	1. Full control over operations. 2. Keep all profits. 3. Greater ability to maintain brand consistency.	1. High initial costs. 2. Higher risk due to lack of local market knowledge. 3. Longer time to establish a presence.	This method often requires substantial initial investment for setting up operations, hiring staff, marketing, etc. The company keeps all revenue but also bears all operational costs and risks.
JV/ Partnership	1. Access to local partner's market knowledge and resources. 2. Shared risks and costs. 1. May be easier to comply with local regulations.	1. Need to share profits with partner. 2. Potential conflicts with partner. 3. Less control over operations.	Costs and risks are typically shared according to the partnership agreement. Profits are also split with the local partner as agreed upon. The exact split can vary widely depending on the deal negotiated.
Distributor	1. Quick way to access market. 2. Lower initial investment. 3. Distributor takes care of logistics and local regulations.	1. Lower control over marketing and customer service. 2. Dependency on distributor's performance. 3. Need to share a portion of revenue with distributor.	In this method, the company usually sells its products to the distributor at a discount, and the distributor then resells the products at a markup. The exact discount or markup can vary but it's often a percentage of the product's retail price.

There is no right answer and each situation is different.

If your intent is to maintain a permanent presence and grow the market, it may make sense to do a direct entry. The trade off is typically slower growth unless you can find the right country leads. JV is a happy mid ground, which allows you to keep the majority of the upside. This is a great method when you may already have some business, but it is not yet economic for you to do a direct entry. The JV can be structured however you want (dependent on local country laws) and you can have your partner pick up a lot of the back office and other workload, similar to a distributor model. However, you maintain ownership and the ability to influence the experience provided.

However, one thing to consider is that for new market entry or for countries with limited revenue, entries facilitated with distributor relationships check a lot of boxes for private equity firms. These entries tend to be cheaper. The distributor partner will typically invest, or you can contractually oblige them to invest, to help grow your revenue in the market. The distributor will also typically take care of the logistics and compliance with local regulations. Finally, the time to market is just the time it takes to find, identify, and contract with the partner and gain regulatory approvals. Once complete, you can typically begin selling product into the distributor and thereby the market.

The biggest downside to distributor relationships is when you would like to dissolve the relationship or if you grow well and want to take over the operation. For both of these situations, it makes sense to ensure that the divorce clause in distributor contracts is as favorable to you as the economics and entry. The best answer is to ensure you have a quick way to assess their performance and mechanisms to rapidly dissolve the relationship if their performance is not meeting your expectations. This could dissuade investment. So, the best option is to contractually obligate and even pay for some of the investment to grow the market.

Direct Entry, Legal Entity Establishment, and Intellectual Property Jurisdiction

Direct entry to a market requires you to typically establish a permanence in the new market through people or presence in the market. This can be done by way of an adjacent country, as long as the appropriate legal vehicles and treaties between the countries are in place. A common example is the entry into Canada from the U.S. You do not need to establish a Canadian presence to sell goods or services across the border because of the U.S.-Canada income tax treaty. A lot of which is tax exempt in Canada from the U.S. However, once you solicit sales through an agent or employee in Canada, produce/manufacture, or provide services you trigger a clause of doing business in Canada and require filing in Canada for tax. Working with established legal teams to help you navigate these complexities is critical. In addition, your tax advisor can help you structure these entities well to minimize tax liabilities.

If you plan to establish a permanent presence, also known as permanent establishment (PE), you will typically need to establish a legal entity that can employ the resources and your company will fall under all of the auspices of that country's legal and tax code. For small-scale operations, this can be cost prohibitive. Typically, you need to have plans of employing at least 40 to 50 employees in that country to have that make sense.

For smaller scale operations, there are services provided through companies like Globalization Partners Papaya Global and Velocity Global that can let you use one of their existing network of legal entities to employ resources in a region. The cost to use this service is high. However, you can begin operations in a matter of weeks with those companies acting as your employer of record in the jurisdiction versus months to wait on your legal entity to be approved. In addition, they have benefit packages and all the HR services needed to support the team locally. If you know you will eventually scale, it is often better to start the country leveraging these services, build out your own infrastructure, and then ramp them down quickly once your legal entities are established and you have met all regulatory requirements.

Business contracting can be with any legal entity that you have for most jurisdictions. It is not uncommon for a UK company or French company to enter into an agreement with a U.S. entity. Before entering into these contracts, it is important to leverage your tax advisor. They may recommend that you utilize a different legal entity to contract through versus a local legal entity. In addition, the tax advisor will likely work with you on transfer pricing to the other legal entities for goods and services to minimize your tax liability.

Once the legwork is set up, it will be up to your country manager to develop the market. The selection of the country manager is a critical hire. They need to have in depth knowledge of the market with access and connections to the key commercial organizations or outlets your company needs. The company needs to diligence this hire well for their capabilities, business connections, ethics, and ability to recruit a team. Someone with limited ability to attract a top-notch team in a key market as you look to build out the capability and capacity may not perform well.

Distributor Selection, Contracts, and Operations

The selection of a distributor should focus on the distributor's capabilities in the market. They will be a key partner for your international expansion and largely responsible for the success or failure of the endeavor. To ensure you pick the right party, you typically want to focus on the relationship that you can develop with that partner. However, you also want to assess in an objective manner their strengths relative to there peers across seven core areas: Specific market knowledge and access, sales and distribution infrastructure, marketing and promotional activities, staff training and support, support for reporting and understanding of product performance in the market, their commitment to your growth, and regulatory compliance track record. Here are some additional details to consider:

Specific market knowledge: The distributor should have a deep understanding of the local market for your core products. For instance, if you are a manufacturer of men's cologne, it may not make sense to work with a distributor that covers men's shoes for the given market. Although they might have access, they may not know how to optimize the operation and grow the market for men's cologne. Your company will pay for this inefficiency through reduced sales or higher overhead costs, leading to less investment.

Sales and distribution infrastructure: When you conduct the diligence on the distributor, you should also evaluate the specific outlets and distribution contracts they have. These outlets and methods of selling your products should align with your company's strategy and position in the market. If they are at Walmart and you are a premium product that is not a distributor you should leverage!

Marketing and promotional activities: The distributor should have a clear plan for promoting and marketing the company's products or services in the new market, including local advertising campaigns, trade shows, or other promotional activities. This plan should be made quantitative and show the explicit growth of your product over the duration of the contract and a few years beyond—typically between three to five years. They should clearly be able to discuss their plans for investment in the products or services and how that will foster growth for your company.

Employee retention, training, and support: The partner should be able to show the company its ability to retain employees. If your partner has significant turnover, that will negatively impact your company's perception in the market. There are highly reputable distributors, specifically in the Asian markets, that have excellent programs that retain employees. The retention should focus on market pay, but also investment in training and support to improve sales. The distributor should show plans to train and invest in the staff to improve their ability to sell your product in line with growth estimates.

Performance metrics and reporting: Given the arm's length contract that will be in place between you and the end market, it is important for the distributor to agree to provide periodic sales reports by outlet and in aggregate. Without these reports, you would not have the ability to understand the market as you would not be able to access this information as the sales would be in their systems and data.

Commitment to growth: The distributor should demonstrate a commitment to growing the market share and actively seeking new customers or business opportunities. This will be quantitatively backed by the marketing and promotional activity plan. They should show their commitment through potential investment. The investment may require a longer contract to ensure the investment is offset with profitable growth for the partner.

Regulatory compliance: Validate the distributor's track record on regulatory and legal compliance. Conduct diligence on the vendor to ensure they are not currently or have recently been afoul of local regulatory requirements. If so, this could complicate your launch and success in the market. The distributor should also have plans and support any regulatory clearance required for your product set. They should also have a method to ensure regulatory compliance for your product set. For countries that require an in-market owner of these regulatory clearances, they should be able to hold these for you. However, these can and often are held hostage in termination discussions. If you have the ability to separate the regulatory ownership from the distributor, then you should strive to do that.

The contract with a distributor is a key lynchpin of success or the beginning of failure in a market. Distributor relationships, although powerful, can and have ended poorly with rights to distribution locked up in a legal morass for years. There are a number of key areas of these contracts that you and your team should review to ensure they are best aligned with your interests.

Parties involved and limitations on distribution: The contract will clearly delineate your partner. In this, you can ask them to clearly articulate which outlets they plan to sell your product in as a cleared distribution channel. In addition, you can put in place a clause that requires them to gain explicit permission from you and your team if they decide to expand into new outlets.

Term: You should define the term including start and end dates. One typical inclination is to use a shorter initial contract, say one or two years. However, this limits the distributors interest in investing in the brand and co-building the brand in the new market. A length closer to three to five years allows for this investment with return for you and them. When you do this you should strengthen the poor performance and termination clauses.

Termination: Outline the conditions under which either party can terminate the contract, such as breach of contract, non-performance, or a notice period. In addition, this portion of the contract should also seek to explicitly outline the payments required upon termination whether for cause or natural termination of the contract. Clearly defining these costs can prevent protracted legal issues upon early termination and excess costs charged to the company at natural contract expiration. It is typical for the company to pay the distributor for the on-hand inventory, any residual marketing and promotional costs, any identified termination fees in the initial contract, this may include legal, professional and transitional costs, if shifting to a new distributor. In some jurisdictions, you may also need to pay for the severance for employees associated with the contract. This will be determined by local labor laws and contractual agreements between the company and distributor.

Territory: Clearly define the geographic area and channels (e.g., brick-and-mortar, specific outlets, online) where the distributor is authorized to sell the company's products or services. This can be a specific country, region, or any other defined market. If you want to split the market between online and brick and mortar, this definition will be a material element of your discussions.

Products/services: Clearly describe the products or services that the distributor is authorized to sell. Include details such as model numbers, specifications, pricing, and any limitations on sales or distribution channels. This can also be highly generalized, such as all products in your brand or within a portfolio of brands.

Exclusivity: Specify whether the distributor has exclusive rights to sell the company's products or services in the defined territory. This could be an exclusive or non-exclusive agreement. For new market entry, you may need to agree for an exclusive agreement. If so, you should seek improved performance mechanisms to minimize time allowed for non-performance. To the extent you can make the agreement non-exclusive that is preferred and allows the company to use other distributors that may be able to access other outlets.

Performance expectations: Outline the distributor's obligations and performance targets, including sales volume, marketing activities, customer support, and any other relevant requirements. This should be tied to the marketing plan discussed before. It should have clear, quantitative targets and clear criteria that allows you to escalate non-performance. You should also seek to reduce time to escalate. It is not uncommon to allow up to two years to hit targets, for rapid international expansion, you may want to decrease this to one year such that if the teams are underperforming, it allows you to rapidly escalate the issue, and if necessary, invoke the termination clauses.

Pricing, payment terms, and incoterms: Detail the pricing structure, including wholesale prices, discounts, and any other relevant payment terms such as payment deadlines, methods of payment, and currency. In this discussion, you should also seek to align on your Incoterms for the contract. The preferred method for delivery is Ex Works, meaning they are responsible for the product as soon as you deliver it to your loading dock.

Intellectual property and brand decisions: Address the protection and use of intellectual property rights, trademarks, copyrights, patents, and any other proprietary information. Typically, they will have limited rights to your IP. They should be able to leverage your trademarks and brand assets to support marketing and promotional activities. However, all brand positioning and decisions should be retained by the company. They should also not be able to make assets with your trademarks. Instead, you should have the ability to see and influence or approve the potential assets.

Marketing and advertising: Specify the marketing and advertising responsibilities of both parties, including the allocation of costs, advertising approval procedures, and any brand guidelines. The company should be investing in the brand, given adequate time horizon in the contract. You should also be willing to invest in the brand, product, or service to accelerate growth.

Confidentiality and non-disclosure: Include provisions to protect confidential information shared between the parties and outline restrictions on sharing or disclosing such information to third parties.

Dispute Resolution: Outline the procedures for resolving disputes, such as negotiation, mediation, or arbitration. Specify the governing law and the jurisdiction for any legal proceedings. Typically, you will want the dispute resolution to be in your local jurisdiction versus theirs.

Liability and indemnification: Define the liability of each party and outline the indemnification provisions, specifying the responsibilities and obligations in case of product defects, injuries, or damages. The company is typically responsible for product defects or inadequacies for service.

Intellectual Property Jurisdiction

Another consideration is where your intellectual property is legally kept. There are jurisdictions that have favorable treatment of income generated from intellectual property. Your tax advisor can provide the best solution for you. However, here are some of the jurisdictions that people have used to create value and minimize tax liability. Please note these are not recommendations or advice in any way shape or form. Please ensure you consult your tax advisor and attorneys on methods to effectively house your IP.

Ireland: Ireland offers attractive tax incentives for companies with IP. The country has a favorable corporate tax rate of 12.5 percent for trading income, which includes income generated from IP. Additionally, Ireland has a "Knowledge Development Box" regime, which allows for a reduced tax rate of 6.25 percent on qualifying IP income.

Switzerland: Switzerland has a beneficial tax regime for IP. The country offers cantonal tax regimes that allow for a substantial reduction in tax liabilities for income derived from IP. Each canton may have its own specific tax rates and incentives, making Switzerland an attractive location for IP-related activities.

Netherlands: The Netherlands has an IP Box regime that provides a significant tax advantage for income derived from qualifying IP. Under this regime, a portion of the profits generated from qualifying IP can be taxed at a reduced rate of 9 percent instead of the regular corporate tax rate.

Luxembourg: Luxembourg has favorable tax policies for IP income. It offers an IP box regime that provides for a partial exemption of qualifying IP income, resulting in a reduced effective tax rate. Luxembourg's IP regime is in line with international standards and OECD guidelines.

Singapore: Singapore has introduced an intellectual property development incentive (IDI) scheme to encourage the development and exploitation of IP. Under the IDI, qualifying IP income can be taxed at a concessionary tax rate, subject to certain conditions.

Cyprus: Cyprus offers a beneficial tax regime for IP income. It has an IP Box regime that provides for an 80 percent exemption on qualifying IP income, resulting in an effective tax rate of 2.5 percent. Cyprus has gained popularity as a jurisdiction for IP holding companies.

CHAPTER 6

Inorganic Growth

Use of additional acquisitions in the private equity space is a typical commercial growth lever to grow the business. As with all mergers, the success and return on the merger is predicated on the roll-up strategy, the rationale for the specific merger, and, of course, the purchase price of the asset. In the private equity setting, there is usually a want for scale and synergies. In one merger that I supported, two top players in a software market combined. The rationale was a bit about scale, but also about improving their competitive position in the market. They were beginning to face pressure from larger companies that were providing "good-enough solutions" that could disrupt their market position. This merger brought some highly regarded capability into the company's product portfolio and gave them two market-leading solutions to strengthen their sale. This merger gave them sufficient product strength to safeguard their position and gave them sufficient scale to compete with those larger players.

Typically, the mergers occur for one of three reasons:

1. There is over capacity in the industry. When you combine, it allows the industry to increase its rents and thereby the profitability of the whole. This is not something an investor will typically look to do. It increases their risk profile for the benefit of a larger whole.

2. The target has specific products, technologies, or market access that the acquiring company needs. This is quite

common as it can (if the merger is executed well) accelerate business growth for the total. In addition, there are often cross-sell and up-sell revenue synergies that can be captured as upside to the transaction.

3.   The target has processes, capabilities or management teams that will help the acquiring company. There are times when the target has a market leading process that is allowing the business to scale. Or they have a stellar management team. The board or investors from the acquiring company could seek to conduct a merger and then take the product or business model from the acquiring company and place it into the better mouse trap or under the guidance of the other company's leadership team. In one instance, I evaluated a merger where the management team from the potential acquisition was better suited for the investment thesis for the private equity investor. They ended up not executing the deal, but had that occurred, there was a probability that the leadership of the company would have transferred to the other asset.

When the opportunity to merge does occur, the private equity company will still need to realize significant bottom line synergies. I will discuss the methods for how to think through synergies later in this chapter. The topline and strategic synergies will likely drive some of the deal. But remember, the investors are economically oriented. There are times when if they can buy an asset on the cheap, buy additional topline and EBITDA, they may execute the deal without significant strategic vision on the acquisition. This would be an arbitrage focused buy and they can and do occur.

More than often, there are times when the investors have a dedicated strategy to grow the topline through acquisition. These are typically referred to as a roll-up strategy. These strategies are executed when the investors develop an investment view that a given industry is strong and has excellent tailwinds. They will look to buy a platform in the industry. The platform is their initial acquisition in that industry. They will work to stabilize the business rapidly and then begin to buy additional assets in the industry creating a portfolio of capabilities, brands, or products to develop into a market leading company.

When executing these strategies there are typically three M&A approaches: 1) Conduct selective mergers when the opportunity presents itself, 2) Buy a large, near-peer competitor, or 3) Establish programmatic M&A and buy a number of small or medium size targets. In a recent McKinsey study, they indicated that a company that leveraged programmatic M&A produced a median excess return of close to 2.1 percent over a 10-year period in total stockholder return (TSR) between 2010 and 2019.[29] In addition, selective and large deal M&A programs typically destroy value with an average -1.3 percent in excess shareholder returns. The worst choice is to rely just on organic growth, resulting in an average -2 percent TSR over the same time period.

Developing a programmatic M&A system is key and allows the company to continue to use market operations to grow its topline and gain the capabilities or portfolio that it needs to succeed in the marketplace. Programmatic M&A consists of developing an internal capability that knows how to rapidly evaluate, ingest and merge companies. In addition, the capability should also seek to tune the back office of the company to support rapid integration. If a team is successful, they can get these integrations into a process and have the entire tuck in or integration completed within six months with limited to no impact to organic growth. This is largely driven by the sophistication of the team and a set process and playbook on how to integrate them. One of the best serial acquirers in recent history was Kinder Morgan. They had a set process that fully completed acquisitions within no more than one year, integrating the scale and capabilities needed to further grow the business.

For those companies that choose large-scale acquisitions, that should be the sum-total of the strategy for M&A. Typically, when conducting a large-scale acquisition, you will see the process take up to two years. During that time, you typically see managerial attention divided and organic growth for both companies be impacted. Over a five-year hold period, you may just be getting through those hurdles before you sell the asset. Often times, the choice to conduct large scale M&A is actually driven by hubris of the executive team. It is always a bigger feather in the cap to say you acquired a $1 billion near-competitor versus 10 $100 million companies that fundamentally transformed your company.

---

29   Robert Uhlaner and Liz Wol, "Programmatic M&A: Winning in the New Normal, McKinsey & Company," March 21, 2022, www.mckinsey.com/capabilities/strategy-and-corporate-finance/our-insights/programmatic-m-and-a-winning-in-the-new-normal.

A HIGHLY-SCALABLE PLATFORM

When creating a highly-scalable platform company, you want to architect the organization and the back end solutions to support rapid integration of service lines, products, and brands. The ability to quickly digest them is key. It is not uncommon for companies to be able to organizationally integrate as soon as day one. The value creation for the deal typically takes longer and requires the capabilities to be integrated.

I will first cover a scalable organizational structure. When putting in place the scalable organizational structure, you want to clearly segment the back office from the front office. Use of global leads for finance (CFO), operations (COO), and administration (CAO) are helpful. Organizing your product lines into distinct lines of business is also helpful. Finally, your go-to market focused on geography is also beneficial. Use of these overarching type of roles also reduces the seams in decision-making for some of the critical capabilities for the combined company.

When the organizational construct is streamlined, the ease of integration of the acquired capabilities quickly are adopted into the combined organization. This then also allows the principal for each of these areas to drive the synergies rapidly.

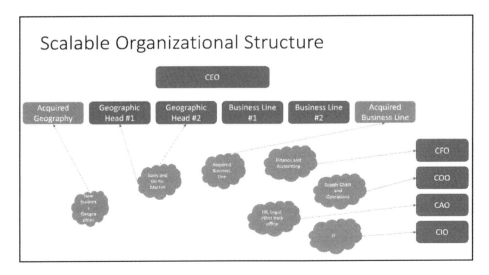

The next layer of a rapidly scalable platform is the back office and middle office ecosystem. The ability to have scalable solutions is critical. Some of the key methods to do this are:

1. Leverage SaaS solutions. When the company leverages a full SaaS and cloud based back-office solution, you can rapidly and horizontally scale the capabilities. In addition, the integration of the new employees into the new platform is simplified. You can quickly provide access and VPN access to their existing platforms. It also allows you to quickly decommission their existing systems, once necessary capabilities are adapted or built into the new architecture. For this, the goal is not to replicate the capability, but give them a good enough capability that is not already resident in your current systems. Optimization can occur later.

2. Leverage 3PLs. For the middle office, you can rapidly integrate the new companies logistics into your own when the infrastructure is not your own. The ability to digest new brands or products into your existing infrastructure is outsourced. The 3PL gets additional business and takes some of the need for integration support onto their shoulders.

3. Leverage outsourced manufacturing. To the extent possible, use of outsourced manufacturing for non-industrial companies allows the operations to rapidly be integrated. If the acquired company has existing production facilities, an economic make versus buy analysis should be conducted in the sign to close phase.

4. Leverage outsourced back office. Accounting should largely be offshored and can be outsourced. When outsourced, it allows you to digest the acquired companies operations more rapidly with the support of your partner. IT for most non-technical companies can be scaled back to an internal resource count less than 10 people for most companies. The key is to leverage a highly flexible managed service provider for the IT infrastructure and application management elements of the business. When you do, they can quickly integrate and scale (some times these providers can even use the acquired company's resources).

5. Leverage a topline consolidation tool. For accounting and finance integration, the use of a topline integration tool obviates the need for rapid ERP integration (typically the longest pole in the tent). This allows the accounting team to maintain the acquired company's books up to the point that the ERP is integrated.

6. Data and Reporting. The use of a data lake repository (unstructured data storage) can improve time to report on the combined entity. The data from all former systems can be mapped to the company's existing data layer. The use of some additional resources and capacity to rapidly replicate prior reports and combined reporting is highly beneficial.

This then leaves the focus on the business integration and the need to consolidate the contracting and the organization into a streamlined business. These elements, specifically the contracting, will take a while. The organizational alignment and restructuring should be able to executed within three months of the close. Some value creation may take longer based on the capability transfer to the new company. Typically, there is a trim reduction in force about one year to 15 months post close. Companies should try to avoid serial layoffs (once per quarter or one ever six months). These work against the growth ambitions and development of the new team.

MERGER SYNERGIES

There are various possibilities of how a merger occurs in a private equity setting. There is an opportunity, that despite potential synergies, it makes more sense for the company to structure the arrangement as a holding company with multiple operating companies versus as a wholly integrated new company. Because of this, when you conduct the analysis, the first step is to look at each company on an individual basis and determine the stand-alone synergies for each company in the potential merger.

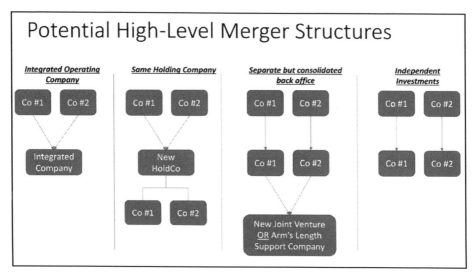

Potential High-Level Merger Structures

Integrated Operating Company | **Same Holding Company** | **Separate but consolidated back office** | **Independent Investments**

Co #1 Co #2 → Integrated Company

Co #1 Co #2 → New HoldCo → Co #1 Co #2

Co #1 Co #2 → Co #1 Co #2 → New Joint Venture OR Arm's Length Support Company

Co #1 Co #2 → Co #1 Co #2

Unlike most public companies, where upon acquisition a merger and integration is assumed, you cannot always assume that to be true for an investor. I have highlighted a few high-level concepts of how they may end up determining that the integration (or lack thereof) may occur. For instance, the investor may decide to just buy the other company and not integrate the asset once bought and operate independently for a period of time before being integrated. There are some options like placing the assets into a new holding company arrangement where the investor owns 100 percent of the holding company and each company then largely operates independently below. In that situation there may be a consolidated executive team at the holding company level or other such synergies. Another is that each company continues to operate independently, but they consolidate back office operations through a joint venture or establishing with assets from both companies a third party, arm's length company that supports the other two through the back office and supply chain. This explanation leaves out a lot of detail on how to structure these types of arrangements and the contracts required, but those are small dollars if these structures yield better potential outcomes for the economics of the assets and the profit for the investor.

When you do the standalone assessment, you will use the entire toolkits of Chapter 4. You will look at offshoring, operating efficiencies, new ERP systems, procurement, and other levers. There are times that you realize that the company acquiring or being acquired was not run that efficiently. It also gives you an excellent understanding of both operations. When you need to implement the work and improvements you have identified, you know (to the best of your ability) what the setup is for each of the companies.

Now, the combined assessment is relatively straightforward. The real delta will be the target operating model of an integrated entity, the consolidated executive management team, and the operational redundancies. Let's look at each of these in more detail.

Target Operating Model Design

With the standalone assessment, you will have a good understanding of each company and their relative inefficiencies. This provides you with a great position of visibility across the two entities and you can leverage experience and judgment to know who has best of breed and who maximizes operating leverage. This allows you to make better-informed decisions than just using the acquirer's management team to make the call. They will have a self-interest in keeping their job, role, and team.

The target operating model (TOM) is defined as the final conceptualized way of operating in the combined entity. Typically, you will bring on board all resources and systems on day one. The companies will largely operate the way they have been because nothing has been integrated at that point. There may be a few exceptions to this relative to leadership and some processes required for a combined entity.

To define the TOM, you will need to focus on four key elements for the TOM. This effort needs to be thought through for the total company and then for each function. The five key areas are:

1. *Strategic vision* for the combined entity. Define the key strategic objectives of the new entity. This can be loosely understood. However, as you define the roles and responsibilities of the combined executive team, you may want to think through the key elements of what these positions require. More often than not, the current executive team will not meet all of the needs of the new responsibilities.

2. Define the *organizational structure* including the hierarchy, reporting lines, and the division of responsibilities. This structure can sometimes change as you may have new strategic objectives. These discussions should typically occur with the investors and the CEO or a trusted executive like a chief transformation officer.

3. For the new TOM, you will need to think about how *key activities and processes* will continue to function and what they will look like in the future state. Some of the key elements to over index on are the mainline operations of the company—goods, services, customer service, sales, marketing, HRIS/payroll, and finance and accounting.

4. Thinking through the *technology and systems* is also key. You will want to understand the roadmap for integration and build in of the capabilities to allow for system consolidation. There are a lot of opportunities once systems are consolidated. This will also be key for day one (specifically HRIS and payroll)

5. With the lines drawn and the systems thought through, you will also need to ensure that the *governance* is clear.

Executive Team Consolidation

Once you are aware of the strategic intent, you should begin to design the organization and also what the executive consolidation will look like. This helps the investors begin to think through who the team will be. This should not just default to the acquiring company's leadership team. Oftentimes, there are great leaders in the acquired company. More often than not, the investor may just default to take the current management team with a few exceptions where the other resource was just objectively better. However, that is not always the case.

In one instance, there was an investor that bought a company with a strategic asset and then reduced the entirety of the acquiring company's leadership team. The strategic vision had shifted and the product set they were responsible for was going to be deprecated. In another, the management team of the acquired company had specific experience that was better than the current management team. The deal fell through, but the general view was to conduct a reverse take over with the acquired management team assuming a large number of the executive roles.

From an assessment perspective, I look at this through two separate lenses that bound the upside and downside scenarios. First, I look at this from a strategic objective perspective. I think through the system and process that the CEO will need to be successful for the strategic objectives stated by the PE firm. I provide two or three courses of action that are cost optimized. I then develop a TOM recommendation and discuss it with the appropriate stakeholders.

The second perspective is to look at the bare minimum number of executives needed for that size organization. When looking at this, begin with the spans and layers analysis and identify the minimum number of executives required to meet the needs of the company. Oftentimes, you will find that the number of executives employed to be significantly higher than that required. For instance, if you look at a 1,000 person company, you will find that that size organization can be run with a four person executive leadership team (exclusive of the CEO). You then make strategic tradeoffs against cost structure to add additional executives to meet strategic objectives. This is an aggressive, cost focused way to look at it. There are scenarios when this is required. However, the final decision should be based on the strategic needs of the organization.

The actual decision for the executives resides with the PE firm. The major focus for the assessment is to understand the high level needs for each of the positions based on the understanding of the strategic objectives. This assessment is helpful for the PE firm's human capital team. They can then ensure the current executive suite is consistent with those needs or if they need to recruit for a better fit.

Here are some additional thoughts:

1. Try to avoid situations with two in a box (e.g., two CEOs). There is an adage that says that when you have two CEOs, you have no CEO. Even if you divide the world by function, it will cause confusion in the rank and file. The political games will be afoot with both vying for the pole position. The best call is to just pick a horse and place your bet.

2. Strive to eliminate direct functional responsibilities reporting directly into the CEO (e.g., legal, HR). The better option is to

layer these functions under an aggregating executive like a
chief administrative officer, a chief operating officer, or a chief
financial officer. These functions are largely self-sufficient and
led by experts.

3. Leverage merger integration to recalibrate levels. Do you
    really need presidents, SVP or EVPs? Or are VPs sufficient
    across the organization? Do you need a large number of
    CxOs? Or can these be changed to VP, Human Resources?

4. Always try to get the organization into a scalable layout with
    clear lines of responsibility. In periods of growth, it streamlines
    decision-making. This also helps with accountability when
    things do not perform well.

Operational Redundancies

This is the largest area of opportunity in the organization. When
you assess this area, you will start with the stand-alone optimization
opportunities. Oftentimes, you can leverage merger scenarios to unlock
some value that may have been trapped in the organization such as use
of 3PL providers, labor cost arbitrage or improved system investment to
reduce large inefficiencies. This will give you the full opportunity and also
sometimes provide the push necessary to be successful for those trapped
value elements. For instance, if the acquired company has an offshore
service for customer service, it may be better to leverage a successful
operation and then add additional headcount to it versus starting a new
one with the acquirer's company.

When you look at the opportunities available in the combined entity,
you will usually find more value and opportunity in the organization. It is
not uncommon for a particular function to see a 30 to 50 percent reduction in force. These opportunities typically occur in redundant capabilities between the enterprises. For instance, you do not need two people
covering the same account on the salesforce. The benchmarks will help
you understand the areas to hunt. However, you will need to get more
granular to understand what is driving the cost out.

For instance, with the example of the two executives covering the
account, the decision makers may be different for the sale. This requires
some additional thought on how to extract the cost from the system. Do

you keep them and transition the relationship? Or are the sales fundamentally different and you actually need to keep both? How do you bridge this gap? Maybe you can bridge the gap with a combination of training on the new technology or product and a focused relationship transition program for the sales teams.

For other areas, you will need to think through timing. For instance, finance and accounting will be redundant. However, it will likely take between six months and a year to integrate their operations into a combined ERP. This means you will need to keep that headcount around until the systems have been integrated. Once done and the operation stabilized, you can reduce those resources. Typically close to a year after day one of the new entity.

For some, you will need to think through capability migration. For instance, if one company has a 3PL and you plan to shift the acquired company to the 3PL, but the capability is currently in house. You will need to factor in time to complete the contract negotiations (around one to three months, depending on relationships), and then integration into the operations of the 3PL and your operation. This could be another three months or nine months, if installation and migration is required. Now you have a view as to a six to 12 month window with more detailed planning to occur once you begin discussions and understand the full details of the operation.

This is a significant opportunity, but to get to a better understanding and assessment, you will need to understand the actual operations and implications before you can discuss the opportunity and timeline to implement.

One key thing to watch out for, specifically for sales, is that when assessing cost out, do not use the fully burdened cost. Only use the salary for the reduced resources. You do not typically get 100 percent capture of the bonus for the reduced resource as some of that upside needs to be provided to the smaller salesforce.

Third Party Spend Opportunities

The final major area to consider is the third party spend consolidation. This will occur through the same mechanisms we discussed previously: negotiation, consolidation or elimination of requirement, and reduction of volume. The largest by dollar value in a merger is typically consolidation or elimination of requirement. For instance, you will have a large number of duplicate type services. You will typically be able to reduce that spend. In a consolidation play, you can usually work with the vendor and see how you can reduce your rate at the same time.

The largest area that requires attention in the assessment and execution is the elimination of need. The systems will be a key area where once capability is integrated; you will be able to reduce the need for one or both of the legacy systems.

For consolidation, depending on the industry and vendor overlap, this can be a sizable opportunity as well. The key will be to understand the commodity spend and what is being bought where. You can do the mapping and then work to consolidate the spend for efficiency.

Topline Synergies

Topline synergies are often understood through the same mechanisms of commercial excellence. There are a few that I will also highlight that have more prevalence in a merger situation. Please remember, these occur in due course. They will and likely should be elements of the investment consideration for an upside scenario. Typically, a base case is a rationalized (meaning remove all "extra" growth proposed by the prospectus or CIM) combined growth estimate. For the upside case, you can consider a number of typical growth levers.

Some of the optimal growth levers are where the acquirer or acquired company has some capability that the other can exploit. For instance, when the acquirer has a global footprint with logistics and a global network of distributors or access to key markets, then the ability to take the existing product set of the acquired company and route that through your distributors and logistics network can all be considered upside, if the acquired company has not conducted international expansion.

Another core area of opportunity is in product or service set. Often, there will be complementary services or products in each company's portfolio. This allows the acquiring company to quickly train their sales team and sell that product into existing account management structures that could be in the market for the new service or product. The key focus for this will be in the training and the development of the combined go-to-market and sales actions to make this happen. The implementation once the team is formed can be rapid—three to six months with positive effect to topline. The converse is also true. It is not uncommon for there to be products or services that have significant capability overlap. When that occurs, the company will also seek to reduce the unneeded complexity. This has significant savings opportunities where new projects can be cancelled. It also requires the go-to-market teams to with the support of the product and operations teams to understand and plan the sunsetting of those products and the retention and cross-sell of the remaining product set.

CHAPTER 7

Carve-Outs

Corporate divestitures are a great source of opportunity and value for private capital investors. A corporate divestiture occurs when a relatively large company separates and sells a portion of their company. These sales can be healthy elements of the company or portions that are or may be on the verge of decline. Sometimes, the company just wants to sell assets. These assets can be brands or assets such as infrastructure.

The value comes through a few mechanisms:

1. **Increased management and board focus:** In the selling company the assets are a lower priority. Because of this, they typically do not receive sufficient attention from the existing management team to have their strategic and operational needs met. By creating a sole focus on these assets, the private investors and their attention can help spur the right decision-making for revenue and profit growth. In addition, the private investors can also seek to improve the talent and managerial capacity of the leadership team

2. **Increased capital investment:** Because the assets were deprioritized, they typically do not receive the necessary investment for them to succeed. The private investor with incentives aligned to improve the outcomes for these assets will typically invest in the needs of the business. They will also

buy down the past debt of investment over time to improve the asset.

3. **The actual carve-out:** the carve-out typically unburdens the asset from corporate allocations and will provide it with a new, state of the art back office that provides proper operating leverage, usually at a reduced cost point. The interesting part is that these assets typically appear to be losing money or providing a negative contribution to the desired profit margins for the larger company. When unburdened with the allocations and what could be an unachievable profit margin for its given industry, the asset can and does perform well.

However, carve-outs come with significant operational risk. The carve-out process is messy. There are a large amount of operational, organizational, and system entanglements that need to be thought through and unwound. On the receiving side, you need to ensure that with your target operating model that you have all of the requirements to run the new enterprise. This element of the diligence and assessment requires significant thought and insight to get right. In others, the investor may take over a distressed asset in the carve-out and conduct a full financial transformation whilst standing up the company and operations. In one of my last assignments, we had to get the asset out of a projected negative $100 million EBITDA hole for year one.

The assets themselves are still not always healthy. There are times when you will buy the asset and it will be on a prolonged negative revenue trajectory and requires a turnaround. There are other times when the assets may be healthy, but the underlying infrastructure and back-office elements will need to be completely overhauled. Investors that seek to conduct takeovers of carved-out assets should have a top-notch operational capability or leverage the best advisors for this type of work. The advisors will depend on the situation and the complexity of the carve-out.

Because of the complexity of the takeover, there will be a set of transition service agreements that the new owner will establish with the seller. Because of the level of entanglement, you need this dedicated period to unwind the systems, organizational elements, and establish independent operations.

The transition service agreement (TSA) is an area of value for the seller and could be an area where the deal economics get made more attractive. We will discuss the typical mechanisms of value in this phase and the long-term. Now, we will go through each element and help to identify where the value comes from.

Carve-Out Boundary and Structure

One of the first elements that needs to be aligned is what you are buying. There will be a specific element of the purchase agreement that details the boundary and what is and is not included in the transaction. This discussion will require some baseline understanding of the company and its operations. It will also need for the seller to tell you where certain things are and show you the evidence of how contracts and intellectual property is assigned. The ownership of key accounts and which legal entities have the cash and which do not.

For instance, in some transactions the company is selling a business unit. The business unit may have a defined legal entity structure with all of the intellectual property, assets, and contracts assigned to that legal entity structure. The other thing to consider is that when the company has an established legal entity and financials, it will also have credit, bank accounts, and other core elements of conducting business. They will also come with a balance sheet with assets and liabilities. You will need to work through those elements and what should be in these accounts upon deal close. The other interesting item is where the headcount exists. Often, headcount is legally assigned to just one legal entity, but may be technically doing work for others. Diligence is needed to understand what you are truly buying and what is or is not in the entity you are acquiring.

There are some situations were the assets the company wants to sell are not that attractive because of declining revenue or extremely low margins. When this occurs, there is an option to explore bundled purchases of assets. For instance, the end deal may include one declining business line, one growth, and one under invested. However, the sum total is economically viable and attractive for purchase.

In other situations, the company may desire to just sell assets. If they are selling a business or infrastructure, this can be effective. You just need to tuck that asset into your operation. However, if they are selling a business or business line through its assets this can be one of the most operationally intense methods to acquire assets from the seller, depending on what the investor is receiving these assets into. For instance, if there is a platform they have already purchased in the industry, this may not be difficult at all. However, if they need to stand up the full operation this will require the management and leadership team to establish the full legal entity structure, the bank accounts, the working capital, and then all of the back office operations for this new entity. The capital outlay to establish and fund the company is something the investor needs to consider. In addition, this will require significant investment to establish all of the back office. This needs to be thought through in total and considered in the economics of the transaction.

Carve-Out Financials and Allocations

When the boundary is aligned or close enough, the seller will develop pro-forma financials for the asset for sale. Carve-out financials are notoriously lousy. Think about your own business. How easy would it be to say the exact profitability of a business line. The difficulty is that a lot of the expense in a large corporation is allocated to the business lines. Take for instance finance and accounting—how much of the millions of dollars really is attributable to that one business line? There is no easy way to identify the actual cost. So, the allocation is approximate, at best. Complicating this, the seller can allocate their expenses however they want. The financials have to be auditable, but the allocation method can be described and that substantiates the need. They can shift the allocation to look favorable or bloated, depending on the story they want to tell. If they want to indicate that the company would be highly profitable except for the allocations then the allocations can be more robust to the business line. However, if they want to show a highly profitable business line, the allocations may be less. This will be situationally dependent.

The goal of your assessment should be to understand what the actual cost profile for the company will be. I have provided a conceptual diagram of what typically happens.

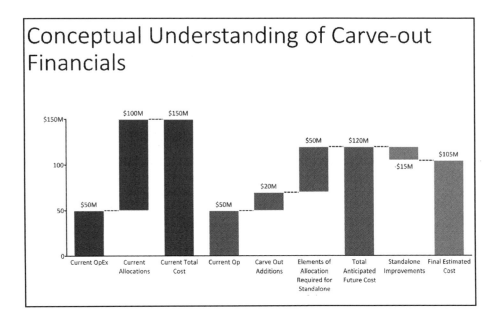

Conceptual Understanding of Carve-out Financials

Typically, the company's current operating expense will flow across to the new entity. For simplicity I have treated that as such in the conceptual drawing of carve-out financials.

The second element is that, in addition to the stated operating expense, there will be additional costs once the company is stand-alone. There is potential that some of these overlap with the conceptual bucket coming from the allocation, but for some things its just easier to specify exactly what those additions will be. For instance, the executive management team or the expansion and upgrading of the team may sit here. New facilities that are not currently in the budget may also need to be in here. Some of these may also be associated with the investment thesis. For instance, for one investor, there was a want to conduct a build out of the existing infrastructure. To support that, we built in additional resources to support those needs.

The allocations are always the difficult part. The best way to work through this is to understand what is captured in the allocation. For instance, the allocation may include the back office, warehouse overhead, R&D, executive spend, T&E, and a number of other things. Depending on the carve-out situation, you may be recreating this structure in its entirety. One way to think about it is to do a zero-based budget for the functions captured in the allocation. Using benchmarks and projected resource costs, you can develop the total cost structure. This allows you to understand the anticipated cost of the total company. Oftentimes, the allocation is a source of value as you streamline the operations of the company and establish a back office that scales.

Another method is to look through the trial balances and get a granular build of the allocation. Often, the company may not give you this level of detail. However, you should seek to try to understand as much as possible of the allocations relative to the remainder of the accounts for the carved out entity.

You end up usually doing both of these methodologies to get to the final answer of what is required to support the company once the corporate support from the larger company is removed.

On the revenue side, the scenario is typically more straightforward. There are some allocations that can occur for bundled products or services. In this situation, you have to remember that there is a chance that not all of that revenue will be replaced as the bundle is no longer relevant in the future state, if across business lines.

This will be a first draft of the cost structure. The reality is that as you go through the organizational, system, and operational entanglements, you will find more costs or efficiencies for the company and management to consider.

Organizational Entanglements

In a carve-out, you typically do not get the full organization you need. Naturally the company will not give you some of the leadership it needs to run its own operation after the sale. What you will end up with is Swiss cheese organization. The transition service agreement will cover you and ensure business stability as you build out the team and organization. The key is to understand where the holes will be and ensure that you have the right coverages in the TSA.

The other consideration is that the divesting company will likely never give you their best players. Often, you will get the junk drawer of resources from the divesting company. If you were on the other side, you would likely do the same. When you are given access to the people, you will also want to understand who you are inheriting and see if you need to reinforce key positions. In carve-outs, it is not uncommon for investors and management teams to hire additional treasury, FP&A, and accounting resources to support and stabilize the teams. Given the critical nature of the function and the uncertainty of the ingoing financials, it helps to have a source of truth that is independent of the past and what may have been provided in the transaction. Another key area is in operations with demand and supply planning. It helps to ensure you reinforce that area with strong talent as you stabilize the company post close.

In addition, carve-outs typically require the build out of the management team. For a business line, you might have all of the business leadership. However, you may not have the CFO. If you are buying assets, you may need to hire the entire leadership team for the company. In addition, the investors should review the needs of the positions and ensure that the team you are inheriting is capable of delivering the value creation plan.

The organization will take some time to stabilize. The initial stabilization will typically occur within about three to six months post close with everyone adjusting to the new operating reality. Typically, it will take about a year to hire the right people across all of the functions and get them onboarded and helping to drive the company in the right direction.

You may not have that much time in the transition service agreement. When you do not have the time needed, there are ways to accelerate this with interim staffing through places like ContinuServe and Randstad. These organizations can rapidly get you resources. A place like Contiu-Serve can quickly spin up resources when you need them leveraging an offshore labor rate. With the Randstad model, you can also do a temp to perm solution and take them on full time as you spin up the rest of your resources.

System and Data Entanglements

One of the largest efforts in a carve-out typically will relate to the information technology backbone of the existing company. The majority of companies have a consolidated, interconnected set of applications that provide the necessary capabilities for the company to run efficiently. These capabilities have to be transferred or stood up for the new enterprise. This is highly dependent on the current company's IT config-uration. Remember, the current company can have a consolidated system (optimal) or they can have a large number of independent systems. The latter is more challenging because the business is actually being run by multiple actual enterprises across their given geographic expanse.

There are several paths that this typically will take. I will discuss it from the easiest to the hardest operational path, but realize the manage-ment team, advisors, and the negotiation with the seller on what they are willing to do will dictate how you approach this. There is also a discus-sion on the timing of the separation and how it will be handled in the interim.

1. The seller decides not to transfer the system to you. When this occurs, it would require the seller to have an extended transition support agreement that allows time for the acquiring company to build out their own set of systems that replicate the required capabilities for the new company. This is convenient because it allows you to build the system from scratch and remove the technical debt that typically resides in a system. It also allows you to put in place a new (typically), lower cost structure as the system you use will be able to be tailored to the new environs. In addition, there are smaller scale options like NetSuite and Microsoft Dynamics that are simple to implement and have what is typically required to support operations. The critical element is that your company will operate its books through the seller for an extended period of time. They will be the system of record. You have to ensure that your transition support agreement is very robust for finance and accounting and that they provide you the required reports and financials in a timely manner. The system implementation for this is relatively straightforward. The seller will need to logically partition their current ERP, set up a new company and route all of your financials through that company code. For the remainder of the IT ecosystem, they will need to keep the workflows through their current systems and then allow the new company access. Or they have a choice to replicate the systems for the new company.

For some critical systems like work management systems or systems core to operations that are unique or homegrown like an oil and gas pipeline nomination and scheduling system or a telecommunication operational system network, this will be a better choice. Because these systems are core to the area and the cash flow of the business, having that capability stabile on Day one without threat of a TSA is helpful to all.

2. They will transfer the systems to you prior to close. This is the heaviest lift for the divesting company. It typically requires their IT teams to have replicated the ecosystem for the operational entity. For the buying company, it is one of the best options. This does not occur frequently as it could prolong the timeline to close. For companies that have preplanned the divestiture, they may have done this years ago and minimized or eliminated the system entanglements. Coming out of the pandemic, a number of large companies made the investment upfront to separate operations within their portfolio to enable rapid sale of assets. This is a smart move when interest rates increase. It is a relatively cheap source of capital if you can find the right buyer.

3. They will transfer the systems to you after close. This is one of the most operationally complex ways of making this transition. The timeline can easily take 18 to 24 months for a large global and complex company. In this scenario, the buyer will continue to leverage the company's existing systems as in part one. However, instead of building new, they will at some point assume the systems. This can be complex because the systems will not typically all come on line at once. You will bring on your WMS then you ERP then your e-commerce. This then requires the two IT teams to reroute the linkages between the companies and the technologies. It can be done, but as you can get a sense, it has the highest likelihood of issues arising during the execution of the plan. In one situation, there were advisors brought in to a large Fortune 300 company to recover the IT ecosystem migrations. The project management for the effort required a significant team with dedicated support over a 14-month period to execute. The more ERP systems the

company has the less likely that this will be your best option. The interesting part is that the company staff will want to push for this because it keeps their systems the way they have always been.

If you do venture down this path, having an enterprise service bus (ESB) for the new company will be critical and allow you to plug and play the systems together. The one issue is that you will need to retain the current company's data model.

Data is a differentiator in today's market. Ensuring that the company has full access to its historical and proprietary customer data is critical to its long-term success. The seller should have in place a method to provide this to you. The best ask is for them to provide you all of the customer data for their larger company. This will provide you the most insight for the new enterprise.

Some companies will not agree to provide that to you. They may even reject the idea that you should receive customer data. I would recommend not accepting that. Sometimes a happy medium and justified is to ask them for the customer data relevant to the products or service business lines that you are acquiring. In some essence, this is an intellectual property of that asset being acquired. To do this, they will need to partition the data that they have. This will require an effort by their IT or advisory team to segment the data and provide that to you.

Operational Entanglements

The majority of modern large companies will have comingled logistics, warehouses, and operational elements. The actual elements co-mingled will vary based on the business model and industry for the company. Please refer to the relevant section of Chapter 4 for a refresher on what this could mean for any company you are reviewing.

The ideal setup for a carve-out is that the actual operation of the company is a clean separation before day one or that the operation has minimal entanglements. For instance, a company in the telecommunications space may ensure that within the carve-out boundary the company will have the required people, warehouses, truck fleet, maintenance assets, the network operations center is fully staffed or replicated to support the new companies operations, the operational systems are replicated and calculating costs and pricing properly, and the actual backbone networks are ascribed to the new entity. Despite best efforts, you will not likely achieve this in full.

I will use the example of a warehouse to help you think through what will need to occur prior to transition. This part will depend on the level of entanglement of the operations. There are some companies where each business unit does have their own operational set up. For instance, a large industrial supplier where the aerospace division has a dedicated warehouse and the subsea supplier has a separate and distinct warehouse. In this instance, the separation will occur because of the transaction and each component will have their independent warehouse. However, if those operations are comingled, there may be a situation where the buyer will leverage a TSA to supply its operation out of that warehouse for a period of time. For this, there are two outcomes: one where the seller chooses to divorce itself from one of the warehouses, and one where they keep the two.

For a situation where the seller decides to divorce itself from the second warehouse, the buyer would seek to either buy or include the unwanted warehouse in the perimeter of the transaction, if not already included. From there, you would leverage the TSA to continue to provide those services and as part of the transition service agreement you would include transportation and separation support for the warehouses. In that agreement, the seller would help the buyer rearrange the goods between the warehouses such that the business lines were separated and then conduct the official separation of the warehouses and operation.

The other situation is one where the seller decides it wants to keep both of the warehouses. In this situation, the buyer will need to procure and establish its own base of operation. The buyer will be fully dependent on the seller for the delivery of its business until it buys or gains use of its own facility. In this situation, the company can seek to buy or build its own warehouse. This process will take a long time—typically on the order of 18 to 24 months—if a full greenfield build of a site and then outfitting for logistics capability. Typically, you will not have that length of time under a TSA. Nor do you really want to be in a TSA for that long.

The other choice is to leverage a 3PL. 3PLs will often buy and build speculative buildings or if the operation is small enough have excess capacity in one of its existing buildings. These operators can typically quickly set up the requirements and ingest the products. They can shrink the 18 to 24 months down to about six to 12, depending on the operational requirements and lead times for the core components of the operation.

There is also the need to transition the inventory while maintaining the ability to operate. You will need to ensure the new warehouse management system works, but then you will begin to transition the inventory. Typically, you will want to start with the lower volume components and SKUs. You will then need to think through the high volume. This planning will require some detailed analysis of projected volume during the transition period and a hard cutover date. You will then begin to build stockpile of the high volume in the new facility. Leading into the cutover date, you will let the high volume in the old facility get used up. There may be a need to shift volume between the facilities to make an order, but in general this is a good strategy. The key element is to have sufficient volume in the new facility to cover about two to three weeks of volume as you shift the remainder of the inventory from old to new post cutover.

Transition Service Agreements

The transition service agreement (TSA) for a carve-out is one of the most critical elements for the success of the new company. Without the TSA, the new company does not have everything it needs to function. TSAs can also be used in mergers. However, the biggest difference and why I did not cover TSAs in the inorganic growth section of this book is that in a merger, the acquired company typically has everything it needs to function. There are times you will need a TSA, but in general they are relatively minor. In a carve-out, the services provided in the TSA will enable the new management team to run the company efficiently whilst standing up the new company and providing time for the company to take over operations seamlessly across all of the core functions.

Every TSA will be different, as each carve-out will have different holes in its Swiss cheese. The key is to ensure that anything you anticipate needing after the close to be specifically spelled out in the TSA. This document will be one of the sole documents that compel support after the close of the deal. The TSA may also be supported by distribution, manufacturing, or shared service agreements, as well.

The first element of the TSA will be a general section which outlines the scope of services offered, penalties if services are not provided, service standards, and general services that will be provided. Often, this will include specific responsibilities of the seller to support the transition of the business and reporting requirements associated with the TSA. There will also be something that dictates the governance of the TSA. Typically, each party will have a relatively senior executive as their party's TSA manager. These resources manage escalations or issues that arise because of the TSA.

In the general or administrative section of the transition service agreement, there will also be specific protocols for how to terminate a service. To finish the TSA and stop incurring cost, it will be required that each individual service is officially terminated by the buyer. Typically, there will also be a section that discusses the cost of ad hoc services and cost per hour for the seller's resources. Services can be added post close. However, the pricing from the seller can be punitive. A helpful way to prevent that is to agree on rate caps for additional services.

Another critical element of these services is the support needed to exit. The buyer should clearly articulate what services it will need from the seller to support the transition. For instance, post close there will need to be data transfers for customer and historical data. The agreement should spell out what is needed and this will then be considered a service under the TSA. The pricing of the service might be incremental to a TSA access fee. Additionally, if it is covered, then the seller cannot deny you the service. This is critical as the length of the TSA wears on.

Typically, the functional elements of the TSA will be arranged by function (e.g., finance, accounting, operations, marketing). The TSA will dictate what services the new company will receive from the seller and for the period of time the service will be provided. The TSA will also specify a standard of service. For instance, an invoice should be routed within 24 hours of receipt. Depending on how the TSAs are drafted, the standard of service can be at the individual TSA level or in an upfront section.

Penalties are important to ensure you can enforce the TSA and any of the associated agreements. There are times when you can waive the penalties for TSAs. However, when you do, remember that your only recourse if the other company decided not to provide services would be a formal legal escalation. Legal escalation can be time-consuming and is usually a painful process. It can often be better just to leave the penalties in place and put in place a cure period before the penalties are enforced. In addition, you can also chose when to enforce them or limit the reporting such that a violation is not an immediate impact to the TSA profit and loss statement. A typical penalty may be loss of the monthly service fee or some pre-negotiated penalty value.

Most of the time, there will be a fee for the services outlined in the TSA. The fees can be a monthly access type fee or they can be a usage-based mechanism—for instance, the new company pays for each invoice processed. Sometimes it can be a mix of these. The monthly access fee is the simplest method. To avoid overcharges, it is best to have the fees provided at a high level functional grouping, such as accounts receivable services. Getting below that level can be hard and may become an administrative issue to manage. The other consideration is how and what elements can be cancelled together. The billing should follow the segmentation on what can be cancelled together.

The pay per usage model can and does work. However, it will require a significant amount of administration. Every month there will need to be a bill presented to the buyer who then will need to pay it. They can challenge elements of the bill. The usage model typically ends up with a significant number of challenges. The service line level minimizes the billing disputes and reduces the amount of overhead needed to manage the TSA.

The other area to try to streamline is the reporting on the standards of service. You can ask for a monthly report on the standards of service. Or, you can work between the TSA managers to identify when there are operational issues that are potentially being caused by a certain service and ask for a deep dive and assessment of the standard of service. Depending on the relationship and how you want to approach it, this may be one of the better methods to manage the reporting. However, the monthly reporting is helpful and allows direct oversight of the TSA. With penalties, this is the best method to manage the oversight as the seller will report on itself that it is either in compliance or not with the standards of service. When asked for these reports, you can also charge for them to be produced.

Typically, TSAs are set for between 12 and 18 months. There are some services that may only need three months or six months post close. If that is the case, then you can only ask for that amount of time. It is always better to be conservative on how long you will need the service. The worst-case scenario is that the seller is unwilling to extend the service and it becomes a risk to your business. Typically, the seller will understand and then just charge a punitive charge. However, there are times that they cannot extend without impacting their own business plans.

Although you want to be conservative on the timing, you also want to get out of them as quickly as possible. The first six months post close is typically friendly and accommodating. However, after about six months in the TSA arrangement, the seller will begin to get impatient. They are incented to get you out of the TSA as quickly as possible. They will honor what is in the agreement, but not much more. Given this, it is usually best to think about trying to complete everything needed by the year point. There are some industries where that will never be the case. For instance, in the telecommunications space, I have seen a three-year TSA for the operational systems portion of the services. It would just take that long to get the new systems implemented and get the required approvals.

The TSA should include a method for resolving any disagreements or disputes that arise during the transition period. The first step will be escalation between the TSA managers. But, this could involve escalation procedures, mediation or arbitration processes, or other dispute resolution mechanisms.

Given that the seller will likely be handling sensitive data during the transition, the TSA should include provisions for maintaining confidentiality and ensuring data security.

International Distribution Service Agreements

There are times when you are acquiring a divested asset that you will not own all of the international contracts or the contract exists in the selling company outside of the boundary of your transaction and will not transfer. In these situations you will need to work with the selling company to maintain access to those markets during the transition period or account for that loss in the transaction value, if acceptable to the investor.

Typically, you will want to maintain that access. The orchestration of this will occur through a distribution agreement, similar to what you will establish with your distributors in the future. The selling company will be your intermediary and leverage its existing commercial contracts for your products or services with their partners, maintaining the sales and sales trajectory. The economics of this transaction should be neutral to you, so they are providing this service as part of the transaction. Leveraging this arrangement similar to a TSA will allow you to build out the needed legal entities and operations in the given geography to make your own contracts and continue to grow the business independent of the other company.

These agreements do not necessarily need to just be transitional. There are times when it benefits both the seller and buyer to continue to distribute the product through the existing channels. There are times where the seller may be contractually required to maintain access to the product set. When this occurs, you should enter into those agreements with the same diligence and assessment you would with other distributors for other markets. In addition some of the economics may be different with longer dated agreements.

There are a few areas to watch out for in these arrangements. The first is to ensure you are truly economically neutral. Typically, distributor contracts have markups for additional profit. To ensure this is true you will need to do an economic margin analysis for the region based on volumes and average discounts. For service companies, you will also need to ensure that any services they provide are given at cost with no or agreed upon overhead markups. If the seller insists upon making a profit, it may be needed to meet the asks of their international team members, then look at tradeoffs on the purchase or other areas to make it overall economically neutral.

Second, ensure that the seller makes efforts to maintain the same market access. There are instances where the selling company has sought to ruin the assets post close in foreign markets. Ensure there are significant penalties for these infractions including loss of business claims. The new company should also have full say on the branding and business decisions. For instance, if the selling company wants to enter a new distribution channel, the new company should have an approval. Just imagine a worst-case scenario where the selling company began distributing a premium product in a discounter. It may be the right business decision, but the new company should have the final say.

Third, end of distribution costs should be negotiated and understood. You have already bought the business. There should be no further costs to you except what is reasonable. For instance, you will need to buy back the inventory. You may also need to buy the assets if they have not already been purchased. However, there should be no significant additional charges unless contractually required and agreed upon.

Manufacturing Service Agreements

Manufacturing facilities do not always transfer with an asset. When they do not, you will likely need to put in place a manufacturing services agreement (MSA) with the seller. You can integrate this into the TSA document, if desired. There are several reasons why it does not make sense to put this into the larger TSA:

1. The MSA will have a number of agreements on the conduct of the order and forecasting for inventory and production rates.
2. There are specific limitations and indemnifications for a manufacturing service agreement. These indemnifications will be limited to the products manufactured and may cause confusion in the drafting of the TSA.
3. There is usually a list of pricing that would be independent of the pricing of the TSA.
4. The MSA will typically last longer than the TSA or could be long duration; essentially they become a contract manufacturer.
5. If you just need products ordered from their third party manufacturers, this can and should be done through the TSA.

For the MSA, you will treat it just like you would a third party contract manufacturing contract. Given that this is a part of the transaction agreement, there should be little to no markup on the pricing. The one watch out for here as you negotiate pricing is the absorption.

Depending on how this is being structured, the seller may attempt to have more of its absorption covered by the products being manufactured for them. As such, you should look at the cost accounting for the production. In addition, you should seek to lock in a standardized price on the product for a period of time. This will prevent the seller from increasing price unless necessary.

Depending on what is being produced, there may be a choice to continue production with the seller versus finding another third party. If this is a choice, you need to negotiate the MSA to support that. This will also include a markup for products purchased through the MSA with periodic opportunities to revisit the pricing.

Shared Service Agreements

A shared service agreement is an extended TSA for back office functions. These are less common, as you typically want to have a full separation of the business at a certain point. There are times that you would use this with a private investor. Sometimes, there is a need to keep the companies tightly integrated because part of the true value of the company still lies with the main company. In others, this may be utilized because you have agreed to have a joint venture where the systems or some element of the operation will continue to be co-managed post separation.

Contract Separation

During a separation, you have to evaluate all of the contracts for the divesting enterprise. The contracts are a critical element of business continuity and will be something that needs to be in place to support day one and definitely needed for the exit of your TSA. Each contract will need to be evaluated as to whether the contract can be kept as is, transferred, requires novation, or can be eliminated. When evaluating, it is helpful to put together a contract database and gather all of the terms to include, change of control provisions, assignment rights, there are tools and services that can go through contracts and provide all of these relevant elements.

In general, contracts follow legal entities. To the extent that you acquire a legal entity and that legal entity has a contract it conveys. There are times where the contract has provisions that require approval before sale or change of ownership. These conditions and approvals will need to be met by the seller.

However, not all of the contracts will be within a legal entity that you are buying. In this instance you will need to have a dedicated effort with a prioritized focus on getting the required contracts transferred or novated when needed. There will be some contracts that may need to be in place for day one. For instance, you may have decided to have all of your employees on your company's payroll with health and benefits for day one. If so, then you will need to have the required contracts in place to support that under the new company.

For other contracts you will need to novate the contract for the company. This may require you to negotiate with the counterparty. The majority of counterparties will often just accept the prior terms. However, some will want to modify. For capabilities in your company that are critical, they may feel that they have an advantage and use this point for leverage. As you takeover an asset, you are usually a price taker. There are benefits if you are part of a group purchasing organization (GPO) that has certain prices already negotiated with key vendors. You can leverage this to minimize the potential for costs to increase. One strategy to minimize price increase is to enter into short-term contracts on the outset and then get yourself in a position where in the future you can negotiate the rate down.

For your existing commercial contracts, most customers want to maintain the product flow and maintain the pricing. They will largely just transfer or novate the contract. This is something they see often. However, there are times when the customer may use this as a leverage point and seek concessions. In these situations, the best choice is to try to get a temporary agreement in place and then buy time to negotiate once product continues to flow. In general, you will end up giving them some concessions as you do not really have any leverage at that juncture where you need to transfer the contract and there is nothing in the contract that compels them to accept the transfer. This approach will also be dependent on how much relative power the company has on the customer. For instance, they are not likely to do this to a company where their products account for a relatively significant portion of their revenue.

CHAPTER 8

Generative Artificial Intelligence

As I was writing this book, I began to see the opportunity in the next two to 10 years for generative AI. I also spoke with some industry experts and those knowledgeable about the technology. The wide spread adoption and use of large language models (LLM) on proprietary data sets will likely be a game changer for companies and even enhance value creation for some functions I have discussed in this book.

I do not like to be a futurist, but capitalism does what capitalism does. The integration of LLMs and proprietary data sets has the potential ability to reduce workforce size and requirements by about 20 to 30 percent in the next decade. In addition, it is not just the lower skill level positions that will be impacted. Those have been the focus up until now because of the limitations of technology and its ability to understand what we want. These tools with the right targeted development and integration with proprietary data sets have the ability to reduce the need for finance, marketing, legal, investment, and other higher paid positions.

There is already a CHATGPT enabled service for legal firms that streamline an attorney's support needed for database analysis, contractual review, legal research, and meeting preparation. Look at CoCounsel by Casetext—as of March 2023, it had already been used at least 50,000 times in day to day work by practicing attorneys. The model thinks like a good junior lawyer—it does not yet replace good judgment, which is of course required by more senior attorneys. The current iterations of the technology reduce the need for junior lawyers to go and conduct hours of legal research or contract review. The chatbot can do it in minutes. Over time, this will reduce the number of required junior lawyers needed at firms. At this point in the technology's maturation, it will not eliminate the need for junior resources.[30]

The current technology is still immature. As a test, one executive asked for one of her staff to develop a report on the impact of the EPA on a given industry. The person went away and developed a 100 percent answer over the course of one week. At the same time, she went and input a well-worded question into ChatGPT-4 and it returned a 70 to 80 percent correct answer, but it took less than three minutes. That level of efficiency if employed across the board is already a game changer. Teams and people should not be hesitant to use it.

Another of my contacts is the CEO of a company that is leveraging LLMs to streamline customer service operations. When a call comes in there is a service that transcribes what the caller is saying in real time. That script is provided to a backend LLM solution. This then allows the solution to pull relevant cases or articles to support the customer service representative serving a voice customer. The representative can solve the problem in less time, and when this occurs across the board, the total need for customer service representatives will reduce. In a chat or email, the AI tool can essentially fully address the question with oversight and quality control by a person, reducing their overall handling time. The other use is improved understanding of issues and improved ticket routing. This improvement alone has already caused a reduction in misrouted volume of about 90 percent.

The singularity I am looking toward that unlocks additional efficiency gains in an organization is when you can integrate the LLM with proprietary data sets at a company or elsewhere. Just imagine that you need to put together a presentation on last month's financials. You enter a single question into a ChatGPT window and the back end of the LLM integrates with last month's financials and populates an answer or integrated with Microsoft Copilot, it automatically creates a chart that can be presented on the topic at the presentation in an hour. The work that an analyst might have taken a day on now takes less than 30 minutes, including quality assurance and positioning on the slide. This is a game changer and fundamentally reduces the need for large teams in almost all functions.

This is not a distant reality; it is beginning to occur now. There are three main ways companies are leveraging LLMs to unlock this capability now.

The first is through training a proprietary LLM. This will also be the most expensive way of developing the internal capability. However, it will be the most thorough and not reliant on the training of an existing LLM. Bloomberg is launching BloombergGPT. This is a service that is now being provided through Bloomberg terminals that can analyze financial data. Bloomberg has over 40 years worth of financial data, news, and documents in addition troves of financial filings and reports. To train the model, it used 350 billion words, 50 billion parameters, and about 1.3 million hours of graphics processing time. Most companies do not have the resources to make this occur.[31]

If a company does not have the resources to do this, then they can "add on" to an existing LLM. This starts with an existing LLM and then you use some data and examples to train the model for some new content. This has had mixed results. In a Google example, they were only able to get to about 85 percent against a medical licensing exam question set. Please note, ChatGPT does not allow users to add on or tune their latest models. A number of companies are using prompt-tuning which requires some add-on software enabling vector embedding of content prior to being provided to OpenAI. This is kind of a band-aid fix until a company comes with a breakthrough to train LLMs on proprietary data sets that do not require significant resources.

At this juncture, a large number of companies are already working to complete some implementation of a LLM into their company. They see the potential. However, unless your company has vast resources, you will likely be working with a model that will not ever be 100 percent accurate with its product. However, this does not mean you cannot achieve efficiencies.

The key is to first put in place the capability and then assess the productivity gain you are seeing from your team. If positive, reduce hiring or do not fill open gap positions and see if they maintain the same output

---

31   Tom Davenport and Maryam Alavi, "How to Train Generative AI Using Your Company's Data," *Harvard Business Review*, July 6, 2023, hbr.org/2023/07/how-to-train-generative-ai-using-your-companys-data.

with similar hours. If productivity improves or hours decline, then look at efficiencies or improving quality of service. Both are beneficial to the company.

The key for the technology in this tranche is to ensure that you have adequate human oversight on the output. The technology can do the junior resource labor-intensive portion such as research, analytics, or reviews. However, the decision-making and judgment should remain with the human managers and team.

ABOUT THE AUTHOR

With over two decades of experience in the vortex of high-stakes business, Will Bundy stands as an acclaimed expert in the field of large-scale operational transformation. His latest tenure as the Chief Transformation Officer and interim Chief Supply Chain Officer for a Consumer Products company backed by a leading Private Equity investor testifies to his ability to execute powerful strategies, recover fragile operations, and implement substantial transformations.

Known for his knack in assessing operations pre-acquisition and assisting investors and management teams to stabilize critical operations post-crisis or transactions, Will's expertise is unmatched. His credentials further shine with previous leadership roles at AlixPartners, a renowned Private Equity operational improvement advisor, and strategy consulting at Bain & Company.

A sought-after thought leader, Will's insights have graced Bloomberg's discussions on the U.S. Carve Out market, and he is a frequent presence at conferences as a content expert. His writings, covering a gamut of topics from 'Distress by Design' to 'Value Creation Strategies for Growth-Oriented Investments,' have been featured in various Private Equity journals.

Before stepping into the private sector, Will served with distinction as a nuclear-trained submarine officer and Pentagon strategist in the United States Navy. He holds a bachelor's degree in Systems Engineering from the United States Naval Academy and an MBA from the Wharton School of Business at the University of Pennsylvania.

Beyond his professional accolades, Will harbors a zest for life that has led him to summit Mt Kilimanjaro, hike the Inca Trail, and participate in Pamplona's Running of the Bulls. His love for travel reflects his desire to explore and appreciate the world's myriad beauties.

Beyond the business world, Will is an active contributor to the community, having served on various non-profit boards and being an influential member of the Executive Committee of Minorities in Restructuring and Alternative Investment. His diverse interests and experiences make Will a relatable figure who speaks not just to the mind, but also to the heart of the business professional.

Made in the USA
Columbia, SC
14 March 2024

e9b7c0f9-fbe6-4df1-9a4b-83fbd61a2b42R02